Deuteronomic Theology and the Significance of *Torah*

Deuteronomic Theology and the Significance of *Torah*

A Reappraisal

PETER T. VOGT

Winona Lake, Indiana
EISENBRAUNS
2006

BS
1275.52
.V64
2006

Library of Congress Cataloging-in-Publication Data

Vogt, Peter T., 1968–
    Deuteronomic theology and the significance of Torah : a
reappraisal / Peter T. Vogt
      p. cm.
    Includes indexes.
    ISBN-13: 978-1-57506-107-8 (hardback : alk. paper)
    1. Bible. O.T. Deuteronomy—Criticism, interpretation, etc.
  2. Bible. O.T. Deuteronomy—Theology. I. Title.
    BS1275.52.V64 2006
    222′.1506—dc22

                         2006022191

Contents

Preface

It is with great delight that I take this opportunity to thank some of the people who have been so generous in providing assistance to me as I have worked on this project. I simply could not have completed this work without the assistance I received. While the shortcomings of this study that remain are my own, I am indebted to many people for helping me to strengthen this work by eliminating other weaknesses.

I want to thank, first, Prof. J. Gordon McConville for his encouragement, assistance, and supervision of the doctoral dissertation on which this book is based. His expertise was invaluable, and his passion for Deuteronomy was infectious. I would also like to thank Prof. Ronald E. Clements, whose wisdom and experience were also of tremendous help.

Having lived on two continents while engaged in the writing of this project, I have people on both sides of the Atlantic who must be thanked. I am grateful to my colleagues and friends in the Biblical Studies Seminar and the International Centre for Biblical Interpretation in Cheltenham, who provided useful stimulation, encouragement, and criticism along the way. In particular, Dr. Karl Möller has been a tremendous blessing to me and has helped me develop ideas related to this project; he has also stimulated my thinking in other areas besides biblical studies (a welcome diversion in times when reflecting on Deuteronomy was overwhelming!). The faculty of Bethel Theological Seminary in St. Paul, Minnesota, also provided much-needed encouragement, support, and wisdom. I am grateful to the entire Bethel community for all the encouragement I have received. I wish especially to thank teaching assistants Alicia Petersen and Matthew MacKellan for their assistance and the students who participated in the course on Deuteronomy. The stimulation of students has contributed immeasurably to this project.

I am grateful, as well, for the support of various church communities of which I was a part. I want to thank the people of Cambray Baptist Church, Cheltenham, for their prayers and for giving me opportunities to teach and preach. I especially appreciate the support of Dr. David Shoesmith, Alex Keiller, Alan Pilbeam, and Tammy Wylie, who all participated in the Greek study group that I taught. Their enthusiasm and interest in biblical studies helped stimulate and enrich my work. The friendship of Gary, Karen, and Kim Hotham was a "life support" during challenging and difficult times. In addition, the people of the Oikos house church provided a loving community that was essential to the completion of this project. There I was challenged to see things from new perspectives and was helped to see God in exciting and awesome ways.

I would also like to thank my parents-in-law, Bob and Gwen Richardson, for their steadfast support and encouragement. There are, as well, other family, friends, and brothers and sisters in Christ too numerous to name here who have faithfully prayed for me and supported me throughout this project. I could not have completed this work without their assistance and, though I cannot name them all, I am profoundly grateful to each one.

Finally, I want especially to thank five people without whom this book would never have seen the light of day. My parents, Tom and Sandy Vogt, provided the financial resources necessary for living and working in England. In addition, they taught me the value of hard work and the need for perseverance, and encouraged me to believe in myself. Their love, selflessness, and generosity (in every way) made this project possible. My wife, Cami, is a precious gift from God. She is both עֵזֶר and רְעָיָה, and she believed in me even during the times (and there were many) when I did not. Her contributions to this project cannot be numbered. Our children, Joshua and Charis, were born in the midst of this project. Their direct contributions were, of course, minimal, but they and their mother made life delightful. It is to these five people, and to the glory of God, that I dedicate this work.

Peter T. Vogt
May 2006

Abbreviations

General

ANE	ancient Near East (or ancient Near Eastern)
DtH	Deuteronomistic History
Dtr	the Deuteronomist
EA	El-Amarna letters
ET	English translation
FS	Festschrift
LXX	Septuagint
MT	Masoretic Text
NASB	New American Standard Bible
NIV	New International Version
OT	Old Testament
Urdt	*Urtext* Deuteronomy
VTE	Vassal Treaties of Esarhaddon

Reference Works

AB	Anchor Bible
ABD	*Anchor Bible Dictionary*. Ed. D. N. Freedman. 6 vols. New York: Doubleday, 1992
AnBib	Analecta biblica
ANET	*Ancient Near Eastern Texts Relating to the Old Testament*. Ed. J. B. Pritchard. 3rd ed. Princeton: Princeton University Press, 1969
AOAT	Alter Orient und Altes Testament
AOTC	Apollos Old Testament Commentary
AbOTC	Abingdon Old Testament Commentaries
AJBI	*Annual of the Japanese Biblical Institute*
ASTI	*Annual of the Swedish Theological Institute*
ATD	Das Alte Testament Deutsch
BA	*Biblical Archaeologist*
BBB	Bonner Biblische Beiträge
BBR	*Bulletin for Biblical Research*
BDB	F. Brown, S. R. Driver, and C. A. Briggs. *Hebrew and English Lexicon of the Old Testament*. Peabody, MA: Hendrickson, 1979
BETL	Bibliotheca ephemeridum theologicarum lovaniensium
Bib	*Biblica*
BibInt	*Biblical Interpretation*
BLH	Biblical Languages: Hebrew

BN	*Biblische Notizen*
BO	Berit Olam: Studies in Hebrew Narrative and Poetry
BR	*Bible Review*
BSac	*Bibliotheca Sacra*
BST	The Bible Speaks Today
BTB	*Biblical Theology Bulletin*
BWANT	Beiträge zur Wissenschaft vom Alten und Neuen Testament
BZAW	Beihefte zur Zeitschrift für die alttestamentliche Wissenschaft
CBQ	*Catholic Biblical Quarterly*
CurBS	*Currents in Research: Biblical Studies*
EC	Epworth Commentaries
EncJud	*Encyclopaedia Judaica.* Ed. C. Roth. 21 vols. Jerusalem: Keter, 1971
ETL	*Ephemerides theologicae lovanienses*
ETS Studies	Evangelical Theological Society Studies
ExpTim	*Expository Times*
FAT	Forschungen zum Alten Testament
FRLANT	Forschungen zur Religion und Literatur des Alten und Neuen Testaments
HAR	*Hebrew Annual Review*
HAT	Handbuch zum Alten Testament
HBS	Herders Biblische Studien
HKAT	Handkommentar zum Alten Testament
HSM	Harvard Semitic Monographs
HUCA	*Hebrew Union College Annual*
ICC	International Critical Commentary
IDBSup	*Interpreter's Dictionary of the Bible: Supplementary Volume.* Ed. K. Crim. Nashville: Abingdon, 1976
IEJ	*Israel Exploration Journal*
Int	*Interpretation*
Interp	Interpretation: A Bible Commentary for Teaching and Preaching
IOS	*Israel Oriental Studies*
IOSOT	International Organization for the Study of the Old Testament
ITC	International Theological Commentary
JAOS	*Journal of the American Oriental Society*
JBL	*Journal of Biblical Literature*
JBQ	*Jewish Biblical Quarterly*
JCBRF	*Journal of the Christian Brethren Research Fellowship*
JETS	*Journal of the Evangelical Theological Society*
JNSL	*Journal of Northwest Semitic Languages*
JR	*Journal of Religion*
JSOT	*Journal for the Study of the Old Testament*
JSOTSup	Journal for the Study of the Old Testament Supplement Series
LBI	Library of Biblical Interpretation

NAC	New American Commentary
NCB	New Century Bible Commentary
NIB	*The New Interpreter's Bible: General Articles and Introduction, Commentary, and Reflections for Each Book of the Bible, Including the Apochryphal/Deuterocanonical Books in Twelve Volumes.* Ed. L. E. Keck et al. Nashville: Abingdon, 1998
NIBC	New International Biblical Commentary
NICOT	New International Commentary on the Old Testament
NIDOTTE	*New International Dictionary of Old Testament Theology and Exegesis.* Ed. W. A. VanGemeren. 5 vols. Grand Rapids: Zondervan, 1997
NSBT	New Studies in Biblical Theology
OBO	Orbis biblicus et orientalis
OBT	Overtures to Biblical Theology
OTL	Old Testament Library
OTG	Old Testament Guides
OTS	Old Testament Studies
RB	*Revue Biblique*
SBL	Society of Biblical Literature
SBLDS	Society of Biblical Literature Dissertation Series
SBLMS	Society of Biblical Literature Monograph Series
SBT	Studies in Biblical Theology
SBTS	Sources for Biblical and Theological Study
SOTBT	Studies in Old Testament Biblical Theology
ST	*Studia theologica*
TDOT	*Theological Dictionary of the Old Testament.* Ed. G. J. Botterweck and H. Ringgren. Trans. D. E. Green. 12 vols. Grand Rapids: Eerdmans, 1974–2003. ET of *Theologisches Wörterbuch zum Alten Testament.* Ed. G. J. Botterweck and H. Ringgren. Stuttgart: Kohlhammer, 1975–77
TLOT	*Theological Lexicon of the Old Testament.* Ed. E. Jenni and C. Westermann. Trans. M. E. Biddle. 3 vols. Peabody, MA: Hendrickson, 1997. ET of *Theologisches Handwörterbuch zum Alten Testament.* Ed. E. Jenni and C. Westermann. 2 vols. Munich: Chr. Kaiser, 1971–76
TWOT	*Theological Wordbook of the Old Testament.* Ed. R. L. Harris, G. L. Archer Jr., and B. K. Waltke. 2 vols. Chicago: Moody, 1980
TynBul	*Tyndale Bulletin*
VT	*Vetus Testamentum*
VTSup	Vetus Testamentum Supplements
WBC	Word Biblical Commentary
ZAW	*Zeitschrift für die alttestamentliche Wissenschaft*

Introduction

One of the few areas of consensus in modern Deuteronomy scholarship is the contention that within the book of Deuteronomy there is a
program of reform that is nothing short of revolutionary.[1] Although
there are divergent views as to the specific details of this revolutionary
program, there remains agreement that in fundamental and profound
ways, Deuteronomy is radical in its vision.

The Deuteronomic revolution is seen as broad-sweeping in its
scale. Theology, worship, politics, and even social and moral values
are seen as being dramatically altered in Deuteronomy.[2] The essential
aspects of this revolution are usually described as demythologization,
centralization, and secularization. Although the details of the various
views are presented in the following chapters, it will be useful at this
point to present a general description of the broad contours of scholarly consensus on the nature of the Deuteronomic revolution.

Deuteronomy, according to the influential perspective of Moshe
Weinfeld and others, alters the conception of God found in earlier
sources. In earlier sources, God is presented in a rather crude, anthropomorphic fashion. He has need of a dwelling place, and so he orders
the construction of the tabernacle (Exod 25:8).[3] In the theophany at
Sinai, Yahweh is described as actually having come down upon the
mountain (Exod 19:18, 20). In addition, there is great concern in the
earlier material about the danger of seeing God. Thus, Exod 33:20
warns that "you cannot see my face, for no one may see me and live."

---

1. See, for example, M. Weinfeld, *Deuteronomy and the Deuteronomic School* (Oxford:
Oxford University Press, 1972; repr. Winona Lake, IN: Eisenbrauns, 1992), 191–243; idem,
Deuteronomy 1–11: A New Translation with Introduction and Commentary (AB 5; New York:
Doubleday, 1991), 37–44; J. H. Tigay, *Deuteronomy* דברים: *The Traditional Hebrew Text with
the New JPS Translation* (Philadelphia: Jewish Publication Society, 1996), xvii–xviii; R. E.
Clements, "The Book of Deuteronomy: Introduction, Commentary, and Reflections," *NIB*,
2: 271–87, esp. 285; idem, *Deuteronomy* (OTG; Sheffield: Sheffield Academic Press, 1989),
60–63; A. D. H. Mayes, *Deuteronomy* (NCB; Grand Rapids: Eerdmans / London: Marshall,
Morgan & Scott, 1979), 57–60.

2. M. Weinfeld, "Deuteronomy's Theological Revolution," *BR* 12/1 (1996): 38.

3. Exodus 25:8 is normally seen as belonging to P, which is held to be later than Deuteronomy. Weinfeld, however, sees P as prior to, or contemporaneous with, D. See Weinfeld, *Deuteronomic School*, 179–83.

Worship is seen in the earlier sources as being, in part, a means of providing for the deity. In this view, the bread and vessels for wine in the tabernacle provide food and drink for Yahweh. In addition, fragrant offerings and lamps are seen as being for the (actually) present deity. Finally, the cherubim serve as a throne for the seated God, while the ark functions as his footstool. [4]

All this is dramatically altered in Deuteronomy as a result of a deliberate effort at reinterpretation and a repudiation of the anthropomorphic view of the earlier sources. Disparate elements of the faith are gathered, harmonized, and "purified" theologically. [5] The earlier conceptions of God were "demythologised and rationalised"; [6] so, it is argued, the portrayal of God in Deuteronomy is radically altered in an attempt to repudiate the earlier views. One example frequently cited as evidence for this shift is the theophany at Horeb/Sinai, where the presence of Yahweh is seen as exclusively aural rather than visual, and Yahweh is said in Deut 4:36 to have spoken "from heaven." [7] Noting the differences between the theophany presented in Exodus and the theophany in Deuteronomy, Hurowitz concludes that

> [t]he accounts of the theophany in Exodus and Deuteronomy thus differ significantly from one another both in specific details and in underlying theological outlook. Exodus portrays Mt. Sinai as if it were a temple precinct where God and man come into immediate and intimate contact. Deuteronomy, in keeping with its own innovative conception of the Temple and the transcendent deity, confines God to the highest heaven even when he is revealing himself to his people at Horeb. [8]

The author(s) of Deuteronomy, then, are deliberately reinterpreting the presence of Yahweh in light of the more abstract theological thinking of the time. Other examples of demythologization are discussed in detail in chap. 1; it is sufficient for the present to simply note that demythologization is seen as central to the Deuteronomic program.

A second element of the revolutionary program is centralization. Major social and political upheaval is seen to have occurred as a result of the law of centralization in Deut 12. In the earlier sources, it is maintained, worship of Yahweh was carried out at a variety of loca-

---

4. Ibid., 191–92.

5. G. von Rad, *Studies in Deuteronomy* (trans. D. M. G. Stalker; Chicago: Henry Regnery / London: SCM, 1953), 37.

6. Ibid., 40.

7. Weinfeld, "Theological Revolution," 39. See also V. Hurowitz, "From Storm God to Abstract Being: How the Deity Became More Abstract from Exodus to Deuteronomy," *BR* 14 (1998): 40–47.

8. Ibid., 47.

tions, including local altars. Exodus 20:24–25 is understood as calling for the erection of altars in multiple locations, albeit only at the locations in which Yahweh "caused his Name to be remembered."[9]

In Deut 12, however, a different conception is seen to emerge. There, worship is limited to a single sanctuary. Since de Wette, this has commonly been understood to be a result of the reforms undertaken by Josiah in the 7th century B.C., and the impact on the life of the nation cannot be overstated.[10] By eliminating all local shrines and sanctuaries, Josiah transforms the political and religious life of the nation. Prior to the reformation, priests in the local shrines would be consulted when elders, serving as judges in the city gates, could not reach a verdict due to a lack of witnesses or evidence.[11] The removal of the local sanctuaries also means that the local priests are no longer available to serve in this capacity, so Deuteronomy calls for the appointment of judges in every town and provides for the consultation of the priests or judges in the central sanctuary in difficult cases (Deut 17:8–9).

Worship was also dramatically affected, as might be expected. The elimination of local altars meant that sacrifice could not be carried out as before. So, the "law of profane slaughter" (Deut 12:15–25) allows for the nonsacrificial slaughter of animals in the locations now deprived of a local altar. In addition, pilgrimages to the central sanctuary

---

9. See, e.g., M. Noth, *Exodus* (OTL; London: SCM, 1962; ET of *Das zweite Buch Mose: Exodus* [ATD 5; Göttingen: Vandenhoeck & Ruprecht, 1959]), 176. See also F. Crüsemann, *The Torah: Theology and Social History of Old Testament Law* (Minneapolis: Fortress, 1996), 173, who argues, from a very different perspective, that the law in Exod 20:24 is dealing with a number of sites. Where Noth presents the widely held view that the Book of the Covenant is earlier than Deuteronomy and that Deuteronomy is a revision of the earlier view, Crüsemann argues that the Book of the Covenant is later than Deuteronomy and represents a reaction *against* centralization.

10. De Wette argued for the connection between Deuteronomy and the Josianic reforms of the 7th century B.C. in a lengthy footnote in his doctoral dissertation ("'Dissertatio critica qua a prioribus Deuteronomium Pentateuchi libris diversum, alius cuiusdam recentioris auctoris opus esse monstratur,' pro venia legendi publice defensa Ienae a. 1805," in W. M. L. de Wette, *Opscula Theologica* [Berlin: G. Reimer, 1830], 149–68), completed at the University of Jena in 1804. He argued that the altar law of Deut 12 could only come from a later period than the rest of the Pentateuch due to the fact that centralization is neither assumed nor especially valued there. This idea was further developed in his two-volume work *Beiträge zur Einleitung in das Alte Testament* (Halle: Schmimmelpfennig und Compagnia, 1806–7). For an analysis of de Wette and his contributions to the study of the Old Testament, see J. W. Rogerson, *W. M. L. de Wette, Founder of Modern Biblical Criticism: An Intellectual Biography* (JSOTSup 126; Sheffield: Sheffield Academic Press, 1992).

11. Weinfeld, *Deuteronomic School*, 233. See also the discussion in B. M. Levinson, *Deuteronomy and the Hermeneutics of Legal Innovation* (Oxford: Oxford University Press, 1997), 98–143.

became necessary and are therefore required by Deuteronomy (e.g., Deut 12:26; 14:25).

An additional effect of centralization was what is often called secularization. While this term is understood differently by various critics, "secularization" generally refers to a tendency in Deuteronomy to downplay the sacred and the removal of certain institutions from the realm of the sacred. Thus, Weinfeld describes Deuteronomy as having a

> distinctly secular foundation. Not only do we encounter institutions of a manifestly secular character such as the judiciary (16:18–20; 17:8–13), the monarchy (17:14–20), the military (20) and civil and criminal laws which treat of the family and inheritance (21:10–21; 22:13–29; 24:1–4; 25:5–10), loans and debts (15:1–11; 24:10–13), litigations and quarrels (25:1–3 and 10–12), trespassing (19:14) and false testimony (19:15–21) and the like; but . . . even institutions and practices which were originally sacral in character have here been recast in secularized forms.[12]

In short, the effects of centralization were so far-reaching that they had a dramatic impact on nearly every facet of life.

As noted, the idea of a Deuteronomic revolution marked by centralization, secularization, and demythologization has achieved widespread acceptance, though there are, of course, differences among the various points of view. Indeed, on the surface, the case for this view appears strong, if not irrefutable. In recent years, however, some of the data adduced in favor of centralization and demythologization in support of the Jerusalem Temple have been shown to be susceptible to very different interpretation. For example, recent research on Deut 12 has raised questions about whether the prevailing view represents the best explanation for the data of the text. Recent studies have argued that this chapter may plausibly be read as stressing the sovereignty of Yahweh in determining where he will be worshiped, rather than restricting the number of permitted worship sites.[13] Similarly, the nature

---

12. Weinfeld, *Deuteronomic School*, 188.

13. See, e.g., J. G. McConville, *Law and Theology in Deuteronomy* (JSOTSup 33; Sheffield: JSOT Press, 1984); J. G. McConville and J. G. Millar, *Time and Place in Deuteronomy* (JSOTSup 179; Sheffield: Sheffield Academic Press, 1994); J. J. Niehaus, "The Central Sanctuary: Where and When?" *TynBul* 43/1 (1992): 3–30; G. J. Wenham, "Deuteronomy and the Central Sanctuary," *TynBul* 22 (1971): 103–18. Two of the most recent studies on the issue of centralization in Deuteronomy are P. M. A. Pitkänen, *Central Sanctuary and the Centralization of Worship in Ancient Israel: From the Settlement to the Building of Solomon's Temple* (Gorgias Dissertations Near Eastern Studies 5; Piscataway, NJ: Gorgias, 2003), and S. Richter, *The Deuteronomistic History and the Place of the Name* (Ph.D. diss., Harvard University, 2001). The prevailing view was challenged already by A. C. Welch, *The Code of Deuteronomy* (London: James Clarke, 1924), who maintained that only Deut 12:1–7 needs to be taken as referring to one central "chosen place." Another early case against the centralization view was G. T. Manley, *The Book of the Law: Studies in the Date*

of Deuteronomy's theology of the presence of God has been shown to be far more subtle and complex than usually thought. Rather than repudiating the idea of Yahweh's actual presence, Deuteronomy may be seen as describing Yahweh's presence as being both in heaven *and* with his people in battle, on Horeb, and at the chosen place.[14]

In addition, although there is broad consensus regarding the fact of centralization and secularization, there is no consensus on other key related questions. Thus, among those who see in Deuteronomy a program of centralization and demythologization, there is disagreement as to the fundamental nature of the program. Some maintain that this program should be understood as a utopian ideal,[15] while others see it as a realistic program of reform.[16] Similarly disputed is the question whether or not the reform should be seen as favoring or opposing the Judean monarchy.[17] In addition, the issues of setting and audience are disputed even among those who see centralization and demythologization at the core of the Deuteronomic program. This lack of consensus on these issues and on the basic meaning of centralization and demythologization in the interpretation of the book calls into question whether or not centralization and demythologization as usually understood should be viewed as the central tenets of the theology of the book.

This suggests that perhaps the time has come to reevaluate the theology of Deuteronomy and to explore the possibility that what lies at the heart of the theology of Deuteronomy is not centralization and demythologization but something else. In this book, I will attempt to articulate an alternative to the prevailing view of the theology of Deuteronomy and will argue that at the core of Deuteronomy is a theology of the supremacy of Yahweh, expressed in the life of Israel through

---

of Deuteronomy (London: Tyndale, 1957). Extensive analysis and references are found in chap. 4 below.

14. See I. Wilson, *Out of the Midst of the Fire: Divine Presence in Deuteronomy* (SBLDS 151; Atlanta: Scholars Press, 1995), and chap. 3 of this work.

15. E.g., N. Lohfink, "Distribution of the Functions of Power: The Laws concerning Public Offices in Deuteronomy 16:18–18:22," in *A Song of Power and the Power of Song: Essays on the Book of Deuteronomy* (SBTS 3; ed. D. L. Christensen; Winona Lake, IN: Eisenbrauns, 1993), 336–52. See also idem, "The Laws of Deuteronomy: A Utopian Project for a World without Any Poor?" (Lattey Lecture 1995; Cambridge: St. Edmund's College, 1995); and idem, "Das deuteronomische Gesetz in der Endgestalt: Entwurf einer Gesellschaft ohne marginale Gruppen," *BN* 51 (1990): 25–40.

16. One of the most recent examples is B. M. Levinson, *Deuteronomy and the Hermeneutics of Legal Innovation* (Oxford: Oxford University Press, 1997).

17. Weinfeld, for example, sees the Deuteronomic reform as supporting the Judean monarchy, whereas Levinson sees the program as opposing the monarchy. See Weinfeld, *Deuteronomic School*, 168–71; and Levinson, *Legal Innovation*, 138–43.

adherence to *Torah*. In this understanding, Deuteronomy *does* in fact represent a revolutionary program but not in the way that the program is usually understood. It is in its deliberate rejection of ANE models of kingship and institutional permanence, its emphasis on the holiness of all life lived out before Yahweh, and its elevation of the supremacy of Yahweh and his *Torah* that Deuteronomy reveals itself to be a truly revolutionary text.

Historical Background

It may be useful at this point to survey briefly the history of research on Deuteronomy in an effort to discern the way in which the prevailing consensus, described above, emerged. An exhaustive study of the history of interpretation of Deuteronomy would be a full-length study in itself. Therefore, I will limit myself to a brief description in order to highlight the works that have been most influential on Deuteronomic studies.[18]

Modern study of Deuteronomy is associated with the work of de Wette, who, as noted above, argued that Deuteronomy was to be associated with the reform of Josiah. Although Jerome had speculated that the law book found in the temple was Deuteronomy,[19] de Wette is credited with the idea that Deuteronomy was not simply a blueprint for the Josianic reforms but was, rather, a product of the period in which it was used. As noted above, de Wette based this conclusion on the fact that Deut 12 stands out from the rest of the Pentateuch in its demand for centralization. The rest of the Pentateuch, he argues, does not presuppose centralization, and it does not seem to value the idea. Hence, Deut 12 must have been written by a different author. He further argues from the style of presentation that Deuteronomy is the work of a different author from Genesis–Numbers (which he sees as a unity, as he also sees Deuteronomy); neither Genesis–Numbers nor Deuteronomy is to be seen as having been written by Moses.[20]

---

18. For a succinct description of the present state of research into Deuteronomy, see M. A. O'Brien, "The Book of Deuteronomy," *CurBS* 3 (1995): 95–128.

19. Noted in M. Weinfeld, "Deuteronomy: The Present State of the Inquiry," *JBL* 86 (1967): 249. Reprinted in D. L. Christensen, ed., *A Song of Power and the Power of Song: Essays on the Book of Deuteronomy* (SBTS 3; Winona Lake, IN: Eisenbrauns, 1993), 21–35.

20. See the helpful presentation of de Wette and his contribution to Deuteronomic studies in G. J. Wenham, *The Structure and Date of Deuteronomy: A Consideration of Aspects of the History of Deuteronomy Criticism and a Re-Examination of the Question of Structure and Date in Light of that History and the Near Eastern Treaties* (Ph.D. diss., University of London, 1970), 16–43. See also Rogerson, *de Wette*.

Modern study of Deuteronomy saw significant advance through the work of Julius Wellhausen, who argued for the existence of three sources in the Pentateuch: JE, D, and P.[21] Wellhausen himself acknowledged that this idea was not unique to him.[22] However, he may be credited with popularizing the now famous "Documentary Hypothesis" and articulating the significance of this view for the understanding of the history of Israel and the development of the literature of the Pentateuch. Furthermore, it was Wellhausen who saw centralization in Deuteronomy as being a key to understanding the nature of the reforms in support of which the book was composed.

For Wellhausen and those who followed him, Deuteronomy emerged as an important starting point for the study of the Old Testament. Wellhausen saw Deuteronomy as being a midpoint between JE and P. That is, JE was earlier than Deuteronomy, originating in the period of the monarchy but prior to the destruction of the Northern Kingdom by Assyria in the eighth century B.C.[23] Deuteronomy was "composed in the same age as that in which it was discovered," namely, during the reign of Josiah.[24] P was written at a later time and assumes many of the innovations presented in Deuteronomy.

Wellhausen further argued that the development of the religion in Israel can be traced through the source documents of the Pentateuch. He saw in the sources an evolution (or, more accurately for Wellhausen, a devolution) from a free, spontaneous, and natural religion to a more formalized, artificial expression of faith. This transition may be seen through a comparison of worship as presented in the sources. For example, Wellhausen argues that JE assumes that many altars will be built for the worship of Yahweh, based on Exod 20:24–25.[25] Deuteronomy, however, changes this law and insists on one central sanctuary and delegitimizes all other sanctuaries in chap. 12. This, again, firmly fixes the date of Deuteronomy in the 7th century B.C. and associates it with the reforms of Josiah, according to Wellhausen.[26] In P,

---

21. J. Wellhausen, *Prolegomena to the History of Israel* (Edinburgh: Black, 1885; repr. Atlanta: Scholars Press, 1994). While Wellhausen does acknowledge that E once existed as an independent source, he notes that we know of it only as "extracts embodied in the Jehovist narrative" (ibid., 8).

22. Ibid., 4. Some of his conclusions were anticipated by Eduard Reuss and his student Karl H. Graf. However, neither of these scholars had published widely, as noted by R. E. Clements, "Wellhausen, Julius (1844–1918)," in *Historical Handbook of Major Biblical Interpreters* (ed. D. K. McKim; Downers Grove, IL: InterVarsity, 1998), 380–85.

23. Wellhausen, *Prolegomena*, 9.

24. Ibid.

25. Ibid., 29.

26. Ibid., 33.

however, the centralization of worship to the one "chosen place" is assumed and never argued.[27] Wellhausen concludes that this can only mean that the transformation of religion envisioned by Deuteronomy had become a reality by the time P was composed. Thus, the different sources, which represent different stages in the history of religion in Israel, each present a different view of the religion. Moreover, a progression from greater freedom to more restriction can be discerned. Using largely the same method, Wellhausen seeks to demonstrate this same tendency in his examination of sacrifice, sacred feasts, the priesthood, and the relationship of Levites to it, firstlings, and Levitical cities.

The Documentary Hypothesis emerged as the dominant method in pentateuchal criticism and remained so until about 1970. There were, to be sure, modifications of the theory as posited by Wellhausen. But the development of the traditiohistorical approach by the Alt school, which argued for the essential continuity between the events and their description in the pentateuchal sources, as well as archaeological discoveries by the Albright school together helped secure the position of the Documentary Hypothesis in modern biblical interpretation.[28] Most notable is the fact that these newer approaches (exemplified by the Alt and Albright schools) sought to harmonize their findings with the traditional sources and dates postulated in the 19th century.[29]

While consensus emerged regarding the composition of the Pentateuch as a whole, questions remained regarding the composition of Deuteronomy in particular. Some followed earlier scholars (such as Steuernagel and Staerk) who sought to understand the growth of Deu-

27. Ibid., 34–35.

28. For a discussion of the modern development of the Documentary Hypothesis, see G. J. Wenham, "Pondering the Pentateuch: The Search for a New Paradigm," in *The Face of Old Testament Studies: A Survey of Contemporary Approaches* (ed. D. W. Baker and B. T. Arnold; Leicester: Apollos / Grand Rapids: Baker, 1999), 116–44.

29. Beginning in the 1970s, serious concerns began to be expressed about the Documentary Hypothesis. Some questioned the basic methodology of source analysis, particularly in light of ANE texts held to be unitary on other grounds but that nevertheless exhibit some of the same characteristics of the biblical texts. Others questioned the archaeological parallels that were thought to support the analysis of source critics. In the 1980s, the consensus began to break down further as some argued that the J source was in fact the latest source and was actually postexilic and post-Deuteronomic. One of the most significant critiques of the Documentary Hypothesis emerged in this time. R. N. Whybray (*The Making of the Pentateuch: A Methodological Study* [JSOTSup 53; Sheffield: JSOT Press, 1987]) presents a powerful argument against the Documentary Hypothesis. Whybray sees the entire Pentateuch as a comprehensive work composed by a single author (*Pentateuch*, 232–33). As Wenham notes, "the academic community is looking for a fresh and convincing paradigm for the study of the Pentateuch, but so far none of the new proposals seems to have captured the scholarly imagination" (Wenham, "Pondering the Pentateuch," 119).

teronomy in terms of sources, not unlike the approach to the Pentateuch as a whole. They based their conclusions on the presence of the *Numeruswechsel*, the change in form of address between second-person singular and plural.[30] The oldest version of Deuteronomy, it is argued, used the singular pronoun, while a later one used the plural. This analysis of literary strata was combined with analysis of the development of the legal section of Deuteronomy to develop a hypothesis about the origin of the book. In this view, Deuteronomy is the product of a redaction of earlier sources. Recent proponents of this view include Minette de Tillesse and Veijola.[31]

This view has been challenged, however. Some, such as Lohfink, see the variation in number as a deliberate stylistic device used to capture the attention of the "listener."[32] Moreover, Mayes has noted that number change cannot be relied upon as a criterion to identify underlying sources in at least some cases in Deuteronomy (such as 4:1–40), which are seen on other grounds as being a unity, despite the use of singular and plural address.[33] In addition, it has been noted that a similar phenomenon is found in extrabiblical texts such as the Hittite and Sefire treaties.[34]

More recently, the phenomenon of *Numeruswechsel* has been explained on rhetorical grounds as well.[35] Lenchak notes that

30. C. Steuernagel, *Der Rahmen des Deuteronomiums: Literarcritische Untersuchungen über seine Zusammensetzung und Entstehung* (Halle a.S.: J. Krause, 1894); and W. Staerk, *Das Deuteronomium—Sein Inhalt und seine literarische Form: Eine kritische Studie* (Leipzig: Hinrichs, 1894). See the description and analysis of this approach in A. D. H. Mayes, *Deuteronomy* (NCB; Grand Rapids: Eerdmans / London: Marshall, Morgan & Scott, 1979), 34–38; D. L. Christensen, "Deuteronomy in Modern Research: Approaches and Issues," in *A Song of Power and the Power of Song* (SBTS 3; Winona Lake, IN: Eisenbrauns, 1993), 3–5; and, more recently, C. T. Begg, "1994: A Significant Anniversary in the History of Deuteronomy Research," in *Studies in Deuteronomy: In Honour of C. J. Labuschagne on the Occasion of His Sixty-Fifth Birthday* (VTSup 53; ed. F. García Martínez et al.; Leiden: Brill, 1994), 1–11.

31. G. Minette de Tillesse, "Sections 'tu' et sections 'vous' dans le Deutéronome," *VT* 12 (1962): 29–87, and T. Veijola, "Principal Observations on the Basic Story in Deuteronomy 1–3," in *A Song of Power and the Power of Song* (SBTS 3; Winona Lake, IN: Eisenbrauns, 1993), 137–46. A very different perspective is advocated by D. L. Christensen, *Deuteronomy 1:1–21:9* (2nd ed.; WBC 6a; Nashville: Thomas Nelson, 2001), ci, who sees the *Numeruswechsel* as "structural markers, particularly of boundaries between rhythmic units of the text, and sometimes the center, or turning point within specific structures."

32. N. Lohfink, *Das Hauptgebot: Eine Untersuchung literarischer Einleitungsfragen zu Dtn 5–11* (AnBib 20; Rome: Pontifical Biblical Institute, 1963).

33. Mayes, *Deuteronomy*, 36.

34. K. Baltzer, *The Covenant Formulary in Old Testament, Jewish, and Early Christian Writings* (Philadelphia: Fortress, 1971), 33 n. 71; and Mayes, *Deuteronomy*, 35–36.

35. Since Muilenburg's programmatic essay (J. Muilenburg, "Form Criticism and Beyond," *JBL* 88 [1969]: 1–18), Old Testament rhetorical criticism has tended to emphasize style, and has been, in many ways, a form of literary criticism. In recent years, however,

[e]very change of number is an assault on the listener. The singular is considered to have been the standard form by which the cult community was addressed: Israel was viewed as one person before Yahweh in worship. In the plural then the community is no longer addressed as an entity but as a collection of individuals. Thus in the plural form the individual Israelite is emphasized and the approach is more personal.[36]

So, rather than being understood as a mark of different sources, number change may be a deliberate attempt on the part of the author to persuade his audience. More than being a matter of style, the change in address is part of the author's attempt to convince his audience that all Israel—as individuals and as a collective—must live lives that are radically devoted to Yahweh.[37]

It was Martin Noth who made the most significant contribution to Deuteronomy studies after Wellhausen. In his landmark work, *Überlieferungsgeschichtliche Studien*,[38] Noth argued that Deuteronomy was best seen not as a work of the so-called Hexateuch but rather as the first part of a Deuteronomistic History (DtH) that consists of the books Deuteronomy–Kings. This work, he argued, is the product of an author, not an editor, who "brought together material from highly varied traditions and arranged it according to a carefully conceived plan."[39] According to Noth, the book of Deuteronomy was compiled in such a way as to serve as the introduction to the larger work. Thus, chaps. 1–3 of Deuteronomy are seen not simply as an introduction to the book of Deuteronomy but primarily as an introduction to DtH.[40] This introduction was placed into an older version of the Deuteronomic law that is essentially the same as that found in Deut 4:44–

---

there has emerged an emphasis on the persuasive, as opposed to stylistic, aspects of rhetoric. It is in this latter sense that I use the word "rhetorical" here. For a helpful discussion of the two "schools" in OT rhetorical criticism, see D. M. Howard Jr., "Rhetorical Criticism in Old Testament Studies," *BBR* 4 (1994): 87–104. See also C. C. Black Jr., "Rhetorical Criticism and Biblical Interpretation," *ExpTim* 100 (1988–89): 252–58; and W. Wuellner, "Where Is Rhetorical Criticism Taking Us?" *CBQ* 49 (1987): 448–63. For a detailed discussion of contemporary rhetorical criticism, see K. Möller, *A Prophet in Debate: The Rhetoric of Persuasion in the Book of Amos* (JSOTSup 372; Sheffield: Sheffield Academic Press, 2003), 2–46.

36. T. A. Lenchak, *"Choose Life!": A Rhetorical-Critical Investigation of Deuteronomy 28,69–30,20* (AnBib 129; Rome: Pontifical Biblical Institute, 1993), 13.

37. Ibid., 16.

38. M. Noth, *Überlieferungsgeschichtliche Studien* (2nd ed.; Tübingen: Max Niemeyer, 1957). References here are to the ET of the first 110 pp., which appears as *The Deuteronomistic History* (2nd ed.; JSOTSup 15; Sheffield: JSOT Press, 1991). The remainder of the work appears in ET in idem, *The Chronicler's History* (JSOTSup 50; Sheffield: JSOT Press, 1987).

39. Idem, *Deuteronomistic History*, 26.

40. Ibid., 27–33.

30:20.[41] Noth further postulated a purpose for this entire composition: to explain the fall of Jerusalem in 586 B.C. as being a result of failure to keep the covenant. As the introduction to DtH, Deuteronomy helps explain the nature and terms of that covenant.

Noth's approach was a significant departure from the approach of his predecessors. After Wellhausen and prior to Noth, study of Deuteronomy focused largely on identifying the various sources thought to lie behind the final form of the text. In particular, there was an effort to identify the earliest form of Deuteronomy (sometimes called Urdt) and to identify other sources that were combined with it in order to form the present version of the text. Noth, however, argued for a basic Urdt that was modified by a single author whose purpose, as noted above, was to explain the fall of Jerusalem and the catastrophe of the exile. Noth's analysis, then, consisted to a great degree of identifying what was Deuteronomistic and what was earlier.

In many respects, Noth's approach was adopted by subsequent critics. Some have suggested that there were in fact two (or more) versions of DtH that have been woven together in the final form of the text. F. M. Cross, for example, argues for two versions of DtH. The first, Dtr[1], was composed in the time of Josiah and in support of the Josianic reforms. It is marked by an emphasis on the themes of judgment and hope. The second version, Dtr[2], was composed during the exile, about 550 B.C. It is seen as being far less hopeful in its outlook than Dtr[1]. Cross notes, however, that he follows Noth in seeing the author of Dtr[1] as a truly creative author and does not challenge the general implications of Noth's theory for the book of Deuteronomy.[42]

---

41. Ibid., 31.

42. F. M. Cross, *Canaanite Myth and Hebrew Epic: Essays in the History of the Religion of Israel* (Cambridge: Harvard University Press, 1973), 274–89. See also A. D. H. Mayes, *The Story of Israel between Settlement and Exile: A Redactional Study of the Deuteronomistic History* (London: SCM, 1983). A more recent work by N. Lohfink ("The Cult Reform of Josiah of Judah: 2 Kings 22–23 as a Source for the History of Israelite Religion," in *Ancient Israelite Religion: Essays in Honor of Frank Moore Cross* [ed. P. D. Miller Jr., P. D. Hanson, and S. D. McBride; Philadelphia: Fortress, 1987], 459–75) comes to similar conclusions, seeing a Josianic Dtr[1] and an exilic Dtr[2].

Subsequent scholars have modified Cross's views substantially. R. D. Nelson, *The Double Redaction of the Deuteronomistic History* (JSOTSup 18; Sheffield: JSOT Press, 1981), argued for two redactions of DtH, but articulated different redactional methods between Dtr[1] and Dtr[2]. G. N. Knoppers, *Two Nations under God: The Deuteronomistic History of Solomon and the Dual Monarchies* (HSM 52; Atlanta: Scholars Press, 1993), sees two redactions but sees the Josianic Dtr[1] as having incorporated some preexilic traditions that were critical of the monarchy.

Other critics moved in the direction of seeing even more redactions. This approach was first advocated in R. Smend, "Das Gesetz und die Völker: Ein Beitrag zur deuteronomischen Redaktionsgeschichte," in *Probleme biblischer Theologie* (ed. H. W. Wolff; Munich:

The significance of Noth's approach for the study of Deuteronomy
is that he brought the idea that different voices could be heard in
Deuteronomy into general acceptance.[43] In addition, Noth postulated that the exilic redactor of Deuteronomy and DtH had a purpose
in view (viz., to explain the exile in terms of failure to keep the terms
of the covenant). This, too, became a criterion used by subsequent
critics to identify layers. That is, perceived changes in perspective or
purpose were used to separate out layers of the text. Each perceived
layer of the text was consequently seen to represent a particular
ideology. As O'Brien notes, "since Noth, the trend has been to concentrate on separating the deuteronomistic (dtr) redaction from the
earlier material."[44]

Chr. Kaiser, 1971). Smend argued for an initial redaction, DtrG, that was roughly equivalent to Noth's Dtr. Interest in legal matters in certain texts in Joshua and Judges (Josh 1:7–
9; 13:1bβ–6; 23; and Judg 1:1–2:9; 17; 20–21; 23) were the result of a second redaction,
DtrN (nomistic). Smend's approach was later modified by W. Dietrich (*Prophetie und Ge-
schichte* [FRLANT 108; Göttingen: Vandenhoeck & Ruprecht, 1972]), who saw an additional, intermediate redaction (DtrP) associated with prophetic interests. More recent
proponents of this view include R. Klein, *1 Samuel* (WBC 10; Waco, TX: Word, 1983). This
view has been criticized because it largely ignores the possibility of a preexilic edition, as
well as because the putative sources are not clearly differentiated from one another.
    Finally, there is the perspective of a single, late Deuteronomist, advanced by J. Van
Seters, *In Search of History: Historiography in the Ancient World and the Origins of Biblical History* (New Haven: Yale University Press, 1983; repr. Winona Lake, IN: Eisenbrauns, 1997).
Van Seters follows Noth in seeing DtH as being the product of a creative author but maintains that the exilic author was the original author and was not editing earlier material
(though sometimes the editor used preformed traditions). In Van Seters's view, the instances in which earlier critics saw different literary strata are the result of the writing of
Dtr. As a result, Van Seters sees great unity in DtH, because it is the product of a single,
creative author writing at a single time. This view has been criticized for its insistence on
the priority of DtH over the Pentateuch, which stems, at least in part, from an assumption
that any text demonstrating any literary or theological sophistication must necessarily be
late. For helpful overviews of these various positions, see S. L. McKenzie, "Deuteronomistic History," *ABD* 2: 160–68; J. G. McConville, "The Old Testament Historical Books in
Modern Scholarship," *Themelios* 22/3 (1997): 3–13; and T. Römer, "The Book of Deuteronomy," in *The History of Israel's Traditions: The Heritage of Martin Noth* (JSOTSup 182; ed.
S. L. McKenzie and M. P. Graham; Sheffield: Sheffield Academic Press, 1994), 178–212. A
more extensive treatment of the issues is found in M. A. O'Brien, *The Deuteronomistic History Hypothesis: A Reassessment* (OBO 92; Freiburg: Universitätsverlag / Göttingen: Vandenhoeck & Ruprecht, 1989); and A. F. Campbell and M. A. O'Brien, *Unfolding the Deuteronomistic History: Origins, Upgrades, Present Text* (Minneapolis: Fortress, 2000).
    43. J. G. McConville, *Grace in the End: A Study in Deuteronomic Theology* (SOTBT; Grand
Rapids: Zondervan, 1993), 34.
    44. O'Brien, "Deuteronomy," 97.

While Noth thought primarily in terms of two sources in the present form of Deuteronomy (Urdt and Dtr), subsequent scholars such as Cross, Smend, and Dietrich[45] began to discover many more layers in Deuteronomy and DtH. In principle, the number of layers could be unlimited. It appears, however, that efforts to identify pre-Deuteronomic, Deuteronomic, and Deuteronomistic layers in Deuteronomy (and DtH) are at an impasse.[46] Despite broad agreement about a later redaction of an Urdt, conclusions about the identification and number of literary strata are diverse and, at times, contradictory.[47] To cite just one example, Cross maintained that 1 Kgs 2:4; 8:25b; and 9:4–5 should be assigned to Dtr^2, since they make the promise to David conditional.[48] Others, however, maintain that these same passages should be assigned to Dtr^1 instead.[49] Similar disagreement may be seen when considering the ideology underlying the redactions. Consequently, some have sought to move in a different direction, with positive results.[50]

Beginning with the important work of Polzin, synchronic readings of Deuteronomy have become more common.[51] According to Polzin, Deuteronomy shows a careful and deliberate interplay between the voice of Moses and that of the narrator of the book, such that the

45. See n. 42, above.

46. See, e.g., C. Conroy, "Reflections on the Exegetical Task: Apropos of Recent Studies on 2 Kings 22–23," in *Pentateuchal and Deuteronomistic Studies: Papers Read at the XIIIth IOSOT Congress, Leuven 1989* (BETL; ed. C. Brekelmans and J. Lust; Leuven: Leuven University Press, 1990), 256–57. H. Seebass ("Vorschlag zur Vereinfachung literarischer Analysen im dtn Gesetz," *BN* 58 [1991]: 83–98) maintains that literary-critical analysis of the Deuteronomic law code has become too complex due to multiplication of the criteria. He identifies three criteria for the identification of literary strata in the Deuteronomic code: (1) a contradiction or the presence of a doublet; (2) marked differences in style; and (3) the judicial sense of a passage.

47. The fact of a later redaction of DtH has also been called into question recently. A. G. Auld ("The Deuteronomists and the Former Prophets, or What Makes the Former Prophets Deuteronomistic?" in *Those Elusive Deuteronomists: The Phenomenon of Pan-Deuteronomism* [JSOTSup 268; ed. L. S. Schearing and S. L. McKenzie; Sheffield: Sheffield Academic Press, 1999], 116–26) argues that the influence should be seen as going in the opposite direction—that is, that Kings has influenced Deuteronomy.

48. Cross, *Canaanite Myth*, 287.

49. Cf. R. E. Friedman, *The Exile and Biblical Narrative* (HSM 22; Chico, CA: Scholars Press, 1981), 12–13; and Nelson, *Double Redaction*, 118.

50. According to O'Brien, "Deuteronomy," 101, "interest in tracing the contours of dtr and pre-dtr layers throughout Deuteronomy seems to be waning."

51. R. Polzin, *Moses and the Deuteronomist: A Literary Study of the Deuteronomic History, Part One: Deuteronomy, Joshua, Judges* (Bloomington: Indiana University Press, 1980); and idem, "Deuteronomy," in *The Literary Guide to the Bible* (ed. R. Alter and F. Kermode; Cambridge: Harvard University Press, 1987), 92–101.

"separate voices of Moses and the narrator gradually fuse as the book progresses toward its conclusion."[52] Apparent contradictions, so often used to identify disparate sources or layers in the book, are, in Polzin's view, the result of a deliberate effort to preserve a "plurality of viewpoints, all working together to achieve a truly multidimensional effect."[53] Polzin's work was significant in that it presented a plausible synchronic reading of the text.[54]

Since Polzin, there has been an increasing tendency to read Deuteronomy as an organized whole, as more and more scholars are recognizing the subtleties of argument and the skill of the author(s) or editor(s) of the book. Lohfink has posited that the book can in fact be read as a whole in which the various parts are seen to be interconnected and support a coherent argument.[55] Olson's work presents a theological reading of the book that seeks to take seriously the development of thought from beginning to end.[56] In addition, recent works by Millar, Barker, and Wright[57] stress the unity of thought of the book, which suggests that a synchronic reading of the text as a whole may be a fruitful avenue to pursue.

The Aim and Method of the Present Work

As noted above, it is my contention that the prevailing consensus regarding the nature of the Deuteronomic program and, therefore, the understanding of the theology of the book has not adequately accounted for the data of the text. One of my primary aims is to demonstrate the reasons why the prevailing consensus on Deuteronomy fails

---

52. Ibid., 92.

53. Ibid., 93.

54. Polzin notes, however, that such a synchronic reading cannot ignore diachronic considerations, and he maintains that the two approaches are complementary to one another. See Polzin, *Moses*, 2–5.

55. N. Lohfink, "Zur Fabel des Deuteronomiums," in *Bundesdokument und Gesetz: Studien zum Deuteronomium* (HBS 4; ed. G. Braulik; Freiburg: Herder, 1995), 65–78. His understanding of how particular texts relate to the *Fabel* of the book may be found in "Zur Fabel in Dtn 31–32," in *Konsequente Traditionsgeschichte: FS für Klaus Baltzer zum 65. Geburtstag* (OBO 126; ed. R. Bartelmus et al.; Freiburg: Universitätsverlag / Göttingen: Vandenhoeck und Ruprecht, 1993), 255–79; idem, "Moab oder Sichem: Wo wurde Dtn 28 nach der Fabel des Deuteronomium proklamiert?" in *Studies in Deuteronomy: In Honour of C. J. Labuschagne on the Occasion of His 65th Birthday* (ed. F. García Martínez et al.; Leiden: Brill, 1994), 139–53.

56. D. T. Olson, *Deuteronomy and the Death of Moses: A Theological Reading* (OBT; Minneapolis: Fortress, 1994).

57. J. G. Millar, *Now Choose Life: Theology and Ethics in Deuteronomy* (NSBT 6; Leicester: Apollos, 1998); P. Barker, *Deuteronomy: The God Who Keeps Promises* (Melbourne: Acorn, 1998); C. J. H. Wright, *Deuteronomy* (NIBC 4; Peabody, MA: Hendrickson / Carlisle: Paternoster, 1996).

to account adequately for the textual data. In so doing, I will be analyzing in chap. 1 some of the primary arguments adduced in favor of centralization, secularization, and demythologization as presented by major interpreters of Deuteronomy.

The second objective is to present a viable alternative to the prevailing view that will, hopefully, better account for the data of the text. This will be based primarily on a synchronic reading of the text, though I will necessarily engage the views of those who adopt a diachronic approach throughout my argument. Because an exhaustive exegesis of the entire book of Deuteronomy is clearly beyond the scope of this project, in chaps. 2 through 5 I will concentrate primarily on the texts that have most often been interpreted as demonstrating the Deuteronomic revolution as commonly understood, in an effort to show how they may be differently interpreted. There are, to be sure, many other texts that would support my understanding as well. I will, however, limit my inquiry to the texts that have been understood as being foundational to the prevailing view of the book. In the final chapter I will discuss the implications of this interpretation of the texts for the theology and ideology of the book as a whole.

Ideology and Structure in Deuteronomy

As a foundation and background to the discussion about the theology of Deuteronomy, an examination of the structure of the book is necessary. Understanding the structure of the book is vital to understanding the message of the book itself. Similarly, understanding the structure of the book helps in the identification of the ideology of the book.

The Meaning of Ideology

It is important at the outset to clarify just what is meant by *ideology* here. This is, in reality, no simple task, for as Barr notes, "the entry of the concept of ideology into biblical scholarship cannot be said to have been a happy event. That there is such a thing as ideology and that the term may well be useful for biblical exegesis may be freely granted. But the way in which it has actually worked, so far at least, has been little short of chaotic."[58] Imposing order on the chaos is beyond the scope of this work, but I will seek to explain how I am using the term and describe how that usage relates to the contemporary scene.[59]

---

58. J. Barr, *History and Ideology in the Old Testament: Biblical Studies at the End of a Millennium* (Oxford: Oxford University Press, 2000), 139.

59. Barr further notes that if the term "ideology" is used, "it should be properly analysed and clearly explained, and the advantages expected from it should also be explained" (ibid., 140). The following will attempt to do what Barr advocates. There is, of course, a

An early attempt at understanding the role of ideology in the Old Testament was that of Miller.[60] Miller defined *ideology* as "a description of the way things are in a society, the values, ideas, and conceptions of a society which cause it to do or act as it does."[61] He goes on, however, to draw a contrast between faith and ideology, arguing that faith is "those impulses which force Israel's theology out beyond the limits of its own self-interest."[62] In Miller's view, then, the ideology of a particular group of people (as reflected in a text) cannot include any sense of self-sacrifice. Rather, ideology is inherently self-interested; thus, Miller identifies faith by drawing a contrast with ideology on the basis of three criteria:

1. the presence of self-criticism;
2. a positive sense of relationship between Israel and the world, so that the interests of Israel are not seen as paramount in defining its goals and so that concern for the nations is part of the understanding of Israel's place in the world;
3. the moral demand for justice and righteousness as the central characteristics of conduct.[63]

In Miller's view, faith is marked by the presence of these three criteria, and ideology by their absence. The problem, in my estimation, is that this strict differentiation between faith and ideology is rather artificial.[64] It seems possible that concern for others could easily be a part of the values or beliefs of a society that cause it to act as it does. Moreover, the religious beliefs and the practices that express these beliefs are undoubtedly important in shaping the values that are reflected in their ideology. Thus, it is not helpful to define *ideology* in a way that contrasts it with the faith of the society.

---

tremendous amount of literature available on ideology. Some important works on this subject include: T. Eagleton, *Ideology* (London: Verso, 1991); J. Plamenatz, *Ideology* (New York: Plaeger, 1974); P. Ricoeur, *Lectures on Ideology and Utopia* (New York: Columbia University Press, 1986). Classic works that form the basis for more recent discussion are K. Marx and F. Engels, *The German Ideology* (London: Lawrence & Wishart, 1938; ET of *Die Deutsche Ideologie*, 1846); K. Mannheim, *Ideology and Utopia* (London: Routledge, 1936).

60. P. D. Miller Jr., "Faith and Ideology in the Old Testament," in *Magnalia Dei—The Mighty Acts of God: Essays on the Bible and Archaeology in Memory of G. Ernest Wright* (ed. F. M. Cross, W. Lemke, and P. D. Miller Jr.; New York: Doubleday, 1976), 464–79.

61. Ibid., 465.

62. Ibid., 467.

63. Ibid., 467–68.

64. Miller does acknowledge that "the line between faith and ideology is never drawn completely" but sees in the later period of Israel's history a greater tendency toward differentiation between the two. See ibid., 467.

A second problem lies in the fact that Miller's association of ideology with self-interest suggests a materialist understanding of ideology. But the materialist view has rightly been criticized for being reductionist. It is too simple to say that one's material conditions "cause" one to think or act in a particular way, not least because to make this claim is to deny the importance of the "subjective, conscious, human activity in the creation of those material conditions which are reckoned to cause human thinking."[65]

Ideology has also been seen as "symbolic representation through which reality is experienced and brought to expression."[66] This view, associated with Ricoeur, sees ideology as serving to integrate a community by providing a common set of symbols, then legitimating a ruling authority, and, finally, distorting by obscuring the processes of life. Religious ideology distorts by disguising self-interest in the form of a divine mandate.[67]

While Ricoeur, Geertz, and Gottwald see ideology functioning in principle to integrate a community, it appears that its true effect is conflict and distortion. Thus Ricoeur asks whether "we are allowed to speak of ideologies outside the situation of distortion and so with reference only to the basic function of integration" and goes on to argue that conflict between ideologies is necessary for there to be ideology at all.[68] This view is taken up and adapted somewhat by Clines, who sees ideology as expressing the self-interest of one group at the expense of another group. Texts, in this view, are ideological statements that are in the interest of a powerful group in society (since societies are not homogeneous) and either hint at or repress some type of social conflict.[69]

It is debatable, however, whether this model of conflict and distortion is really the best understanding of ideology or, more importantly,

65. A. D. H. Mayes, "Deuteronomistic Ideology and the Theology of the Old Testament," *JSOT* 82 (1999): 60. Cf. I. Robertson ("Ideology," in *Encyclopedia of Anthropology* [ed. D. E. Hunter and P. Whitten; New York: Harper & Row, 1976], 214), who maintains that many social scientists "believe that the relationship between belief systems and their material base may be more complicated and subtle than Marx envisaged."

66. Mayes, "Deuteronomistic Ideology," 61.

67. Ibid., 62–63. A similar view is advocated by C. Geertz, *The Interpretation of Cultures* (New York: Basic Books, 1973); and N. Gottwald, *The Tribes of Yahweh: A Sociology of the Religion of Liberated Israel, 1250–1050 B.C.E.* (London: SCM, 1980).

68. Ricoeur, *Lectures*, 259.

69. D. J. A. Clines, "Biblical Interpretation in an International Perspective," *BibInt* 1/1 (1993): 84–86. A more succinct definition of *ideology* is presented in J. B. Thompson, *Ideology and Modern Culture: Critical Social Theory in the Era of Mass Communication* (Palo Alto: Stanford University Press, 1990), 7, who says that ideology is "meaning in the service of power."

the basis on which texts should be interpreted. For example, Clines cites the Ten Commandments as a text that reflects self-interest on the part of Israelite elites and somehow represents (either by repressing or highlighting) social conflict.[70] But this supposes, as Barr notes,[71] that there was a faction or group in Israel that was opposed to the ideology represented in this text. Yet, it is hard to imagine factions that were in favor of adultery, stealing, disrespect toward parents, and so forth. Rather, it is in *everyone's* interest (not just the elites') that adultery and murder be condemned. It seems, then, that consensus, not conflict, lies at the heart of a text such as the Decalogue.[72]

One view of ideology that stresses consensus has been suggested by Lemche. He defines ideology as "that set of opinions which dominated Israelite society and which made up the 'system' of values with which the Israelite actions corresponded."[73] This view of ideology is attractive because it recognizes that ideology may represent a consensus in society. This is not to suggest that there were no differences among various groups in Israelite society, but it does imply that there was some prevailing or commonly held view. Second, Lemche notes that ideology includes opinions (or beliefs) and that these beliefs were part of the framework of values that undergirded life in Israel. He goes on to note that *"ideology, religion,* and *theology* are to a large extent synonyms."[74] This represents an advance on Miller's view in that it makes it possible for altruism and religious beliefs to be an integral part of the ideology of a people, not something antithetical to it.

Although Lemche warns against the danger of equating ideology with theology,[75] the danger nevertheless exists. It is possible that in so conceiving ideology, one will tend to think of theology *as opposed to* "practical" and secular issues. But this distinction between sacred and secular is a distinctly modern phenomenon. No such distinction was known in the ancient world; rather, the pervasive reality of God or the gods was accepted as a matter of course, and this belief had an impact on other aspects of life as well.

---

70. Clines, "Biblical Interpretation," 85.

71. Barr, *History and Ideology,* 134–35.

72. The fact that some texts reflect consensus rather than conflict suggests that caution should be exercised when drawing conclusions regarding the ideology represented by the text. Texts may represent the prevailing attitudes of the community as a whole, or they may reflect a minority or dissenting viewpoint of a subculture of the community. It is not necessary to conclude, however, that conflict and repression are at the center of the expression of ideology.

73. N. P. Lemche, *Ancient Israel: A New History of Israelite Society* (The Biblical Seminar; Sheffield: JSOT Press, 1988), 34 n. 1.

74. Ibid.

75. Ibid.

It seems to me, then, that a preferable definition of *ideology* would be one that sees it as synonymous not with theology but with *world view*. In this theory, ideology represents the system of beliefs (including religious beliefs), attitudes, values, and assumptions of a community or part of a community.[76] As Wright notes, world views deal with the "ultimate concerns of human beings."[77] They give expression to several basic issues, including questions of identity (Who are we as a community? What are our basic needs? What is the solution to our problems?) as well as practice (Given who we are, how are we to live? How do we put into practice the solutions to our problems?).[78] Ideology, then, is more than theoretical but has tremendous practical implications as well.

Ideology and Text

Before examining the structure of Deuteronomy and the ways in which the structure of the book may shed light on its underlying ideology, we must briefly consider the way texts reflect ideology. As noted above, ideology may be thought of as synonymous with world view. It is to be expected, then, that texts will reflect the world view or ideology of the community or culture (or subculture) in which the text was produced. Indeed, all human writing may be thought of as the expression of world views and often includes the attempt to persuade others to accept the articulated world view.[79]

Furthermore, a text is the product of an author's intention to communicate something to an audience; it is *"social discourse."*[80] There is, in addition, a persuasive element to this communication, because the

76. Cf. K. J. Vanhoozer, *Is There a Meaning in This Text? The Bible, the Reader and the Morality of Literary Knowledge* (Leicester: Apollos / Grand Rapids: Zondervan, 1998), 175. This is similar to (although less cumbersome than) the definition of *ideology* provided by G. Duby, "Ideologies in Social History," in *Constructing the Past: Essays in Historical Methodology* (ed. J. Le Goff and P. Nora; Cambridge: Cambridge University Press, 1974), 152; cited in M. Z. Brettler, *The Creation of History in Ancient Israel* (London: Routledge, 1995), 13. See also M. Sternberg, *The Poetics of Biblical Narrative: Ideological Literature and the Drama of Reading* (Bloomington: Indiana University Press, 1985), 37. It should be clear that this understanding of ideology is not a negative one. Although a negative connotation is often intended by scholars using the word, no such connotation is intended here.

77. N. T. Wright, *Christian Origins and the Question of God*, vol. 1: *The New Testament and the People of God* (London: SPCK, 1992), 122.

78. Ibid., 123–24.

79. See ibid., 65; and Sternberg, *Poetics*, 37. The persuasive element need not be explicit to function as "rhetorical." Even when writing texts that seek to inform, authors want the reader to accept the information as true and valid.

80. Wuellner, "Rhetorical Criticism," 462.

author seeks to convince the audience of the truth of his or her perspective.[81] The content and form of this communication is largely influenced by the ideology or world view of the author and audience.[82]

Interpreting texts, then, involves identifying what the author intended to communicate to his or her audience. But, because texts are reflections of ideology or world view, it is necessary to consider this world view when one interprets the text. This means, first, being aware of the cultural context in which the text was written. But it also means taking into consideration the rhetorical purpose for which a text was written. Clines notes that the phrase "'Bus stop' will mean one thing when attached to a pole at the side of the road, another thing when shouted by an anxious parent to a child about to dash out into that road."[83] While Clines argues that this demonstrates the indeterminacy of textual meaning, it seems to me that considering the purpose for which the words were written (or spoken) grounds the meaning. While the *words* "bus stop" are indeed indeterminate (i.e., they are capable of a variety of interpretations), they become grounded by the context in which they are uttered. It is inconceivable that those words affixed to a pole would be interpreted as being meant to warn of impending danger to a child running toward the road, just as the context clearly establishes that a parent shouting the words at a running child is not intending to inform the child that this is the place at which he or she may board a bus. Proper interpretation demands an awareness of the rhetorical purpose (to inform, to warn, etc.) for the utterance.

Finally, understanding the rhetorical purpose and the intended meaning of the utterance helps us understand the ideology or world view represented by the text. Because texts reflect the world view of the author, a careful analysis of the text, paying attention to rhetorical purpose and context, will provide clues regarding the major values, beliefs, and interests of the author.[84]

81. On the different types of persuasive speech, see C. Perelman and L. Olbrechts-Tyteca, *The New Rhetoric: A Treatise on Argumentation* (trans. J. Wilkinson and P. Weaver; Notre Dame: University of Notre Dame Press, 1969), 21–51; E. P. J. Corbett and R. J. Connors, *Classical Rhetoric for the Modern Student* (4th ed.; Oxford: Oxford University Press, 1999), 15–24; G. A. Kennedy, *New Testament Interpretation through Rhetorical Criticism* (Chapel Hill: University of North Carolina Press, 1984), 19–23.

82. It should be noted that this presumes, to some degree, correspondence between the world view of the author and his or her audience. That is, an author assumes that the conventions, imagery, and allusions of his or her text will be understood by the audience reading it.

83. Clines, "Biblical Interpretation," 78.

84. What I am suggesting is similar in some respects to the methodology of ideological criticism. There are, however, crucial differences. Ideological criticism as usually construed presupposes a materialistic conception of ideology and seeks, therefore, to focus on

The Structure of Deuteronomy

We can turn our attention now to the issue of the structure of Deuteronomy and what the structure of the book may suggest about the ideology represented in it.

There have been many varied attempts to describe the structure of Deuteronomy. The variety of approaches undoubtedly stem from the book itself, which Wright aptly notes is "so rich in content and texture that, like a rich fruitcake, it can be sliced in various ways."[85] The question that I want to consider is: what meaning is suggested by the various proposals for the structure of the book? This is a question that has not usually been considered. Attention has often been given to the structure of the Deuteronomic law,[86] but less attention has been paid to the interpretive implications of the structure of the book as a whole.[87]

Superscriptions

One of the simplest and most natural ways of understanding Deuteronomy is as a record or collection of the speeches of Moses. Thus, the structure of the book would be identified by the markers used to introduce these speeches. These include the phrases אֵלֶּה הַדְּבָרִים (1:1); אֵלֶּה דִבְרֵי הַבְּרִית (28:69); וְזֹאת הַמִּצְוָה הַחֻקִּים וְהַמִּשְׁפָּטִים (6:1); וְזֹאת הַתּוֹרָה (4:44); and וְזֹאת הַבְּרָכָה (33:1). So, a typical proposal for the structure of the book based on the superscriptions is:

---

the aspects of the text that reveal a struggle for power in the community in which the text was written. The effect of this approach is largely to eliminate consideration of the communicative intention for which the text was written in favor of analyzing something that lies behind the text. Others have also extended ideological criticism to include an evaluation of the ideology of the reader, which, again, has the effect of focusing attention on something other than the communicative intention for which the text was written. My interest is in the message intended to be communicated through the conventions (grammatical, rhetorical, literary, etc.) of the text, a message I take to be ideological as defined above. On ideological criticism, see G. A. Yee, "Ideological Criticism," in *Dictionary of Biblical Interpretation* (ed. J. H. Hayes; Nashville: Abingdon, 1999), 1:534–37; and R. P. Carroll, "An Infinity of Traces: On Making an Inventory of Our Ideological Holdings. An Introduction to *Ideologiekritik* in Biblical Studies," *JNSL* 21 (1995): 25–43.

85. Wright, *Deuteronomy*, 1.

86. See, e.g., S. A. Kaufman, "The Structure of the Deuteronomic Law," *Maarav* 1–2 (1978–79): 105–58; J. H. Walton, "Deuteronomy: An Exposition of the Spirit of the Law," *Grace Theological Journal* 8 (1987), 213–25. Walton here counters Kaufman, who saw the correlation to the Decalogue simply as a literary device. G. Braulik, "Die Abfolge der Gesetze in Deuteronomium 12–26 und der Dekalog," in *Das Deuteronomium: Entstehung, Gestalt und Botschaft* (ed. N. Lohfink; Leuven: Leuven University Press, 1985), 252–72, argues that the legal section represents an authoritative interpretation of the Decalogue.

87. One important exception to this is Olson, *Death of Moses*. Olson maintains that the structure of the book helps elucidate its meaning.

1:1–4:43   A historical review, followed by exhortation
4:44–28:68 Exhortation to covenant loyalty, followed by the law,
            covenant renewal, blessings, and curses
29:1–30:20 Summary and concluding challenge[88]

According to this view, the remainder of the book functions as a sort of epilogue.

The strength of this view is that it is simple and straightforward. It allows the text to determine the structure, rather than any external factors. On the other hand, it does not take into account changes in content, which may also be indicators of structure. For example, this understanding of structure does not recognize a major structural break at chap. 12, despite the fact that there is a clear transition in terms of content. In my estimation, structure should be identified on the basis of form *and* content, not simply in terms of one or the other. Moreover, this understanding of structure relegates the final chapters of the book to the status of an appendix or epilogue. While they may, of course, actually be nothing more than that, it seems to me once again to be necessary to assess their place in the book in terms of content as well as form.

This understanding of structure clearly stresses the authority and pivotal role of Moses. Emphasis is on the fact that the words proclaimed are not just any words but the words spoken by Moses, who enjoyed a unique relationship with Yahweh (Deut 34:10–12). Each of the introductory phrases cited above is associated in important ways with Moses. In some instances, Moses is credited by the narrator with saying what follows (Deut 1:1; 4:44; 33:1). In another case, Deut 6:1, Moses in the first person identifies what follows as the words that Yahweh commanded him to teach, but Moses is nevertheless highlighted as the bearer of the words of Yahweh. Finally, in Deut 28:69, it is the narrator who identifies Moses as the one who brings Yahweh's word to the people.

This understanding of the structure of the book clearly emphasizes the role of Moses. But it is important to note that it is primarily Moses as teacher of *Torah* that is emphasized in Deuteronomy. While Moses is recognized as leader of the people in the recollection of the post-

---

88. Wright, *Deuteronomy*, 2. Similarly, Olson (*Death of Moses*, 15) sees the structure as based on the superscriptions, although he sees another section beginning with the superscription at 33:1, which Wright does not acknowledge. Other works that see the structure in terms of superscriptions are P. D. Miller, *Deuteronomy* (Interp; Louisville: John Knox, 1990), 10–15; I. Cairns, *Word and Presence: A Commentary on the Book of Deuteronomy* (ITC; Grand Rapids: Eerdmans / Edinburgh: Handsel, 1992), 2–4; Tigay, *Deuteronomy*, xii; S. K. Sherwood, *Leviticus, Numbers, Deuteronomy* (BO; Collegeville, MN: Liturgical Press, 2002), 220. In most cases, additional subheadings are identified.

Horeb experiences (Deut 1:6–3:29), there is greater emphasis on his role as messenger and interpreter of Yahweh's word (cf. Deut 1:5). Indeed, Moses' second speech has been seen as a statement of the command of Yahweh (chap. 5) followed by its explication by Moses.[89] Thirty-six times in chaps. 4–30 Moses says, "I command you," thus stressing the authority of his own teaching.[90] Moses' significance is due primarily to his role as mediator, messenger, and teacher of Yahweh's *Torah*.

It is necessary at this point to engage the important argument advanced by Polzin, who posits a very different understanding of the ideology suggested by a structure based on superscriptions.[91] As a result of a close literary examination of Deuteronomy, Polzin identifies three voices in the book: Moses, God, and the narrator. According to Polzin, the three voices in Deuteronomy are engaged in a complex, subtle interplay. The voice of Moses (and, because he is God's messenger, the voice of God as well) represents the point of view of retributive justice and stresses the unconditional election of Israel as the people of God and the immutability of God's word.[92] The voice of the narrator, on the other hand, represents the point of view of "critical traditionalism," which mediates the election of Israel with knowledge of its disobedience and stresses the need for ongoing interpretation of the divine word.[93] In Polzin's view, these voices compete in Deuteronomy, but the voice of the narrator emerges as the final voice and authority. This is accomplished through subtle shifts, in which Moses' authority to interpret the word of God is paralleled with the narrator's authority to report (and to interpret) those words. By subtly marginalizing the authority of Moses by showing himself to be an equally authoritative reporter/interpreter of God's word, the narrator prepares the audience to listen to his voice in the subsequent Dtr.[94] This process culminates in the narration of the death of Moses, where the teaching authority is seen to shift from Moses to the narrator. In this way, the narrator emerges as the prophet like Moses (Deut 18:15).[95]

89. As noted above, there are those who see the Decalogue as the key to understanding the structure of Deuteronomy, because the rest of the book (including the legal code) is seen as an explication and elaboration of the basic law presented in Deut 5. See Walton, "Exposition," 214–24.

90. D. M. Beegle, "Moses," *ABD* 4: 915.

91. Polzin, *Moses,* 25–72. Polzin is not explicitly engaged in discussion of the relationship between structure and ideology, but his argument about the nature of the narrative voices and ideology is relevant to our discussion here.

92. Ibid., 67.

93. Ibid., 53–57.

94. Ibid., 57, 72.

95. Ibid., 35–36.

If this reading is correct, then the conclusions I suggested above regarding the nature of the ideology presupposed by a structure based on
superscriptions would need to be revised substantially, because then
the structure would only superficially emphasize Moses' authority to
promulgate and interpret *Torah*. There are, however, some compelling
reasons to question whether Polzin's treatment, though challenging
and thought-provoking, is the best explanation of the data of the text.

Part of Polzin's argument is based on the idea that the voices of
Moses and God are blurred in Deuteronomy. But as Olson notes, a distinction between the authority of the words of God and the words of
Moses appears to be retained.[96] This may be seen by the fact that the
Ten Commandments, the direct words of Yahweh, are stored inside
the ark (Deut 10:1–5), as "a sign of their unique authority."[97] But the
book of *Torah*, which was written by Moses' hand, was to be stored
next to the ark (Deut 31:24–26). This suggests a fundamental difference between the words of Yahweh and those of Moses.

This difference may also be seen in the fact that in Deut 29:29
Moses maintains that "the secret things belong to Yahweh our God,
but the things revealed belong to us and to our sons forever, that we
may observe all the words of this *Torah*." This suggests that Yahweh's
revelation through Moses is partial and limited, which implies that
there is an important distinction between the voice of Moses and the
voice of Yahweh. Moses is the servant of Yahweh par excellence but
remains a servant.[98]

Furthermore, in the closing chapters of the book, Yahweh emerges
as the decisive figure, even as Moses' death draws near. It is he who
chooses Joshua as successor to Moses (Deut 31:7–8, 14–15, 23), and
the portrayal of Yahweh in the covenant at Moab (chaps. 29–32) emphasizes Yahweh's supremacy and his judgment (chap. 32). Significantly, when the narrator describes Moses' death in chap. 34, the only
direct quotation is of Yahweh's reference to the earlier promises to the
patriarchs (Deut 34:4). Yet this reference appears to emphasize the immutability of God's word (the promise to the patriarchs) and the
unique status of Israel, which, in Polzin's view, were the very elements
the Deuteronomistic narrator was trying to subvert.

Finally, it is not clear that the authority of Moses and the narrator
are merged, as Polzin claims. Deuteronomy 34:10–12 makes the claim
that *no* prophet like Moses has emerged. Olson rightly notes that

[e]ven if Polzin is correct in identifying the Deuteronomic narrator as
the new "prophet like Moses" promised in Deut 18:15, that prophet

96. Olson, *Death of Moses*, 15, 179.
97. Ibid., 179.
98. Ibid.

must be subject to the tests of true and false prophecy (Deut 18:20–22). Moreover, future authority within the community will not be confined only to this one prophet's words. Authority will be distributed among several "voices" in the Deuteronomic program: judges, officials, priests, and king (Deut 16:18–22). Just as Moses redistributed his centralized authority among tribal leaders in the first narrative in Deuteronomy (1:9–18), so the Deuteronomic narrator as prophet will also share authority with other "voices" in the community.[99]

Once again, important claims regarding the unique identity and authority of Moses are made precisely in the portion of the text (Deut 34) in which Moses is gone, and the authority of the narrator is at its highest. This suggests, perhaps, that the fusing of voices in Deuteronomy is not as complete as Polzin contends.[100]

It seems likely, then, that the structure of Deuteronomy based on superscriptions suggests an emphasis on Moses as mediator and interpreter of *Torah*. There are, however, other ways of understanding the structure of the book, which we will now examine.

Covenant/Treaty Form

Since Mendenhall's seminal work recognizing the significance of ANE treaty structure for the understanding of the Old Testament,[101] much scholarly discussion has centered around the relationship between it and Deuteronomy. Kline took up Mendenhall's approach and applied it to the book of Deuteronomy, arguing that it, as a whole, has the form of the second-millennium treaties.[102] Others see closer analogies in first-millennium treaties.[103]

---

99. Ibid., 180.

100. A major problem with Polzin's analysis is that he cannot seem to conceive of God as being in some fashion concerned about the unique identity of Israel while at the same time interested in inclusivity. Thus, the two streams of thought are seen to represent different points of view, in which, as noted, the critical traditionalist point of view of the narrator (and, perhaps, Polzin himself) is seen to emerge as the dominant one. In some respects, Polzin's analysis is not so very different from that of traditional source-critics, who assigned different points of view to different authors and sources. Neither Polzin nor the traditional source-critics whose methods and conclusions he rejects are able to conceive of a world view that is capable of holding different facets (such as justice and mercy) in tension with one another, and so they must posit disparate voices or sources. Another perspective on Polzin's argument is found in J. P. Sonnet, *The Book within the Book: Writing in Deuteronomy* (Biblical Interpretation Series 14; Leiden: Brill, 1997), 238–43. Sonnet argues that the narrator's insertions (in the "frame breaks," at least) serve to reinforce and highlight the authority of Moses.

101. G. E. Mendenhall, "Covenant Forms in Israelite Tradition," *BA* 17 (1954): 50–76.

102. M. G. Kline, *Treaty of the Great King* (Grand Rapids: Eerdmans, 1963).

103. See, for example, Weinfeld, *Deuteronomic School*, 59–81, especially p. 60; and idem, *Deuteronomy 1–11*, 6–9. There (p. 9), Weinfeld argues that Deuteronomy is based both on the old Hittite model (via the "old biblical tradition") and the Assyrian model.

While there are different views about exactly how to compare Deuteronomy with the ANE treaties, it is common to compare their forms. Craigie presents a typical view of the structure of Deuteronomy in terms of the treaty form:

1. Preamble (1:1–5)
2. Historical Prologue (1:6–4:49)
3. General Stipulations (chaps. 5–11)
4. Specific Stipulations (chaps. 12–26)
5. Curses and Blessings, with exhortation (chaps. 27–30)
6. Witnesses and Provisions for the Continuity of the Covenant (see 30:19; 31:19; 32:1–43)[104]

In light of the remarkable parallels between the ANE treaty forms and Deuteronomy, it is virtually undeniable that the book is influenced in a significant way by this form. It is also undeniable that Deuteronomy in its present form is not a treaty document. It is much longer than any of the extant ANE treaties. In addition, it includes within it material that is not present in ANE treaties, such as poetry, itineraries, admonitions, and parenesis.[105] Most importantly, the extensive legal section of Deuteronomy (chaps. 12–26) is not present in ANE treaties. Weinfeld rightly notes that, while this section is "functionally equivalent" to the specific stipulations of ANE treaties, it is very different in content.[106] The specific stipulations in ANE treaties are much briefer and contain instructions concerning payment of tribute, territorial boundaries, military obligations, and other obligations placed on the vassal by the sovereign.

For these reasons, it is impossible to sustain the claim that the treaty form represents the best understanding of the structure of Deuteronomy. Simply put, the book does not read like a treaty because it is not a treaty.[107] Miller helpfully suggests that one may think of Deu-

---

104. P. C. Craigie, *The Book of Deuteronomy* (NICOT; Grand Rapids: Eerdmans, 1976), 24. Other works that see the structure of Deuteronomy in terms of the treaty pattern are E. H. Merrill, *Deuteronomy* (NAC 4; Nashville: Broadman & Holman, 1994), 38–40; Wenham, "Structure and Date," 199; J. A. Thompson, *Deuteronomy: An Introduction and Commentary* (London: Inter-Varsity, 1974), 19; R. Brown, *The Message of Deuteronomy: Not by Bread Alone* (BST; Leicester: Inter-Varsity, 1993), 15. Miller (*Deuteronomy*, 13) sees the treaty form as a substructure of Deuteronomy. It should be noted that these works differ about exactly how Deuteronomy is to be compared with the ANE treaties, but they all see the treaty form somehow as underlying the structure of Deuteronomy.

105. Merrill, *Deuteronomy*, 29.

106. Weinfeld, *Deuteronomic School*, 148.

107. See D. L. Christensen, "Form and Structure in Deuteronomy 1–11," in *Das Deuteronomium: Entstehung, Gestalt und Botschaft* (ed. N. Lohfink; BETL 68; Leuven: Leuven University Press, 1985), 135.

teronomy as having an explicit literary structure centered around the superscriptions, a substructure based on the treaty pattern, and a theological structure focused on the Ten Commandments and the Shema.[108] The treaty elements in Deuteronomy, then, are best understood as a substructure of the book, not the primary structure.

This is not to suggest, however, that the parallels with the treaty form are incidental to the book. The parallels are too numerous to dismiss as coincidence. Rather, it seems likely that the treaty pattern informed the structure of the book because of the author's familiarity with the political treaties, or possibly that the author of Deuteronomy deliberately reflected the treaties to create a substructure for the book.[109] We must now consider the implications of this substructure for the interpretation of the book. Again, our concern is with the world view represented by the proposed structure.

The ANE suzerain-vassal treaties commonly defined the relationship between two parties in order to "consolidate the hegemony of the suzerain."[110] McCarthy notes that these treaties were *very* heavily weighted in favor of the suzerain. The vassal, typically not in a position to negotiate more favorable terms, accepted the treaty and the obligations demanded by the suzerain.[111]

The interests of the suzerain are advanced in the treaty in several key ways. First, the historical account of relations between the two powers serves parenetic and rhetorical purposes. Although there are, of course, differences in the various ANE treaties, the historical accounts have in common a reminder of the generosity and beneficence of the suzerain, often referred to as the "Great King," toward the vassal.[112] The historical account has the effect of making clear that "equity and self-interest are on the side of remaining faithful" to the suzerain.[113]

---

108. Miller, *Deuteronomy*, 10.

109. It is not necessary for the present analysis to delve into the question of exactly *which* treaty form may have been the basis for the parallels in Deuteronomy. What matters for this study is that ANE suzerain-vassal treaties (or the treaty form) were familiar to the author and audience and served as the basis for the parallels in Deuteronomy. On the antiquity and prevalence of the treaty pattern in the ANE, see D. J. McCarthy, *Treaty and Covenant* (AnBib 21a; Rome: Pontifical Biblical Institute, 1981), 25–36, and H. Tadmor, "Treaty and Oath in the Ancient Near East: A Historian's Approach," in *Humanizing America's Iconic Book: Society of Biblical Literature Centennial Addresses* (ed. G. M. Tucker and D. A. Knight; Chico, CA: Scholars Press, 1982), 127–52.

110. M. L. Barré, "Treaties in the ANE," *ABD* 6: 654.

111. McCarthy, *Treaty*, 51.

112. Ibid., 53. McCarthy notes as well that in some instances a reminder of the power of the Hittite king is included in the historical account.

113. Ibid.

Second, the treaties regulate the relationship between suzerain and vassal. This follows naturally from the recitation of the historical relationship between the two parties. The power and generosity of the Great King suggest that he is in a position to make demands of the weaker power. The stipulations include both mundane, practical matters as well as more general demands of exclusive loyalty and devotion to the Great King and to his descendants. In return, the vassal will come under the protection of the suzerain, and the vassal's heir (usually) will inherit the throne.[114]

The adoption of this treaty pattern, however loosely, suggests that the author of Deuteronomy sought to emphasize the role of the sovereign (Yahweh) in establishing the relationship with the vassal (Israel). In the ANE treaties, the emphasis was on the requirements of the vassal and the right of the suzerain to establish requirements. Deuteronomy demonstrates remarkable parallels with the treaty pattern: the book opens with a recounting of the gracious acts of Yahweh on behalf of Israel, and then spells out the ways in which Israel was to live out a relationship with Yahweh that was marked by absolute loyalty to him. The use of the treaty pattern served a powerful rhetorical purpose in encouraging devotion to Yahweh on the part of every Israelite (and the nation as a whole). The political treaties were established by the Great King; in using the pattern, the author of Deuteronomy is making the claim that Yahweh is the Great King, who has authority to impose obligations on his people. In addition, the Decalogue and the legal section of Deuteronomy, while more extensive and different in many respects from the stipulations of the political treaties, served to teach the people how to live out their lives in the presence of and in loyalty to the Great King.[115]

The use of the treaty pattern in Deuteronomy, then, suggests an attempt to highlight the supremacy of Yahweh as the Great King and to demonstrate his authority to impose obligations and demand loyalty of his people. We will now consider a final way of analyzing the structure of the book.

Literary Concentricity

A very different approach is taken by Christensen. He argues that Deuteronomy is best understood as having a concentric pattern of five parts:

---

114. Mendenhall, "Covenant Forms," 59. Mendenhall notes (p. 56) that there is no "legal formality by which the Hittite king binds himself to any specific obligation." The legal obligations, then, are on the side of the vassal.

115. Cf. McCarthy, *Treaty*, 15.

A   The Outer Frame: A Look Backward (Deut 1–3)
  B   The Inner Frame: The Great Peroration (Deut 4–11)
    C   The Central Core: Covenant Stipulations (Deut 12–26)
  B′   The Inner Frame: The Covenant Ceremony (Deut 27–30)
A′   The Outer Frame: A Look Forward (Deut 31–34)[116]

This view takes into account the apparent unity of the book in its final form and recognizes a careful attempt to communicate the message of Deuteronomy with a tremendous degree of literary skill. It also accounts for the repetition of key themes and even terminology in the later sections of the book.[117]

Another strength of this perspective is that it accounts for the entire book. That is, the final chapters of the book are not viewed as an appendix to the main thrust of the book but are central to the argument of the book as a whole, as the author looks forward to the future of Israel.

In this view, the theological center of the book is the legal section, Deut 12–26. Chapters 1–11 are carefully designed to lead to this important stage in the development of the book. Chapters 1–3, for example, recount the history of the relationship between Yahweh and his people. There seems to be particular emphasis on the earlier disobedience of the people and the consequences of that disobedience (Deut 1:26–46; 2:14–15; note also the contrast in the form of an emphasis on the blessings resulting from obedience in 2:24–3:11). Chapter 4 introduces the חֻקִּים and מִשְׁפָּטִים that will be discussed in chaps. 5 and 12–26 but does not describe them.[118] Instead, chap. 4 emphasizes the twin themes of the importance of obeying the commands of Yahweh and the absolute supremacy of Yahweh.[119] Chapter 5 sets forth the Decalogue and is preceded and followed by exhortations to obedience and loyalty on the basis of the fact of Yahweh's supremacy and election of Israel.

---

116. Christensen, *Deuteronomy 1:1–21:9*, lviii. Christensen sees the book as a whole as a didactic poem that was originally set to music. This idea, while intriguing, has not gained widespread acceptance. See O'Brien, "Deuteronomy," 96.

117. For example, Joshua is a major figure in the "outer frame" (chaps. 1–3 and 31–34), and blessings and curses are prominent in both parts of the "inner frame" (chaps. 11, 27–30). Christensen argues (*Deuteronomy 1:1–21:9*, lviii) that the two parts of each frame may be read as a single document.

118. The significance of the phrase הַחֻקִּים וְהַמִּשְׁפָּטִים will be examined below. For now it is sufficient to note that the phrase functions in a rhetorically significant way that highlights the Deuteronomic conception of *Torah* as encompassing much more than rigid prescriptions. See McConville and Millar, *Time and Place*, 36–40.

119. See chap. 3 below (pp. 113ff.) for a detailed examination of the text.

In this way, chaps. 1–11 set the stage for the promulgation of the laws in chaps. 12–26. There is a progression in these chapters that highlights the importance of what follows. The first eleven chapters of the book highlight the importance of obedience and rhetorically put the audience at the place of deciding whether to obey Yahweh or not.[120] Obedience and loyalty, the important themes of chaps. 1–11, demand knowledge of what is required of the people, which is spelled out in chaps. 12–26.

The significance of the *Torah* of chaps. 12–26 is further evident when considered in light of the structure proposed by Christensen. In chaps. 27–30, the emphases of the inner frame are picked up again, as the covenant renewal in Moab is narrated. Obedience and loyalty are once again at the fore and highlighted dramatically through the description of blessings and curses in chaps. 27 and 28. More importantly, the renewal of the covenant describes a first step of obedience to Yahweh. The significance of the central core (chaps. 12–26) is highlighted because keeping the terms of the *Torah* described there is precisely the means by which Israel will demonstrate loyalty and obedience to Yahweh.[121]

Again, we want to consider the implications that this understanding of structure has for the understanding of the ideology or world view of the book as a whole. The emphasis on *Torah* suggested by this structure implies that the authority for Israel is the *Torah*.[122] Loyalty to Yahweh, expressed through adherence to *Torah*, is what will define the nation in the context of surrounding nations and will ensure Israel's continued existence in the land (Deut 4:5–8, 26–28).

Israel's identity is further defined by the content and presentation of *Torah*. For example, Israel in Deut 12–26 is a community of brothers.[123] Many of the laws, such as those dealing with indebtedness, slavery, and the poor demand specific treatment for members of the community based on the fact that the community is bound by ties of brotherhood. In this way, Israel's identity is shaped by *Torah*.[124]

120. See Millar, *Now Choose Life*, 44–47; and Mayes, *Deuteronomy*, 217.

121. Millar, *Now Choose Life*, 46. The fact that chaps. 12–26 may be seen to reflect (in some fashion at least) the Decalogue suggests that *all* of the commands of Yahweh (not just those in chaps. 12–26) are part of the *Torah* that Israel is to follow in order to live out its relationship with Yahweh.

122. Anticipating some of the conclusions that I will endeavor to prove in subsequent chapters—I believe that *Torah* in Deuteronomy refers to the words of Yahweh mediated by Moses. The content of the *Torah*, then, includes not only the legal stipulations of chaps. 12–26 but also the parenesis and exhortation of the framing material.

123. See, e.g., Deut 15:7, 9, 11; 19:18–19.

124. This emphasis on loyalty expressed through adherence to *Torah* represents a break from the prevailing conception of deity-national relations in the ANE. As D. I. Block

The emphasis on *Torah* has other ideological implications as well. If *Torah* is indeed the authority for Israel, this suggests that other authorities are reduced in their importance to the life of the nation. Thus we find in Deuteronomy a view of kingship that emphasizes the king's role in studying *Torah* and exemplifying adherence to it (Deut 17:14–20). In Deuteronomy's program, the king is not the supreme figure of other ANE nations but is, rather, under the authority of *Torah*.[125]

Implications of Structure

We have seen that the three major ways of conceiving structure have important implications for the understanding of the ideology or world view of the book. The superscriptions identifying the speeches of Moses emphasize Moses' authority as teacher and mediator of *Torah*. The parallels with the ANE treaty form highlight the authority of Yahweh and the nature of the relationship between him and his people. Finally, the concentricity in the literary arrangement serves to highlight the crucial place of *Torah* in the life of the nation.

In my estimation, these are helpful ways of examining the book, though they do, to some extent, cut across each other formally. The concentric pattern identified by Christensen, for example, takes no account of the superscriptions. What is especially telling is the fact that these differing views of structure have in common an emphasis on the supremacy of Yahweh and the importance of *Torah*. This suggests that these themes should be seen as central to the book as a whole.

This brief examination of structure suggests that we are likely to find in a careful exegetical analysis an emphasis on the things that are highlighted through the various conceptions of structure. That is, while our exegesis cannot, of course, be predetermined by the implications of structure, we might expect that the ideology revealed in our exegesis will emphasize the sovereignty of Yahweh, expressed in the life of Israel through adherence to *Torah*. But understanding the ideology or world view of the text can finally come only through careful exegesis of that text. We will shortly turn our attention to this task, but first we must examine the arguments adduced in favor of the prevailing view of Deuteronomy, in order to see whether they adequately account for the data of the text.

(*The Gods of the Nations: Studies in Ancient Near Eastern National Theology* [2nd ed.; ETS Studies; Grand Rapids: Baker, 2000], 21–33) notes, the emphasis in most ANE societies was on the relationship between the god and the land. The inhabitants of the land were assumed to be the people of that god simply by virtue of their dwelling in the land. In the OT, by contrast, and in Deuteronomy in particular, the identity of the people is paramount, and adherence to *Torah* is an important aspect of maintaining this identity.

125. See the detailed interpretation of this text in chap. 5 below.

Chapter 1

Centralization, Secularization, and Demythologization in Deuteronomy

As we have seen, the issue of cult centralization in Deuteronomy has emerged as one of the main pillars supporting the prevailing view of the book as a revolutionary program of reform. Like the law code in the Book of the Covenant in Exod 20:22–23:19, the legal section of Deuteronomy begins with an altar law. But since the time of Wellhausen, the altar law in Deut 12 has been seen as radically altering the nature of worship in Israel by demanding worship of Yahweh in a single place.[1] This demand for centralization is understood as having far-reaching consequences affecting every aspect of life.

Despite a broad consensus about the fact of centralization and secularization and the demythologization that results from it, fundamental disagreement remains on some crucial questions. How should the Deuteronomic reform be understood in relationship to the monarchy? Is it positive toward the institution of kingship or negative?[2]

---

1. Though not identified in Deuteronomy, the place chosen by Yahweh has long been understood to be Jerusalem. This is based in large part on the association of the book with the 7th century and in particular the reforms of Josiah. See, for example, M. Weinfeld, *Deuteronomy and the Deuteronomic School* (Oxford: Oxford University Press, 1972; repr. Winona Lake, IN: Eisenbrauns, 1992), 4–9; idem, *Deuteronomy 1–11: A New Translation with Introduction and Commentary* (AB 5; New York: Doubleday, 1991), 50–57; S. R. Driver, *A Critical and Exegetical Commentary on Deuteronomy* (3rd ed.; ICC; Edinburgh: T. & T. Clark, [1901]), xxvii–lvii; W. Brueggemann, *Deuteronomy* (AbOTC; Nashville: Abingdon, 2001), 18–20; J. H. Tigay, *Deuteronomy* דברים*: The Traditional Hebrew Text with the New JPS Translation* (Philadelphia: Jewish Publication Society, 1996), xx–xxii; R. E. Clements, "The Book of Deuteronomy: Introduction, Commentary, and Reflections," *NIB* (Nashville: Abingdon, 1998), 278–80; idem, *Deuteronomy* (OTG; Sheffield: Sheffield Academic Press, 1989), 70–76; A. D. H. Mayes, *Deuteronomy* (NCB; Grand Rapids: Eerdmans / London: Marshall, Morgan & Scott, 1979), 85–103. I. Cairns (*Word and Presence: A Commentary on the Book of Deuteronomy* [ITC; Grand Rapids: Eerdmans / Edinburgh: Handsel, 1992], 18) argues that the final form of Deuteronomy "clearly" identifies the chosen place with Jerusalem, despite the fact that the place is *never* identified and the construction of an altar outside of Jerusalem (on Mount Ebal) is commanded.

2. Weinfeld, for example, sees the Deuteronomic reform as supporting the Judean monarchy, whereas Levinson sees the program as opposing the monarchy. Crüsemann

32

Should this program be understood as a realistic program of reform or a utopian ideal?[3] Finally, issues of setting and audience are disputed even among scholars who see centralization, secularization, and demythologization as the core of the Deuteronomic program.

In this chapter, I will focus on centralization, secularization, and demythologization in Deuteronomy and will identify and analyze the main arguments for their being seen as the heart of the Deuteronomic revolution. I will then attempt to determine whether these arguments adequately account for the data of the text. I will also examine the ideologies suggested by these interpretations and will evaluate the extent to which these ideologies are supported by the text and the cultural and historical context in which Deuteronomy originated.

Centralization in Deuteronomy

The examination of the issue of centralization in Deuteronomy will begin with an analysis of the positions of several major modern interpreters of the text of Deuteronomy.[4] Given the pervasiveness of the idea of centralization and its importance for the interpretation of the book as a whole, I will select five representative interpretations of a single text, to make the investigation manageable. Thus, I will use the interpretations of Deut 16:18–18:22 as a basis for examining the positions of the interpreters. This text is a useful starting point because it is recognized almost universally as a distinct unit, it represents the heart of the changes resulting from centralization, and most effectively highlights the differences among the various interpreters. It will, of

---

sees the reforms as supporting the interests of the people of the land against claims of the state authorities. See Weinfeld, *Deuteronomic School*, 168–71; B. M. Levinson, *Deuteronomy and the Hermeneutics of Legal Innovation* (Oxford: Oxford University Press, 1997), 138–43; F. Crüsemann, *The Torah: Theology and Social History of Old Testament Law* (trans. A. W. Mahnke; Minneapolis: Fortress, 1996), 219–24 (ET of *Die Tora: Theologie und Sozialgeschichte des alttestamentlichen Gesetzes* [Munich: Chr. Kaiser, 1992]).

3. Levinson (*Legal Innovation*) and Crüsemann (*Torah*) see the Deuteronomic program as realistic, whereas N. Lohfink ("Distribution of the Functions of Power: The Laws concerning Public Offices in Deuteronomy 16:18–18:22," in *A Song of Power and the Power of Song: Essays on the Book of Deuteronomy* [ed. D. L. Christensen; SBTS 3; Winona Lake, IN: Eisenbrauns, 1993], 336–52) sees the book as presenting a utopian ideal. See also idem, "The Laws of Deuteronomy: A Utopian Project for a World without Any Poor?" Lattey Lecture, 1995 (Cambridge: St. Edmund's College, 1995); and "Das deuteronomische Gesetz in der Endgestalt: Entwurf einer Gesellschaft ohne marginale Gruppen," *BN* 51 (1990): 25–40.

4. It is somewhat artificial, I realize, to separate the elements of centralization, secularization, and demythologization, because they are to a great degree bound up with one another. For the purpose of analysis, however, it is necessary to examine them separately but with the understanding that they are interrelated.

course, be necessary to refer to other texts as part of this examination, but this section will serve as the starting point.[5] So, I will focus on the interpretation of Deut 16:18–18:22 and will describe the ways in which this section has been understood as contributing to the program of centralization. I will then analyze these perspectives in order to determine if, in fact, this section is best understood as contributing to a program of centralization. (I will return to Deut 16:18–18:22 in chap. 5.)

Five Views of Centralization

S. R. Driver

Like many other commentators, Driver sees 16:18–18:22 as a discrete unit, which he titles "The Office Bearers of the Theocracy."[6] In Driver's view, centralized worship at the Temple in Jerusalem was a necessary corollary to the near monotheism taught in Deuteronomy. This was due to the "conditions of the time," in which worship in many different places would lead to syncretism.[7]

In Driver's view, the centralization program envisioned by Deuteronomy is in response to the excesses and abuses of the reign of Manasseh.[8] The idolatrous practices of Manasseh included the building of altars to pagan gods even in the court of the Temple itself (2 Kgs 21:1–9). For the loyal devotee of Yahweh, urgent reform was necessary, and it was to this end that the book of Deuteronomy was produced. Driver insists, however, that Deuteronomy is more than simply a "pious fraud." Rather, he argues that what was produced and placed in the Temple (and later found by Hilkiah) was within the stream of Mosaic teaching and, therefore, can rightly be identified with him. Deuteronomy, he argues, is not new in terms of its content but in its form. There are laws that were updated, modified, or even originated in the 7th century, but the laws in Deuteronomy, including the centraliza-

5. Deuteronomy 12 is, of course, the text that legislates centralization. I will be dealing with this text in chap. 4 but want here to focus on a text that most clearly demonstrates the wide variety of positions held even by those who agree generally on the fact of centralization.

6. Driver, *Deuteronomy*, 199–230. However, Driver argues (p. 201) that 16:21–17:7 have been moved from an original location, probably before 13:2.

7. Ibid., xxix. Driver's assessment of the "conditions of the time" and the impact of centralization on the Jews' ability (or, more accurately in Driver's view, their *in*ability) to appreciate the "more spiritual" teaching of Christ represents a particular understanding of religious development prevalent at the time and is clearly articulated by Wellhausen (see below, n. 13).

8. Ibid., xxvii. He argues that the book was written either during the reign of Manasseh or during the early years of the reign of Josiah, but in any event prior to 621 B.C. (ibid., xlv–xlvi).

tion law, were consonant with Mosaic law and, indeed, ultimately derived from Moses.[9] On this view, then, Deuteronomy represents an attempt to actualize the ideals advocated by the 8th-century prophets, and Deuteronomy's law of centralization is the logical extension of the prophetic criticism of the בָּמוֹת. The book itself is a "prophet's reformulation of the 'law of Moses,' adapted to the requirements of that later time."[10]

In Driver's view, Deuteronomy was "a great manifesto against the dominant tendencies of the time."[11] It was an attempt to reaffirm the values and ideals on which the nation was founded in a new context and a call to repudiate practices that were inconsistent with the unconditional loyalty to Yahweh called for by Moses. Given the new context and changed circumstances, the older laws of the Book of the Covenant were "adjusted" in order to meet the needs of the time.[12] Driver argues that, in some respects, Deuteronomy's program had unintended consequences. He argues that the goal of Deuteronomy was to spiritualize religious life in Israel but that the necessity of centralization (to prevent idolatrous worship at the בָּמוֹת) led to formalization of worship and resulted in a loss of spontaneity.[13]

Driver thus sees in Deut 16:18–18:22 a realistic program for the theocratic government of a nation under Yahweh. If the book of Deuteronomy represents a continuation of the prophetic call to live life in exclusive loyalty to Yahweh, then this section may be seen as the means by which the nation is to express this loyalty in terms of the structures of government. Driver sees this as a realistic, not utopian, program; this is evidenced by his comparison of the law regarding the "central tribunal" in Deut 17:8–13 with the Chronicler's description of Jehoshaphat's judicial reforms in 2 Chr 19:8–11.[14] Throughout his

---

9. See ibid., lvi–lvii.
10. Ibid., liii. See also xxvii.
11. Ibid., liii.
12. Ibid., lii.
13. Ibid., lxiv. Here, again, it appears that Driver is influenced by Wellhausen and a particular view of the development of religion in which religion is initially free and spontaneous but later becomes formalized, ritualistic, and therefore (in this view) less spiritual. See J. Wellhausen, *Prolegomena to the History of Israel* (Edinburgh: Black, 1885; repr. Atlanta: Scholars Press, 1994). Wellhausen's influence has been, of course, immeasurable. Assessment of his influence may be found in E. W. Nicholson, *The Pentateuch in the Twentieth Century: The Legacy of Julius Wellhausen* (Oxford: Clarendon, 1998). See also *Semeia* 25 (1982), which is devoted to Wellhausen and his influence on the study of the Old Testament.
14. Driver, *Deuteronomy*, 200, 208. Because of Driver's understanding of the date of Deuteronomy, he never considers the possibility that Deuteronomy may have been the basis for the judicial reforms instituted by Jehoshaphat, described in 2 Chr 19:5–11. If the account in Chronicles is reliable, Jehoshaphat appointed judges in the cities of the land,

analysis of Deuteronomy, Driver clearly envisions the legislation as being a realistic program for the nation. He consistently identifies features in Israelite history and polity that reflect the Deuteronomic program as evidence that this was, and presumably was intended to be, a program that was to be carried out in the life of the nation.

In the same way, Deuteronomy's "Law of the King" (Deut 17:14–20) is understood by Driver to be in keeping with the theocratic program undertaken in the book. As a theocracy, Israel was to have been governed by Yahweh; a human king, of course, was unnecessary to theocratic government. For this reason, Driver argues, a king is not required by Deuteronomy but only permitted.[15] If the people do elect to have a king, he is not to "imitate the great despots of the East"[16] but is to carry out his reign in keeping with the principles laid out in Deuteronomy.

So we can conclude that Deuteronomy (and especially Deut 16:18–18:22), according to Driver, is a realistic program for theocratic government of the nation, and centralization is a key component of this program. The program of centralization envisioned in the book is in response to the excesses and idolatry of the reign of Manasseh (and was written either in his reign or in the early years of Josiah) and is the culmination of the exhortations of the 8th-century prophets. The significance of *covenant* in the theology of Deuteronomy is not as heavily emphasized by Driver, because his work was carried out prior to the identification of the significance of the ANE political treaties. The arguments of the representative interpreters will be evaluated below. We now turn our attention to another perspective.

G. von Rad

A different approach was taken by Gerhard von Rad. Using the method of form criticism, he sought to identify the Sitz im Leben of

---

as well as in Jerusalem. In keeping with the judicial law (though not the explicit language) of Deuteronomy, he exhorted the newly appointed judges to act with impartiality, righteousness, and to eschew bribes. While the book of Kings is clear that Jehoshaphat did not eliminate the בָּמוֹת (1 Kgs 22:43), the book of Chronicles portrays him as having carried out some judicial reforms that are in keeping with the Deuteronomic law. One major difference, however, is that Deuteronomy seems to give authority to the people as a whole to appoint judges, whereas this authority is assumed by the king in the account in 2 Chronicles. J. Bright argues for the historicity of the Chronicler's account of these judicial reforms in *A History of Israel* (3rd ed.; London: SCM, 1980), 251; see also G. T. Manley, *The Book of the Law: Studies in the Date of Deuteronomy* (London: Tyndale, 1957), 114–16.

15. Ibid., 209.

16. Ibid.

Deuteronomy. He argued that the form of Deut 4–30[17] reflects a traditional cultic pattern, perhaps a covenant-renewal ceremony. This, he contended, accounts for the homiletic style of the book, the use of the standard treaty formula (albeit in a "mutilated form"[18]), the frequent exhortations even in the presentation of law, and the repetition of key phrases and ideas. In its present form, however, the cultic setting has been largely abandoned, and the older material has been reworked as an instructional address to the people as a whole.[19]

In von Rad's view, it was the Levites who were responsible for the composition of Deuteronomy (i.e., chaps. 4–30). He bases this contention on the fact that they would have had access to the sacral literature as well as the authority to interpret ancient traditions in light of contemporary concerns. The emphasis in Deuteronomy on holy war also suggests to von Rad that the authors of Deuteronomy were Levites, given the close association between the theology of the holy war and the ark, and the fact that it was the Levites who maintained the ark.[20]

More specifically, von Rad argues, the authors of Deuteronomy were "country Levites," who sought, with the support of the עַם הָאָרֶץ (people of the land), to revive the "old patriarchal traditions" of Yahwism that date back to the amphictyonic period.[21] He bases this argument on the relative insignificance of the king in Deuteronomy and the absence of any apparent reference to the Davidic covenant and the Messianic implications thereof. Most importantly, he argues for this understanding of provenance based on the fact that it is the country Levites who could have possessed the resources and authority to reinterpret and reintroduce older traditions in light of a new context. Country Levites would be in just such a position and, von Rad contends, would have had the support of the עַם הָאָרֶץ.[22]

---

17. Von Rad follows Noth in seeing the first three chapters of the present book of Deuteronomy (as well as chaps. 31–34) as an introduction to the Deuteronomistic History (DtH). He sees, however, significant growth in Deuteronomy during the period of its independent existence prior to its incorporation into DtH in the sixth century. See G. von Rad, *Deuteronomy: A Commentary* (London: SCM, 1966), 12.

18. Ibid., 23.

19. Ibid., 15–23.

20. Ibid., 24–25. See also G. von Rad, *Studies in Deuteronomy* (trans. D. M. G. Stalker; Chicago: Henry Regnery / London: SCM, 1953), 66–67. There is no textual basis, however, for von Rad's speculative contention that the "warlike spirit of Deuteronomy" (*Commentary*, 25; and *Studies*, 60–61) was a result of a Josianic reorganization of the military following Assyrian conquests in or around 701 B.C.

21. Von Rad, *Studies*, 66–67.

22. Ibid., 62–67. This view has been challenged. See, for example, the critique of Weinfeld, *Deuteronomic School*, 53–58.

Centralization holds a paradoxical place in von Rad's interpretation of Deuteronomy. On the one hand, he holds that it was "the most important special feature of Deuteronomy"[23] and was a necessary result of Deuteronomy's uncompromising insistence that "Yahweh is One" (Deut 6:4).[24] It was decidedly far-reaching in its consequences for the religious life of Israel, and the centralizing laws are to be understood as "a fresh interpretation . . . of the old cultic system, an interpretation which had become necessary owing on the one hand to abuses introduced . . . and on the other to quite new perceptions of Yahweh and his relationship to Israel."[25] These "abuses" and "new perceptions" are presumably the anthropomorphic conception of Yahweh's presence and the rejection of that by the authors of Deuteronomy.

On the other hand, von Rad cautions against seeing centralization as a theological center of the book. He argues that Deuteronomy's demand for centralization represents a relatively late period in the development of the book and is "comparatively easy to remove as a late and final adaptation of many layers of material."[26] This, he argues, is seen by the fact that the demand for centralization, far from pervading even the entire legal corpus in Deuteronomy, is known for certain only in seven areas: the altar law (chap. 12), tithes (14:22–29), firstlings (15:19–23), feasts (16:1–17), the central judicial tribunal (17:8–13), provision for priests (18:1–8), and cities of refuge (19:1–13). Moreover, the demand for centralization is unknown or contradicted in other laws.[27]

In addition, von Rad raises the question whether or not centralization per se was best understood as being new in Deuteronomy. After all, he argues, prior to the establishment of the temple under Solomon, the ark in its various locations may have served as the cultic center to which the tribes journeyed for pilgrimage festivals.[28] Also, the Book of the Covenant begins with its own altar law (Exod 20:24). While von Rad allows that the altar law in Deuteronomy is indeed different, he nevertheless maintains that

> it is not right to regard as its primary aspect . . . an abrupt discontinuance of old usages. There is probably, after all, much that is traditional in this Deuteronomic rule which appears to be so revolutionary. This is

---

23. Von Rad, *Commentary*, 16, 88–89.
24. Idem, *Old Testament Theology*, vol. 1: *The Theology of Israel's Historical Traditions* (trans. D. M. G. Stalker; New York: Harper & Row, 1962), 226–27; idem, *Commentary*, 91.
25. Idem, *Commentary*, 91.
26. Idem, *Studies*, 67.
27. Idem, *Commentary*, 16, 89. See, e.g., p. 115 on Deut 16:21–22.
28. Ibid., 16–17.

evident in the resemblance of the form of the basic Deuteronomic law to the law of the altar in the Book of the Covenant. When compared with the latter, the formulation in Deuteronomy appears to be only a fresh wording.[29]

Thus, there appears to be a sense of caution on von Rad's part regarding the nature of centralization in Deuteronomy and its significance. For von Rad, the idea of covenant and the need for loyalty to Yahweh is more significant in Deuteronomy than the idea of centralization.

Similar ambiguity surrounds the question of the nature of Deuteronomy. On the whole, von Rad seems to have a utopian (rather than realistic) understanding of Deuteronomy. He sees the book in its present form as a record of preaching, couched in the liturgical form of a covenant-renewal ceremony. The aim of this preaching is to inculcate in the people obedience and loyalty to the commands of Yahweh.[30] In this respect, Deuteronomy is highly realistic, because the purpose and tenor of the exhortation is to bring people to real obedience to Yahweh. However, von Rad further sees in Deuteronomy an attempt "by a 'utopian' anachronism" to revert back to the old amphictyonic order.[31] In other words, the reformers of the 7th century seem to have sought to recover the lost glory of an earlier, better age, in which Israel was devoted to Yahweh and in which the security of his protection could be relied upon. But it would, of course, be a practical impossibility for a monarchic state to revert to the institutions and practices of the premonarchic period.[32] Thus, the vision of Deuteronomy is ultimately a utopian one.

The utopian nature of Deuteronomy is further seen in von Rad's analysis of the preaching of the book. He notes that in its present form the preaching in Deuteronomy is not addressed to the state of the monarchic period in the 7th century (when, according to von Rad, the book was written), although he argues that the preaching does in fact reflect the issues of that period. Rather, the preaching in Deuteronomy is ostensibly aimed at Israel on the border of the land, prior to the conquest of Canaan. The effect is such that the 7th-century audience of Deuteronomy is addressed as if they were, in fact, on the border of the

29. Ibid., 90–91. Von Rad holds that, of the three "centralizing ordinances" in Deut 12 (vv. 1–7; 8–12; 13–19[20–28]), the third is the earliest due to the fact that it is worded in the singular. See ibid., 16.

30. Idem, *Theology*, 225.

31. Idem, *Studies*, 64 n. 2.

32. The idea that the political structure of early Israel was an amphictyony, as promulgated by Noth and as understood by von Rad, has been largely rejected. The idea of an Israelite amphictyony was first introduced by M. Noth, *Das System der zwölf Stämme Israels* (BWANT; Stuttgart: Kohlhammer, 1930).

land. Von Rad notes, "Israel is set once more at Horeb to hear Jahweh's word of salvation which has not yet lost its power."[33] Deuteronomy speaks to each generation as if the people were in the period of the Israel addressed in the book, between the promise from Yahweh on the one hand and the fulfillment of that promise on the other. This, then, helps account for what von Rad sees as the "theoretical character" of the book.[34]

At the same time, however, he sees the book as fiercely realistic in its opposition to syncretism and the influence of Canaanite religion. He notes that "Deuteronomy is in no sense a theoretical compendium of the will of Jahweh: rather it develops its demands" against Canaanite religion, which represented a threat to Yahwism.[35] In von Rad's view, then, Deuteronomy may be seen as utopian in terms of the era to which it seems to want to return and the way in which it envisions Israel in every generation as being on the verge of the fulfillment of divine promises. On the other hand, it is fiercely realistic in its expectation that the people of Yahweh are to be uncompromisingly loyal to Yahweh.

Thus for von Rad, there is a division between the moral/spiritual realm and the political realm. Deuteronomy is realistic in terms of the moral and spiritual issues but utopian in terms of the political. This differs from more-recent treatments of the nature of the program (see below).

The complexity of the "realistic-versus-utopian" question may be seen in von Rad's handling of the material in Deut 16:18–18:22. In his commentary, he deals with each chapter on its own and does not set this section out as a discrete unit, as other interpreters tend to do.

With regard to the law of judges in 16:18–20, von Rad does not address the setting in which this ordinance originated and does not specifically address how this does or does not relate to centralization. He does argue that a corps of professional (or pseudoprofessional) judges was not the original means by which justice was administered in Israel. Thus the command to appoint judges and officers (שֹׁפְטִים וְשֹׁטְרִים) may represent, in von Rad's view, the encroachment of the monarchy on the administration of justice. He maintains, however, that "no earlier legal system can be detected behind v. 18."[36] Despite the fact that

---

33. Von Rad, *Studies,* 70. Cf. also idem, *Commentary,* 28.
34. Ibid., 27.
35. Idem, *Theology,* 227–28.
36. Idem, *Commentary,* 114.

all Israel is addressed throughout chap. 16, von Rad seems to think that it is the king who is to appoint judges in 16:18.[37]

He does connect the central tribunal (Deut 17:8–13) with the Deuteronomic program of centralization. However, he says that Deuteronomy does not provide much information about the function of this tribunal.[38]

The law of the king (Deut 17:14–20) provides one of the most interesting examples of the way in which the Deuteronomic program is envisioned. The Deuteronomic program, in von Rad's view, seeks to revive the traditions of the amphictyonic period that knew no king. Thus the presence of the law of the king is described as "astonishing."[39] But as a "concession to historical reality," a king is permitted, though the role of the king is portrayed in a very unrealistic, nonhistorical manner that is, in his estimation, nearly a distortion.[40] In this sense, then, von Rad's view of Deuteronomy must be seen as utopian. It seeks to revert back to an idealized, "golden age," in which no king was necessary in Israel and in which the many failures of the people to live out their lives as the people of Yahweh were yet to come. The authors grudgingly recognize the reality of the king and the intervening years of history and allow a role for a king, albeit one that is limited in function and power.

With respect to priests (Deut 18:1–8), von Rad sees at least a portion of this law as reflecting the Deuteronomic program of centralization. Verses 6–8, in von Rad's view, reflect the demand for centralization, though he cautions that this text should not be thought of in connection with 2 Kgs 23:8, because there is no evidence in Deuteronomy that the arrival of the priests in the central sanctuary was forced (as he argues is the case in 2 Kgs 23:8), and, furthermore, there is no evidence to suggest that all the Levites living in the towns were priests of the high places.[41]

Finally, von Rad examines the role of the prophet (Deut 18:9–22). This section, he argues, dates to the earliest period of the monarchy because certain practices unknown in the earliest days of Israel's history are here taken for granted. He sees in this law a hope for *a* prophet "like Moses," one who serves the nation in a special capacity,

37. Ibid., 118.
38. Ibid.
39. Ibid.
40. Ibid., 119.
41. Ibid., 122.

and he argues against seeing this as a vision of the prophets of judgment.[42]

For von Rad, then, centralization is a key aspect of the Deuteronomic program (but it is important to note his caution in seeing it as *the* key theology of the book). The book seeks to revive ancient traditions and ideals of the amphictyonic period. It is, therefore, utopian in its view of an earlier period and its desire (which is an unrealistic desire and is recognized as such by the authors in the laws promulgated) to reinstitute the practices of the earlier period. It is realistic, however, not in its political aspirations but in its call for complete loyalty to Yahweh.

M. Weinfeld

In Weinfeld's view, the Deuteronomic program of centralization was a key part of a wider reform that had far-reaching and significant consequences. This program as understood by Weinfeld is one marked by "demythologization and secularization." He notes:

> The centralization of the cult was in itself, of course, a sweeping innovation in the history of the Israelite cultus, but its consequences were . . . decisively more revolutionary in nature, in that they involved the collapse of an entire system of concepts which for centuries had been regarded as sacrosanct. . . . [Israelite religious life] was freed from its ties to the cult and was transformed into an abstract religion which did not necessarily require any external expression. Indeed the very purpose of the book of Deuteronomy . . . was to curtail and circumscribe the cultus and not to extend or enhance it.[43]

Centralization, in Weinfeld's view, was part of an attempt to reform religious life in Israel that sought to repudiate older traditions and concepts that did not comport with the more sophisticated theological understanding of the authors of Deuteronomy.

Weinfeld sees the authors of Deuteronomy as being Jerusalem court scribes who were versed in wisdom literature and were also familiar with trends of thought in society, including the ideas brought to Judah by refugees from the North following the Assyrian conquest of the Northern Kingdom. This, he argues, explains the presence in Deuteronomy of parallels with wisdom literature (both biblical and ancient Near Eastern) as well as elements that reflect the thinking of the Northern Kingdom.[44] He bases this understanding on the perception that the "school" that created Deuteronomy "could not conceive a regime without a king" and thus advanced a legal code and political

---

42. Ibid., 123–24.
43. Weinfeld, *Deuteronomic School*, 190. See also idem, *Deuteronomy 1–11*, 37.
44. Idem, *Deuteronomy 1–11*, 62–65; 44–50.

system reflecting "typical monarchic rule." Moreover, he argues, the didactic nature of the book points to the scribes as authors, because scribes were involved in both secular and religious education.[45]

Weinfeld holds that Deuteronomy was written during the time of Hezekiah and was rediscovered during the rule of Josiah. However, like von Rad and Driver, Weinfeld acknowledges that Deuteronomy contains in it some ancient material, portions of which date as early as the time of Moses.[46] But the ancient material was reworked in a deliberate attempt to address the priorities and reflect the thinking of the later era. Specifically, Deuteronomy seeks to repudiate earlier ideas about God that did not conform to the more advanced theology of the era in which it was created. Deuteronomy is, in Weinfeld's view, a manual, based on ancient traditions but updated for a more modern time, for the king and people regarding the way they are to live under Yahweh.[47]

Deuteronomy's program is, in Weinfeld's understanding, eminently realistic and practical. The book in some form served as the basis for the reforms of Josiah.[48] Indeed, the connection between Deuteronomy and Josiah's reform is so strong that Weinfeld argues that Josiah's reform "might well be called the Deuteronomic Reform."[49] He further argues that

> the book of Deuteronomy appears indeed to have the character of an ideal national constitution representing all the official institutions of the state: the monarchy, the judiciary, the priesthood, and prophecy. These institutions are successively referred to in Deut. 16:18–18:22 and are depicted not only in realistic terms but also in terms of the ideal at which this neutral circle of scribes was clearly aiming—a national regime which incorporated all the normative, spiritual, and religious circles of the period.[50]

---

45. Ibid., 55. See also idem, *Deuteronomic School*, 298–306.

46. Idem, *Deuteronomy 1–11*, 83–84.

47. Ibid., 55, 57.

48. Weinfeld states that the form of Deuteronomy that served as the basis for the reforms included "an introduction, a law code (certainly chapters 12–19, which embody the principles of the reform) and the admonition in chapter 28 regarding the rewards for obedience and punishments for violation of the [covenant]" (M. Weinfeld, "Deuteronomy's Theological Revolution," *BR* 12 [1996]: 38). See also Weinfeld, *Deuteronomy 1–11*, 9–13, where he argues that Deut 4:44–28:68 constituted the original book, which was later supplied with additional introductory and concluding material, and the entire work was (still later) subjected to a Deuteronomi(sti)c redaction.

49. Idem, "Theological Revolution," 38. He notes, however, that at least one aspect of the reforms, the eradication of alien cults, was undertaken *prior* to the discovery of the book of the *Torah*. See also idem, *Deuteronomy 1–11*, 73–74.

50. Idem, *Deuteronomic School*, 168.

Thus, it is clear that in Weinfeld's view the revolutionary reform undertaken by Josiah was in some measure the application of the requirements of the form of Deuteronomy that existed at that time and was in keeping with the theological understanding of the book.[51]

As noted above, centralization was at the heart of the Deuteronomic reform program and was, therefore, at the center of the Josianic reforms as well. Josiah's reform began with the eradication of alien cults (2 Kgs 23:4–14) and proceeded with the centralization of the Yahweh cult through the destruction of the high places. This led, in Weinfeld's view, to a transformation of Israelite religion, as the day-to-day life of the people became less and less affected by cultic matters.

This may be seen clearly in the judicial reform mandated by Deuteronomy (16:18–20; 17:8–13). Weinfeld holds that, prior to centralization, priests of the local sanctuaries would be consulted when elders, serving as judges in the city gates, could not reach a verdict in a case, due to lack of witnesses or evidence. The removal of local sanctuaries, required by centralization, meant that local priests were no longer available to serve in that capacity, leading to the need for judges and officers to be appointed.[52] If, after the reform, the local judges could not render a verdict, the priests and judges of the central sanctuary were consulted (Deut 17:8–13). Thus, he argues, the laws of judicial reform must be interpreted in light of the centralizing program of Deuteronomy.[53]

Another key element of the Deuteronomic program was the monarchy.[54] In Weinfeld's view, the monarchy was held in high esteem by

51. It would be reductionistic, however, to suggest that Weinfeld sees in Josiah's reform simply the application of Deuteronomic principles. Rather, he maintains that there was a more dynamic relationship between the reform and the book of Deuteronomy in which the reform itself (which was inspired and based in large part on some form of the book) reshaped the book and contributed to its development. See, for example, his comments on the law of the king (Deut 17:14–20; ibid.).

52. Ibid., 233–35. He argues there that the Deuteronomic reform left only "patriarchal and family litigation" (p. 234) under the jurisdiction of the elders, all other cases being adjudicated by the newly appointed judges.

53. Ibid., 235–36. This is also seen as evidence of secularization (see below).

54. In large part, Weinfeld sees in Deuteronomy a reinterpretation of the so-called "Jerusalem Cult Tradition." Many elements held to be a part of that tradition (the ark as a symbol of Yahweh's presence and, hence, an anthropomorphic view of God; Jerusalem as a specially-chosen cult center; the prominent role of the Davidic king) are dealt with in new ways in Deuteronomy. While some elements of that tradition, in Weinfeld's view, are rejected because they do not comport with the thinking of the author(s) of Deuteronomy (such as the conception of an "actual presence" of Yahweh in the Temple), some are strengthened and reinforced (such as the prominence of Jerusalem as the central sanctuary). The institution of the monarchy, a central part of the Jerusalem cult tradition (or Zion tradition), is critiqued in light of past excesses but not rejected (see below). On the Zion

the scribal circles responsible for the book. He argues that "the scribes . . . regarded the institution of monarchy as essential for the proper functioning of society."[55] This, he maintains, may be seen partly in the important "centralization law" in Deut 12:8–9, where it says, "You shall not do as we all are doing here today, every man doing whatever is right in his own eyes, for you have not yet come to the resting place and to the inheritance which the Lord your God is giving you." The phrase "every man doing whatever is right in his own eyes," in Weinfeld's view, expresses the same view as that of the Deuteronomist in Judges. There, the phrase is used to highlight the anarchy of the period of the judges and to demonstrate the need for a king. In Deuteronomy, then, the phrase is used to refer back to the period of the Judges, when anarchy reigned and provincial or private altars abounded. Only after the monarchy was established could there be "rest," and only then could the requirement for centralization be met. And it was only under the centralized rule of a monarch that all the requirements of the book of the *Torah* could be implemented.[56]

In Weinfeld's view, then, Deuteronomy presents a positive view of the monarchy. Even the law of the king (Deut 17:14–20), which is so shocking in its limitation of the role of the king, is not to be seen as being antimonarchical per se. Indeed, he argues that the law, which clearly limits the role of the king, presumes the existence of the institution of the monarchy and provides for its continuation through dynastic succession. The limitations on the king reflect the anti-Solomon bias of Josiah's court. That is, the law in Deut 17 is directed against the specific excesses of a specific king, Solomon. It is not a polemic against kingship in general. This, he argues, may be seen through the close correlation between the prohibitions against wives, money, and horses in the law and the description of Solomon's reign in 1 Kgs 10–11. Moreover, Josiah was the only one of the Judean kings to move against the high places erected by Solomon for his foreign wives (2 Kgs 23:13).[57]

While Weinfeld holds that Deuteronomy is in the main a realistic program, he also recognizes that there are utopian elements within it. The most significant of these is the notion in Deuteronomy that the

---

tradition, see von Rad, *Theology*, 46–48. See also R. E. Clements, "Deuteronomy and the Jerusalem Cult Tradition," *VT* 15 (1965): 300–312. For a critique of this understanding, see J. G. McConville, "Jerusalem in the Old Testament," in *Jerusalem Past and Present in the Purposes of God* (ed. P. W. L. Walker; Carlisle: Paternoster / Grand Rapids: Baker, 1994), 21–51.

55. Ibid., 169.
56. Ibid., 170–71.
57. Ibid., 168–69.

entire Canaanite population was to be considered חֵרֶם and, therefore, exterminated (Deut 7:1–2; 20:16–17). Weinfeld argues that this is a utopian policy that was never actually practiced or intended to be. The ancient Israelites did follow a doctrine of חֵרֶם, but never was it applied to an entire population automatically, independent of a vow or an oath, as is mandated in Deuteronomy. Weinfeld argues that this is a utopian ideal adapted from a Gilgalite tradition and is used by the Deuteronomic author(s) in support of a revival of patriotic fervor.[58]

Centralization is, then, crucial to the Deuteronomic program as envisioned by Weinfeld. The entire program sought to reinterpret and revolutionize faith and practice in Israel during the era of Hezekiah–Josiah. Old traditions and theology that did not comport with the thinking of the day were reinterpreted in favor of a more abstract, spiritual understanding, or they were ignored. The scribes of the royal court sought to support the monarchy through the radical reform envisioned by Deuteronomy. At the heart of that reform was centralization. Thus, the Temple in Jerusalem and the king who reigned there were given primacy in the religious and political life of the nation. Worship was centralized at the Temple in Jerusalem; consequently, all local sanctuaries were outlawed. The administration of justice was centralized as well, with new (royal) magistrates replacing elders in the adjudication of cases in the towns, and a central tribunal was established to serve as a court of appeal. Deuteronomy is thus a realistic program for reform and served in large measure as the basis for the Josianic reforms.[59]

At the same time, there is something of a curious tension in Weinfeld's treatment. On the one hand, he sees Deuteronomy as eminently realistic in terms of its political program and therefore sees the book as supporting the reforms of Josiah in the 7th century. On the other hand, he maintains that Deuteronomy seeks to advance a more abstract, spiritual religion. It seems as though Weinfeld envisions a dichotomy between the political and the spiritual, though it is not quite like that of von Rad, where the distinction is more explicit.

N. Lohfink

Like the other interpreters discussed above, Lohfink sees in Deuteronomy a program of centralization. Its final redaction dates to the period of the exile, although much in the book is ancient. Indeed, the book and its central ideology may be understood as having been de-

---

58. Weinfeld, *Deuteronomy 1–11*, 51–52; 382–84. See also idem, *Deuteronomic School*, 166–67.

59. But see the caution in n. 51, above.

veloped through interaction with older literary works and the ideas contained therein.[60] He bases this date on the fact that the Deuteronomic law of the king calls for the *Torah* to be copied from a scroll kept by the Levitical priests. This, he argues, connects Deuteronomy with the Deuteronomistic History, which is typically dated to the beginning of the exilic period. Moreover, he argues that Deuteronomy appears to know nothing about the emergence of the Zadokites and so should be dated prior to the end of the exilic period.[61]

The authors of the early form of the work are understood by Lohfink as being Jerusalem court officials (scribes) familiar with wisdom literature and expressions but also priests.[62] The nature of this group, he argues, may be seen in the repetitious use of stock phrases and in the similarities between Deuteronomy and wisdom literature, particularly the use of motivational phrases and clauses.[63] He sees the period of Hezekiah (ca. 715–687 B.C.) as being the most likely time when theological reflection and literary effort were combined in an early form of the book.[64] He holds that "many texts in the book of Deuteronomy were . . . exactly that which they now appear to be: legal and liturgical texts which were to be read before large assemblies of Israel."[65]

Deuteronomy, in Lohfink's view, represents an attempt to reinterpret and "systematize" old traditions in the face of dramatically altered circumstances. He argues that the theological reflection found in Deuteronomy is the result not of an evolutionary development of religious traditions but as a reaction to a threat to a traditional world view.[66] The sudden removal of the Assyrian threat and Josianic moves toward independence led to a resurgence of traditional faith. This traditional faith was repackaged in an early form of Deuteronomy in such a way as to make it appealing to the people (who were accustomed, after generations of being dominated, to the Assyrian world view and practices) and at the same time to neutralize the threat of

---

60. See N. Lohfink, "Deuteronomy," in *IDBSup*, 229. See also idem, "Distribution of the Functions of Power," 343, 345–46; and "Utopian Project," 18. In the latter work (p. 18), he suggests that the final form of Deuteronomy could possibly be dated as late as during Plato's lifetime (427–347 B.C.).

61. Idem, "Distribution," 345–46.

62. Idem, "Deuteronomy," 229; idem, "Culture Shock and Theology: A Discussion of Theology as a Cultural and Social Phenomenon Based on the Example of a Deuteronomic Law," *BTB* 7 (1977): 14.

63. Idem, "Deuteronomy," 229–30.

64. Ibid., 229.

65. Ibid.

66. Idem, "Culture Shock and Theology," 12–22.

the competing world view.[67] Lohfink does not address this issue, but it seems logical to conclude, based on this model, that the final form of Deuteronomy (which he dates to the early exilic period) included further theological reflection in light of the "culture shock" experienced in the Babylonian exile and the threat to the traditional world view manifested by Babylonian culture.

Lohfink sees Deut 16:18–18:22 as representing a coherent constitutional scheme that deliberately seeks to distribute the functions of power. He avers that this "draft constitution"[68] is the result of critical engagement with the constitutional system extant during the period of the monarchy. Its present form, however, represents significant growth. This may be seen partly, he argues, in the "abrupt" transition to the law concerning judges (16:18ff.) from the previous law dealing with the celebration of the feast (Deut 16:1–17).[69] At the time of Deuteronomy's redaction in the early exilic period, the laws concerning offices were brought together and integrated into a comprehensive, consistent constitutional theory.

It was, however, a "utopian theory" because, from the time it was accepted as law in the early exilic period, the monarchy in Israel had ceased to exist, never to be restored.[70] Given that "the lack of one element affects all others in a system, the constitutional theory in Deuteronomy was never concretely realized."[71] In Lohfink's view, then, the laws contained here may have originated in the monarchic period, but in their present form they are intended to be read as a coherent system that is the result of reflection on and engagement with the monarchical system. The result of this engagement is the utopian scheme of the distribution of the functions of power found in Deuteronomy.[72] It is clear that Lohfink's utopianism is different from von

---

67. Ibid., 20.

68. Idem, "Distribution," 346.

69. Ibid., 339, 343. This "abrupt" transition has led some to see Deut 16:17 as the end of the original Deuteronomic law book. Cf. G. Braulik, "The Sequence of the Laws in Deuteronomy 12–26 and in the Decalogue," in *A Song of Power and the Power of Song* (SBTS 3; Winona Lake, IN: Eisenbrauns, 1993), 313–35.

70. The view of Deuteronomy as a postexilic, utopian program was advanced already in 1923. See G. Hölscher, "Komposition und Ursprung des Deuteronomiums," *ZAW* 40 (1923): 161–225. See also N. Lohfink, "Zur neuren Diskussion über 2 Kön 22–23," in *Das Deuteronomium: Entstehung, Gestalt und Botschaft* (ed. N. Lohfink; Leuven: Leuven University Press, 1985), 25.

71. Lohfink, "Distribution," 346.

72. Lohfink's understanding that the Deuteronomic program is a postexilic utopian program is based in part on literary-critical questions of the wording of the laws (see Lohfink, "Distribution," 345–46). For a critique of this understanding, see Crüsemann, *Torah*, 210.

Rad's, because Lohfink maintains that Deuteronomy is a utopian expression of kingship that was never reestablished, whereas von Rad
maintained that Deuteronomy was utopian in its idealization of the
amphictyonic period.

The Deuteronomic scheme, according to Lohfink, serves to redefine power relationships in Israel. The powers of the king and the
priesthood are scaled back in Deuteronomy, while at the same time
the offices of judge and prophet are given greater authority. This is
evident in the fact that the law of the king provides for no judicial
role for the king, whereas formerly he had exercised such a function.[73] Indeed, the only roles that Deuteronomy envisions for the
king, Lohfink maintains, are to carry out administration, study the
Torah, and serve as a symbol of the prosperity of the state.[74] Similarly,
in Lohfink's view, the priestly role is curtailed in favor of the prophet.
He suggests that the priests had formerly "served the oracle" and so
provided contact between an individual and God. In Deuteronomy's
law concerning priests, there is no mention of oracles, and it is the
prophet, in Lohfink's view, whose realm of responsibility includes
contact with God. Moreover, Deuteronomy expressly prohibits spirit-
ism and divination in Israel. The only legitimate means by which Israel can determine the divine will is through the prophet, who
interprets *Torah* (see below).

This redefinition of power relationships, he argues, helps account
for the order of the laws in this section of Deuteronomy, in which the
ideas raised by one law lead, through association, to another. Thus,
the law of the king follows the law of judges, because the king formerly exercised a judicial function. Similarly, the law regarding prophets follows the law of priests due to the association of the priests'
historical function with the prophets' present role.[75]

While the roles of the king and the priests are diminished, the role
of judges is enhanced in Deuteronomy. This is evident, Lohfink notes,

---

73. Lohfink, "Distribution," 348.

74. Lohfink does not comment on how the king, through his harem and wealth,
functions as a symbol of the state in light of Deut 17:7. In this text, the king is prohibited
from having a large harem or much wealth. If the king's harem and wealth serve as symbols of the state's prosperity, then Deuteronomy appears to ensure that the state has no
outward symbol of wealth. It is likely, however, that Deuteronomy is here reacting against
ANE conceptions of the status of nations in favor of its own unique understanding of the
prosperity of the state. In Deuteronomy, the prosperity of the state is measured not by the
wealth of the king but by the way in which the powerless and the Levites are cared for. See
Lohfink, "Laws of Deuteronomy," and also J. G. McConville, *Law and Theology in Deuteronomy* (JSOTSup 33; Sheffield: JSOT Press, 1984), 149–51.

75. Lohfink, "Distribution," 348.

in the fact that in Deuteronomy the judicial system is independent of the king. Nowhere is the king given the authority to appoint judges or to remove them; this responsibility lies with Israel as a whole (although Lohfink argues that the judges in the central tribunal are not appointed by the people or the king but their office is best understood as being hereditary). The judges are given authority to judge the people but are called to do so righteously, in keeping with the tenets of *Torah* (see below).[76]

In a similar way, the role of the prophet is enhanced in Deuteronomy. As noted above, individual contact with God, formerly the province of the priest, is now the responsibility of the prophet. Lohfink argues that the prophets in Deuteronomy are the successors to Moses. Both the office of prophet and *Torah* itself originated at Horeb, and the prophets are described as being "like" Moses. Their role is to interpret the immutable *Torah* for changing times and circumstances. In Lohfink's understanding, the prophets serve as a sort of legislature, though they represent Yahweh, not the people. The prophets serve as a "counterbalance" to the power of the other offices.[77] Through the legislative role of the prophets, "God reserves for himself the possibility of exercising his sovereignty in ever new ways, as occasions arise."[78] The significance of their role may be seen in the fact that those who disobey the prophet are judged by Yahweh himself (18:19), whereas those who fail to heed the instructions of the central tribunal are judged and punished by the people.[79]

Key to Lohfink's understanding of Deuteronomy's constitutional scheme is the role of *Torah*.[80] In Deuteronomy, *Torah* is the ultimate authority. All offices are subordinate to it, including even the king. The king is to read from the *Torah* daily and learn thereby to fear Yahweh and keep his commandments (Deut 17:18–20). The priests are to have custody of the *Torah*, and they are given the responsibility of teaching the generations to come the stipulations of the *Torah* (Deut 31:10–13). Similarly, Deuteronomy assumes that judges will render verdicts that are in keeping with the *Torah* (Deut 17:11). Finally, the prophets are also bound to *Torah*, though Lohfink argues that they are "less subordinate to it than parallel to it. . . . the prophets seem to be thought of as a means of concretizing and actualizing the will of God, as set out in general terms in the Torah."[81]

---

76. Ibid., 349.
77. Ibid.
78. Ibid., 350.
79. Ibid., 342.
80. Ibid., 350–51.
81. Ibid., 351.

To summarize: Lohfink sees Deuteronomy as representing in part a redefinition of power relationships in Israel: power is distributed among the offices of judge, king, priest, and prophet. The ultimate authority in Israel, however, is not the offices or officeholders but *Torah*. All the offices are subject to *Torah*, although the prophet is viewed as equal to *Torah* because his task is to hold the nation accountable to the terms of the *Torah*. This program is a utopian ideal, however, because the office of the king was never reestablished following the exile.

B. Levinson

The final perspective to be considered in this presentation of views of Deuteronomy and centralization is the perspective of Bernard Levinson. Levinson associates Deuteronomy (that is, a form of the book that included a law of centralization) with the reforms of Josiah on the basis of the close association between the requirements of the legal corpus of Deuteronomy and the reform measures actually carried out by Josiah.[82] The authors of this work, he believes, were scribes who drew on other texts (particularly the Covenant Code) in an effort to transform Israelite law, religion, and social structure in radical ways. This transformation was without precedent in the history of Israel.[83]

Levinson's work is unique, not because it sees the Judean scribes as having effected a revolution in the political and religious life of Israel (this view is shared by Weinfeld and others) but because of his understanding of the way that this was accomplished. He argues that the scribes responsible for Deuteronomy deliberately used older legal material but reworked it in support of their own agenda. The use of older material was critical to ensure support for the program through the guise of continuity with the old tradition. But, he argues, the *way* in which the older material is used and reworked demonstrates that the material is used tendentiously. He notes in particular two literary techniques that identify the editorial transformation of a text. The first is repetitive resumption, in which a sequence of ideas is interrupted by a digression or interpolation, and then one or two clauses from the material preceding the digression is repeated to mark the resumption.[84] The other (which is in effect a subcategory of the first) is Seidel's law, in which an interpolation or digression is followed by the reversal of the elements that preceded it. Levinson maintains that repetitive resumption is generally attributed to redaction of material in both Israelite and cuneiform legal texts.[85]

82. Levinson, *Deuteronomy and the Hermeneutics of Legal Innovation*, 9.
83. Ibid., 3–22.
84. Ibid., 18.
85. Ibid., 18–19.

The Deuteronomic authors, then, used the older laws of the Covenant Code to demonstrate continuity with tradition. But they used these laws in such a way as to actually break with, rather than affirm, that tradition. He notes:

> The authors of Deuteronomy employed the Covenant Code . . . not merely as a textual source but as a resource, in order to purchase the legitimacy and authority that their reform agenda otherwise lacked. The reuse of the older material lent their innovations the guise of continuity with the past and consistency with traditional law. The authors of Deuteronomy cast their departure from tradition as its reaffirmation, their transformation and abrogation of conventional religious law as the original intent of that law.[86]

In this way, then, the Deuteronomic program may be seen as particularly revolutionary and unprecedented.

At the heart of this program, as Levinson understands it, is centralization of the cult. Local sanctuaries were outlawed, requiring a major shift in all aspects of life. As a result of this proscription, concession had to be made to allow for the slaughter of animals for food. Just such a law is part of the centralization law in Deut 12, as Levinson sees it. In addition, the removal of local altars and sanctuaries meant that cultic festivals, previously held at local sanctuaries, had to be reworked and directed to the central sanctuary. Finally, the loss of local altars and the desire of the reformers to redefine the social structures of the old clan order led to a restructuring of the judicial system, because prior to the Deuteroromic reforms court cases would be heard at local sanctuaries.

In dealing with this restructuring, Levinson begins with an analysis of the problem posed by Deut 17:2–7. It was long ago suggested that the material in Deut 17:2–7 represents an interruption of the sequence of laws in Deuteronomy and, given its thematic ties to chap. 13, should be relocated there. If this were carried out, the section on judges (Deut 16:18–20) would be followed by the material dealing with the central tribunal (17:8–13)—all material belonging to the same theme. At the same time, the relocation of 16:21–17:7 to chap. 13 would also ensure continuity of theme, because both chap. 13 and the first verses of chap. 17 deal with the issue of idolatry. This, according to Levinson, has become the "standard solution" adopted by most interpreters representing a variety of methodologies.[87]

---

86. Ibid., 21.

87. Ibid., 104–7. Levinson does not mention the commentators who do not apply the "standard solution" but attempt to account for the presence of the apparently intrusive verses through analysis of the text and its context. See, e.g., E. H. Merrill, *Deuteronomy*

Levinson challenges the "standard solution" by contending that it is based on two assumptions, neither of which can be upheld. The first assumption is that Deut 17:2–7 is the completion of a series of laws on apostasy found in chap. 13. The second is that chap. 13 and 17:2–7 "derive from the same literary stratum."[88] But this solution, he argues, is not viable because it creates more problems than it solves. If Deut 17:2–7 were inserted between 13:1 and 13:2, as is sometimes proposed, then the laws concerning actions by lay people interrupt a law concerning a prophet's incitement to apostasy. Moreover, he notes that inserting Deut 17:2–7 *before* 13:7–12 does not solve the problem either, because it places a case dealing with actual apostasy into a series that deals only with incitement.[89] Thus, he argues, the "standard solution" fails to resolve the existing problem of lack of coherence in the laws because it introduces its own incoherence and simply shifts the problem from one chapter to another.

The second assumption, that the two texts derive from the same literary stratum, is shown to be false, he argues, based on the shared terminology of Deut 16:18–20, 17:8–13, and 17:2–7. Technical terms for the secular sphere and the cultic sphere are used consistently in Deut 16–17 but are absent from chap. 13 (see below). In addition, the term בְּקִרְבְּךָ ("in your midst") is used consistently in chap. 13 but in a way that cannot be construed as parallel to the use of the technical vocabulary of Deut 16–17. This may be seen readily in Deut 17:2, where the author has retained the term בְּקִרְבְּךָ from the earlier law in Deut 13 but added the distinctive technical term בְּאַחַד שְׁעָרֶיךָ.[90]

In order to avoid the problems wrought by the standard solution, Levinson proposes an alternative understanding. He argues that Deut 17:2–7 represents an original part of the structure of the chapter and that it and the following section (vv. 8–13) represent two alternatives to a problematic case. Verses 2–7 present a case in which there is reliable evidence in the form of the testimony of two witnesses. This is the "secular" resolution. The second alternative (vv. 8–13) is a case in which there is ambiguity of some sort that makes it impossible for

---

(NAC 4; Nashville: Broadman & Holman, 1994), 257–58; P. D. Miller Jr., *Deuteronomy* (Interp; Louisville: John Knox, 1990), 142–44; C. J. H. Wright, *Deuteronomy* (NIBC 4; Peabody, MA: Hendrickson / Carlisle: Paternoster, 1996), 204–7. Still others, while accepting that the laws in 16:21–17:7 may have originated elsewhere, seek to account for the presence of the laws in the final form of the book but in a different way from Levinson's. See Clements, "The Book of Deuteronomy," 420–21; idem, *Deuteronomy*, 23–31.

88. Levinson, *Legal Innovation*, 108.

89. Ibid.

90. Ibid., 131–33.

the secular judges to render a verdict. In this case, Deuteronomy provides for resolution of the case in the central tribunal through the
mediation of the Levitical priest or judge in office (Deut 17:9), presumably through recourse to cultic inquiry. The function of Deut
17:2–7, Levinson argues, is to "define the conditions for evidentiary
certainty."[91]

Levinson bases this contention on the fact that the Covenant
Code, which he understands as being revised by Deuteronomy, includes laws with a similar structure, albeit dealing with different subject matter. He notes that Exod 22:6–7 includes a protasis marked by
כִּי, followed by two alternative subordinate clauses marked by אִם.[92] In
the case of Exodus, the first alternative represents a case in which
there is incontrovertible evidence (the apprehension of the thief who
stole property). In the second, ambiguity exists, and so the owner of
the house is required to approach God to determine whether or not
he did, in fact, misappropriate the property. He argues that Deut 17
similarly presents two parallel conditional clauses, each of which
deals with different conditions. The first, vv. 2–7, begins with a כִּי
clause and deals with a case in which there is irrefutable evidence.
The second, also beginning with כִּי, deals with an ambiguous case that
requires recourse to a cultic setting. The cultic setting, however, has
been reinterpreted in Deuteronomy in light of its unique centralization law that eliminated the local sanctuaries, which were formerly
the places at which the ambiguous cases were resolved. He further
notes that a similar construction (of two parallel conditional clauses
dealing with alternative scenarios) is found in the Akkadian *Laws of
Eshnunna*.[93]

Thus, in this understanding, Deut 17:2–7 is in fact a revision not
only of the Covenant Code but also of Deut 13:7–12 (which is itself a
revision of earlier law[94]). The latter text is concerned with the case of
enticement to apostasy by a close family member or close friend.
Levinson argues that the text requires that "the person to whom the

---

91. Ibid., 116.
92. Ibid., 115.
93. Ibid., 115–16. An English translation of the *Laws of Eshnunna* is found in *ANET*,
161–63.
94. Levinson, *Legal Innovation*, 122–23. Levinson sees in Deut 13 a revision of the law
in Exod 19:22 that prohibits sacrifice to foreign gods. In his discussion of this (p. 123), he
assumes that Deut 13:7–12 is in part a restrictive interpretation of Exod 19:22, in that the
later text does not provide for the destruction of the entire family, as, he assumes, does
Exod 19:22. However, this assumption is highly speculative, and Levinson himself notes
(p. 123 n. 67) that there "is no conclusive evidence that the punishment does extend to
the family" in Exod 19:22.

incitement is addressed ... take summary action to execute the in-
citer, acting in self-defense on behalf of the entire community to de-
fend it from a mortal threat."[95] The key phrase is found in Deut 13:10–
11a, which commands:

[A] יָדְךָ תִּהְיֶה־בּוֹ בָרִאשׁוֹנָה לַהֲמִיתוֹ וְיַד כָּל־הָעָם בָּאַחֲרֹנָה:
[B] וּסְקַלְתּוֹ בָאֲבָנִים וָמֵת

This phrase appears again, in almost identical form, in Deut 17:5b–7.
But here, in Levinson's interpretation, the phrase is cited chiastically
and with a reversal of elements, in accordance with Seidel's law. But,
as is the case when Seidel's law is used to mark textual reuse, there is
an interrupting element that is innovative. Thus, Levinson sees the
following chiastic structure with an innovative element (here denoted
as X) in Deut 17:5b–7[96]:

[B′] וּסְקַלְתָּם בָּאֲבָנִים וָמֵתוּ:
[X] עַל־פִּי שְׁנַיִם עֵדִים אוֹ שְׁלֹשָׁה עֵדִים יוּמַת הַמֵּת לֹא יוּמַת עַל־פִּי עֵד אֶחָד:
[A′] יַד הָעֵדִים תִּהְיֶה־בּוֹ בָרִאשֹׁנָה לַהֲמִיתוֹ וְיַד כָּל־הָעָם בָּאַחֲרֹנָה

According to Levinson, this text represents a reuse of Deut 13:10–11a,
with an additional requirement of a minimum of two witnesses interpolated into the revised text. Given the revision, it is the "hand" of the
witnesses (plural) that are to be the first to cast the stones. This revision, he argues, "establishes the legal-historical distance between the
two texts."[97]

According to this interpretation, the focus of Deut 17:2–7 is not
apostasy but the rules of evidence. Deuteronomy 13:10–11a, in his
view, deals with summary execution. The later passage seeks to reinterpret the law concerning summary execution and introduce into
it the requirement for multiple witnesses, and it does so using the
very wording of the earlier text. That the case in question deals with
apostasy, the most vile crime imaginable under the terms of the covenant, demonstrates, in Levinson's view, the paradigmatic nature of
the text. If two witnesses are required even for apostasy, the importance of the requirement is easily seen.[98]

Levinson contends that this reinterpretation was part of a deliberate effort on the part of the authors to redefine the nature and role of
the judicial system at the local level. Part of the function of Deut
17:2–7 is to demonstrate that there is still a judicial function to be

95. Ibid., 118.
96. See ibid., 118–19.
97. Ibid., 119–20.
98. Ibid., 121.

exercised locally; even capital cases dealing with apostasy may be adjudicated locally, as long as the evidence in the form of two or more witnesses is available. But Deuteronomy still is seen as radical in that it transfers to the central tribunal the authority to adjudicate ambiguous cases and, importantly, it supplants the clan-elder role in the judiciary through the requirement that judges and officers be appointed in each town (Deut 16:18).[99] He notes that Deuteronomy is completely silent on the role of clan elders and that the authors "impose their professionalized judicial system upon the city gate as if it were a tabula rasa without traditional legal-historical occupants."[100] This silence about the elders, in Levinson's view, can "only constitute a deliberate polemic."[101] The purpose of the authors of Deuteronomy is to create an independent judiciary that is free from control by the institution of the monarchy. The result is a political system in which the judge does not serve the king; instead, both offices, king and judge, are subject to the authority of *Torah*.[102]

While transforming local judicial procedure, Deuteronomy transfers authority for adjudicating ambiguous cases to the central tribunal. This change, Levinson argues, is not as dramatic because ambiguous cases formerly were resolved at the local sanctuary. Thus, the authors of Deuteronomy simply shift the location to the central sanctuary.[103] Levinson argues that it is the parties to the dispute, not the local judges, who are to go to the central tribunal for resolution of the case. He bases this on the idea that the earlier law, here being reworked, included a requirement for the swearing of a judicial oath. Thus, he argues, the parties to the case would likely be required to proceed to the central tribunal. Moreover, he argues that, because Deut 19:17 requires that in the case of a single (malicious) witness both parties must stand "before the LORD" (לִפְנֵי יְהוָה) to determine the veracity of the accusations, the same requirement is most likely present here.[104]

Together, Levinson argues, Deut 17:2–7 and vv. 8–13 form a coherent whole that establishes the jurisdiction of the various judicial spheres. The first text, vv. 2–7, assigns all cases in which the evidence

---

99. Ibid., 124–27.
100. Ibid., 125.
101. Ibid., 126.
102. Ibid., 126–27.
103. Ibid., 127. Although most commentators assume that the central sanctuary and the central tribunal were coterminous, Merrill argues that this is not necessarily the case. He notes that the "place" of the central tribunal is not specifically identified, as is the location of the sanctuary: "where the LORD placed his Name," as in Deut 12:5. See Merrill, *Deuteronomy*, 261–62; and Cairns, *Word and Presence*, 163–64.
104. Levinson, *Legal Innovation*, 129–30.

is readily available, including cases involving religious issues such as apostasy, to the local sphere. At the same time, vv. 8–13 assign all ambiguous cases (whether dealing with religious or civil/"secular" matters) to the central tribunal for disposition via cultic measures.[105] Thus, the two sections function together in a dialectical structure. Furthermore, Levinson argues that key phrases found in either section function as technical terms denoting the cultic and secular realms, respectively. The phrase "in the place" (בַּמָּקוֹם) functions to identify the cultic sphere in the legal section of Deuteronomy. Similarly, the phrase "in your gates" (בִּשְׁעָרֶיךָ) serves as a technical term for the secular sphere.[106] All this demonstrates, Levinson contends, that Deut 17:2–7 is a deliberate reinterpretation of the apostasy laws of Deut 13 in light of centralization.

For Levinson, the program of centralization of justice envisioned by Deuteronomy is both realistic and utopian. It is utopian in its subjugation of all offices to the *Torah*. On the other hand, he sees it as realistic in its systematic and deliberate reinterpretation of the Covenant Code and the judicial system and procedures described there. He sees in Deuteronomy both a "draft constitution" and a description of the office-bearers of theocracy. He notes that "the Deuteronomic agenda is thus both cultic and judicial, both utopian and practical; it is concerned both with the rewriting of texts and with the transformation of public life."[107]

Finally, Levinson addresses the judicial role of the king in Deuteronomy. He notes that the Deuteronomic presentation of the judiciary provides no role whatsoever for the monarch. This, he notes, stands in marked contrast to the judicial role played by the king throughout the ANE and in Israel prior to the writing of Deuteronomy. He argues that the denial of any meaningful judicial role to the king is intelligible in light of the authors' intention to draw out the implications of centralization in every sphere of life. This may be seen even in the sequence in which the offices are discussed in Deut 16:18–18:22. Levinson argues that the order of the offices (judge, king, priest, prophet) and the order of topics in the section (local justice, central justice, king, priests, prophet) do not reflect ascending or descending organization, which is often present in cuneiform law codes and even in earlier biblical codes.[108] Thus, the point is not to highlight the

---

105. Ibid., 130.
106. Ibid., 131.
107. Ibid., 137.
108. Ibid., 142. He cites Exod 21:28–32 as an example of a descending organizational pattern.

supremacy of any office per se but to argue for the supremacy, both judicial and textual,[109] of the cultic center. The very presence of the law of the king, following the laws concerning the central tribunal, is a reflection of the role the king formerly played in the judicial system.

Evaluation

It is now necessary to evaluate briefly the nature of the arguments and cases for centralization summarized above. Thorough evaluation of the arguments of each of these interpretations would be vastly beyond the scope of this chapter. I will, therefore, simply highlight significant difficulties with some of the interpretations discussed.

It appears to me that some of the interpretations have not consistently evaluated the data of the text. As noted above, Weinfeld understands the centralization program in Deuteronomy to include as a corollary an attempt by scribes to reinterpret old traditions and theology in favor of a more sophisticated, spiritual religion. Part of this reinterpretation includes a repudiation of the ostensibly anthropomorphic conception of Yahweh found in earlier strata and in P. In Weinfeld's view, much of the Deuteronomic program is designed to counter the view that Yahweh was actually present in the temple and, instead, to promote the idea that Yahweh dwells in heaven, not in the temple. This proposed shift in understanding of the presence of Yahweh has tremendous implications for Deuteronomy's presentation of cult and theology. Indeed, Weinfeld states that the removal of Yahweh's actual presence (immanence) means the collapse of the entire Priestly code. All cultic function would cease, and all the social laws of the code would also cease to be operative.[110]

Because Deuteronomy has ostensibly reinterpreted the presence of Yahweh, many of the rituals that presupposed his presence are eliminated. Actions that formerly were to be performed in Yahweh's presence are reinterpreted in light of the fact that he is no longer actually present. To put it more simply: if the purpose of the sacrificial rituals was to satisfy a locally present deity, those rituals must necessarily be reinterpreted if the deity is absent. This, according to Weinfeld and others, explains much of what we see in Deuteronomy. Methods of sacrifice and sacral service are missing from Deuteronomy.[111] When

109. Levinson argues against any descending organizational pattern in the these laws but claims that the fact that the laws concerning the central tribunal are textually prior to the law of the king demonstrates the eclipse of monarchical judicial authority in favor of the central tribunal. But the laws concerning the *local* judiciary are textually prior to both the central tribunal and the law of the king.

110. Weinfeld, *Deuteronomic School*, 185.

111. Idem, *Deuteronomy 1–11*, 55.

sacrifice is mentioned, the author of Deuteronomy presents it in a different way than does P or the holiness code. Weinfeld argues that sacrifice in Deuteronomy is not practiced for its own sake. Rather, sacrifice is reinterpreted in Deuteronomy and is understood as a personal transaction between the offerer and God; it serves a largely humane, not religious, purpose.[112] That is, according to Weinfeld, the obligation to share the offering brought to "The Place" with the underprivileged and the Levite is stated so often and emphatically that it appears to be a central purpose of the offering itself. Moreover, it is a personal matter, not inherently a communal concern; it functions as a gift from the offerer to Yahweh.[113] All this, again, may be seen to derive from the fact that God is not seen as actually being present in the temple.

Weinfeld sees support for his view in the fact that there is no discussion of expiatory sacrifice in Deuteronomy. The only rite analogous to a sin or guilt offering is found in the law of unsolved murder. However, in this law he sees evidence of a changed attitude to sacrifice in general and expiation in particular. Whereas the priests in P and earlier codes played a mediatorial role, in Deuteronomy, he argues, they are simply present to provide a religious environment to the ceremony, which itself is actually performed by elders (who represent the political, not religious, realm).[114] Forgiveness comes as a result of the prayers of the elders who represent the city, not as a result of the sacrifice of the heifer.

It is here that an important objection may be raised. Weinfeld's argument is based in part on an argument from silence. That is, because Deuteronomy does not present a complete or systematic description of sacrifice, it must be repudiating the practice or, at least, the theology behind it. But the data of the text will admit of other explanations. Weinfeld sees Deuteronomy as being a manual for the king and people.[115] Given the audience that Weinfeld himself assumes, it is not surprising to find a less than systematic presentation of sacrifice. Even the "revolutionary" centralization law in Deut 12:6 calls for the presentation at "the place" of "your burnt offerings, your sacrifices, your tithes, the contribution of your hand, your votive offerings, your freewill offerings, and the firstborn of your herd and of your flock." The emphasis Weinfeld sees on humanitarian concerns need not necessarily imply that this was the only, or even primary, motivation for sacrifice.

112. Ibid., 40–41.
113. Ibid., 41.
114. Ibid., 40.
115. Ibid., 46.

In the case of the law of unsolved murder, Weinfeld argues that sacrificial ritual is transformed in Deuteronomy because 21:8 calls for expiation of the *people*, not the land. But it is not at all clear that this chapter is best understood as reflecting Deuteronomy's understanding of sacrifice in general. The case may instead be exceptional (it is, after all, not presented as a discussion of sacrifice but of the exceptional case of unsolved murder), even if Weinfeld's interpretation of the text is correct. But Weinfeld's interpretation—that the text is about the expiation of the people instead of the land—is not necessarily correct. Milgrom rightly notes that the ritual described in Deut 21 "is incomprehensible without the assumption that the blood does contaminate the land on which it is spilt and that this ritual transfers the contamination to the untillable land."[116] Furthermore, the same chapter later indicates that the rationale for not exposing the corpse of an executed criminal overnight is to avoid contamination of the land (וְלֹא תְטַמֵּא אֶת־אַדְמָתְךָ). Even if these two sections derive from different stages in the development of the book, the final redactor was not concerned with avoiding the implication that the land could be defiled, despite the fact that this was the view espoused in earlier sources supposedly rejected by Deuteronomy.

In addition, Deuteronomy's understanding of divine presence and its relationship to P is an exceedingly complex matter. Wilson has challenged the prevailing view that Deuteronomy represents a different understanding of the presence of God than do other sources in the Pentateuch.[117] His careful examination of the historical sections of the book (which are widely held to be "Deuteronomistic" and, so, would reflect the theology of the Deuteronomists that Weinfeld and others have understood as rejecting earlier concepts of the presence of Yahweh[118]) demonstrates that the author(s) of Deuteronomy do not seem to have been constrained to use different terminology from that of parallel sources. Rather, similar language is used in Deuteronomy and in the Tetrateuch when describing the presence of Yahweh with Israel. Significantly, the language used in both the Tetrateuch and in Deuteronomy in parallel passages is used for similar functions and to convey the sense that Yahweh was actually present among his people.[119]

116. J. Milgrom, "The Alleged 'Demythologization and Secularization' in Deuteronomy (Review Article)," *IEJ* 23/3 (1973): 157.

117. I. Wilson, *Out of the Midst of the Fire: Divine Presence in Deuteronomy* (SBLDS 151; Atlanta: Scholars Press, 1995).

118. M. Weinfeld, "Presence, Divine," *EncJud* 13: 1020, notes: "[T]he abstract notion of the Divine Presence associated with the so-called 'Name' theology found its full expression in Deuteronomy and the Deuteronomic school."

119. Wilson, *Midst of the Fire*, 24–28, 32–36, 45–50, 114–15, 200.

Similarly, Wilson's examination of the use of the phrase לִפְנֵי יְהוָה in the legal section of Deut 12–26 demonstrates that Deuteronomy understands the cultic actions described (eating, rejoicing, etc.) as taking place in the presence of Yahweh, and "thus . . . they point to the localized Presence of the Deity at the 'chosen place.'"[120] He notes:

> This preference for acting *before* God, and thereby using a preposition whose possible range of meaning undoubtedly includes the literal "in the presence of," is consistent with a belief in the Deity being localized in the immediate vicinity of the worshipper, but is antithetical to a concern to emphasize his *absence* from the earthly sphere.[121]

That such expressions occur both in the historical sections (which are understood to be Deuteronomi[sti]c) and in the legal section calls into question the understanding that Deuteronomy has "relocated" God to heaven[122] and challenges the view that the book presents a radically different understanding of the presence of Yahweh.

Weinfeld appears to be inconsistent at another point as well. In his reconstruction of Deuteronomy's judicial reform, he argues that centralization "created a judicial vacuum in the provincial cities, and the law providing for the appointment of state judges in every city was apparently designed to fill it."[123] But according to his own reconstruction, centralization resulted in the loss of local *sacral* authorities, not local judicial authorities. The "judicial vacuum" ostensibly created by centralization was filled by the enhanced role of the central tribunal, since that body fulfilled duties previously exercised by the local sanctuaries. Thus, centralization did not *require* the appointment of judges in the cities. The local authorities who, according to this interpretation, formerly exercised judicial authority could have continued to do so.[124] Instead of consulting a local shrine or sanctuary in cases too difficult for the local judges, centralization would simply require that they consult the central tribunal. Weinfeld's theory of centralization does not adequately account for the requirement that judges be appointed in the cities (Deut 16:18).

He further assumes that the jurisdiction of elders was limited as part of the centralizing reform to "patriarchal and family litigation" and that Deuteronomy assigns to the royally appointed magistrates

---

120. Ibid., 204.
121. Ibid.
122. T. N. D. Mettinger, *The Dethronement of Sabaoth: Studies in the Shem and Kabod Theologies* (Lund: CWK Gleerup, 1982), 47.
123. Weinfeld, *Deuteronomic School*, 234.
124. T. M. Willis, *The Elders of the City: A Study of the Elders-Laws in Deuteronomy* (SBLMS 55; Atlanta: Scholars Press, 2001), 44.

"all cases requiring a clear cut verdict (such as the establishment of guilt or innocence . . .)."[125] But this interpretation stands in contrast to Deut 19:11–12, which deals with the case of a murderer who seeks asylum in one of the cities of refuge inappropriately—because the killing was intentional, not accidental. The elders are given responsibility for delivering the offender to the avenger. But this text seems to presuppose that the elders are in fact establishing the guilt or innocence of the offender; presumably, it would not be immediately known that the person intentionally killed his neighbor. The elders would therefore have to investigate the case and determine whether or not the killing was accidental or intentional.[126] This is not a case of family litigation but of determining the guilt or innocence of a suspected offender. The same is true for other cases explicitly assigned to the elders (Deut 21:19–20; 22:15–21; 25:8–9). Although Weinfeld considers them to be cases of "patriarchal and family litigation," they all are dealing with establishing guilt or innocence (and therefore, in Weinfeld's view, would be the responsibility of the magistrates, not the elders) and can even involve a sentence of death. Whatever the true relationship between the "judges" required in Deut 16:18 and the elders described elsewhere, Weinfeld's reconstruction seems improbable and does not account for the textual data.

Objections may be raised about certain points of Levinson's treatment as well. He argues that Deuteronomy's radical innovation is apparent in the supposed reinterpretation of Deut 13 in chap. 17. As noted above (pp. 52–54), Levinson sees Deut 17:2–7 as a reinterpretation not just of the earlier Covenant Code but also of Deut 13:7–12. He argues that Deut 13:7–12 requires summary execution of a person who incites another to apostasy. He concludes that, in cases of incitement to apostasy in which there are no witnesses, "even immediate summary execution—taking the law into one's hands—is mandated."[127]

---

125. Weinfeld, *Deuteronomic School*, 234.

126. D. Patrick (*Old Testament Law* [Atlanta: John Knox, 1985], 73) argues that this is implied in the similar passage in Exod 21:12–14. There, he notes, "when the avenger sought the killer at the sanctuary, a trial could be convened to determine whether the person taking sanctuary should be removed." Similarly, Crüsemann maintains that "the control of avengers and their vendettas by public councils is necessarily and inseparably connected with the distinction between intentional and unintentional murder. This distinction can only be effective if all homicides are subject to thorough public investigation of a claim. . . . Furthermore, the distinction between intentional and unintentional had the purpose and function of *determining who was guilty and what the nature of the guilt was*" (Crüsemann, *Torah*, 175–76, emphasis mine). He further notes (p. 177) that Deut 19:12 maintains that the elders of the place where the crime was committed have the responsibility to carry out the proceedings to determine the guilt or innocence of the offender.

127. Levinson, *Legal Innovation*, 134.

This command is then reinterpreted in favor of more stringent evidential requirements in Deut 17:2–7. But is this really what Deut 13:7–12 is requiring?

Verse 10 is a key to this section. It says, כִּי הָרֹג תַּהַרְגֶנּוּ יָדְךָ תִּהְיֶה־בּוֹ בָרִאשׁוֹנָה לַהֲמִיתוֹ וְיַד כָּל־הָעָם בָּאַחֲרֹנָה ("But you shall surely kill him. Your hand shall be first against him to put him to death, and afterward the hand of all the people."). Even if it is conceded that the MT and not the LXX (which renders the first clause ἀναγγέλλων ἀναγγλεῖς περὶ αὐτοῦ, "You shall surely *report* him") is the correct reading, as Levinson argues,[128] it is still possible that summary execution is not in fact in view here. The text stresses that "your hand" (i.e., the person who was invited by a close friend or family member in secret [בַּסֵּתֶר] to serve other gods) is to be the first against the offender and then "afterward the hand of all the people." The very fact that "all the people" are to take part in the execution may imply that a judicial procedure did in fact precede the execution. A judicial procedure would bring this section in line with vv. 13–19 of the same chapter, where a thorough investigation is called for prior to punishment. As Tigay notes, "the investigation is not mentioned here because the present paragraph does not focus on the role of the court but on the duty of the person approached by the instigator."[129] At the very least, this text prohibits immediate, private, summary action; the entire community is to be involved.

Moreover, this passage emphasizes the importance of demonstrating allegiance to Yahweh. It is a forceful argument that loyalty to Yahweh is more important even than loyalty to family. Furthermore, the enticement to apostasy was made in secret (בַּסֵּתֶר), so there would have been a real temptation to cover it up. What the text is stressing is that covenant loyalty to Yahweh means exposing the idolatrous inclinations of even close family or friends, even if those inclinations would otherwise remain secret.[130] Given the thrust of this passage in

---

128. Ibid., 120 n. 60. On this issue, see also idem, "'But You Shall Surely Kill Him!': The Text-Critical and Neo-Assyrian Evidence for MT Deut 13:10," in *Bundesdokument und Gesetz: Studien zum Deuteronomium* (HBS 4; ed. G. Braulik; Freiburg: Herder, 1995), 37–63; Weinfeld, *Deuteronomic School*, 91–100; P. E. Dion, "Deuteronomy 13: The Suppression of Alien Religious Propaganda during the Late Monarchical Era," in *Law and Ideology in Monarchic Israel* (JSOTSup 124; ed. B. Halpern and D. Hobson; Sheffield: Sheffield Academic Press, 1991), 147–216, esp. 149–56. Levinson's preference for the MT goes against the "nearly absolute scholarly consensus" that the LXX reading, not that of the MT, is correct (*Legal Innovation*, 120 n. 60).

129. Tigay, *Deuteronomy*, 132.

130. Cf. Wright, *Deuteronomy*, 175–76; P. C. Craigie, *The Book of Deuteronomy* (NICOT; Grand Rapids: Eerdmans, 1976), 224–25.

the context of the argument of the chapter, it is then not surprising that any judicial procedure that may have preceded execution is not spelled out. Doing so would have detracted from the main focus of the passage, which is the need for absolute loyalty to Yahweh. Judicial procedure and evidential requirements would interrupt the flow of thought of the passage; such topics could be and are dealt with elsewhere. To argue thus is not improper harmonization but simply interpreting the text in its context.

It is also important to note the motivation for the execution. The author says (Deut 13:12) that, as a result of the execution, "all Israel will hear and will be afraid, and they will not again do anything like this evil in your midst." Thus, the motivation is deterrence. The author is seeking to persuade his audience to avoid going after other gods, even in secret. The threat is that even disloyalty to Yahweh perpetrated in secret will be brought to light and the offender executed, even if the offence is "only" an incitement to apostasy (rather than actual apostasy). A careful presentation of the judicial procedures that may have preceded the execution would serve only to diminish the tension raised by the author and undermine its rhetorical effect on his audience.[131]

In addition, Levinson asserts that Deuteronomy's program seeks to supplant the local elders with judicial professionals.[132] Thus, the silence on the role of elders in this section of Deuteronomy "can only constitute a deliberate polemic."[133] In criticizing Weinfeld's reconstruction of separate jurisdictions for the professional judges and the elders, Levinson argues that "such a synchronic harmonization overlooks the diachronic issues involved in the composition of the legal corpus."[134] But it seems to me that Levinson is guilty of completely overlooking synchronic concerns in favor of diachronic analysis. Deuteronomy's "polemical silence" regarding the role of elders is limited to this section only. There are several texts that assume the continued participation of elders in the judicial realm (Deut 19:11–13; 21:1–9; 22:13–21; 25:5–10). In one instance, Deut 21:2, the offices of judge and elder are mentioned together because both participate in

---

131. I am not suggesting, as have some, that the chapter is to be understood as only rhetorical. Rather, I am saying that the author is using strong language that emphasizes harsh consequences in order to persuade his audience to be loyal to Yahweh. Hölscher argues that the text reflects a lack of realism and emerged only in an exilic setting as theoretical speculation. See his "Ursprung des Deuteronomiums," 192–93, cited in Dion, "Deuteronomy 13," 148.

132. Levinson, *Legal Innovation*, 124–27.

133. Ibid., 125, 126.

134. Ibid., 125.

the ritual following an unsolved murder. Even if these texts are assigned to different literary strata of the book, Levinson does not address why the final redactor(s) of Deuteronomy included a judicial role for elders while at the same time including the text that ostensibly eliminates any judicial role for them whatsoever.

Willis further notes that in the entire corpus of the laws of Deuteronomy fewer than ten laws specify who is to adjudicate.[135] He argues that it is possible that Deuteronomy assumes the continuation of an earlier system in which elders adjudicated many cases. The fact that the text only rarely states who is to adjudicate means that caution must be exercised in drawing conclusions about who is thought to be acting and what constitutes "polemical" silence. Indeed, Willis notes that Levinson's interpretation is based on

> the prior assumption that the introduction of something new to the judicial system eliminates the need for (or even prohibits the possibility of) the continuation of what already existed. For some, it might be just as logical to argue that the laws calling for adjudication by elders were written later than Deut 16:18–20, and that those laws use "polemical silence" to prohibit continued adjudication by professional judges.[136]

A further objection to Levinson's reconstruction of the relationship between Deut 13:7–12 and 17:2–7 may be raised. Levinson himself concedes a "methodological difficulty" regarding the relationship between these texts.[137] The problem in his view is whether 17:2–7 should be considered Deuteronomistic because it dates later than Deut 13:7–12 or whether it should be considered Deuteronomic because it furthers the Deuteronomic program of centralization.[138] In my estimation, this is a serious methodological problem that Levinson downplays.

Levinson contends that Deut 13 is "very much a literary text: a deliberate composition in which Josianic authors appropriate the literary and political model of the neo-Assyrian state treaties . . . and transfer that loyalty oath . . . to Yahweh."[139] He further notes that Deut 17:2–7 is part of the deliberate reinterpretation of earlier material in support of centralization.[140] But he contends that the centralization program is best understood as being associated with the

---

135. Willis, *Elders*, 68 n. 78.
136. Ibid., 44.
137. Levinson, *Legal Innovation*, 136–37 n. 97.
138. Ibid.
139. Ibid., 122.
140. Ibid., 109, 116.

reforms of Josiah.[141] This raises a legal-historical difficulty. If both texts are to be associated with Josiah's reform, to what extent could Deut 13:7–12 be said to have "achieved sufficient authoritative status that subsequent editors made new law through the reinterpretation of" it?[142] The hermeneutical method of the authors as outlined by Levinson was a careful reworking of earlier authoritative texts in order to foster the appearance of continuity (even to the extent that the very words or lemmas are used) while in fact radically revising the earlier law. It seems improbable to me that Deut 13, a product of Josiah's time and, in Levinson's view, requiring summary execution for incitement to apostasy, would have become so entrenched as a legal text that it would need to be carefully reworked by scribes of the same school who worked later in Josiah's time.

The problem may be put differently. Who is the audience to whom this verbal-literary "sleight of hand"[143] is directed? Anyone familiar with what Levinson sees as an "authoritative text" (such as Deut 13:7–12) would immediately be aware of the discrepancies between the older text and the revised text, the reuse of lemmas notwithstanding. If Levinson's interpretation is correct, the older text mandates summary execution, while the later text requires due process. The disparity is not obscured even by the fact that the terminology of the earlier text is tendentiously reworked in the formulation of the later. If the text is addressed with an audience in mind that is not intimately familiar with the requirements of earlier texts, then presumably such a careful reworking of earlier legal material is unnecessary. If the text is composed with a king in mind, tendentious reuse of lemmas probably would be insufficient to convince him to embrace a document that denies him any legal role whatsoever.

The criticisms raised here do not, of course, disprove the thesis of centralization. But I have demonstrated that there are problems with certain understandings of centralization and with seeing centralization as being at the heart of the Deuteronomic revolution. It is now necessary to examine some of the implications of the various views of centralization and the objections identified.

Centralization and the Interpretation of Deuteronomy

The previous discussion has demonstrated that, while there may be consensus that centralization is at the core of the Deuteronomic pro-

---

141. Ibid., 9.

142. Ibid., 122.

143. J. Barton, "Review of *Deuteronomy and the Hermeneutics of Legal Innovation*, by B. M. Levinson," *JR* 79 (1999): 651.

gram, this has not led to consensus on other key aspects of the book. I will now attempt to show the ways in which these representative views differ from one another in key areas of interpretation of the book.

Setting

The various representative interpretations described above provide no solid consensus on the setting of the book. Von Rad contends that the book is the product of Northern country Levites,[144] hence positing a priestly/cultic setting, while Weinfeld and Levinson see the setting of the book as the Judean court. Driver proposes a prophetic setting for the book; Lohfink, on the other hand, argues for a postexilic setting.

More importantly, each of these commentators (naturally) understands centralization in terms of the provenance he posits. For example, according to Driver, centralization is an attempt to reform the cult in the light of the prophetic critique of its excesses.[145] It is shaped by the particular abuses and idolatry of Manasseh's reign and represents an attempt to spiritualize the cult and prevent syncretism. Von Rad is cautious about seeing centralization as the theological center of the book and even says that the altar law in Deut 12 is in large measure a "fresh wording" of the altar law in Exod 20:24.[146] This stands in marked contrast to Levinson's understanding of centralization as a "comprehensive program of religious, social, and political transformation that left no area of life untouched."[147] Thus centralization, while certainly innovative in all of these interpretations, is understood differently by the various interpreters depending, in part, on their understanding of the setting of the book.

Audience

Another area of disagreement, related to the first, has to do with the audience of the book. This important issue is largely ignored by the representative interpreters described above.

Weinfeld sees Deuteronomy as a manual for the king and the people.[148] Similarly, von Rad sees the book as preaching and, consequently, as being addressed to an audience consisting of the people. Driver sees the book as continuing in the prophetic tradition of the 8th-century prophets and, therefore, as having the people in view.[149]

---

144. A more recent proponent of the Northern hypothesis for the origin of Deuteronomy is E. Nielsen, *Deuteronomium* (HAT 1/6; Tübingen: Mohr Siebeck, 1995).

145. Driver, *Deuteronomy*, xxvii.

146. Von Rad, *Commentary*, 90–91.

147. Levinson, *Legal Innovation*, 20.

148. Weinfeld, *Deuteronomy 1–11*, 55, 57.

149. Driver, *Deuteronomy*, xxvi.

Likewise, Lohfink believes that the book had a popular audience, on the basis of the instruction that the text was "to be read before large assemblies of Israel."[150]

Levinson, however, has in mind a more specific audience than the people as a whole. The program he envisions is based on careful re-working of existing legal texts, using even the lemmas of the earlier works. This seems to presuppose great familiarity with the existing texts. In addition, he notes that these texts "may not yet have had the status of actual public law; they may have been only prestigious texts, part of the curriculum of scribal schools."[151] Thus the texts being modified were, in some instances, familiar only to the scribes, so it is this audience (initially, at least) to which Deuteronomy addresses its hermeneutical and legal innovation.

The interpreters described above do not go far enough, in my esti-mation, in recognizing the significance of the audience presumed by the text of Deuteronomy. In the section concerning offices (Deut 16:18–18:22), it is the *people* who are consistently addressed. Deuter-onomy 16:18 commands the people to appoint judges and officers. The second-person singular address is used, which is usually under-stood as addressing the whole people.[152] Thus, it is all the assembled people who are to do the appointing, a fact overlooked by von Rad, for example, when he asserts that the king is to appoint judges in 16:18.[153] Moreover, the assembly of the people (again note the use of second-person singular address) is given the responsibility of choos-ing a king according to Deut 17:15. Deuteronomy thus seems to grant extraordinary power to the people in assembly. This stands in remark-able contrast to ANE conceptions of political power, in which the monarch wielded tremendous power.[154] The extraordinary role of the

---

150. Lohfink, "Deuteronomy," 229.

151. Levinson, *Legal Innovation*, 5.

152. On the use of second-person singular and plural in Deuteronomy, see T. A. Len-chak, *"Choose Life!": A Rhetorical-Critical Investigation of Deuteronomy 28,69–30,20* (AnBib 129; Rome: Pontifical Biblical Institute, 1993), 12–16, and references there.

153. Von Rad, *Commentary*, 118.

154. The centrality of the king in ANE political systems is highlighted by K. W. White-lam, "Israelite Kingship: The Royal Ideology and its Opponents," in *The World of Ancient Israel: Sociological, Anthropological and Political Perspectives: Essays by Members of the Society for Old Testament Study* (ed. R. E. Clements; Cambridge: Cambridge University Press, 1989), 119–39, who notes (p. 130) that "the king's role in the protection of society as warrior, the guarantor of justice as judge and the right ordering of worship as priest are the fundamen-tal roles which cover all aspects of the well-being of society. It is well known that this triple function of kingship, with particular emphasis on the roles of the king as judge and war-rior, is common throughout the ancient Near East and is expressed in a great deal of royal literature from Mesopotamia through the Levant to Egypt." It is especially interesting to note in this regard that Deuteronomy provides no role for a king as judge or warrior.

assembly is all too often overlooked in reconstructions of the Deuteronomic program.[155]

Nature of the Program: Utopian versus Realistic
As already noted, interpreters differ on the fundamental question: should the Deuteronomic program of centralizing reform be considered idealistic and utopian or should it be seen as realistic? For Lohfink, the judicial reform of Deut 16:18–18:22 represents a utopian ideal because the institution of the monarchy had ceased to exist at the time this text was accepted as law. Levinson, on the other hand, sees the reform as an active engagement with an existing political system that was realistic in intention. Clearly, the nature of the program affects how the book is best interpreted.

Conclusions regarding Centralization

In this section we have examined the views of five interpreters who see centralization as being at the heart of the Deuteronomic revolution. Questions arise at key points about whether these interpretations have adequately accounted for the data of the text. The differences among the pentateuchal sources proposed by Weinfeld and others have been shown to be not what they usually envision. In addition, examples were cited that suggest that Weinfeld has overstated his case for the type of revolution he sees in Deuteronomy. Similarly, concerns were raised about the reconstruction posited by Levinson, because elements remain in Deuteronomy that undermine the sort of radical innovation he envisions.

Centralization is understood very differently by its various proponents. Weinfeld and von Rad maintain that centralization was designed in part to curtail the cult and to advance the interests of the monarchy and the official court that produced the book. That is, the transformation of religious life and practice was not a by-product of centralization but was at its heart. Others, such as Lohfink, see external political reasons—the experience of Assyrian domination and Babylonian exile—underlying the Deuteronomic program. This issue is important, because one's understanding of the nature of the program necessarily has an effect on the interpretation of the book. Deuteronomy is notoriously lacking in any overt explanation of the rationale

155. For an interpretation of Deuteronomy as the charter of the national assembly of Israel, see B. Halpern, *The Constitution of the Monarchy in Israel* (HSM 25; Chico, CA: Scholars Press, 1981). But see also his later essay, "Jerusalem and the Lineages in the Seventh Century BCE: Kinship and the Rise of Individual Moral Liability," in *Law and Ideology in Monarchic Israel* (JSOTSup 124; Sheffield: Sheffield Academic Press, 1991), 11–107.

for centralization,[156] so one's starting point with regard to the nature of centralization is important.

The overall lack of consensus regarding the nature of centralization has led to tremendous diversity in the interpretation of the book as a whole, as we have seen. Centralization need not be understood as leading inevitably to the type of revolutionary reform envisioned by Weinfeld, in which centralization, secularization, and demythologization are linked as part of a royal-scribal reform program. Rather, it is apparent that different conceptions of centralization lead to rather different understandings of the nature of the program envisioned in Deuteronomy.

The fact that certain details in the text have been overlooked or misunderstood, coupled with the fact that there is no agreement on crucial elements of the book, suggests that another conception of the nature, ideology, and implications of centralization in the Deuteronomic program should be sought.

Before moving on to an examination of key texts in Deuteronomy in order to articulate an alternative view of the Deuteronomic program, we must examine the notions of secularization and demythologization, which are often seen as emerging out of centralization. It is to these corollaries of centralization that we now turn our attention.

Secularization and Demythologization in Deuteronomy

In the previous section we have seen that, while there has been widespread agreement among interpreters that Deuteronomy is best understood as mandating a program of centralization, this has not led to consensus on a number of other crucial aspects of the book. These aspects include setting, audience, and the nature of the program (utopian or realistic). Lack of consensus on these issues and on the basic meaning of centralization calls into question whether centralization as usually understood should be viewed as the (or even a) central tenet of the theology of the book.

Similarly integral to many contemporary interpretations of Deuteronomy are the concepts *secularization* and *demythologization*. While these terms are understood somewhat differently by various proponents, *secularization* in Deuteronomy generally refers to a tendency to downplay the sacred and the removal of certain institutions from the realm of the sacred.[157] *Demythologization* refers to the tendency to

---

156. Cf. Tigay, *Deuteronomy*, 459–60.

157. Thus, Weinfeld describes Deuteronomy as having a "distinctly secular foundation. Not only do we encounter institutions of a manifestly secular character such as the

reinterpret earlier theology (which is usually understood as being less abstract in its theological constructs) in favor of a more spiritual, abstract understanding. The tendency toward secularization and demythologization, it is argued, may be seen in the following features of Deuteronomy: profane slaughter, an altered understanding of firstlings, a reinterpretation of tithes, a changed view of the cultic calendar, a humanitarian motivation for laws, cities of refuge, the elimination of priestly involvement in local judicial matters, the changed status of Levites, a more abstract conception of God, and a shift in understanding the presence of God.[158] Deuteronomy's tendency toward secularization and demythologization, coupled with its demand for centralization, makes for a revolutionary program.[159] The result of this revolutionary program was that Israelite religion was transformed from a religion that emphasized sacrifice and ritual into a religion that focused on prayer, a book (Deuteronomy, to begin with), and a more abstract faith.[160]

In this section, I will examine the concept of secularization in Deuteronomy. The interpretation of Moshe Weinfeld will be presented in an effort to discern how secularization has been understood. I will then analyze this perspective to determine if, in fact, Deuteronomy is best understood as presenting a program of secularization and demythologization as envisioned by Weinfeld and others who come to similar conclusions.

The Program of Secularization and Demythologization

It is appropriate again to examine the influential work of Weinfeld and his understanding of the nature of the Deuteronomic program. While attention will here be focused primarily on secularization and demythologization, we must bear in mind the fact that the elements of centralization (discussed above), secularization, and demythologization are integral to the Deuteronomic revolution envisioned by Weinfeld.

---

judiciary . . . the monarchy . . . the military . . . and civil and criminal laws which treat of the family and inheritance . . . loans and debts . . . litigations and quarrels . . . trespassing . . . and false testimony . . . and the like; but . . . even institutions and practices which were originally sacral in character have here been recast in secularized forms. . . . The very book which is so centrally concerned with 'the chosen place' has almost completely ignored the sacral institutions which the chosen place must necessarily imply and without which the conduct of sacral worship is unimaginable." See Weinfeld, *Deuteronomic School*, 188.

158. M. Weinfeld, "On 'Demythologization and Secularization' in Deuteronomy," *IEJ* 23/4 (1973): 230–31. See also idem, *Deuteronomy 1–11*, 37–44.

159. Weinfeld, "Theological Revolution," 45.

160. Ibid., 38. See also idem, *Deuteronomy 1–11*, 78–79.

The way in which these elements combine in support of the Deuteronomic "revolution" will be examined below.

Presence of God
The most dramatic and significant of the Deuteronomic reinterpreta-
tions that Weinfeld sees is a transformation of the understanding of
the presence of God.[161] Indeed, this shift in understanding the presence of God accounts for many of the other changes in Deuteronomy.

Weinfeld sees in P a deliberate "schematization and dogmatiza-
tion" of the earlier conception of Yahweh as being actually present in
the temple.[162] In the earlier sources that antedate P, as well as in P itself, the conception of God was largely anthropomorphic. Thus, all
the elaborate temple rituals are designed to convey the sense of a God
who was actually present in the temple. The Cherubim served as a
throne for a God who is seated on them, with the ark serving as his
footstool. Food (in the form of the Bread of the Presence, grain offerings, and offerings of the fat of sacrificial animals) is provided for Yahweh. Lamps are lighted to provide light for him, and pleasing aromas
of incense are offered to him. All these rituals presuppose that Yahweh is actually present.

It is the divine presence in the sanctuary that requires the strict
observance of purity and holiness, as well as serving as the basis for
the rituals. Yahweh's seclusion in his sanctuary was to be respected.
Only a priest might approach the inner sanctum; the lay person who
did so must die because he had not observed the proper rituals for establishing and maintaining purity (Num 17:12–13; Lev 10:3). The
conception of "graded holiness" is based on the idea of the actual
presence of Yahweh. So central is the presence of God to P's conception of religion that Weinfeld notes "it is the pervading presence of
God in the midst of Israel (viz. the sanctuary) that gives meaning to
the Israelite scene. Remove the divine immanence, and the entire
Priestly code collapses. Not only would the worship of God cease, but
laws relating to the social sphere would become inoperative."[163]

The demythologization posited by Weinfeld may best be seen
through an examination of the ways in which the presence of God is
envisioned in the sources. In P, according to Weinfeld, the essential
concept of the presence of God is corporeal, anthropomorphic, expressed by the term כְּבוֹד יהוה. Thus, Ezekiel (a book that is thought to

---

161. Here Weinfeld picks up on the earlier work of von Rad, who also saw a shift from
a theology of presence to a "Name" theology. See von Rad, *Studies*, 37–44.
162. Weinfeld, *Deuteronomic School*, 193.
163. Ibid., 185.

reflect the ideology of P) describes the Glory of Yahweh as having a human form, seated on a throne (Ezek 1). Weinfeld notes that the theophany of Ezek 1 "comprises all the elements of Israelite theophany . . . but its most singular feature is the anthropomorphic imagery."[164] *Kabod* (כָּבוֹד) is conceived in P as the "body" or "substance" of God and describes the weight and importance of it.[165] There is accordingly a danger of seeing the glory of God. Hence in P the cloud (which is known from the earlier sources as either a guide, a protection for the people, or a means of conveyance for God) serves to prevent human beings from seeing the *Kabod*. Moreover, the priestly literature contains protections against seeing the glory of God in the Holy of Holies. Leviticus 16 contains provisions for Aaron to protect himself with a cloud of incense so that he can avoid seeing the Glory of God.[166]

Deuteronomy, Weinfeld argues, presents a radically different understanding of the presence of God. In contrast to the anthropomorphic view of the actual presence of God, Deuteronomy presents a more abstract understanding in which God himself does not dwell in the temple; only his name (שֵׁם) lives there. The repeated use of the expression לְשַׁכֵּן שְׁמוֹ in Deuteronomy "is intended to combat the ancient popular belief that the Deity actually dwelled within the sanctuary."[167] That is, there is a deliberate effort on the part of the authors of Deuteronomy to articulate a more abstract understanding of God's presence and to repudiate the earlier understandings of Yahweh as actually present in the temple.

Even כָּבוֹד undergoes a transformation in Deuteronomy. No longer does it refer to the body and substance of God, as in P, but rather it refers to Yahweh's splendor and greatness. This becomes clear in examining the Deuteronomic account of the revelation at Sinai. While the account in Exod 19 describes Yahweh's descent onto the mountain (vv. 11, 20), the parallel account in Deut 4 contains no such description. Instead, Deuteronomy makes it clear that God spoke to the people from heaven, not from the mountain itself. This, Weinfeld

---

164. Ibid., 201.

165. Ibid., 202.

166. In Weinfeld's view, P's conception of *Kabod* is an interpretation of earlier conceptions of the presence of Yahweh and rests on ancient traditions. The main difference is not in their fundamental conception of the presence of God (both the earlier traditions and P are anthropomorphic in their understanding of divine presence) but rather in the response that the presence of God elicits. In JE the manifestation of the presence of God is a terrifying experience, whereas in P it is conceived of as something wonderful, a blessing that is to be received joyfully. See ibid., 204–5.

167. Ibid., 193.

argues, represents a shift in the "centre of gravity of the theophany from the visual to the aural plane."[168] This is further seen by the dangers posed by the theophany in the sources. In the earlier sources, the danger lay in *seeing* the form of God and, therefore, perishing (Exod 19:21; 33:20; cf. also Gen 32:31). In Deuteronomy, however, the danger lies in *hearing* the voice of God (Deut 4:33; 5:24–26). This reinterpretation of the danger is due to the fact that Deuteronomy cannot conceive of anyone's being able to see God and has expressed the danger in keeping with its own theological understanding.[169]

Just as Deuteronomy has reinterpreted כָּבוֹד in the light of its theological point of view, so too the ark is presented differently in Deuteronomy, according to Weinfeld. In the earlier sources, the ark was thought to be the seat on which God sat as he went forth against his enemies (Num 10:33–36; 14:42–44). In Deuteronomy, however, the ark serves a didactic function. As the container of the tablets of the covenant, it serves to remind the people of the covenant they have made with Yahweh so that they will learn to fear him (Deut 31:26). The altered function of the ark is apparent when the narratives of the failed attempt at conquest following the initial refusal to enter the land are compared. In Num 14:42–44, the reason for the defeat of the people is the fact that the ark has not left the camp. Deuteronomy 1:42–43, however, says simply that Yahweh was not with the people, completely omitting any reference to the ark. Finally, Weinfeld argues that the revised understanding of the function of the ark is seen in the fact that there is no mention of the ark in Deuteronomy's laws of warfare (23:15). He maintains that "one would expect a passage which speaks of the presence of the Divinity within the military encampment to make some mention of the ark which accompanied the warriors on their expeditions."[170] The role of the ark as a seat or throne for Yahweh did not comport with the thinking of the authors of Deuteronomy, so they depicted the ark in a way that was in keeping with their understanding.

Judicial Reform
As noted above, Weinfeld sees in Deuteronomy a shift from an older judicial system centered largely on local sanctuaries to one in which professional magistrates adjudicated cases (except in instances where a "decisive verdict" could not be rendered by the magistrates, in which case appeal was made to the central sanctuary).[171] Weinfeld notes that

168. Ibid., 207.
169. Ibid., 207–8. See also Weinfeld, *Deuteronomy 1–11*, 37–39.
170. Ibid., 209.
171. Ibid., 234–35.

the "provision for the appointment of secular magistrates over matters which formerly lay within sacral jurisdiction implies . . . that the Israelite judiciary had undergone a process of secularization."[172]

In Weinfeld's analysis, judicial procedure prior to centralization included a sacral component. He maintains that "[c]ivil or family suits which could not be settled by the elders because of a lack of witnesses or evidence were generally submitted to sacral jurisdiction, which decided them by the administration of oaths . . . sacral lot-casting . . . or trial by ordeal."[173] Deuteronomy 16:18, in contrast, provides for the appointment of judges (שֹׁפְטִים) in "all your gates" (בְּכָל־שְׁעָרֶיךָ), who were assigned to adjudicate cases. Because the office of judge is secular (as opposed to priestly), no mention is made of any sacral media being employed by these judges. In the cases that were too difficult for the local judges to decide, a court of appeals was established (Deut 17:8–9). Even in the case of this central tribunal, which could include the the participation of a priest (Deut 17:9), there is no mention of sacral media in the resolution of cases.

The role of elders, then, also changed. According to this analysis, town elders prior to the Deuteronomic revolution had primary responsibility for the adjudication of cases, except in cases in which insufficient evidence was available (in which case the priest(s) of the local sanctuary would be consulted). Following the reforms of Deuteronomy, the elders are relegated to a less central role in the administration of justice, being responsible for "patriarchal and family" litigation only.[174] In such cases, according to Weinfeld, "no professional judgment is necessary . . . ; the elders preside over a case, whose consequences are clear beforehand."[175] The judges assume responsibility for rendering decisions in cases in which the local elders are unable to render a verdict and need a "higher and more objective judicial authority."[176]

Laws of Asylum

A related development in Deuteronomy is the establishment of cities of refuge in the land (Deut 4:41–43; 19:1–10). Weinfeld maintains that Exodus describes the altar in the sanctuary as the place to which the accidental manslayer must flee (Exod 21:13–14). This was later modified in favor of entire "temple cities" in which Levites resided.[177] He

---

172. Ibid., 236.
173. Ibid., 233–34.
174. Ibid., 234. See also idem, "Elder," *EncJud* 6: 578–80.
175. Weinfeld, "Elder," 578.
176. Ibid.
177. Weinfeld, *Deuteronomic School*, 236.

argues that the underlying basis for these laws is that the accidental manslayer must atone for his sin through forced exile in a sacred location. Thus, the purpose of this provision in the Book of the Covenant and in P is not to provide refuge from an avenger but to "[serve] as the place in which he atones for his sin."[178]

The institution has undergone a process of secularization in Deuteronomy, according to Weinfeld. Since local altars and sanctuaries have been abolished by the Deuteronomic reform, they can no longer serve as the basis for asylum. Instead, cities are chosen based on "rational" and geographical grounds.[179] The Priestly terms קָדוֹשׁ and קָרָה, used in this context in Josh 20:7 and Num 35:11, respectively, are absent in Deuteronomy, which uses the Hiphil of בָּדַל (Deut 4:41; 19:2, 7). This term, Weinfeld avers, is more "neutral" and devoid of any sacral connotations.[180] In addition, there is a greater order to the system: the land is subdivided, and a city is assigned in each region, thereby allowing a fleeing manslayer to reach a city of refuge without delay. Finally, the nature of asylum has changed in Deuteronomy. No longer does the exile of the killer serve to atone for his guilt. Rather, the function of the city of refuge is simply to provide an accidental killer with a safe haven, out of reach of any avenger. The altered grounds for the law are further reflected, Weinfeld argues, in the fact that Deuteronomy does not specify how long the accidental killer must remain in the city of refuge. In P, the manslayer must remain until the death of the high priest, because the high priest's death will expiate the guilt. Since Deuteronomy does not share the conceptions of holiness found in P, it omits any reference to the duration of the stay. Presumably, the killer must remain until the avenger's desire for revenge abates.[181] Deuteronomy's alteration of the location of asylum (from a sacred location to a regional center) and the reason for it (from atonement of sin to protection of an accidental killer), in Weinfeld's view, further demonstrates a process of secularization in Deuteronomy.

Feasts and Festivals
Weinfeld sees further evidence of secularization in Deuteronomy's handling of ritual feasts and festivals. The Feast of Unleavened Bread (Maṣṣot) and the Feast of Weeks marked the grain harvest. According to Lev 23:10–14, at the beginning of the harvest season the Israelites

---

178. Ibid., 237.
179. Ibid.
180. Ibid., n. 4. See also ibid., 236 n. 4.
181. Ibid., 237. See also idem, *Deuteronomy 1–11*, 33–34. J. R. Spencer maintains that the asylum is only to protect the accused until a trial can be held. See "Refuge, Cities Of," *ABD* 5: 657–58.

were required to bring in the sheaf of their firstfruits as an offering to Yahweh. It was to be brought to the priest, who would then wave the sheaf before Yahweh on the day after the Sabbath.[182] In addition, a one-year old male lamb was to be offered as a burnt offering (עֹלָה). The close of the season 50 days later was marked by the Feast of Weeks, in which two loaves of bread, as well as animal sacrifices, were offered (Lev 23:15–21). These offerings are described as קֹדֶשׁ יִהְיוּ לַיהוָה לַכֹּהֵן (Lev 23:20). Weinfeld understands Lev 23:14, which prohibits the Israelites from eating new crops until offering is made to Yahweh, as rendering new grain unclean for consumption if the offerings were not made.[183]

The Feast of Booths is the major autumn festival commemorating the ingathering of crops. It is marked by living in booths during the week of the festival, as well as by the use of specific flora in the worship of Yahweh (Lev 23:39–44). This celebration, Weinfeld argues, was originally observed in local sanctuaries. He argues that it is unlikely that the first sheaves of a harvest, the decorative flora, and the loaves of bread were to be brought to a central sanctuary, which might be situated a great distance from some areas. Thus, he argues, the festival is better understood as being celebrated in a local sanctuary.

Finally, there is the presentation of the Passover, which, in Weinfeld's view is the clearest example of Deuteronomic secularization of the feasts.[184] The earlier sources, JE and P, understood Passover to be a

> domestic celebration accompanied by apotropaic rites of an animistic nature: the paschal blood is daubed upon the lintel and doorposts . . . , the animal must be roasted together with its head, legs, and inner parts . . . , it may not be removed from the house, no bone may be broken . . . and a special dress is prescribed for the celebration.[185]

This festival had its origin in the nomadic period of the tribes' existence and thus reflects the mythical and "primitive" thinking of an ancient time.[186]

---

182. It is debatable, however, whether the waving of the sheaf is to be understood as part of the Maṣṣot ordinances or as an introduction to the regulations governing firstfruits (Feast of Weeks). G. J. Wenham (*The Book of Leviticus* [NICOT; Grand Rapids: Eerdmans, 1979], 303–4) sees this regulation as part of Passover/Maṣṣot, in which the intimations of Exod 23:15 and 34:18–20 are made into explicit regulations. McConville (*Law and Theology*, 103) understands the sheaf-waving as an introduction to the regulations about firstfruits. A similar view is advocated by J. Halbe, "Erwägungen zu Ursprung und Wesen des Massotfestes," *ZAW* 87 (1975): 324–45.

183. Weinfeld, *Deuteronomic School*, 218.

184. Ibid., 216.

185. Ibid., 217.

186. Ibid.

In Deuteronomy, however, the feasts are presented differently. Deuteronomy, Weinfeld argues, has completely stripped the Passover of its magical rituals and domestic quality. Instead, Deuteronomy portrays Passover as a communal celebration to be carried out at the central sanctuary, using cattle as well as sheep and goats and cooking the animal as any ordinary sacrifice (Deut 16:1–8). There is a deliberate attempt to recast the celebration in a manner more palatable to the spirit of the times, eliminating the mythical and magical elements in favor of a more rational approach.

In addition, Deuteronomy for the first time combines the festivals of Passover and Maṣṣot, which at an earlier stage were separate festivals (as demonstrated by the earlier sources, JE and P). This, he argues, is shown by the fact that the law of unleavened bread is injected into the regulation concerning Passover, which "appears very artificial."[187] In addition, removing the interpolated verses (Deut 16:3–4) results in a continuous and coherent regulation of Passover that is parallel to that of the Covenant Code.[188]

The other feasts are also refashioned and secularized, in Weinfeld's view. Although it retains the ancient names for the feasts, Deuteronomy presents them in a much different way. There is no mention at all of a sheaf-waving ceremony in connection with the Feast of Weeks; neither is there any reference to the reason for dwelling in booths during the Feast of Booths (i.e., in order to remember the fact that the exodus generation lived in booths). Instead, Deuteronomy has reestablished the feasts as occasions of ceremonial rejoicing marked by voluntary offerings, and the sacral character of the feasts is eliminated entirely.

As evidence of this, Weinfeld notes that the Feast of Weeks is counted as 7 weeks from the start of the harvest in both Lev 23 and Deut 16. In Leviticus, however, the counting has a special purpose that reflects a sacral perspective: the counting is necessary to ensure that the offerings may be presented in the sanctuary at the appropriate time. The sacral nature of the counting is obvious, because the required interval is 7 times 7, reflecting a sacral calendar. Deuteronomy, however, does not mention that the interval is to be 49 days (7 times

---

187. Weinfeld, *Deuteronomy 1–11*, 23.

188. Ibid. Levinson (*Legal Innovation*, 53–97) takes up this issue and argues that integration of Passover and *Maṣṣot* was a crucial element in the Deuteronomic program. But see also the response of J. G. McConville, "Deuteronomy's Unification of Passover and *Maṣṣôt*: A Response to Bernard M. Levinson," *JBL* 119 (2000): 47–58; and the reply of B. M. Levinson, "The Hermeneutics of Tradition in Deuteronomy: A Reply to J. G. McConville," *JBL* 119 (2000): 269–86.

7) but says simply that the Feast of Weeks is to be carried out "seven weeks from the time you begin to put the sickle to the standing grain" (Deut 16:9). The sheaf-waving and the presentation of the new grain offering are eliminated.

Similarly, the Feast of Booths is altered in Deuteronomy. There is no mention of specific types of flora that are to be used in the decorations, as there is in Lev 23.

Most important for his argument, however, is the fact that Deuteronomy appears to have altered the basis for the festivals. There is in Deuteronomy a constant emphasis on the communal and social nature of the festivals, implying that this is the primary reason for their observation. This, Weinfeld argues, is evidence that Deuteronomy has secularized the festivals by eliminating the earlier sacral bases for the feasts in favor of secular, humanitarian grounds. This is in keeping with the theological perspective of the authors, who rejected primitive conceptions of holiness and the sacred.

A similar tendency is seen by Weinfeld in Deuteronomy's presentation of the Sabbath and the sabbatical year. Earlier sources emphasize a sacral basis for observing the Sabbath, noting that God worked six days and then rested in the seventh (Gen 2:1–3 [P]; Exod 31:17 [P]; Exod 20:8 [E]). Thus, the rationale for the Sabbath observation in P and E is to reenact God's rest on the seventh day. In Deuteronomy, however, the rationale for Sabbath observation is a humanitarian one. Deuteronomy 5:12 enjoins Sabbath observation (using שָׁמוֹר, where P uses זָכוֹר) "so that your male servant and your female servant may rest as well as you" (v. 14). This, in turn, is tied to remembrance of the experience of slavery in Egypt (v. 15). In Deuteronomy, then, the Sabbath commemorates a historical event, whereas in P it reenacts a sacral event.[189]

In like manner, the sabbatical year is reinterpreted in Deuteronomy, according to Weinfeld. According to Lev 25:2–7, the land was to have a "Sabbath to Yahweh" (שַׁבָּת לַיהוָה) in every seventh year. Since Lev 26:34–35 states that the period of exile of the people was partially in order to allow the land to "satisfy" its sabbath years denied by disobedient Israelites, Weinfeld concludes that the sabbatical year is a

---

189. Weinfeld, *Deuteronomic School*, 222. See also idem, *Deuteronomy 1–11*, 301–9. Weinfeld notes that the two bases are not incompatible with each other and that the two grounds could have coexisted. But he argues that the emphases of the sources reflect their theological underpinnings, and the fact that Deuteronomy emphasizes the social/humanitarian element over the sacred illustrates the theological priorities of the author of the book. See chap. 3 for a detailed analysis of Weinfeld's interpretation of the Sabbath law in Deuteronomy.

"taboo year, a year in which all agricultural work must cease."[190] Deuteronomy, in contrast, speaks not of a release of *land* but only of a release of *debts* (Deut 15:1–3). Thus, Deuteronomy reinterprets the earlier law in a social, humanitarian way and ignores the sacral conception of the release of the land. Thus, the institution is divested of its sacral importance in favor of a humanitarian rationale.[191] In short, the institution has been secularized.

Tithes and Firstlings

In addition to a reinterpretation of feasts and festivals, there is also, in Weinfeld's view, a secularization in Deuteronomy's conception of the tithe and firstlings. Leviticus 27:30–33 states that the tithe is "holy to Yahweh," and if a person wishes to redeem part of the tithe, he must pay an additional twenty percent of the value. If he seeks to exchange the tenth animal for another one, he then forfeits both. Therefore, Weinfeld concludes that in P the sanctity of the tithe is an "inherent quality of the grain or animal."[192] In addition, Num 18:21–32 (which Weinfeld assigns to a separate, later stratum of P[193]) states that the tithe is to be given to the Levites "as an inheritance." From this tithe, the Levites are to present a tithe to the priests.

With regard to firstlings, as with tithes, Weinfeld argues that P considers sanctity an inherent quality of the animal. Thus, he argues, Lev 27:26 views a firstling as holy by virtue of birth; consequently, humans cannot make it holy by consecration or "secularize it by redemption,"[194] which is specifically forbidden in Num 18:17. In addition, the firstling is seen by both JE (Exod 22:29; 34:19) and P (Num 18:15–17) as belonging to the priests.

Deuteronomy, however, has reinterpreted tithes and firstlings according to its own theological point of view. The sacral conception of the tithe in P has been rejected by Deuteronomy. This, Weinfeld argues, may be seen by the fact that, in Deuteronomy, the tithe "may be secularized and used for profane purposes on payment of an equivalent monetary value (without the addition of the fifth-part required by P . . .)."[195] The holiness of the tithe in Deuteronomy is not a quality that "inheres in things which by nature belong to the divine

---

190. Idem, *Deuteronomic School*, 223.
191. Here again Weinfeld notes that the two conceptions of the sabbatical year are not incompatible. But, he argues, the fact that each author chose to emphasize different elements is illustrative of the ideologies of the authors. See ibid., 224.
192. Ibid., 215.
193. Ibid., 214; and idem, "Tithe," *EncJud* 15: 1159.
194. Idem, *Deuteronomic School*, 215.
195. Ibid.

realm, but is rather a consequence of the religious intentions of the person who consecrates it." In this way, the cult in Deuteronomy is divorced from its "intimate ties to nature."[196]

In addition, the ownership of the tithe is altered in Deuteronomy. Whereas P understood the tithe to be "holy to Yahweh" (Lev 27:30–33) and to be given to the priests and Levites (Num 18:21–32), Deuteronomy envisions the tithe as being eaten in the chosen place by the giver and his family (Deut 14:22–27). Thus, according to Weinfeld, the institution is altered from one that emphasizes inherent sanctity based on taboo to one that focuses on celebration and joy, with no mention of inherent qualities of holiness.

Firstlings, too, are conceived of differently in Deuteronomy, and the reconception is typical of the secularization that Weinfeld describes throughout the book. Weinfeld argues that Deut 15:19 stands in apparent contradiction to the earlier regulation in P. Leviticus 27:26 states, "However, a firstborn among animals, which as a firstborn belongs to Yahweh, no man may consecrate; whether ox or sheep, it is Yahweh's." Deuteronomy 15:19, however, says, "You shall consecrate to Yahweh your God all the firstborn males that are born of your herd and of your flock." The difference between these texts, Weinfeld argues, is due to the fact that the authors of Deuteronomy do not share the theological view of the authors of P, who regarded the firstlings as inherently sacred. For the authors of Deuteronomy, the sanctity of the firstlings is not an inherent quality but a state deriving from the will of the person who consecrates the animals. In this way, the authors of Deuteronomy are distancing themselves from the earlier understanding of sanctity in favor of an understanding that better reflects their own theological point of view.

Holiness and Purity
Curiously, however, when it comes to the people as a whole, Deuteronomy conceives of holiness as an inherent quality, where the earlier sources do not. As evidence Weinfeld cites the laws concerning consumption of נְבֵלָה. Leviticus 22:8 prohibits priests from eating נְבֵלָה. But other passages permit lay Israelites to eat it, provided that they do not eat the fat or the blood (Lev 7:24–27; 11:39–40; 17:15). The different requirements for priests and lay people is explained, Weinfeld argues, by the fact that the priests must minister in proximity to God and his dwelling place and they, therefore, must maintain a greater degree of holiness than other Israelites. In P, holiness is understood to be determined by "physical proximity to the divine presence and preservation

---

196. Ibid.

of that proximity through ritual means."[197] Thus, the priests are prohibited from rendering themselves unclean through eating the נְבֵלָה.

In Deuteronomy, however, the situation is altered. Deuteronomy
14:21 prohibits all Israelites, not just priests, from eating נְבֵלָה. Weinfeld explains this difference on the grounds that Deuteronomy regards all people, not just priests, as inherently holy, and consequently
all must avoid what is unclean. Moreover, Deuteronomy rejects earlier
conceptions of the divine abode on which the Priestly understanding
of holiness is based (see below) and therefore reinterprets holiness in
this manner. The holiness of Israel in Deuteronomy is a result of having been chosen by Yahweh to be his people, and the condition of holiness therefore extends to all Israel. So, Weinfeld maintains, holiness
in P is "a condition that can be secured only by constant physical pu-
rification and sanctification, whereas in Deuteronomy it . . . devolves
automatically upon every Israelite."[198]

Weinfeld observes further evidence of this shift in the understanding of holiness in the ways in which holiness is discussed in the various sources. P speaks of the holiness of the land, because Yahweh
dwells in the land (Josh 22:19). As a result, all people who live in the
land are subject to the tenets of the sacral law. Moreover,

> residence in the land is deemed to be an automatic recognition of the
> god of the country on the part of the resident and thus also entails the
> obligation to worship him . . . ; conversely an Israelite who resides out-
> side the land of Yahweh is deemed to dwell in an unclean land and be
> the worshipper of foreign gods.[199]

Deuteronomy, however, makes only Israelites subject to the *Torah*. The
foreigner (גֵּר) is not obligated to observe the stipulations of *Torah*,
though he may do so if he desires.

Once again, the laws concerning נְבֵלָה are cited as evidence to support this contention. As noted above, Deut 14:21 prohibits all Israelites from eating the נְבֵלָה but permits foreigners to eat it. Leviticus
17:15, on the other hand, mandates that, "when any person eats an
animal which dies, or is torn by beasts, whether he is a native or an
alien, he shall wash his clothes and bathe in water, and remain unclean until evening; then he will become clean." In the regulations of
the Holiness Code, an Israelite or a foreigner may eat the נְבֵלָה, but

---

197. Ibid., 227. See also P. P. Jenson, *Graded Holiness: A Key to the Priestly Conception of
the World* (JSOTSup 106; Sheffield: Sheffield Academic Press, 1992). For a comparative view
of ANE conceptions of holiness, see E. J. Wilson, *"Holiness" and "Purity" in Mesopotamia*
(Neukirchen-Vluyn: Neukirchner Verlag, 1994).

198. Ibid., 226–27.

199. Ibid., 229.

both will become ritually unclean and must bathe in order to restore cleanliness. Deuteronomy forbids the Israelite to eat the נְבֵלָה at all, and there is no ritual prescribed for the foreigner who eats it. The difference, Weinfeld says, is due to the different viewpoint of the two sources. He maintains that "P is concerned only with the ritual problem of impurity involved: all who eat *nebelah*, whether Israelite or resident alien . . . carry impurity on them. . . . But Deuteronomy regards the prohibition only as a *noblesse oblige*. Israel must abstain from eating *nebelah* because it is an act unbecoming to a holy people, and not because it causes impurity from which one must purge oneself by ritual bathing."[200] Thus, Deuteronomy has rejected the underlying theology of the earlier source and framed the regulations in a way that comports with its own theological perspective.

Evaluation

Weinfeld's thesis of secularization and demythologization resulting from centralization in Deuteronomy has attracted broad support. Indeed, it has become the mainstream view of the book, though some have, of course, understood various aspects of the book differently.[201] In this section, I will evaluate Weinfeld's thesis in an attempt to determine whether or not the idea of *secularization* best accounts for the data of the text.

---

200. Ibid., 230. See also idem, *Deuteronomy 1–11*, 32.

201. For example, Tigay (*Deuteronomy*, xvii) notes, "The limitation of sacrificial worship to a single place would inevitably remove a sacral dimension from the life of most Israelites. . . . Deuteronomy's aim is to spiritualize religion by freeing it from excessive dependence on sacrifice and priesthood"; R. E. Clements ("Deuteronomy," 285) maintains that "[Deuteronomy] may be held to have desacralized religion, removing much of the mystical and quasi-magical notions of cultic power. As such it promotes a rather 'secularized' interpretation of religious commitment"; Mayes (*Deuteronomy*, 59) argues that "there is a tendency in Deuteronomy towards the liberation of religious institutions and practices from primitive magical elements, taboo regulations and so on. . . . This may be called secularization provided that the term is understood . . . not to imply opposition to religion"; V. Hurowitz ("From Storm God to Abstract Being: How the Deity Became More Distant from Exodus to Deuteronomy," *Bible Review* 14 [1998]: 45) maintains that "[t]he different locations of God in the theophany accounts is important because it reflects different views of God in Exodus and Deuteronomy. Deuteronomy views God as transcendent and abstract; thus, God remains in heaven. Exodus presents an intimate, immediate view of God, who has a physical presence on earth"; L. J. Hoppe ("The Levitical Origins of Deuteronomy Reconsidered," *Biblical Research* 28 [1983]: 32) notes that "Deuteronomy then opposes a mythological notion of a divine relationship to the land which seems to have been supported in and through the cult" and cites "other examples of demythologization" pointed out by Weinfeld.

The thesis of secularization rests on two premises, as is clear from the above description of Weinfeld's analysis of Deuteronomy. The first premise is that the sources earlier than Deuteronomy present a fundamentally sacral perspective of the institutions of religious life and, furthermore, the divine presence is largely anthropomorphic and immanent. The second premise is that Deuteronomy presents institutions in a way that is inherently secular—that is, divorced from the realm of the cult—and that its concept of God is largely abstract and transcendent. Both of these premises have been challenged. We will begin with an examination of the ways in which the first premise has been challenged.

In his commentary on Leviticus, Milgrom argues strenuously that "P makes a concerted effort to *avoid* anthropomorphisms."[202] This, he argues, is supported by the fact that P conspicuously avoids the presentation of any sustenance-type offerings (i.e., food and drink) in the inner sanctuary. Instead, "all sacrifices are to be offered on the outer altar in the open courtyard, visible to all worshipers and removed from the Tent, the Lord's purported domicile."[203] Exodus 30:9, which regulates the inner altar, expressly forbids placing burnt offerings, cereal offerings, or drink offerings on it. This, Milgrom argues, is a deliberate attempt to show that the food offerings are *not* to provide food and drink for Yahweh.

In addition, the use of כָּבוֹד in the earlier sources is more nuanced than Weinfeld allows. Prior to Weinfeld, von Rad identified P's *Kabod* theology as totally different from a theology of actual presence. Indeed, von Rad argued that it was a means of repudiating the idea of actual presence, just as Deuteronomy's "Name" theology avoided the notion of actual presence. Von Rad concluded that in P, "the Tabernacle is neither the dwelling place of Jahweh himself nor of his name, but the place on earth where, for the time being, the appearance of Jahweh's glory meets with his people."[204] Similarly, Eichrodt maintained that כָּבוֹד in the Priestly material refers to "*the reflected splendour of the transcendent God*, a token of the divine glory, by means of which

---

202. J. Milgrom, *Leviticus 1–16: A New Translation with Introduction and Commentary* (AB 3; New York: Doubleday, 1991), 59; emphasis mine. Milgrom elsewhere maintains that Weinfeld's evidence from P "is not rendered correctly and borders at times on the inaccurate" and that one can conclude that there is demythologization in Deuteronomy "only if D's premises are ignored and P's are misconstrued." See idem, "Alleged 'Demythologization and Secularization,'" 157–58. See also the reply of Weinfeld, "Demythologization and Secularization."

203. Ibid.

204. Von Rad, *Studies in Deuteronomy*, 39.

Yahweh declares his gracious presence,"[205] and itself represented a spiritualization of earlier, anthropomorphic conceptions of God.

This has been further developed by McConville. He has shown that JE and P both use כָּבוֹד to describe an "unusual manifestation of God," whereas God's שֵׁם is used in connection with ordinary worship.[206] Thus, for example, Exod 33:18–23 juxtaposes the two terms in surprising ways. Moses requests to see God's "glory" but is refused permission. Instead, God determines to have his "goodness" (טוֹב) pass before Moses, and at the same time he will proclaim his *name*. Moses is allowed to see Yahweh's back (אָחוֹר) but not his face (פָּנִים). Here, the word כָּבוֹד seems to be used to parallel פָּנִים (vv. 20, 23) in the sense of divine presence.[207] That it is *not* used in the sense of physical presence is clear from the fact that Moses is denied the right to see God's כָּבוֹד but is allowed to see his back and hand.

More important, however, is the fact that Yahweh freely and graciously proclaims his name to Moses and reveals his goodness (i.e., attributes). Indeed, the articulation of the Name of Yahweh may be seen as the climax of the section Exod 33:18–34:9.[208] This expression of Yahweh's Name has the function in the text of resolving the dilemma about how Yahweh could continue with his people after their failure in the incident with the golden calf (Exod 32). The issue in this text is about human sin and how Yahweh can in any sense continue to "be with" Israel in light of their sin. The revelation of Yahweh's Name and Moses' response in Exod 34:6–9 show that God is gracious, merciful, and forgiving but is at the same time "other." So the use of כָּבוֹד here is not concerned with expressing an anthropomorphic understanding of God but with resolving the tension raised by the holiness of Yahweh on the one hand and the reality of human sin on the other. Similarly, the use of שֵׁם is to show that God will continue to be with his people precisely because he is the kind of God he is (i.e., gracious and forgiving). McConville rightly notes that this text is not about anthropomorphic versus antianthropomorphic understandings of God.[209]

205. W. Eichrodt, *Theology of the Old Testament* (London: SCM, 1967), 2: 32.

206. J. G. McConville, "God's 'Name' and God's 'Glory,'" *TynBul* 30 (1979): 156.

207. Cf. J. I. Durham, *Exodus* (WBC 3; Waco, TX: Word, 1987), 452. See also C. J. Collins, "כבד," *NIDOTTE* 2: 581–83; and Eichrodt, *Theology*, 2: 38. B. S. Childs, *Exodus: A Commentary* (London: SCM, 1974), 596, sees כָּבוֹד as parallel to "goodness" (טוֹב). However, he is in agreement that the divine revelation to Moses is not in terms of physical appearance but of divine attributes.

208. Cf. J. J. Niehaus, *God at Sinai: Covenant and Theophany in the Bible and the Ancient Near East* (Grand Rapids: Zondervan / Carlisle: Paternoster, 1995), 245–47.

209. McConville, "God's 'Name,'" 155 n. 32.

McConville demonstrates that what is true in this text (assigned to JE) holds in other sources as well, including P. Thus, Exod 40:34–35 demonstrates that God's glory is unapproachable, even by Moses, as does Exod 33:18ff. In the same way, the books of Psalms and Chronicles contain both the terms כָּבוֹד and שֵׁם with no difficulty. McConville thus concludes that "'name' seems to be used in contexts where the kind of revelation of and response to God is that of normal, ongoing worship. 'Glory' occurs . . . for dramatic, exceptional divine manifestations, or when some emphasis is laid on God's majesty."[210] Thus, it is doubtful that Weinfeld's thesis that P and earlier sources are inherently anthropomorphic best accounts for the data.

Moreover, the radical distinction between the Book of the Covenant and Deuteronomy that Weinfeld posits[211] has been challenged by recent scholarship. Otto, for example, argues that the Book of the Covenant reflects Deuteronomistic interpretation and redaction.[212] Thus, he notes that the Book of the Covenant, like Deuteronomy, stresses the lordship of Yahweh over every aspect of life and shares with it an understanding of Yahweh as transcendent Lord. For example, he sees in Exod 22:28–23:12 a chiastic structure that emphasizes Yahweh's transcendence, demonstrating that the issue of Yahweh's transcendence is of particular concern to the author(s) of the Book of the Covenant.[213] In addition, he notes that the introduction to the Book of the Covenant, Exod 20:22–23, has important links to the preceding verses (of the Sinai pericope) and stresses themes similar to those in Deuteronomy. Thus, the saving act of Yahweh in the exodus is related to the chosen status of Israel, and there are similar

210. Ibid., 161.

211. "Deuteronomy would be seen as replacing the old book of the covenant and not as complementing it. . . . What is clear is that Deuteronomy used laws identical in formulation with those of the book of the covenant and revised them according to its ideology" (Weinfeld, *Deuteronomy 1–11*, 19).

212. E. Otto, *Wandel der Rechtsbegründungen in der Gesellschaftsgeschichte des antiken Israel: Eine Rechtsgeschichte des "Bundesbuches" Ex XX 22–XXIII 13* (Studia Biblica 3; Leiden: Brill, 1988). Cf. also J. A. Soggin, *Introduction to the Old Testament: From Its Origins to the Closing of the Alexandrian Canon* (3rd ed.; London: SCM, 1989), 143–45. For more recent analysis of the issue, see M. Vervenne, "The Question of 'Deuteronomic' Elements in Genesis to Numbers," in *Studies in Deuteronomy: In Honour of C. J. Labuschagne on the Occasion of His 65th Birthday*" (ed. F. García Martínez et al.; Leiden: Brill, 1994), 243–68; H. Ausloos, "Deuteronomi(sti)c Elements in Exod 23,20–33: Some Methodological Remarks," in *Studies in the Book of Exodus: Redaction-Reception-Interpretation* (ed. M. Vervenne; BETL 126; Leuven: Leuven University Press, 1996), 481–500; M. J. Oosthuizen, "Law and Theology in the Covenant Code," *Skrif en Kerk* 17/1 (1996): 160–90.

213. Otto, *Wandel der Rechtsbegründungen*, 46.

prohibitions of images and demands for exclusive loyalty to Yahweh (Exod 20:23; 23:13).[214]

Similarly, although he denies Deuteronomistic editing of the Book of the Covenant, Crüsemann has identified important parallels in theology and world view between Deuteronomy and the earlier Book of the Covenant. He argues, for example, that the Book of the Covenant

> demanded social justice as the most important of its own accents. The protection of foreigners (Exod 22:20f.; 23:9) and the poor (Exod 22:24f.) as well as the correction of the slave law (Exod 21:24f.) are the main accents in the contents, the formulation of principles for judicial practice (Exod 23:1–8) is a central judicial tool. The exclusive veneration of Israel's God is identified here with a relationship aimed at social justice for the socially and legally impoverished.[215]

Many of these themes, of course, are identified as being especially or uniquely present in Deuteronomy and are considered by Weinfeld and others to be part of the revolutionary Deuteronomic program.

Crüsemann's interpretation of the altar law in the Book of the Covenant reveals further parallels. He notes, for instance, that the "place" (מָקוֹם) of God is a significant theme in the Book of the Covenant and stresses throughout a connection between God's sovereign choice of the place and his speaking to his people. The fact that discussion of the "place" occurs in significant locations in the Book of the Covenant (the beginning, Exod 20:24; the end, Exod 23:20ff.; and in the middle of the section of the Mishpatim, 21:13–14) demonstrates the importance of the concept for the collection as a whole.[216] Moreover, he argues that the significance of the "place" in the Book of the Covenant is "not the place as such, or the proper altar and cult that guarantees the divine presence, but only the fact that God causes his name to be remembered there."[217] He goes on to argue that the altar law in the Book of the Covenant is an implicit indictment of purely cultic conceptions of holy places. That is, he argues, the fact that sites engage in cultic ritual or have long been associated with tradition does not guarantee Yahweh's presence. Rather, the sites that still proclaim his name are the only subjects of divine blessing. He notes that "[t]his is not a critique of the deuteronomic understanding, but rather an—incomplete—parallel to it. If we draw a correlation using the fact that the divine *name* is what constitutes a true shrine, then we are justified in

---

214. Ibid., 57–58. On the unity of the Sinai pericope, see also T. D. Alexander, "The Composition of the Sinai Narrative in Exodus XIX 1–XXIV 11," *VT* 49 (1999): 2–20.

215. Crüsemann, *Torah*, 170.

216. Ibid., 171.

217. Ibid., 173.

speaking of a pre- or early form of the deuteronomic demand for centralization together with its underlying theology."[218]

Finally, it is appropriate to mention the view of J. Van Seters. In contrast to most scholars, who agree that the Book of the Covenant precedes Deuteronomy, Van Seters maintains that the Book of the Covenant is actually later than, and may be understood as a theological correction of, Deuteronomy.[219] This, he argues, may be seen in the fact that there are many instances in which the Book of the Covenant seems to be based on Deuteronomic laws and not vice versa, as is usually maintained. To cite just one example, Van Seters sees the presentation of the Sabbath law in Exod 23:12 as being based on the Sabbath law in Deuteronomy. This, he argues, is supported by the fact that the 8th-century prophets present the Sabbath as a religious holiday, a time of "cultic convocation" (Isa 1:13; Hos 2:13; Amos 8:5), completely devoid of any humanitarian or social connotations.[220] The Book of the Covenant in Exod 23:12, on the other hand, has as its primary motivation a humanitarian concern; no mention is made of the inherent sanctity of the Sabbath. This, Van Seters argues, can only be because the presentation of this law in the Book of the Covenant is based on the presentation of the Sabbath in Deut 5:12–15, where the motivation for the Sabbath is humanitarian.[221]

Van Seters further argues that the Sabbath law in the Book of the Covenant actually goes beyond Deuteronomy and may be seen as *more* humanitarian. He bases this on the fact that the Sabbath law in Exod 23:12 does not refer to the sanctity of the day (whereas Deut 5:12 does refer to the day as sacred) and then expands the humanitarian motivation for the law to include rest for animals and strangers, not just slaves. He argues that, while Deut 5:12 does refer to rest for animals and strangers, the alteration of the order in which they are presented in the Book of the Covenant, with animals presented first,

218. Ibid.

219. J. Van Seters, "Cultic Laws in the Covenant Code and Their Relationship to Deuteronomy and the Holiness Code," in *Studies in the Book of Exodus: Redaction-Reception-Interpretation* (ed. M. Vervenne; Leuven: Leuven University Press, 1996), 319–45. Van Seters presents his case for a late (both sequentially and temporally) J source in these additional works: *Abraham in History and Tradition* (New Haven: Yale University Press, 1975); *Prologue to History: The Yahwist as Historian in Genesis* (Louisville: Westminster John Knox, 1992); *The Life of Moses: The Yahwist as Historian in Exodus–Numbers* (Louisville: Westminster John Knox, 1994). For a concise analysis of the impact of Van Seters's work, see G. J. Wenham, "Pentateuchal Studies Today," *Themelios* 22/1 (1996): 3–13, esp. 4–8.

220. Van Seters, "Cultic Laws," 334.

221. Ibid.

demonstrates that the later code has expanded the humanitarian concern of the earlier law.[222]

It is clear from the foregoing discussion that the data of the text are capable of being interpreted in a variety of ways. That P, for example, is capable of being fairly interpreted as seeking to avoid anthropomorphisms, and the Book of the Covenant may be seen as having significant affinities with the theology of Deuteronomy demonstrates that the differences between the sources are not of the kind that Weinfeld supposes. That there are differences is, of course, undeniable, and these differences must be accounted for in any coherent interpretation of Deuteronomy. But it is equally undeniable that it is not necessary to conclude, as does Weinfeld, that the JE and P material is inherently mythological, anthropomorphic, and "sacred."

The second premise for Weinfeld's thesis of secularization, that Deuteronomy presents institutions in a way that is inherently secular (i.e., divorced from the realm of the cult) and that its concept of God is largely abstract and transcendent, has been challenged as well. We will now examine the arguments raised against this premise.

One of the most important critiques of Weinfeld's thesis has come from N. Lohfink.[223] Because Lohfink's work is an important and fundamental critique of Weinfeld's thesis, an in-depth examination of the grounds of his argument is in order.

Lohfink sees in Deuteronomy an *extension* of the concepts of the *sacred* and *holiness*, not a reduction of them. At the same time, the "center of gravity" of holiness is shifted in Deuteronomy from an emphasis on cultic ritual to a concentration on the people gathered in unified, joyful celebration.[224] He maintains, moreover, that Deuteronomy establishes a new ritual, that of pilgrimage to the central holy place. It is in this unified, joyful gathering of Israel that the nation may best be understood as being "before Yahweh," and this, Lohfink maintains, is a new conception of holiness for Israel.[225]

---

222. Ibid.

223. N. Lohfink, "Opfer und Säkularisierung im Deuteronomium," in *Studien zu Opfer und Kult im Alten Testament mit einer Bibliographie 1969–1991 zum Opfer in der Bibel* (ed. A. Schenker; Tübingen: Mohr [Siebeck], 1992), 15–43. In his review of Weinfeld's *Deuteronomy and the Deuteronomic School*, Milgrom also challenged Weinfeld's characterization of Deuteronomy as representing an attempt at secularizing the institutions of Israel. But, as Lohfink rightly notes ("Säkularisierung," 17), Milgrom was more concerned about correcting Weinfeld's misinterpretation of P than in examining the true nature of Deuteronomy's attitude toward the cult. See Milgrom, "Alleged 'Demythologization and Secularization.'" See, again, Weinfeld's reply in "Demythologization and Secularization."

224. Lohfink, "Säkularisierung," 36.

225. Ibid., 34–35.

Lohfink notes that, in the context of the so-called centralization laws, one can discern a distinct emphasis on feasts, joy, and the participation of all Israel, including especially those who cannot subsist on their own property.[226] The prevalence of these themes in a variety of laws dealing with a variety of topics leads Lohfink to conclude that this is the essence of sacrifice in Deuteronomy.

At the heart of cultic celebration in Deuteronomy is the unity of all Israel. Lohfink notes that Deuteronomy pointedly seeks to integrate people who, for whatever reason, cannot support themselves on their own property. Typically, these groups (slaves, widows, orphans, strangers) are thought of as "marginal groups" or, more simply, the "poor." Lohfink, however, demonstrates that these people are not considered "poor" in Deuteronomy. Indeed, the Hebrew terminology for the poor is used in Deuteronomy only in connection with debt slavery. Those who are to be included in the feasts are people who are in need of some other support system, since they cannot support themselves with their own property. This is evident, he argues, in the fact that the Levites are included in this group. The Levites are excluded from owning property because of their calling to minister before Yahweh. This is, he notes, an honorable and quite acceptable thing in Israel. At the same time, a support system must be set up in order to provide for the Levites, and Deuteronomy does just that, requiring that the Levites be allowed to participate in the celebrations with "all Israel." In the same way, other so-called "marginal groups" are to be provided for as well.[227]

Thus, the feasts at the central holy place emerge as the high point in the life of the nation. There, according to Deuteronomy, all Israel participates in joyful celebration, without distinction in social status. But this unity "before Yahweh" is not limited to the feasts at the holy place. Lohfink notes that the Sabbath law (Deut 5:14) extends the

---

226. Ibid., 26–30. The texts evaluated are Deut 12:4–7, 8–12, 13–19, 20–28; 14:22–27; 15:19–23; 16:1–8, 9–12, 13–15, 16–17; 17:8–13; 18:1–8; 26:1–11; 31:10–13.

227. Ibid., 32–33. Lohfink has developed this idea further in "Das deuteronomische Gesetz in der Endgestalt: Entwurf einer Gesellschaft ohne marginale Gruppen," *BN* 51 (1990): 25–40; and "Utopian Project." McConville has rightly argued that the Levites function in Deuteronomy partly as a measure of the obedience of the people. Because Yahweh has promised to bless the land, the Levites should be cared for well. If the people obey the command to care for the Levites and to share the blessings with them, they will not be "poor." He notes that a "poor Levite could not be an ideal figure, for his poverty, far from portraying devotion to Yahweh, would actually be a consequence of disobedience and godless independence on the part of the whole people." See McConville, *Law and Theology*, 151. If Lohfink's analysis is correct (and I believe it is), then the way in which all the "property-less" people (not just the Levites) are cared for becomes a measure of the obedience of the people in sharing the blessings of Yahweh.

idea of rest to the slaves and the sojourner (who might not otherwise be allowed the rest), thus providing rest for all Israel, regardless of status. In so doing, Deuteronomy is deliberately seeking to make the joyful, unified celebration of the thrice-yearly feasts a reality for all people at all times. As at the feasts, all social barriers are broken down on the Sabbath.[228] In the same way, the holiness of unified worship of Yahweh is extended to the whole of life and is not limited to celebrations at the holy place.

The expansion of the concept of holiness is seen further in the laws of Deut 14:1–21. There, Lohfink argues, the close connection between the regulations concerning mourning, dietary laws, and food preparation and the statement of the holiness of the people serves to illustrate how holiness has been expanded. Here again the holiness of unified worship in the holy place (which emphasizes the unified eating of a feast) described in Deut 12 is extended to all Israel through the regulations of Deut 14:1–21. In this passage, he notes, the term טָמֵא is applied to the entire people, not just priests, in order to show that holiness is extended to the whole people. Thus, he concludes, the boundary of holiness is not in the midst of Israel but between Israel and the rest of the nations.[229] All the people and all of life are brought into the realm of the sacred.

Lohfink therefore disputes the idea that Deut 12 permits "profane slaughter," arguing that this view reflects pre-Deuteronomic conceptions of the sacred and profane. Deuteronomy, he notes, seeks to leave nothing in the realm of the profane. The center of gravity of the sacred is simply shifted to an emphasis on the people of Israel. This implies a widening of the realm of the sacred so that nothing in Israel is outside the realm of the sacred.[230]

The wider conception of holiness in Deuteronomy may be further seen in the way in which the topic is addressed in the legal corpus of Deuteronomy. Lohfink notes that holiness terminology in Deuteronomy is more than simply the term קָדוֹשׁ. Instead, negative terms such as תּוֹעֵבָה, which is a sacral term, demonstrate the expansion of the holiness concept in Israel. There is, moreover, a close connection between the laws demanding centralization of sacrifice and the command to rid the land of heathen cultic centers.[231] In addition, the fact that the word כָּפַר appears in Deuteronomy only in connection with the regulations pertaining to an unknown murderer (Deut 21:1–9)

---

228. Lohfink, "Säkularisierung," 33.
229. Ibid., 36.
230. Ibid. See also chap. 4 of this volume.
231. Ibid., 36–37.

demonstrates this new conception of the sacred. In this text, the guilt is expiated without a sacrifice, but the context (due in part to the use of the term כָּפֵּר) demonstrates that "holiness" is nevertheless part of the concern.[232] He goes on to note that the laws in Deut 24:4 (on divorce) and 25:13–16 (on false weights and measures) demonstrate that violations of the commands affect the holiness of the whole land.[233] Finally, he notes that the final sentence of the legal code (Deut 26:15) contains a petition that Yahweh look down and bless the people and the ground (אֲדָמָה). It is followed immediately by a ceremony of covenant ratification in which the terminology of Israel as a "holy people" is most pronounced (Deut 26:16–19). Thus, he concludes that there is a close relationship in Deuteronomy between the purity of the land and the way in which the "holy people" live in it.[234]

Conclusions regarding Secularization and Demythologization

In this second section, we have examined secularization and demythologization in Deuteronomy as conceived by Weinfeld. We noted that Weinfeld's conception of secularization and demythologization rests on two fundamental premises. The first premise is that the sources that predate Deuteronomy demonstrate a fundamentally sacral view of life and are marked by an understanding of the divine presence that is largely anthropomorphic and stresses divine immanence. The second premise is that Deuteronomy presents a secularized view of life and institutions, in that they are divorced from the realm of the cult, and presents God in a way that is markedly more abstract and stresses divine transcendence.

Both of these premises have been challenged. Contrary to the usual understanding of the nature of the sources, P has been seen as conspicuously attempting to avoid anthropomorphisms, and the use of כָּבוֹד in both JE and P has been shown to be far more nuanced than Weinfeld allows. Rather than being an attempt to present the presence of Yahweh anthropomorphically or nonanthropomorphically, the use of כָּבוֹד and שֵׁם may be fairly seen as emphasizing aspects of Yahweh's revelation of himself: the latter term, שֵׁם, "Name," appears

---

232. Ibid., 37. He also argues (p. 21) that this law may actually be seen as a "sacralization" of ANE law, since Hammurabi's Code (§§22–24), for example, requires no ceremony at all in dealing with an unknown murderer but instead mandates that the city and governor pay restitution. The fact that Deuteronomy requires a ceremony involving priests suggests to Lohfink that this is an instance of "sacralization," not secularization.

233. Ibid., 37.

234. Ibid., 38.

in the context of normal worship, while the former, כָּבוֹד, "glory," describes dramatic instances of divine manifestations.

The validity of the first premise (difference between the earlier and later sources) has also been challenged due to the fact that some commentators have seen far greater continuity between the Book of the Covenant and Deuteronomy than Weinfeld allows. The fact that both texts appear to share an emphasis on the lordship of Yahweh and the need for exclusive loyalty to him suggests that the differences are not as stark as Weinfeld maintains. In addition, the fact that the Book of the Covenant appears to stress issues of social justice and humanitarian concerns raises doubts regarding the legitimacy of the idea that the two texts are as radically different as Weinfeld proposes, because he argues that these themes are exclusively or especially present in Deuteronomy.

The second premise (secularization of institutions in Deuteronomy) has been challenged as well. As we have seen, Deuteronomy may plausibly be viewed as extending, rather than curtailing, the concepts of the sacred and holiness. The fact that the holiness of unified worship is extended to all Israel points to an expansion rather than a reduction of the idea of holiness. Moreover, several of the laws in Deut 12–26 appear to reflect this expanded concept of holiness, with the result that a close relationship between the purity of the land and the way the "holy people" live in it is described.

As was the case with centralization, the fact that Deuteronomy is capable of such interpretation calls into question whether Weinfeld's position best accounts for the data of the text. Once again the differences between the other pentateuchal sources and Deuteronomy may not be as radical or of the sort that Weinfeld envisions. Since this radical reinterpretation of other sources by Deuteronomy is at the heart of the revolution envisioned by Weinfeld, the fact that the differences are not of the sort he posits undermines the credibility of his thesis as a whole. This, in turn, suggests that a new way of looking at the Deuteronomic revolution is in order.

The Ideology(ies) of Centralization, Secularization, and Demythologization

We have seen to this point that no consensus has emerged on key issues in the interpretation of Deuteronomy, despite broad agreement on the general fact that Deuteronomy supports a program of centralization (of some kind), coupled with secularization and demythologization. The various conclusions on these key issues have important implications for the consideration of ideology in Deuteronomy. I argued in the introduction that ideology consists of the system of beliefs, attitudes, values, and assumptions that a community holds. It is now necessary to examine the various views on centralization, secularization, and demythologization in an effort to discern what ideology(ies) are suggested by these interpretations.

Ideological Implications of Centralization, Secularization, and Demythologization

Weinfeld and von Rad, as we have seen, both understand Deuteronomy as supporting the monarchy. For them, then, one of the crucial ideological components of the book is the preservation and support of the institution of kingship. Weinfeld is most explicit in noting that the scribal authors of Deuteronomy "regarded the institution of monarchy as essential for the proper functioning of society."[235]

The idea that Deuteronomy is a product of the royal court and serves to strengthen the claims of the monarchy is extremely important in understanding Weinfeld's perspective on the book of Deuteronomy. This idea does not simply explain who wrote the book and when (though it does that); it also provides an ideological basis for the interpretation of the book. This underlying general understanding of the book as supporting the monarchy[236] naturally influences interpretive decisions made about specific portions of it.

Levinson, on the other hand, sees centralization primarily as supporting the interests of the central cult. He sees Deuteronomy as presenting a negative critique of the institution of kingship. Levinson's approach suggests an ideology geared not toward the secular institutions of king and judiciary but toward the cult. He argues that Deuteronomy "reflects the strategy of the text's authors: they divest the king of his judicial authority and reassign it to the Temple. The authors of Deuteronomy grant pride of place . . . to the cultic center."[237]

Lohfink's emphasis on the distribution of powers represents yet another ideology, though he, like Levinson, sees Deuteronomy as undermining the role of the monarchy.[238] Lohfink's conception of Deuteronomy suggests an ideology that emphasizes *Torah* and limits the various offices that are regulated by *Torah*.

---

235. Weinfeld, *Deuteronomic School*, 169.
236. The promonarchical stance is, of course, just one aspect of the ideology or world view implied by Weinfeld's thesis.
237. Levinson, *Legal Innovation*, 143.
238. Lohfink, "Distribution," 346–48.

The differences among the various interpreters about whether or not Deuteronomy should be seen as a realistic program or a utopia has implications for ideology as well. If Deuteronomy is a realistic program (as argued by Levinson and, to some degree, Weinfeld), this implies that the authors of the book envisioned that it could and should be implemented in the community. The choices and consequences are realistic for the audience of the book (however conceived). If, on the other hand, Deuteronomy is seen as a utopian ideal, then the rhetoric may be understood as attempting to convince the audience to embrace the ideals lying behind the utopian scheme rather than the specifics of the program. These different views have implications beyond the interpretation of the texts in question, because they reflect different understandings of the fundamental ideology (or world view) of the text.

In the same way, the idea of secularization and demythologization necessarily presupposes an ideology. As we have seen, in Weinfeld's view centralization led to secularization: the sacral bases for life in the nation were eliminated as the central sanctuary was elevated. While Weinfeld is careful to note that secularization did not imply an atheistic tendency or opposition to religious institutions,[239] his understanding of secularization in Deuteronomy intimates a world view that separates life into the spheres of secular and sacred.

It is questionable, however, whether this world view can be ascribed accurately to the author(s) of Deuteronomy. As we have seen, Lohfink has argued that Deuteronomy extends rather than curtails the idea of holiness. The fact that the people are regarded as "holy" in Deuteronomy (Deut 7:6; 14:2, 21; 26:19) due to their election by Yahweh suggests that all of life is to be considered within the realm of the sacred. The fact that the dietary regulations and laws regarding clean and unclean animals in Deut 14 apply to all the people, not just priests, demonstrates that the entire people was considered to be holy. The laws of Deut 14 make clear that the status of the people as holy meant that the choices they made with regard to diet and other practices were not religiously insignificant.[240]

In addition, the legal section of Deut 12–26 itself suggests that the secular/sacred distinction is questionable. The legal code seeks to regulate life in the nation and includes matters of great religious significance (such as the importance of exclusive loyalty to Yahweh, to the extent that even incitement to apostasy is punishable by death according to Deut 13) as well as the more "common" aspects of life

---

239. Weinfeld, "'Demythologization and Secularization,'" 230.
240. See, again, Lohfink, "Säkularisierung," 36.

(requirements to return a stray ox or sheep and regulations about types of clothing, Deut 22:1–4, 11–12). But it is important to note that these regulations all appear in the *Torah* given by Yahweh. It is according to these standards that the nation will be judged concerning loyalty to Yahweh. Miller notes that the law, to some extent, is seen as a surrogate for Yahweh.[241] Therefore, adherence to *Torah* and the regulations therein is of great religious significance, and it is difficult, if not impossible, to maintain that in the ideology of Deuteronomy any aspect of life is to be thought of as secular and divested of religious significance.

This may be further seen in Deut 16:18–20. In Weinfeld's view, the appointment of judges is necessary due to centralization and represents Deuteronomy's tendency toward secularization. But the actions of the people and judges in Deut 16:18–20 are of great religious significance. Failure to pursue צֶדֶק properly will result in death and expulsion from the land (Deut 16:20); this is the same as the punishment for failing to honor Yahweh and his covenant with fidelity. So, the actions of the people and the judges (the appointment of whom ostensibly points to secularization) are seen as being of great religious import.[242]

In this respect, the perspective of Deuteronomy is in keeping with the general world view of the ANE. While there are, of course, important and significant differences between the cultures of the ANE and their perspectives, it is generally accepted that there are some important features common to most of the societies of the ANE. One of these is a belief in the pervasive influence and presence of the gods in the lives of human beings. Sumerian gods were seen as powerful because of their ability to wield the powers of nature, and they were believed to "cut" the destinies of human beings as well as the cosmos as a whole. The Sumerian term *giš-hur*, a "numinous term for the order," refers to the design or plan of the gods.[243] The Babylonians saw the gods as manifesting qualities important for human life. Thus the sun god Shamash was also the god of justice and law,[244] and proper administration of justice was seen as a way of honoring the deity.[245] Similarly, in most ANE cultures, kingship was viewed as a divine institution in which the king represented the gods, and service to the king

241. P. D. Miller, *The Religion of Ancient Israel* (London: SPCK / Louisville: Westminster John Knox, 2000), 158. See also idem, *Deuteronomy*, 56–57.

242. Deuteronomy 16:18–22 will be discussed in greater detail in chap. 5 below.

243. W. von Soden, *The Ancient Orient: An Introduction to the Study of the Ancient Near East* (Grand Rapids: Eerdmans, 1994), 177.

244. Ibid., 180.

245. Cf. L. K. Handy, *Among the Host of Heaven: The Syro-Palestinian Pantheon as Bureaucracy* (Winona Lake, IN: Eisenbrauns, 1994).

was seen as service to the god(s).[246] There was apparently no distinction between the secular and the sacred in this world view.

It seems to me that Weinfeld has ascribed to the author(s) of Deuteronomy a world view that they were rather unlikely to possess. While there are, of course, important differences between the theology and world view of ancient Israel and the other cultures of the ANE, we must also bear in mind that there was engagement between Israel and the neighboring cultures and some basic elements of world view common to both. Deuteronomy, to be sure, could and did innovate in comparison with ANE theology and ideology. But caution must be exercised when determining exactly how far Deuteronomy's innovation extended vis-à-vis ANE parallels. The distinction between the sacred and the secular is modern, not ancient. Indeed, it is hard to conceive of the program envisioned by Deuteronomy as "secular" in any sense of the term, given its fundamentally theocentric outlook. The program of secularization envisioned by Weinfeld seems more at home in the post-Enlightenment modern realm than in the ANE milieu in which Deuteronomy was written.

Conclusions regarding Ideology(ies)

In this section, we have examined the theses of centralization, secularization, and demythologization and have seen that there are important ideological implications associated with the various views of centralization. Among the various views are several ideologies of centralization, some of which are diametrically opposed to others (pro- versus anti-monarchical views, for example).

We have also seen that there are significant problems with the ideology implied by secularization, because it ascribes to the author(s) of Deuteronomy a world view that represents a radical departure from the prevailing world view in the ANE and is more reasonably akin to modern, rather than ANE, perspectives.

The fact that there is such a diversity of world views implied by the modern interpretations of Deuteronomy and the fact that certain interpretations seem to make improper assumptions about the world view of the authors suggest that an alternative ideology should be sought. I will begin by interpreting key texts in Deuteronomy and will describe in subsequent chapters how these texts support an alternative ideology.

---

246. F. A. M. Wiggermann, "Theologies, Priests, and Worship in Ancient Mesopotamia," in *Civilizations of the Ancient Near East* (ed. J. M. Sasson et al.; New York: Scribner's, 1995), 3: 1859–61.

Chapter 2

The Appointment of Judges and *Torah*: Deuteronomy 1:9–18

We have now seen that there are some serious difficulties with the prevailing view of Deuteronomy as representing a revolutionary program of centralization, secularization, and demythologization. Given the problems identified in chap. 1, I argued that an alternative conception of the book should be sought. In this and the following chapters, I will examine several key texts in Deuteronomy that have often been understood as supporting the view of Deuteronomy as a centralizing, secularizing book. I will examine the views of major interpreters in an effort to determine if the interpretations they provide are the most consistent with the textual data. Then I will seek to demonstrate how these same texts may be seen as supporting the idea that at the heart of Deuteronomy is the theology of the supremacy of Yahweh and an emphasis on keeping *Torah* as a means of demonstrating loyalty to him. I will begin with an examination of Deut 1:9–18.

Prevailing View: Secularization of Judicial Procedure

The opening chapter of Deuteronomy identifies Moses as the speaker of the words that follow (1:1) and briefly identifies the setting of the utterance (both geographically and temporally). The first speech of Moses then begins with a description of Yahweh's command to the people to leave Horeb and to proceed to the land promised to the patriarchs.

The description of Yahweh's command and its execution by the people is interrupted by the narration of the appointment of judges in Deut 1:9–18. The appointment of judges is necessary, according to vv. 10–12, because Yahweh has blessed the nation to such a great extent that Moses is unable to bear the burden of leading and judging the people. The qualifications of the officers are described, and Moses' confirmation of the appointment is narrated. Immediately thereafter, Moses charges the judges to execute their responsibilities impartially and in recognition of the fact (v. 17) that "judgment is God's."

There is a general consensus that this text is a unit and that these verses are integral to the broader narrative of chaps. 1–3.[1] Mayes sees these verses as representing an old tradition that has been incorporated into Deuteronomy to advance the Deuteronomist's purposes, which is (following Noth) to introduce the DtH.[2] Similarly, Weinfeld sees these verses as intrusive but reasons that they highlight the radical nature of Deuteronomy's program.[3]

The radical nature of Deuteronomy is evident, in Weinfeld's view, in the way it uses the sources thought to lie behind this text. Exodus 18:13–27 recounts the selection of judges in a somewhat different way, and Num 11:11–17 describes the selection of 70 leaders, who would be given something of the spirit that was upon Moses to enable them to assist him in the responsibilities of leadership. According to Exodus, the initiative for the idea of appointing judges belongs to Jethro (Exod 18:14–15), whereas in Deuteronomy the impetus for the action lies with Moses. In Numbers, the initiative comes from Yahweh (Num 11:16–17). In addition, in Exodus and Numbers the leaders are chosen by Moses (Exod 18:25; Num 11:16), whereas in Deuteronomy the people are to choose them (Deut 1:13). Similarly, Deuteronomy emphasizes the intellectual qualities of the appointees and stresses the need for impartiality in their judgments. In Exodus the candidates are chosen based on their moral qualities (Exod 18:21), and in Numbers it is the proved leadership qualities of the appointees that will make them worthy choices.[4] No call to impartiality for the elders/judges is recorded in Exodus or Numbers.

Perhaps the most important difference between the sources lies in the understanding of Moses' role in hearing cases too difficult for the newly appointed judges. In Exodus, difficult cases are brought to Moses, who will in turn bring them to God (Exod 18:19–22). In Deuteronomy, nothing is said about bringing difficult cases to God. In Deut 1:17 Moses simply says, "the case that is too difficult for you, bring to me and I will hear it." There is no mention of bringing it to Yahweh for disposition. The passage in Numbers makes no mention

---

1. See D. L. Christensen, *Deuteronomy 1:1–21:9* (WBC 6a; Nashville: Thomas Nelson, 2001), 17–23; and idem, "Prose and Poetry in the Bible: The Narrative Poetics of Deuteronomy 1:9–18," *ZAW* 97 (1985): 179–89.

2. A. D. H. Mayes, *Deuteronomy* (NCB; Grand Rapids: Eerdmans / London: Marshall, Morgan & Scott, 1979), 117–18.

3. M. Weinfeld, *Deuteronomy 1–11* (AB 5; New York: Doubleday, 1991), 137–40.

4. Weinfeld maintains that divine inspiration is what "makes the candidates worthy of their position" in Numbers (ibid., 139). But Num 11:16–17 suggests that Moses is to select elders already known as leaders to receive the spirit and assist Moses. Thus, the giving of the spirit empowers the selected elders to serve but is not the basis of their election.

of any appeal to Moses or Yahweh, as the nature of the appointment seems to be different. Whereas it is clear in Exodus and Deuteronomy that judges are in view,[5] Numbers refers to elders who will help Moses carry the burden of the people, but no judicial function is intimated. It is not surprising, then, that the Numbers account does not make reference to an appeal to Yahweh (or Moses).

In Weinfeld's view, the differences between the accounts may be explained, at least partially, by noting the ideology or world view of Deuteronomy. That Deuteronomy emphasizes the intellectual qualities of the appointees is explained by Deuteronomy's emphasis on wisdom. As Weinfeld sees it, Deuteronomy emerged out of a royal scribal school and therefore reveals many similarities with wisdom literature, both in form and content.[6] It is not surprising, then, that Deuteronomy would emphasize intellectual qualities, given the environment from which it emerged.

Other differences are also explained by Weinfeld on ideological grounds. The fact that Jethro is not mentioned in the account in Deuteronomy is explained by Weinfeld as being the result of the desire of the authors of Deuteronomy to minimize the role of a foreigner. The idea of a Midianite priest playing a central role in the establishment of the judiciary of the people of God was contrary to the nationalistic views of the authors of Deuteronomy, so his role is removed in the account in Deuteronomy. Similarly, the fact that the people, not Moses, choose the men who will serve as leader/judges reflects the more democratic ideals of the book.[7]

Deuteronomy's emphases may be most clearly seen, in Weinfeld's view, when one considers the most striking difference between Deuteronomy and the account in Exodus: the elimination of an appeal to Yahweh by Moses when the difficult cases are brought to him. This is due to the fact that Deuteronomy does not accept the inherent sanctity of judicial procedure. That is, the authors of Deuteronomy are attempting to highlight the natural and intellectual nature of judicial

---

5. There is broad agreement that the judges referred to in Deut 1:9–18 serve military as well as judicial functions. See Mayes, *Deuteronomy*, 124–25; I. Cairns, *Word and Presence: A Commentary on the Book of Deuteronomy* (ITC; Grand Rapids: Eerdmans / Edinburgh: Handsel, 1992), 34; M. Weinfeld, "Judge and Officer in Ancient Israel and the Ancient Near East," *IOS* 7 (1977): 65–88. Here, of course, the emphasis is on the more traditional, judicial aspect of their role.

6. M. Weinfeld, *Deuteronomy and the Deuteronomic School* (Oxford: Oxford University Press, 1972; repr. Winona Lake, IN: Eisenbrauns, 1992), 244–81. A similar view is adopted by J. H. Tigay, *Deuteronomy* דברים: *The Traditional Hebrew Text with the New JPS Translation* (Philadelphia: Jewish Publication Society, 1996), 422–23.

7. Weinfeld, *Deuteronomy 1–11*, 140.

procedure and consequently downplay the role of sacral authority or practice in the adjudication of cases.[8] This, Weinfeld maintains, is a clear example of the tendency toward secularization in Deuteronomy.[9]

Evaluation

We have seen that Deut 1:9–18 has been interpreted as demonstrating the revolutionary tendency toward secularization posited by Weinfeld. We now must examine the arguments adduced in favor of this view in order to determine whether they are supported by the data of the text or whether an alternative explanation should be sought.

It appears that Weinfeld has overstated the differences between the sources in some instances. It is apparent that the account in Deut 1:9–18 is influenced to some degree by the accounts in Exodus and Numbers.[10] But the nature of the differences may not be of the sort that Weinfeld claims.

Weinfeld maintains that Deuteronomy highlights intellectual qualifications of judges, where Exodus stresses moral qualities, due to Weinfeld's understanding that Deuteronomy is the product of scribal schools. However, as Wright notes, the moral qualities explicitly described in Exod 18:21 are implied by Deut 1:16–17.[11] Exodus 18:21 calls for the appointment of men who "fear God, men of truth who hate dishonest gain." These same qualities are part of the exhortation of Deut 1:16–17, where the judges are exhorted not to "fear man, for the judgment is God's." The implication, of course, is that they are to fear God, whom they are representing in their execution of justice (see below). Similarly, the righteous judgment and impartiality to which the judges are called imply a disavowal of dishonest gain (cf. Deut 16:19–20, where this is made explicit).

Moreover, Moses here commands the judges to judge righteously (צֶדֶק). In claiming that Deuteronomy emphasizes intellectual qualities, Weinfeld overlooks the fact that צֶדֶק entails more than intellectual qualities. The nominal forms צֶדֶק and צְדָקָה appear 13 times in

---

8. Weinfeld, *Deuteronomic School,* 233; and idem, *Deuteronomy 1–11,* 138.

9. Idem, *Deuteronomic School,* 233.

10. This may be seen in terms of content but also in terms of language used. The phrase לֹא־אוּכַל לְבַדִּי שְׂאֵת אֶתְכֶם in Deut 1:9 is similar to Num 11:14. See S. R. Driver, *A Critical and Exegetical Commentary on Deuteronomy* (3rd ed.; ICC; Edinburgh: T. & T. Clark, 1901), 15; and Weinfeld, *Deuteronomy 1–11,* 135. McConville rightly notes that the idea of endurance is present in Exod 18:23 as well and concludes that Exod 18:13–27 and Num 11:10–25 have been "collapsed . . . into one." J. G. McConville, *Deuteronomy* (AOTC 5; Leicester: Apollos / Downers Grove, IL: InterVarsity, 2002), 59.

11. C. J. H. Wright, *Deuteronomy* (NIBC 4; Peabody, MA: Hendrickson / Carlisle: Paternoster, 1996), 26.

Deuteronomy.[12] In the majority of these appearances the broader sense, "righteousness," appears to be in view. In Deut 9:4–6, for example, the word צְדָקָה is used parallel with יֹשֶׁר לְבָבְךָ, "uprightness of heart." In addition, it is contrasted with רִשְׁעָה, which usually denotes an abstract sense of evil or wickedness.[13] This suggests that, though the description of the qualifications of judges is indeed different in Deuteronomy, the nature of the qualifications is not as different as Weinfeld maintains. There is more to the qualifications of judges than intellectual qualities.

A further point may be made about Weinfeld's apparent understanding of wisdom literature. He suggests that in its emphasis on intellectual affairs wisdom literature downplays matters of morality or of the heart as he draws a contrast between the moral emphases of Exodus and the intellectual emphases in Deuteronomy. While this emphasis on the intellectual in wisdom literature has been advocated,[14] Waltke rightly notes that "wisdom . . . appeals to the mind, but to know wisdom is more a matter of a loving heart (i.e., a person's center for both physical and emotional-intellectual-moral activities) than of a cold intellect."[15] This may be further seen when it is noted that, according to Prov 1:7 and Job 28:28, "the fear of Yahweh is the beginning of wisdom." Garrett notes that "reverence for God determines progress in wisdom, and this reverence includes the moral dimension of obedience and the spiritual dimension of worship."[16] My point is simply that wisdom literature may encompass aspects of morality and the fear of Yahweh in its conception of the wise person. That is, the "wise man" of wisdom literature is the one who lives out fear and rev-

---

12. Deuteronomy 1:16; 6:25; 9:4, 5, 6; 16:18, 20 (2×); 24:13; 25:15 (2×); 33:19, 21. Although some have maintained a difference in meaning between צֶדֶק and צְדָקָה, Reimer rightly notes that, due to the overlap in usage of the various forms, context rather than morphology should be decisive in determining the meaning of any particular use of the term. See D. J. Reimer, "צדק," *NIDOTTE* 3: 744–69, here p. 746.

13. G. H. Livingston, "רשׁע," *TWOT* 2: 862–64; E. Carpenter and M. Grisanti, "רשׁע," *NIDOTTE* 3: 1201–4.

14. See D. Kidner, *An Introduction to Wisdom Literature: The Wisdom of Proverbs, Job, and Ecclesiastes* (Downers Grove, IL: InterVarsity, 1985), 11.

15. B. K. Waltke and D. Diewert, "Wisdom Literature," in *The Face of Old Testament Studies: A Survey of Contemporary Approaches* (ed. D. W. Baker and B. T. Arnold; Leicester: Apollos / Grand Rapids: Baker, 1999), 300.

16. D. A. Garrett, *Proverbs, Ecclesiastes, Song of Songs* (NAC 14; Nashville: Broadman, 1993), 54. Cf. R. Murphy, "Religious Dimensions of Israelite Wisdom," in *Ancient Israelite Religion: Essays in Honor of Frank Moore Cross* (ed. P. D. Miller Jr., P. D. Hanson, S. D. McBride; Philadelphia: Fortress, 1987), 449–58, esp. 452–56; B. K. Waltke, "The Book of Proverbs and Old Testament Theology," *BSac* 136 (1979): 302–17; and idem, "Fear of the Lord," *JCBRF* 128 (1992): 12–16.

erence for Yahweh. Consequently, the qualifications described in Exodus and Deuteronomy may not be as different as Weinfeld suggests. At the very least, caution should be exercised in drawing contrasts between the world view represented by wisdom literature and other types of literature, because scholars are presently divided about the best understanding of the religious elements of wisdom literature.[17]

Objections may be raised as well about Weinfeld's contention that the elimination of any mention of Jethro is due to the nationalistic tendency of Deuteronomy. While it is undeniable that Deuteronomy contains within it an emphasis on the nation of Israel and a related denigration of the surrounding nations (Deut 7), the nature of the relationship between Israelites and non-Israelites is more complex than Weinfeld seems to allow. Deuteronomy 7 calls for the destruction of the seven nations occupying Canaan, based in large measure on the fact that they worship other gods (Deut 7:4–6; 9:4). But Deut 9 makes clear that Yahweh's judgment on the nations is not to be taken by Israel as a statement of its own righteousness. Indeed, the fact of Israel's unrighteousness and persistent rebellion is made explicit in Deut 9:4–29; 31:14–32:43. In addition, the extensive curses of chap. 28 suggest that the nation is expected to experience the loss of the land, due to the persistent sin of the people and their failure to demonstrate proper loyalty to Yahweh through adherence to his *Torah* (Deut 32:46). As Wright notes, Deuteronomy is clearly "more concerned with the failures of God's people than with the wickedness of the other nations."[18]

---

17. There are, of course, major issues raised here regarding the nature and development of wisdom literature. While thorough exploration of these issues is beyond the scope of this study, it should be noted that there is much debate centered on the relationship between wisdom literature and the worship of Yahweh. W. McKane (*Proverbs: A New Approach* [OTL; Philadelphia: Westminster, 1970], 3–8) maintains that Old Testament wisdom originates in folk wisdom and was essentially international. It was later assimilated into Yahwism, and the development may be seen in Prov 1–9. In a basic sense, then, wisdom literature is seen as being separate from the explicitly religious tenets of Yahwism. As noted above, however (see n. 16), this idea has been challenged. With respect to Deuteronomy, opinion is also divided. Weinfeld sees significant parallels between Deuteronomy and wisdom literature (see, e.g., *Deuteronomy 1–11*, 62–65). J. L. Crenshaw (*Old Testament Wisdom: An Introduction*, [rev. ed.; Louisville: Westminster John Knox, 1998], 29–30), however, argues that Deuteronomy's use of covenantal language and "election categories" (p. 30) excludes it from the category of wisdom literature. Including Deuteronomy in the category of wisdom literature would, in his estimation, "distort the meaning of wisdom beyond repair" (p. 30). For the purposes of the present study, it is enough to note that, because there are many questions about the religious nature of wisdom literature and whether or not wisdom literature should be seen as having a unified character, caution is warranted when drawing conclusions about the nature of wisdom appealed to in Deuteronomy.

18. Wright, *Deuteronomy*, 134.

Moreover, the text in question, as well as the book as a whole, includes a call to treat aliens with compassion and justice in judicial proceedings (Deut 1:16). Craigie notes that aliens were to be treated as equals of Israelites in judicial matters, even if they were not considered equal in other respects.[19] Fair treatment of aliens, it is noted, is to execute justice in Yahweh's name (Deut 1:17; see below). Indeed, as we have seen in chap. 1, there is a sense in which the protection and preservation of so-called marginal groups (aliens, orphans, and widows) may be understood in Deuteronomy as a measure of the obedience of the people to the *Torah* of Yahweh.[20]

The inclusion of aliens extends in Deut 23 to granting permission for the inclusion of the descendents of certain non-Israelites (Edomites and Egyptians) in the assembly of Yahweh. Entry into the assembly is granted after only three generations. The inclusion of Egyptians in the category of those who may ultimately be permitted to join the assembly is particularly striking, because it is based on the fact that the Israelites were themselves once aliens in Egypt. There is no kinship relationship between Israel and Egypt, as there is with Edom. One may not conclude that inclusion in the assembly of Yahweh is based on a broader (Abrahamic) nationalism, because Egypt is included while Ammon and Moab (despite being descendents of Abraham) are not.

Finally, it should be noted that Deut 16 expressly includes the resident alien (גֵּר) in the celebration of the Feast of Weeks at the chosen place (Deut 16:9–12). It seems, then, that Deuteronomy's perspective on aliens is far more nuanced than Weinfeld allows. As Brett notes, Deuteronomy provides "moral resources which can be seen as nationalist and anti-nationalist."[21]

It should also be noted that Weinfeld's argument about the removal of reference to Jethro is an argument from silence. He maintains that the silence about Jethro is a reflection of the nationalistic tendency of the book but does not consider any other possibilities. Driver, for example, maintains that the absence of reference to Jethro is due to the fact that "the stress [in Deut 1:9–18] lies less on the orig-

---

19. P. C. Craigie, *The Book of Deuteronomy* (NICOT; Grand Rapids: Eerdmans, 1976), 98.

20. See, again, N. Lohfink, "Das deuteronomische Gesetz in der Endgestalt: Entwurf einer Gesellschaft ohne marginale Gruppen," *BN* 51 (1990): 25–40; and idem, "The Laws of Deuteronomy: A Utopian Project for a World Without Any Poor?" 1995 Lattey Lecture, Von Hügel Institute, St. Edmund's College, Cambridge. See also J. G. McConville, *Law and Theology in Deuteronomy* (JSOTSup 331 Sheffield: JSOT Press, 1984), 151.

21. M. G. Brett, "Nationalism and the Hebrew Bible," in *The Bible in Ethics: The Second Sheffield Colloquium* (ed. J. W. Rogerson, M. Davies, and M. D. Carroll R.; JSOTSup 207; Sheffield: Sheffield Academic Press, 1995), 159.

inator of the suggestion than on the fact of the organization having been established by Moses, and on the need for it in the numbers of the people."[22] The text must be interpreted in light of the purposes for which it was written, and it is certainly possible that the purposes of the author would not have been advanced by describing the initiation of the idea. Miller takes a similar view, noting that this text highlights *"the need for organization and leadership in the fulfillment of the blessing God promised long before to Abraham."*[23] Thus, there are other, equally probable reasons than those suggested by Weinfeld that explain why Jethro is not mentioned in Deuteronomy's account of the appointment of judges in Deut 1:9–18.[24]

A similar point may be raised in connection with Weinfeld's contention that this text is an example of secularization. As we have seen, he makes this claim because judicial proceedings in this text do not appear to have any sacral component, whereas the earlier material includes reference to appeal to Yahweh. But as with the reference to Jethro, this is an argument from silence. That is, the basis of Weinfeld's contention that this text represents secularization of the judiciary is the fact that there is no mention in Deuteronomy of any appeal by Moses to Yahweh. But depicting an appeal of this kind would be out of place in light of Deuteronomy's emphasis on Moses as the mediator of Yahweh's words to the people (Deut 1:3, 5–6, 19, 34, 42–43).[25] In addition, Deuteronomy consistently depicts the relationship between Yahweh and Moses as unique (Deut 34:10–12). Describing an appeal to Yahweh by Moses would undermine the presentation of Moses as the sole mediator of the words of Yahweh. It is not surprising, therefore, that there is no mention of any appeal.

What should be noted, however, is that mention *is* made of an appeal to Moses by the judges in cases that are too difficult for them to decide (Deut 1:17c). Cairns argues that a case that is "too difficult" is one for which there is no precedent.[26] If there is in fact no precedent, only Yahweh (or his designated mediator, Moses) is in a position to decide the case. Thus, in calling for appeal to Moses and stressing that "judgment is God's," the author is further highlighting the unique role of Moses as mediator of the words of Yahweh.

22. Driver, *Deuteronomy*, 15.

23. P. D. Miller Jr., *Deuteronomy* (Interp; Louisville: John Knox, 1990), 28; emphasis is original.

24. It seems likely, as I will argue below, that Deuteronomy's emphasis on Moses' role as Yahweh's representative is sufficient to explain the absence of reference to Jethro in Deut 1:9–18.

25. Cf. E. H. Merrill, *Deuteronomy* (NAC 4; Nashville: Broadman & Holman, 1994), 70.

26. Cairns, *Word and Presence*, 34.

Moreover, Deut 17:8–13 explicitly calls for appeal to the priests serving in "the place" in cases that are too difficult for the judges to decide. The inclusion of priests in addition to judges in Deut 17:9ff. suggests that in such cases appeal would be made to Yahweh in some fashion; their inclusion is superfluous if this appeal represents simply a recourse to a higher, secular judicial body.[27] There seems, as well, to be a somewhat greater emphasis on the role of the priest in promulgating the decision of the court. It is the priest's pronouncement (v. 12) that is given priority and that carries the weight of greatest authority. The emphasis on priestly (i.e., sacral) authority seems to undermine Weinfeld's contention that secularization of the judiciary is at the heart of the Deuteronomic reform program.[28]

Once again, consideration must be given to the author's purpose in including this material. I will argue below that the focus of this text is on the time of transition and the need for acknowledging Yahweh through adherence to *Torah* in executing judgment. If this is so, it is hardly surprising that all of the details of judicial procedure are not spelled out here. To do so would distract from the purposes for which the text was written.

One of the major problems with most treatments of this text is the fact that there is little discussion about why this section dealing with the appointment of leaders and judges appears here at all. The section clearly interrupts the flow of the narrative, because the command to move forward from Horeb is given in v. 8, and the description of its execution begins in v. 19. Moreover, as Weinfeld notes, the section opens with the phrase בָּעֵת הַהִוא, which often introduces intrusive texts.[29] Indeed, the narrative describing the departure from Horeb is seamless apart from the interpolation of vv. 9–18. Yet scant attention is paid to this fact.[30] Instead, as we have seen, most interpreters focus

---

27. McConville (*Deuteronomy*, 291) rightly notes that the nature of the relationship between the sacral and civil powers (represented by priest and judge) is unclear in Deut 17:8–13. What is clear is that both sacral and civil authorities are to participate in the rendering of a decision in difficult cases.

28. I realize that some (e.g., Mayes, *Deuteronomy*, 267) see Deut 17:8–13 as originating from a hand different from Deut 1:9–18. Regardless of their origins, however, the two texts were placed in the same work by a redactor who presumably understood them to be compatible with each other.

29. Weinfeld, *Deuteronomy 1–11*, 139. See also Driver, *Deuteronomy*, 15.

30. Especially striking is the fact that few commentators posit a separate source for this section. Instead, as we have seen, since Noth there has been general agreement that this section is produced by the Deuteronomist and forms part of the introduction to the Deuteronomistic History (DtH). See M. Noth, *The Deuteronomistic History* (2nd ed.; JSOT-Sup 15; Sheffield: Sheffield Academic Press, 1991); ET of *Überlieferungsgeschichtliche Studien* (Tübingen: Max Niemeyer, 1957), 1–110. Cf. also T. Römer, "The Book of Deuteronomy,"

on the differences between the account in Deuteronomy and the accounts found in Exod 18:13–27 and Num 11:11–17.

But if Deuteronomy is to be considered seriously as a literary or theological work, then one must explain why this passage is included here. Since the book does not present itself as a comprehensive history of Israel but as a compilation of speeches by Moses in a particular time and place intended to serve a particular purpose, it is safe to assume that the inclusion or exclusion of certain events in the narrative must be deliberate on the part of the author or editor(s).[31] That is, it is not enough to account for the differences between the earlier sources and the text in Deut 1:9–18. Rather, consideration must be given to *why* the author or editors chose to include this material here. Serious treatment of this issue is lacking in many interpretations of this text. We will now turn our attention to this question, as I articulate an alternative understanding of this text, including a discussion of the ideological implications of this alternative.

Alternative View:
Yahweh and Torah *for All Times*

I have argued above that scholars holding the prevailing view of this text make some unwarranted assumptions regarding the nature of the differences between the earlier sources and Deuteronomy and that they also fail to account adequately for the fact that Deut 1:9–18 interrupts the flow of the narrative. I will now describe how I see this text functioning in the overall rhetoric of Deuteronomy and how the text highlights the unique ideology of the book.

While the significance of the inclusion of this intrusive section has been largely unrecognized, it has not gone entirely unnoticed. Clements suggests that this section is included in order to highlight the importance of a "fair and acceptable system of juridical authority."[32] Thus, he notes that the legal section of the book (chaps. 12–26)

---

in *The History of Israel's Traditions: The Heritage of Martin Noth* (ed. S. L. McKenzie and M. P. Graham; JSOTSup 182; Sheffield: Sheffield Academic Press, 1994), 178–212, esp. 178–91.

31. I contend, further, that the author's purpose is related to the rest of the book of Deuteronomy—not, as Noth maintained, to introduce DtH. For a discussion of the overall purpose of Deuteronomy and the nature of the book as communication, see T. A. Lenchak, *"Choose Life!": A Rhetorical-Critical Investigation of Deuteronomy 28,69–30,20* (AnBib 129; Rome: Pontifical Biblical Institute, 1993), 1–27. See also P. A. Barker, *Deuteronomy: The God Who Keeps Promises* (Melbourne: Acorn, 1998), 7, who notes that Deuteronomy's presentation of history is selective and serves a rhetorical purpose.

32. Clements, "The Book of Deuteronomy," 297. In a later work, he argues that this text emphasizes justice and wisdom in describing the qualifications of judges and in so doing serves to introduce the authors of the book to the readers by tracing their authority

is greatly concerned with the administration of justice and provides details of institutional responsibilities for it.[33] Olson, on the other hand, sees in this section the first intimation of the impending death of Moses. He sees in the provision of leaders for the nation a "dying to exclusive claim on authority, a dying to self-glorification, a dying to hoarding power for oneself rather than sharing and trusting others with it."[34]

In my estimation, both Clements and Olson have seen important facets of this section and have rightly noted the importance of the inclusion of this section in the narrative. I would suggest, however, that this passage contains the first suggestion of the importance of *Torah* as the successor to Moses in the life of the nation.

Gary Millar has argued persuasively that the theology of Deuteronomy is permeated with a dynamic element.[35] That is, there is a sense in Deuteronomy in which the people of God are constantly seen to be "on the move" toward the land of promise, and the challenge for the people is to live out their lives in obedience to Yahweh even in the face of changing circumstances. The book itself is, of course, set in a moment of tremendous importance and change. The people are addressed at Moab, on the verge of entering the promised land. They are leaving behind the wilderness, the nomadic life, and the experience of slavery in Egypt. Their relationship with Yahweh will change upon their entry into the promised land. Whereas formerly the people had a tangible sense of Yahweh's presence in the form of the pillar of fire and cloud and the Tent of Meeting, they will soon find themselves settling into cities and villages, and their sense of Yahweh's presence will necessarily change. Deuteronomy, then, addresses the people at a crucial turning point in the way in which they live out their lives as the people of Yahweh.

But, as has been recognized, there is more to the exhortations of Deuteronomy than simply an appeal to the audience addressed at Moab. There is a careful blending of the audiences addressed; for example, the Moab generation is described in Deut 5:3–5 as having been

---

back to Moses. See idem, *The Book of Deuteronomy: A Preacher's Commentary* (EC; Peterborough: Epworth, 2001), 4–5.

33. Clements, "Book of Deuteronomy," 297.

34. D. T. Olson, *Deuteronomy and the Death of Moses: A Theological Reading* (Minneapolis: Fortress, 1994), 24.

35. See J. G. Millar, *Now Choose Life: Theology and Ethics in Deuteronomy* (NSBT 4; Leicester: Apollos, 1998), esp. 67–98; J. G. McConville and J. G. Millar, *Time and Place in Deuteronomy* (JSOTSup 179; Sheffield: Sheffield Academic Press, 1994). Cf. Cairns, *Word and Presence*, 32.

at Horeb, despite the fact that, in reality, they were not.[36] In addition, the frequent use of the term הַיּוֹם has been shown to be a rhetorical device that contributes to the sense of contemporaneity.[37] All the important decisions are said to be urgent "today," yet DeVries and others have shown that "today" is more than temporal.[38] In its frequent use of the term הַיּוֹם and the recurrent blurring of the distinction between generations, Deuteronomy evokes the sense that its "today" at Moab is a decisive moment but one that, paradoxically, the people face again and again in their journey with Yahweh. Thus, Millar concludes that "Moab is presented as the place where the past and future of Israel coalesce in a single moment, the place where the decision to follow Yahweh must be reaffirmed in every generation."[39]

In the light of this, Deut 1:9–18 takes on new significance. As Christensen has noted, the section is bracketed by the phrase בָּעֵת הַהִוא, which appears in vv. 9, 16, and 18.[40] This, I believe, serves to focus attention on the particular time when the event occurred and is not used simply to indicate a temporal transition. The repetition of the term in just a few verses argues against the idea that merely temporal transition is being emphasized.[41] Rather, the phrase is used to draw attention to the particular time when Moses made the appointment of officials and exhorted the judges. This has been noted by Tomasino, who demonstrates that the phrase can have more significance than simply as a temporal marker. The use of בָּעֵת הַהִוא in Deut 3:12, 18, 21, and 23 appears to be stressing the particular time when the events occurred, in much the same way that it does here.[42]

The "time" emphasized, when judges are appointed, is one of transition and potential. The people are at Horeb, having experienced a tremendous revelation of Yahweh and having entered into a special

36. The "blending" of generations appears first in Deut 4:9–10, where Moses speaks of the things that the people saw at Horeb and are encouraged to remember. Here, again, this is not actually the case, because 1:35 and 2:14 make clear that the generation that experienced Horeb firsthand had died. The people addressed were the children of those who had experienced Horeb.

37. See, for example, S. J. De Vries, *Yesterday, Today and Tomorrow: Time and History in the Old Testament* (Grand Rapids: Eerdmans / London: SPCK, 1975), esp. 45–47; P. A. Verhoef, "יוֹם," *NIDOTTE* 2: 419–24; Millar, *Now Choose Life*, 76–78; McConville and Millar, *Time and Place*, 42–45.

38. DeVries, *Yesterday, Today and Tomorrow*, 45.

39. McConville and Millar, *Time and Place*, 47.

40. Christensen, *Deuteronomy 1:1–21:9*, 21–22.

41. DeVries (*Yesterday, Today and Tomorrow*, 168) argues that the phrase בָּעֵת הַהִוא is simply used to introduce a new narrative episode and marks the secondary nature of this section.

42. A. Tomasino, "עֵת," *NIDOTTE* 3: 563–67.

relationship with him. Yahweh then commands the people to leave the mountain and go to the land he swore to the patriarchs he would give to them (Deut 1:6–8). The breadth of the land described implies that the Israelites will be spread out over vast distances. Their lives would inevitably change. So, too, the fulfillment of God's promise to Abraham for many offspring (vv. 10–11) necessitates a change in the way in which the Israelites are organized as a society. The growth in numbers since leaving Egypt necessitates a change in the administration of the nation.

In this moment of transition, a new system is put in place. Leaders are selected by the tribes and commissioned by Moses to serve as "heads" over the people.[43] The people, through their "heads," will now be responsible to Yahweh for the way they live out their lives.

Insight regarding the expectations comes in the next verses, the charge to the judges in Deut 1:16–18.[44] The judges are told to "judge righteously" (וּשְׁפַטְתֶּם צֶדֶק) in the cases that will come before them, whether the parties are Israelites or foreigners, "great or small." The rationale for impartial judgment is given in v. 17: כִּי הַמִּשְׁפָּט לֵאלֹהִים. The statement that "judgment is God's" implies that in the cases that the judges will hear, God will render judgment through their agency, and the judges are expected to act in accordance with the law that comes from God.[45] This, Wright notes, "enshrines a major feature of constitutional law, namely, that the law has a transcendent value. Promulgated and administered by humans, it possesses an authority above even those who promulgate and administer it."[46]

Moreover, this historical remembrance is deliberately included in Moses' speech to Israel on the plains of Moab (Deut 1:1). The people gathered on the boundary to the land of promise also face a significant transition. They will engage in fierce battles to take possession of the land that Yahweh swore to their forefathers. Upon entering the land, they will face temptation from the religious practices of the

---

43. On the use of רֹאשׁ as a title for a leader, see J. R. Bartlett, "The Use of the Word רֹאשׁ as a Title in the Old Testament," *VT* 19 (1969): 1–10.

44. It is not explicit from the text, but I think it likely that the judges exhorted here should be understood as being the same people selected in v. 13 and commissioned in v. 15. The qualifications described suggest that judicial as well as military responsibilities are in view. See Mayes, *Deuteronomy*, 124–25; Wright, *Deuteronomy*, 26; Bartlett, "Use of רֹאשׁ"; Weinfeld, "Judge and Officer."

45. Wright, *Deuteronomy*, 27, and Mayes, *Deuteronomy*, 125. Wright notes that the phrase could also be understood to mean simply that God is ultimately responsible for dispensing justice—that is, this is his domain. However, he rightly notes that other texts (e.g., 2 Chr 19:6 and Prov 16:33) argue in favor of the alternative view.

46. Wright, *Deuteronomy*, 27.

people who occupy the land. They will face the temptation to "be like" the nations they are displacing in every way. And they will face these dangers without the leadership and mediation of Moses, who had led them through all the transitions and trials they had yet experienced. Thus, the insertion of Deut 1:9–18 demonstrates that the book is able to address people in ever-new generations.

Despite the fact that there will be transition and trials, some important constants in this text emerge as well. First, there is the faithfulness of Yahweh. This is seen most clearly in the fact that the "burden" of the growing population is described as being a blessing of Yahweh in fulfillment of his promise to the patriarchs (vv. 10–11). This is also suggested by the fact that the judges are seen as being God's representatives in adjudicating the cases that come before them. The fact that judgment through human agents is seen as belonging to God implies that God is interested in the affairs of his people.

Perhaps more significant is the fact that the appointment of judges is described as occurring in connection with the giving of the law at Horeb. While I believe it is correct to see the phrase בָּעֵת הַהִוא as more than a temporal marker, it is not less than that. Thus, the time emphasized is one of transition, but it also refers to the time at which the law is given. There appears to be a connection between the giving of the law at Horeb (the time to which בָּעֵת הַהִוא generally, though not specifically, refers[47]) and its implementation in the form of the appointment of judges. Miller notes that, as the nation moves forward and lives out the blessing of prosperity, "life becomes more complex, requiring leadership, wisdom, structure, order, and fairness to an even greater degree than before."[48] The *Torah*, promulgated at Horeb and expounded at Moab, will serve as the basis for the "leadership, wisdom, structure, order, and fairness" of the new life the people will be facing. The judges are charged here with ensuring that the "land given in promise will be a land kept in *Torah*."[49] *Torah*, then, emerges as a crucial constant in the face of changing circumstances.

---

47. Mayes (*Deuteronomy*, 121) argues that Deut 1:9 agrees with Num 11 against Exod 18 in seeing the appointment of judges as occurring following the departure from Sinai/Horeb. But the time reference here is too vague to be certain what is intended and could refer to the Sinai event as a whole. Given that the use of בָּעֵת הַהִוא appears to function rhetorically to highlight the time as one of transition and only more generally as a temporal reference, caution should be exercised in attempting to reconcile the different events temporally. Moreover, it is not at all clear that the appointment of elders in Num 11 is the same event described in Deut 1:9–18 and Exod 18:13–27.

48. Miller, *Deuteronomy*, 28.

49. W. Brueggemann, *Deuteronomy* (AbOTC; Nashville: Abingdon, 2001), 28.

Conclusions regarding
Deuteronomy 1:9–18

In the rhetoric and world view of Deuteronomy, the people of God are ever on the verge of the promised land and are always at the place of decision. In the face of transition and decision, Yahweh's faithfulness and his *Torah* emerge as constants. In the moment of transition when departing Horeb, a new order is established in Israel. Times have changed, and so must the structures of society. The account of the appointment of officers occurs in the context of speeches by Moses to the people assembled at Moab (yet another moment of transition) and highlights the fact that institutional permanence is not to be a hallmark of life with Yahweh. In addition, Moses will not accompany the people into the land (Deut 3:23–28). More significant, however, is the fact that he will not be replaced by a single person. Instead, the "offices" of Moses (prophet, judge, mediator, political leader) will be replaced by several separate institutions and people, who will all be expected to act in conformity with Yahweh's will expressed in *Torah*.[50] In this way, *Torah* itself is shown to be the successor to Moses. It is the *Torah* that provides for the offices and institutions that replace Moses, and the *Torah* provides the standards by which the tasks should be carried out.

Paradoxically, however, *Torah* itself will not change but will serve continually as Yahweh's revelation to Israel about how they are to live out their lives as the people of Yahweh (Deut 4:2; 12:32). Thus, there is continuity even in the face of discontinuity. In addressing the moment of transition at Moab by looking back to an earlier moment of transition, Deuteronomy demonstrates that it is able to address new times and situations of transition.

In addition, the supremacy of Yahweh is firmly established, since it is his judgment that must be carried out by the judges. They will act as his representatives, rendering decisions in light of his will. They cannot act according to their own desires, preferences, or prejudices but must instead render God's judgment. Thus, in giving the charge to the judges to remember that "judgment is God's," Moses is reminding the people of the solemn responsibility they have to acknowledge the supremacy of Yahweh as they live out every aspect of their lives. That the judges are commissioned with judging in accordance with Yahweh's will intimates that their role is inherently sacred, although perhaps not cultic. This further weakens the case for seeing secularization as being at the heart of the Deuteronomic program.

---

50. Cf. Olson, *Death of Moses*, 21.

Chapter 3

The Presence of Yahweh and *Torah*: Deuteronomy 4:1–6:9

Like Deut 1:9–18, Deut 4:1–6:9 has been associated with a radical program of reform centered on centralization, secularization, and demythologization. In Deut 4, the presence of Yahweh is dealt with, and
this has led some scholars to see there a repudiation of the idea that
Yahweh was actually present in the midst of Israel. Deuteronomy 5:1–
6:9 presents the Decalogue and further deals with the presence of Yahweh. The differences in presentation of the Decalogue in Deut 5 and
in Exodus have been described as evidence of the unique aspects of the
theology of Deuteronomy and as representing secularization and demythologization, as we will see below.

For ease of analysis, I will consider the material in two sections.
Following the analysis of the prevailing view, I will articulate my understanding of the text and attempt to show how each subsection, as
well as the broader section as a whole, contributes to an understanding of Deuteronomy that emphasizes *Torah* and the supremacy of
Yahweh.

Deuteronomy 4

Deuteronomy 4 marks the final section of the first speech of Moses.
There is a clear shift in this chapter from the historical remembrance
of Deut 1–3 to the exhortation of Deut 4. Indeed, chap. 4 may be understood as a transition from the historical reflection that serves as a
basis for Moses' exhortation and the commandments that follow.[1]

The unity of this chapter has been the subject of much debate.
The presence in Deut 4 of the *Numeruswechsel* (the change in form of
address between second-person singular and plural) has suggested to
some that the chapter is a compilation of various sources. Verses 1–28
are predominantly plural, whereas vv. 29–40 are mostly singular. This
change has been used to identify different strata or sources. Begg, for

---

1. R. D. Nelson, *Deuteronomy* (OTL; Louisville: Westminster John Knox, 2002), 61.

example, identifies three blocks of material in the chapter (vv. 1–28, using plural; vv. 29–31, singular; vv. 32–40, singular).[2] In addition, others have identified thematic and linguistic differences in the chapter. Nelson sees evidence of the chapter's composite nature in the shift from an emphasis on the commandments and Yahweh's presence in the early verses to a condemnation of images, Israel's future fate, and then the singularity of Yahweh in the later verses. Moreover, he notes, the understanding of בְּרִית ("covenant") appears to differ in various places in the chapter.[3] Von Rad's perspective is typical of those who claim that the chapter has a composite character when he notes that

> the alternation between the use of the second person singular and the second person plural immediately indicates certain breaks in homogeneity. In fact, the contents do not make a perfect whole, for the admonitions proceed oddly along a double track. On the one hand the law revealed by Yahweh at Horeb is mentioned in comprehensive and general terms (vv. 9–14); but beside it there runs an exhortation which revolves around a single concern, namely that of making the prohibition of images compulsory (vv. 15–20, 23–24). This cannot be the original form.[4]

These issues related to the *Numeruswechsel*, style, and content have led many to conclude that the chapter is not a literary unity.[5]

On the other hand, the data are capable of being read very differently. Mayes, for example, argues that the language, form, and content of the chapter point to its unity.[6] In terms of language, he notes that use of terms and motifs in the chapter is consistent. So, to take just one example, the theme of the giving of the land is described in similar terms (בּוֹא, עָבַר, נָתַן) throughout the whole of Deut 4. In addition,

---

2. C. T. Begg, "The Literary Criticism of Deuteronomy 4,1–40: Contributions to a Continuing Discussion," *ETL* 56 (1980): 10–55. It should be noted that the blocks are not completely uniform in their use of singular or plural, but one or the other predominates.

3. Nelson, *Deuteronomy*, 62.

4. G. von Rad, *Deuteronomy* (OTL; London: SCM, 1966), 49.

5. Other commentators maintaining this view include I. Cairns, *Word and Presence: A Commentary on the Book of Deuteronomy* (ITC; Grand Rapids: Eerdmans / Edinburgh: Handsel, 1992); S. R. Driver, *A Critical and Exegetical Commentary on Deuteronomy* (ICC; Edinburgh: T. & T. Clark, [1901]); D. Knapp, *Deuteronomium 4: Literarische Analyse und theologische Interpretation* (Göttingen: Vandenhoeck & Ruprecht, 1987); S. Mittmann, *Deuteronomium 1:1–6:3 literarkritisch und traditionsgeschichtlich untersucht* (BZAW 139; Berlin: Alfred Töpelmann, 1975); A. Rofé, "The Monotheistic Argumentation in Deuteronomy IV 32–40: Contents, Composition and Text," *VT* 35, 4 (1985): 434–45. This is not to suggest, of course, that these interpreters are in agreement on every point. Rather, there is general agreement that the chapter is the result (somehow) of a combination of sources.

6. A. D. H. Mayes, "Deuteronomy 4 and the Literary Criticism of Deuteronomy," *JBL* 100 (1981): 24–30.

there is the repeated use of significant words, such as עֵינֶיךָ, חָיָה, and יָמִים, in all sections of Deut 4. Such "obvious consistency . . . points strongly to unity of authorship."[7]

The form of the chapter similarly points to its unity. Mayes understands the chapter as breaking down into six sections: vv. 1–4, 5–8, 9–14, 15–22, 23–31, and 32–40.[8] He further notes that five of these sections begin with a warning to obey the law and then follow up the warning with a reference to history.[9] In addition, it has been noted that the entire chapter resembles the pattern of ANE law codes and may be seen as having a prologue (vv. 1–8), a legal core (vv. 9–31), and an epilogue (vv. 32–40).[10] Further, vv. 9–31 resemble the form of an ANE treaty and contain treaty elements such as a prologue (vv. 10–14), stipulations (vv. 15–19, 23–24), and curses and blessings (vv. 25–31).[11]

Finally, the content of the chapter is interpreted as demonstrating its unity. There is in the chapter an emphasis on the law promulgated by Moses, a central tenet of that law (viz., the prohibition of images), and Yahweh's unique status. We will be examining the relationship between these elements in detail on pp. 127–134 below.

Some additional points should be noted in connection with the *Numeruswechsel*. First, it is possible to conceive of the change back and forth between singular and plural as an element of stylistics or rhetoric. Lohfink argued that the *Numeruswechsel* should be considered a stylistic device used to capture the attention of the listener.[12] Similarly, Lenchak argued that the number change serves as a rhetorical device to highlight the intention of the author/speaker: every change in number is "an assault on the listener."[13] Thus, the presence of the *Numeruswechsel* may be seen as part of the rhetorical and stylistic intention of

---

7. Ibid., 25.

8. Ibid. Most commentators see the unity of the chapter as extending to v. 40 only. The remaining verses, vv. 41–49, are usually not included in the analysis because they are not a part of Moses' first speech. A case can be made, however, for seeing the whole of the chapter as a unity, in that vv. 41–49 tie into the ideas of history and journey that are present in the rest of the chapter. Moreover, Deut 4:44–49 echoes the opening verses of the book (Deut 1:1–5) as an inclusio, with the elements of Deut 1:1–5 inverted in Deut 4:44–49. See J. G. McConville, *Deuteronomy* (AOTC 5; Leicester: Apollos / Downers Grove, IL: InterVarsity, 2002), 101.

9. Mayes, "Deuteronomy 4," 25.

10. G. Braulik, *Deuteronomium* (2 vols.; Neue Echter Bibel; Würzburg: Echter Verlag, 1986–92), 1: 38–39. See also D. L. Christensen, *Deuteronomy 1:1–21:9* (WBC 6a; Nashville: Thomas Nelson, 2001), 75.

11. McConville, *Deuteronomy*, 101; Mayes, "Deuteronomy 4," 25–26.

12. N. Lohfink, *Das Hauptgebot: Eine Untersuchung literarischer Einleitungsfragen zu Dtn 5–11* (AnBib 20; Rome: Pontifical Biblical Institute, 1963).

13. T. A. Lenchak, *"Choose Life!": A Rhetorical-Critical Investigation of Deuteronomy 28,69–30,20* (AnBib 129; Rome: Pontifical Biblical Institute, 1993), 13.

the author. Second, number change alone is an insufficient criterion to identify redactional layers, because some discern different strata even when there is no *Numeruswechsel.* Mittmann and Knapp, for example, identify multiple plural strata on theological grounds. [14] Consequently, caution must be exercised when using the *Numeruswechsel* to argue that the chapter is a literary composite. Indeed, Mayes notes that a later editor easily could have modified the putative sources so that there was consistency in number, and he concludes that the *Numeruswechsel* is "only one (and by no means a particularly strong one) of a number of criteria of literary critical division." [15]

Because of the consistency in form, language, and content described above, and because the *Numeruswechsel* has been shown to be an insufficient criterion to identify literary layers, it is reasonable to conclude that Deut 4 is best understood as a unity. [16] In light of this conclusion and in support of the unity of the chapter, the following broad structure for the chapter is posited: [17]

vv. 1–8   *Torah* of Yahweh pointing to uniqueness of Israel
            and presence of Yahweh
vv. 9–14   Divine encounter: the words of Yahweh
vv. 15–24   Worship of Yahweh alone in the manner he
            chooses
vv. 25–31   Idolatry leading to expulsion from land
vv. 32–40   Yahweh alone as God: word and presence
vv. 41–49   Word and history

---

14. Mittmann, *Deuteronomium,* 170–74; Knapp, *Deuteronomium 4,* 30. See the analysis of J. G. McConville, *Grace in the End: A Study in Deuteronomic Theology* (SOTBT; Grand Rapids: Zondervan, 1993), 36–39; and idem, *Deuteronomy,* 101.

15. Mayes, "Deuteronomy 4," 28. D. L. Christensen (*Deuteronomy 1:1–21:9* [2nd ed.; WBC 6a; Nashville: Thomas Nelson, 2001], 73) argues, based on his prosodic analysis of the chapter as a whole, that the *Numeruswechsel* actually *supports* the unity of the chapter rather than interfering with it.

16. Other interpreters holding to the essential unity of the chapter include R. E. Clements, "The Book of Deuteronomy: Introduction, Commentary, and Reflections," *NIB* 2: 271–538; N. Lohfink, "Verkündigung des Hauptgebots in der jüngsten Schicht des Deuteronomiums (Dt 4,1–40)," in *Höre Israel: Auslegung von Texten aus dem Buch Deuteronomium* (Die Welt der Bibel 18; Düsseldorf: Patmos, 1965); McConville, *Deuteronomy;* J. H. Tigay, *Deuteronomy* דברים*: The Traditional Hebrew Text with the New JPS Translation* (Philadelphia: Jewish Publication Society, 1996); M. Weinfeld, *Deuteronomy 1–11* (AB 5; New York: Doubleday, 1991).

17. I am here largely following McConville (*Deuteronomy,* 101–2), because he rightly argues that vv. 41–49 should be included as an integral part of the chapter. See also Christensen, *Deuteronomy 1:1–21:9,* 73, where a more detailed structure that reflects literary concentricity is proposed. At the center of the chiasm that Christensen envisions is the exclusion of Moses from the promised land, highlighting the need for adherence to *Torah.*

Prevailing View: Demythologization

As we have seen in chap. 1 above, one of the features of the Deutero-nomic revolution envisioned by Weinfeld and others is demythologization. In Deuteronomy, it is argued, conceptions of God that were considered "primitive" by the author(s) of the book were rejected, and a more nuanced theological understanding was advanced. We will now examine the ways in which demythologization is distinguished in Deut 4.

Deuteronomy 4 describes the encounter with Yahweh at Horeb and parallels the account in Exod 19. However, there are some important differences between the two texts that point to the particular theological concerns of the author(s) of Deuteronomy.

Corporeal Elements in Exodus

In Exod 19, Yahweh's presence is described in corporeal terms. Exodus 19:11 says that, on the third day, Yahweh would "come down" (יָרַד) on Mount Sinai. The actual descent is described in v. 20: Yahweh "came down" on the mountain. This can only be understood as describing Yahweh's actual presence on Mount Sinai. Weinfeld argues that the principal concern in Exod 19 is the danger that the people will see Yahweh, so Yahweh commands Moses to warn the people, "lest they break through to Yahweh to look (רָאָה) and many of them perish." As a result, boundaries are established in order to prevent people from approaching the mountain and seeing Yahweh.[18] Indeed, Weinfeld argues, in texts prior to Deuteronomy the concern is always the danger of seeing God (cf. Exod 33:20; Gen 32:31).[19]

The character of the Sinai narrative in Exodus is more complex than a simple corporeal understanding, a fact that Weinfeld acknowledges. While Exod 19 is clear in stating that Yahweh descended to the mountain, other texts are equally clear that Yahweh spoke "from heaven." Exodus 20:22 says that Moses is to remind the people that they have seen Yahweh speak "from heaven" (מִן־הַשָּׁמַיִם). In addition, fire and the כָּבוֹד of Yahweh appear in Exod 24:17. Thus, the Sinai narrative in Exodus is complex and nuanced but still conceives of Yahweh's actual descent to the mountain and his actual presence there.[20]

---

18. M. Weinfeld, *Deuteronomy and the Deuteronomic School* (Oxford: Oxford University Press, 1972; repr. Winona Lake, IN: Eisenbrauns, 1992), 206–7; and idem, *Deuteronomy 1–11*, 212–13.

19. Idem, *Deuteronomic School*, 207.

20. Idem, *Deuteronomy 1–11*, 213.

Demythologization in Deuteronomy 4

In Deut 4, however, the presentation is different. There is no reference
to Yahweh's having descended to the mountain. Rather, the emphasis
is on the fact that Yahweh speaks from heaven. Deuteronomy 4:36
notes that "Out of heaven he let you hear his voice, that he might discipline you. And on earth he let you see his great fire, and you heard
his words out of the midst of the fire." In Weinfeld's view, Yahweh
speaks from heaven and the words are heard out of the midst of the
fire on the mountain; he is not actually present there, because there is
no mention of descent.[21] Like the Sinai account in Exodus, Deut 4 includes the ideas of Yahweh's speaking from heaven and the presence
of fire, but it does so in a unique way. Weinfeld maintains that

> the particular contribution of the author of Deut 4:1–40 is the synthesis
> of the various traditions and the explicit manner in which this outlook
> is presented, which is not yet found in Exodus. He combines the speak-
> ing from heaven with the fire on the mountain in order to advance his
> abstract notion of the revelation: neither did God descend upon the
> mountain nor did the Israelites see any image during the revelation,
> they only heard God's words from the fire.[22]

The result is a demythologization of the conceptions of God found in
the earlier sources and a "shift in the centre of gravity of the theophany from the visual to the aural plane."[23] That is, the emphasis has
shifted: the danger in Deut 4 is not in seeing Yahweh, since Deuteronomy cannot conceive of being able to see him, but in hearing his
voice. Deuteronomy 4:32 speaks of the dangers of hearing God's voice
and marvels that the people of Israel were able to hear the voice of
Yahweh and yet live.[24]

A similar view is held by Mettinger. He maintains that, while the
Zion-Sabaoth theology is aniconic, it is still anthropomorphic. In contrast, the theology of Deut 4 is "programmatically abstract: during the

---

21. Idem, *Deuteronomic School*, 207. R. E. Clements, *God and Temple* (Oxford: Black-
well, 1965), 90–92, earlier argued in a similar fashion. Compare, however, the following,
later works, in which he advocates an actual, though invisible, presence at Horeb: *Deuteronomy* (OTG; Sheffield: Sheffield Academic Press, 1989), 51 ("when God revealed his will
to Israel at Mount Horeb . . . he was hidden in fire, and no form was visible"); idem, "Deuteronomy," 317 ("Israel heard a voice but saw no form of deity when the LORD God was
revealed as being present at Mt. Horeb"); idem, *The Book of Deuteronomy: A Preacher's Commentary* (EC; Peterborough: Epworth, 2001), 15 ("the lack of any visible form of God . . .
was important and is in accord with the tradition of Exod. 33:18–23 that the presence of
God can never be seen by human eyes").

22. Weinfeld, *Deuteronomy 1–11*, 213.

23. Idem, *Deuteronomic School*, 207.

24. Ibid., 207–8.

Sinai theophany, Israel perceived no form . . . she only heard the voice
of her God (Deut 4:12,15). The Deuteronomistic preoccupation with
God's voice and words represents an auditive, non-visual theme."[25]
Thus for Mettinger, as for Weinfeld, the absence of form as presented
in Deut 4 represents a shift toward a more abstract conception of God
and an alteration of the sense of his presence. In the theology of Deut
4, God has been "relocated" to heaven.[26]

Further evidence is cited by Hurowitz. While agreeing with Weinfeld's analysis of the location of Yahweh in the theophany, he maintains that the tendency toward demythologization may also be seen
in the "special effects—the sound and light show—that accompany
the theophany."[27] In Exod 19, there are "meteorological" and "seismological" dimensions to the theophany.[28] The descent and presence
of Yahweh are associated with thunder, lightning, smoke, and the
quaking of the earth. Moreover, the terms used to describe Yahweh's
voice are used differently in Exodus and Deuteronomy. In Exodus, the
term קוֹל ("voice," "sound," "thunder") sometimes is used in ways that
clearly indicate that "thunder" (rather than "voice" or "sound") is intended. So, for example, Exod 20:18 refers to the people as seeing
אֶת־הַקּוֹלֹת וְאֶת־הַלַּפִּידִם ("the thunder and the lightning"). Thus, he argues, Exod 19:19 should be translated "Moses would speak, and God
would answer him with thunder [בְקוֹל]."[29]

In Deuteronomy, the picture is very different. There is no mention
of a storm at Horeb. The word קוֹל appears several times in Deut 4, but
it is qualified in its first appearance by the term דְּבָרִים ("words").[30]
This suggests that what is intended is not thunder but a voice speaking intelligible words. Deuteronomy's apparent disinterest in thunder
(through its emphasis on קוֹל as voice and the lack of reference to
lightning) and lack of reference to meteorological phenomena generally in connection with the theophany is best seen, in Hurowitz's
view, as an attempt to distance Yahweh from the storm gods of the
surrounding cultures,[31] unlike the author of the Exodus narrative,

25. T. N. D. Mettinger, *The Dethronement of Sabaoth: Studies in the Shem and Kabod Theologies* (Lund: CWK Gleerup, 1982), 46.
26. Ibid., 47. Like many exegetes, Mettinger sees Deut 4 as belonging to the DtH
(which he refers to as the "D-work"), not to the original form of Deuteronomy.
27. V. Hurowitz, "From Storm God to Abstract Being: How the Deity Became More
Distant from Exodus to Deuteronomy," *BR* 14 (1998): 45.
28. Ibid.
29. Ibid., 46. Hurowitz erroneously says that Exod 19:20 should be so translated,
though Exod 19:19 is in view.
30. Ibid.
31. Ibid.

who has depicted Yahweh's presence at Sinai in the image of a storm god.[32]

Demythologization and the Prohibition of Images

The significance of this demythologizing may be seen in the theology of the chapter. Weinfeld maintains that the more abstract conception of God is the basis for the prohibition of idols in vv. 15 and following.[33] A God who has no visible form cannot be represented through the use of an image, because this would presuppose a form. Weinfeld does not state this explicitly, but an implicit logical conclusion from his argument is that the heavy emphasis on aniconic worship in Deut 4 serves to further the cause of demythologization. According to Deut 4:15–16, the basis for the prohibition of idols is the fact that no form was seen by the people. Moreover, Weinfeld maintains that, in deliberate contrast to Exod 19, Deut 4 omits any reference to a visible form of Yahweh, which would not comport with the thinking of the author(s) of the chapter. So, aniconic worship is intimately connected with and supportive of the demythologization intended by the author(s) of Deut 4.

The connection between aniconic worship and demythologization is made somewhat more explicit by Mettinger. He maintains that the prohibition of images was an attempt to "accentuate [Yahweh's] transcendence."[34] Whereas neighboring ANE cultures had gods in heaven, on earth, and in the underworld, Israel's emphasis on aniconic worship serves to "safeguard the border between God and the world."[35] The prohibition of images presumably serves to distance Israelite worship from overly immanent conceptions of Yahweh or the gods of the nations around Israel.

In this way, then, Deut 4 is seen as contributing to a radical program of demythologization. We will now evaluate the arguments presented in an effort to determine if the data of the text support this conclusion.

---

32. Ibid.

33. Weinfeld, *Deuteronomy 1–11*, 204.

34. T. N. D. Mettinger, "The Veto on Images and the Aniconic God in Ancient Israel," in *Religious Symbols and Their Functions: Based on Papers Read at the Symposium on Religious Symbols and Their Functions Held at Åbo on the 28th–30th of August 1978* (ed. H. Biezais; Stockholm: Almqvist & Wicksell, 1979), 26.

35. Ibid.

Evaluation

The central contention for demythologization in Deut 4 is the idea that, in contrast to the earlier sources, Deut 4 conceives of Yahweh as dwelling in heaven: he did not descend to the mountain, and he was not actually present. This contention has been challenged, however.

Actual Presence in Deuteronomy 4

There are numerous indications that Deuteronomy envisions the people as being in proximity to Yahweh at the declaration of the Decalogue and that he is conceived of as actually present. Wilson has persuasively argued that the terminology of Deut 4 points to this understanding.[36] It is telling that in Deut 4:10 the people are summoned to gather before Yahweh. This is expressed as עָמַדְתָּ לִפְנֵי יְהוָה ("you stood before Yahweh"). Wilson notes that in instances in which this phrase refers to a particular time and place, the sense is literal. Since Deut 4:10 makes reference to a particular time and place, it is probable that a literal sense is intended, and the text refers to the gathering of the people to stand in the (actual) presence of Yahweh.[37]

Another important example is the use of the phrase מִתּוֹךְ הָאֵשׁ ("out of the midst of the fire") in Deut 4:12, 15, 33, 36; 5:4, 22, 24, 26; 9:10; and 10:4. In every instance, the message is conveyed (either explicitly or through the context) that the people heard the voice of Yahweh out of the midst of the fire.[38] If Yahweh is said to be speaking "out of the midst of the fire," or his words are said to be heard from there, it is reasonable to conclude that he is thought to be present there. This is consistent with the six other instances in the Old Testament in which communication "out of the midst of" something is best understood as referring to the presence of the communicator (whether divine or human) in the place from which he speaks.[39]

In addition, Wilson notes that the very fact that the Israelites are prohibited from making images on the basis of the Horeb experience points to an understanding of the actual presence of Yahweh in the depiction in Deut 4. He notes that Deut 4:15–16 says that, "since you saw no form on the day that Yahweh spoke to you out of the midst of the fire, be careful lest you act corruptly by making a carved image." This seems to presuppose that Yahweh was actually present at Horeb,

---

36. I. Wilson, *Out of the Midst of the Fire: Divine Presence in Deuteronomy* (SBLDS 151; Atlanta: Scholars Press, 1995), 45–104.

37. Ibid., 47–49.

38. Ibid., 57–60.

39. Ibid., 60–61. The six instances are Exod 3:4, 24:16; Ps 22:23, 109:30, 116:19; Ezek 32:21.

because it is only on the basis of his presence that the people might be tempted to make an image to represent what they had experienced.[40] Wilson argues that if Yahweh

> were not present on that occasion there would seem to be little reason why the people's lack of perception of his form (i.e., as opposed to a denial of his Presence) should provide the basis for a section on the prohibition of images, or indeed why in that connection their experience at Horeb should be appealed to at all.[41]

But if the intention of the author is to convey Yahweh's invisible presence, then the prohibition of images is more coherent. The problem is that scholars (such as Weinfeld and Mettinger) who see demythologization in Deut 4 tend to equate noncorporeality and invisibility with absence. But invisibility and absence are not the same things. Deuteronomy 4 clearly portrays Yahweh as invisible, but this is not the same as saying he is absent.[42] Indeed, the chapter conceives of exposure to the fire and the voice as dangerous, which is consistent with the conclusion that Yahweh was actually present. Moreover, Deut 4:11–12 stresses that what the people have "seen with their eyes" they are to remember. This implies that their experience was one of the actual presence of Yahweh and that, though invisible in form, his presence was made known through the fire and his speaking from it.

It should be noted, too, that Deuteronomy, like Exodus, describes the mountain as being wrapped in "darkness, cloud, and gloom" (Deut 4:11). Hurowitz cites this as evidence of the shift in theological thinking in Deuteronomy, since, in his view, "in Deuteronomy God remains in heaven but draws up fire from the mountain to cover himself from below."[43] But if Yahweh remains in heaven, why is anything necessary to shield him from view? Covering would be necessary only if Yahweh is somehow actually present on the mountain, the very thing that is ostensibly denied in Deut 4.

The Nature of Differences between Exodus and Deuteronomy
It should also be noted that the differences between the Exodus account of Sinai and the presentation in Deut 4 are not as stark as Weinfeld and others maintain. As we have seen, Weinfeld claims that in Deut 4 the emphasis shifts to the aural plane, due to the desire on the part of the author(s) to deny the actual presence of Yahweh at Horeb. But this contention simply is not adequately supported by the data of

40. Ibid., 63–64.
41. Ibid., 64.
42. Ibid., 62–63.
43. Hurowitz, "Storm God," 44.

the text. Both Exod 19 and Deut 4 contain references to visual phenomena that are remarkably similar. In both chapters, the mountain is
said to be "wrapped" with either smoke (Exod 19:18) or "darkness,
cloud, and gloom" due to the fact that the mountain burned with fire
(Deut 4:18).[44] There is also (as we have seen) a repeated emphasis in
Deut 4 on what the people saw with their eyes and a subsequent exhortation on what they are not to forget.

In addition, it is simply not the case that Exodus stresses the danger of seeing Yahweh, while Deuteronomy emphasizes the danger of
hearing his voice. Exodus 20:19 demonstrates that there is mortal
danger in hearing Yahweh's voice, just as in Deuteronomy. While it is
true that Deut 4 does not describe the voice of Yahweh in terms of
thunder, as does Exodus, but instead emphasizes the *words* of Yahweh,
as Hurowitz rightly maintains,[45] it should also be noted that what
Moses heard as thunder (according to the Exodus account) was understandable to him as *words*. Moses is able to comprehend what Yahweh
says in thunder and then explain it to the people as words. So it is
simply not correct to say that Exodus emphasizes the visual at the expense of the aural. In both texts, there is danger in hearing Yahweh's
voice, and in both chapters Yahweh communicates in audible ways
that can be understood as words.

There are, of course, differences between the two texts. The most
significant perhaps is the fact that there is no reference to Yahweh's
actual descent to the mountain in Deut 4, as there is in Exodus. As we
have seen, Weinfeld and others contend that this is evidence of the
Deuteronomic author's rejection of the theology of the earlier material. But this does not take into consideration the rhetorical or communicative purposes of Deuteronomy.

One important aspect that is relevant here is the narrative perspective of the book. Wilson argues that the emphasis of Deut 4 is on the
experience of the people as a whole. Moses points out to the people,
in Deut 4:12, 15, 33, 36, that they experienced Yahweh speaking out
of the midst of the fire. This is stressed an additional four times elsewhere in the book.[46] There are no statements that "*we* heard his
voice," or "Yahweh spoke to *us*."[47]

Given this emphasis on the experience of the people, it is not so
surprising that details about Yahweh's descent are not present in Deut
4. Moreover, it is important to bear in mind that the references in

44. Wilson, *Midst of the Fire*, 92–93.
45. Ibid., 46.
46. Deut 5:4, 22; 9:10; 10:4.
47. Wilson, *Midst of the Fire*, 58.

Exod 19:11, 18, 20 to Yahweh's descent appear in a narrative description of the event itself. Within this narrative, there is a description of
the words that Yahweh spoke to Moses, which he was to tell the Israelites in preparation for the encounter. But the context of Deut 4 is
different. The description of the Horeb event appears in Deuteronomy in a sermon by Moses to prepare the people for the recitation of
the *Torah* and, ultimately, to prepare them for entry into the land.
Deuteronomy is not attempting to narrate the events of Horeb but
rather to re-present them homiletically in order to make the points of
the author(s). The fact that the author(s) of Deut 4 chose not to include details from the Exodus account may simply mean that they
did not comport with their communicative intentions and so were
left out. This becomes all the more likely when one remembers that in
Deut 4 there is an emphasis on the people as a whole. Simply put, a
description of the descent of Yahweh to Horeb or even a description
of the conversation between Moses and Yahweh regarding the prepa-
rations for the encounter does not involve the people.[48] As a result,
these features of the Exodus narrative were omitted. It is not necessary to conclude that the details were left out in an effort to repudiate
the theology implied by the earlier text.

Divine Presence in Deuteronomy 4
Though it may not be necessary to conclude that demythologization
is in view, in light of the arguments presented above, I have not yet
proved that Deut 4 does not have a demythologizing intent. Whether
demythologization is in view must be based on a more thorough
examination of the specific textual arguments in favor of demythologization. Accordingly, we now turn our attention to more specific features of the case for demythologization.

One of the crucial texts for the case for demythologization, as we
saw above (p. 118), is Deut 4:36. This verse says:

מִן־הַשָּׁמַיִם הִשְׁמִיעֲךָ אֶת־קֹלוֹ לְיַסְּרֶךָּ
וְעַל־הָאָרֶץ הֶרְאֲךָ אֶת־אִשּׁוֹ הַגְּדוֹלָה וּדְבָרָיו שָׁמַעְתָּ מִתּוֹךְ הָאֵשׁ׃

From heaven he caused you to hear his voice to discipline you,
and on earth he let you see his great fire, and you heard his words out
of the midst of the fire.

The relationship between the two lines of this verse is subject to debate. That the lines are meant to be parallel is clear from the fact that
both lines start with an adverbial phrase followed by a *Hiphil* verb. In
addition, in each line the indirect object is incorporated into the verb

48. Ibid., 92–95.

and is marked by a second-person singular pronominal suffix. The direct object in each line is marked by אֶת and includes a third-person singular pronominal suffix. The final point is particularly suggestive, because it is the only place in Deuteronomy in which "his fire" (אִשּׁוֹ) appears, though there are, of course, many other references to fire in connection with Horeb in Deuteronomy. This points to a deliberate insertion of the term here, which in turn suggests that the intention is to express parallelism between the two halves of the verse ("his voice" [קֹלוֹ] is made parallel to "his fire" [אִשּׁוֹ]).[49] In addition, there is parallelism in the terminology used, such as "heaven/earth" and "see/hear."

It is common to see the relationship between the lines as antithetical parallelism. In this view, the two halves of the verse are expressing contrasting ideas. This is the basis of Weinfeld's contention that this verse denies Yahweh's actual presence. In Weinfeld's view, the sense of Deut 4:36 is: "You heard his voice *from heaven*, but on earth all you saw was fire (since he was not actually on earth)"; a contrast is being drawn in the two lines of the verse.

This view, however, is untenable in light of v. 36 itself, as well as Deut 4 as a whole. Verse 36b links the two parts of the verse together, because the "words" (corresponding to the first line) are heard "out of the midst of the fire" (corresponding to the second line). Wilson notes that the adverbial phrase in line one must be taken as referring to the subject and therefore indicates where Yahweh was at the time he spoke. This, of course, is granted by Weinfeld and others. But then the adverbial phrase in line two must also be taken as referring to the subject of its main clause, which again is Yahweh.[50] This indicates that, according to Deut 4:36, Yahweh is present *both* in heaven and on earth. MacDonald concludes that "it is not that the heavenly aspect of the Horeb revelation is substantial, whilst the earthly aspect is superficial. The two aspects of the revelation form a whole."[51] This understanding is further supported by the fact that the phrase מִתּוֹךְ הָאֵשׁ ("out of the midst of the fire") is best understood as referring to Yahweh's actual presence, as we have seen.

In addition, the very chapter containing v. 36, in which an antithetical understanding of "see/hear" is posited, contains evidence that points to a complementary understanding. These same words appear as imperatives in Deut 4:1, 5 and point to the need for all the senses to be involved in apprehending the *Torah*.[52] The words appear

49. Ibid., 67–68.
50. Ibid., 68.
51. N. MacDonald, *Deuteronomy and the Meaning of "Monotheism"* (FAT 2/1; Tübingen: Mohr Siebeck, 2003), 193.
52. Ibid., 194.

again in Deut 4:9–10, where Israel is commanded to remember what it has seen and heard. This suggests that, though no form was seen, the visual component of the revelation at Horeb is not unimportant. Indeed, immediately prior to the verse that is understood as drawing such a stark contrast between hearing and seeing (v. 36), Deut 4:33 and 35 demonstrate that the revelation at Horeb consists of things both heard (v. 33) and seen (v. 35).[53]

It should be further noted that Deut 4:39 contains the claim that יְהוָה הוּא הָאֱלֹהִים בַּשָּׁמַיִם מִמַּעַל וְעַל־הָאָרֶץ מִתָּחַת ("Yahweh is God in the heavens above and on the earth below"). MacDonald has argued that v. 39 is the realization of the demand for acknowledgement contained in v. 35. This realization contains the claim that Yahweh is God of both heaven *and* earth, which finds its contextual and logical support in v. 36. He notes that "if the intention of v. 36 is to argue that YHWH is to be exclusively located in heaven then v. 36 not only fails to provide the logical basis for v. 39, but is in contradiction to it."[54]

On the basis of this, it seems reasonable to conclude that Deut 4 conceives of Yahweh as present *both* in heaven *and* on earth. This theology is known elsewhere in the Old Testament; for example, it finds expression in several Psalms (e.g., Pss 11, 14, 20, 76, 78).[55] As Mettinger notes, the "mythical concept of space" is used to designate the situation in which two spaces are understood as holding the same content at the same time so that the distinction between them is obliterated, and he sees this conception in various Psalms.[56] Indeed, he maintains that the mythical concept of space "may help to explain those passages which so unconcernedly locate God simultaneously on earth and in heaven."[57] Thus, it is entirely plausible that Deut 4 (esp. Deut 4:36) is conceiving of Yahweh's presence in a similar manner. Even if, for the sake of argument, it is granted that the Exodus account of the events at Sinai conceives of Yahweh as descending to earth so that he is no longer in heaven, it is simply not clear that Deut 4 seeks to refute this view with the notion that Yahweh is *only* in heaven. Rather, it is likely that Deut 4 conceives of Yahweh as present in heaven *and* on earth. Given that Weinfeld himself recognizes that the Exodus account is *not* simply asserting that Yahweh is only on

---

53. Ibid.

54. Ibid., 193.

55. See, e.g., J. D. Levenson, *Sinai and Zion: An Entry into the Jewish Bible* (Minneapolis: Winston, 1985), 137–42.

56. Mettinger, *Dethronement*, 30. For a fuller discussion of mythical space, see B. S. Childs, *Myth and Reality in the Old Testament* (SBT 27; London: SCM, 1960), 84–94.

57. Mettinger, *Dethronement*, 30.

earth, as we have seen,[58] it is apparent that the differences between the accounts in Exodus and Deuteronomy are not what is usually claimed. Indeed, it has been argued that the Sinai narrative in Exodus, like the presentation in Deut 4, emphasizes Yahweh's transcendence in rather a similar way.[59]

In light of the foregoing analysis, we have reason to be cautious about seeing demythologization at the center of the intention of the author(s) of Deut 4. Indeed, we have seen that the data are plausibly read quite differently. We will now turn our attention to providing an alternative understanding of the text in an effort to account for the unique aspects of the material in Deut 4.

Alternative View: Presence and Word

I have argued above that the differences between the accounts of the revelation at Sinai/Horeb in Exodus and Deut 4 are not of the sort that is often claimed. Yet there are, of course, differences that must be explained. In this section, I will present an alternative to the view that demythologization is at the center of the chapter and will instead argue that Deut 4 presents a nuanced understanding of the presence of Yahweh that highlights his immanence and transcendence and points to the importance of *Torah*.

As noted above, some of the differences between the presentation of the revelation at Horeb in Exodus and Deut 4 may be explained in terms of the rhetorical and communicative intentions of the author(s). That is, the events at Horeb are presented in Deut 4 in the context of a sermon focused primarily on the experience of the people. It is, therefore, not surprising that certain elements from the narrative in Exodus were omitted; they did not further the purpose of the author(s) of Deut 4. This does not, however, go far enough in explaining the presentation of the theophany of Deut 4.

Actualization of the Presence of Yahweh in Deuteronomy 4

Deuteronomy 4 is at pains to highlight the unique nature of Yahweh and his actions on behalf of Israel. The two themes are actually linked, as we shall see. Yahweh's uniqueness and incomparability are expressed most completely in Deut 4:32–40. As we have seen, Deut 4:36 expresses the idea that Yahweh is present both in heaven and on earth. This in turn leads to the assertion that Yahweh is "God in heaven above and on earth beneath" (יְהוָה הוּא הָאֱלֹהִים בַּשָּׁמַיִם מִמַּעַל וְעַל־

---

58. See p. 117 above.

59. E. W. Nicholson, "The Decalogue as the Direct Address of God," *VT* 27 (1977): 422–33.

הָאָרֶץ מִתָּחַת). This expression is used infrequently in the Old Testament, occurring in just three other instances (Josh 2:11; 1 Kgs 8:23; Eccl 5:1).[60] The first two instances are similar to the usage in Deut 4:39. Ecclesiastes 5:1, however, draws a contrast between the location of God and human beings, implying that the ubiquity of Yahweh's presence is in view in the use of the phrase elsewhere. That Deut 4:36 is intended as a statement of Yahweh's unique status is demonstrated by the final clause of Deut 4:39, which states אֵין עוֹד ("there is no other"). This statement is widely recognized as being a monotheistic assertion, denying the very existence of other gods.[61] Thus, Yahweh is portrayed as utterly unique, being the only God that exists.

The uniqueness of Yahweh is further seen in the rhetorical questions posed in Deut 4:32–34. The actions of Yahweh on behalf of the Israelites in the events surrounding and including the exodus from Egypt are utterly unique. No other god (whose existence is later denied) has ever acted in the way that Yahweh has. In this regard, it is noteworthy that the "outstretched arm" of Deut 4:34 is here applied to Yahweh, as in Exodus it is Moses' "outstretched arm" that is the symbol of Yahweh's power and authority.[62] It seems that Deuteronomy wants to ensure that no mistake is made regarding the source of the powerful acts of the exodus. This further highlights the claims being made about Yahweh's uniqueness.

But these claims regarding Yahweh's distinctiveness are linked with claims of Israel's uniqueness as well. The rhetorical question in v. 33 has to do with Israel's uniqueness. No nation, according to Deut 4:33, has experienced what Israel experienced at Horeb. The people of Israel alone have heard the voice of God[63] and lived.

---

60. MacDonald, *Monotheism*, 195. Ecclesiastes 5:6 is erroneously cited as the third instance of the appearance of the pairing. For an examination of ANE data related to the appellation "Lord of Heaven" and the concomitant claims of singularity being made by using the epithet, see R. A. Oden, "*Ba'al Šāmēm* and *'Ēl*," *CBQ* 35 (1977): 457–73.

61. So Weinfeld, *Deuteronomy 1–11*, 212; E. H. Merrill, *Deuteronomy* (NAC 4; Nashville: Broadman & Holman, 1994), 133; P. C. Craigie, *The Book of Deuteronomy* (NICOT; Grand Rapids: Eerdmans, 1976), 143.

62. McConville, *Deuteronomy*, 112.

63. The translation of vv. 33–34 is often somewhat confused. As C. J. H. Wright (*Deuteronomy* [NIBC 4; Peabody, MA: Hendrickson / Carlisle: Paternoster, 1996], 60) notes, it is best to be consistent in the translation of אֱלֹהִים in vv. 33–34. Many translations render אֱלֹהִים as referring to Yahweh in v. 33 ("God"), but referring to other gods ("gods") in v. 34. Consistency, however, is preferred. In this case, אֱלֹהִים should either be rendered "god" in both cases or "God" in both cases. The first option would stress the unique nature of Yahweh in comparison to other gods. The second option would, as Wright correctly argues, preserve the emphasis on Yahweh's uniqueness, while also stressing the singularity of Israel's experience, which also is in view in vv. 35–40.

The rhetorical questions in Deut 4:32–34 are balanced by the presence of rhetorical questions in Deut 4:7–8. The questions there ask,

כִּי מִי־גוֹי גָּדוֹל אֲשֶׁר־לוֹ אֱלֹהִים קְרֹבִים אֵלָיו כַּיהוָה אֱלֹהֵינוּ בְּכָל־קָרְאֵנוּ אֵלָיו׃
וּמִי גּוֹי גָּדוֹל אֲשֶׁר־לוֹ חֻקִּים וּמִשְׁפָּטִים צַדִּיקִם כְּכֹל הַתּוֹרָה הַזֹּאת אֲשֶׁר אָנֹכִי נֹתֵן
לִפְנֵיכֶם הַיּוֹם׃

What great nation is there that has a god so near to it as Yahweh our God is to us, whenever we call on him? And what great nation is there that has statutes and ordinances as righteous as all this *Torah* that I am setting before you today?

The emphasis is on Israel's unique experience of Yahweh's nearness and their status as recipients of *Torah*.

At first glance, there appears to be little relationship between the two questions; they appear to be raising two different issues. However, there is a syntactical relationship between them that suggests that they are related to one another.[64] Both begin with the interrogative pronoun מִי followed by the identical expression "great nation" (גּוֹי גָּדוֹל). Both contain the relative particle followed by the preposition ל with the third-person masculine-singular pronominal suffix, and this is followed by the specific items being described. On the basis of this close syntactical relationship, it appears that a deliberate parallelism is being drawn. If so, then the sense here is that the nearness of Yahweh and the *Torah* are closely related. That the nearness of Yahweh and the *Torah* may be closely connected is supported by Deut 30:11–14, where the nearness of God is closely associated with "commandments."[65]

The logical inference to be drawn from this is that it is through *Torah* that Yahweh's nearness is experienced by Israel.[66] Yahweh's immanence is somehow expressed and experienced through his word. That the Decalogue, the foremost expression of the statutes and ordinances, is explicitly identified with the covenant in Deut 4:13 is particularly significant. This suggests that demonstrating loyalty to Yahweh through the keeping of the covenant (i.e., by following the instructions of *Torah*) is more than simply a legal requirement. Rather, it is a means of experiencing the nearness of Yahweh. As Miller notes, "The righteous commandments and the keeping of them is the way that God is somehow known and found in the midst of the community."[67]

64. P. D. Miller Jr., *Deuteronomy* (Interp; Louisville: John Knox, 1990), 56.
65. Ibid.
66. Cf. ibid., 56–57; J. G. McConville and J. G. Millar, *Time and Place in Deuteronomy* (JSOTSup 179; Sheffield: Sheffield Academic Press, 1994), 134–35.
67. Miller, *Deuteronomy*, 57.

It should also be noted that the keeping of *Torah* is identified as wisdom in Deut 4:6. Since the keeping of *Torah* is a means of actualizing Yahweh's presence, there is an inherently religious component to wisdom in the conception of Deut 4. That is, to keep the commandments is to experience Yahweh's presence. This, in turn, is wisdom. The logic here is not terribly far removed from the elements of wisdom literature that stress the fear of Yahweh as being the beginning of wisdom (Job 28:28; Prov 1:7).[68]

This understanding of Yahweh's immanence is a radical departure from the view of, for example, Mettinger, who argued that in Deut 4 Yahweh is "relocated" to heaven.[69] In my view, Yahweh's immanent presence is firmly established through *Torah*. He is not "relocated" but is, rather, present in some way through *Torah*—the manner that he, as the unique God, has chosen.

It should be noted that this conception of Yahweh's presence is not in itself a form of demythologization, because it seems clear that Yahweh's presence through *Torah*-adherence is not exhaustive. That is, Deuteronomy here is conceiving of Yahweh's presence qualitatively or experientially rather than spatially or quantitatively. Given the emphasis on Yahweh's actual presence described above, the idea of Yahweh's presence through *Torah* and its adherence should be seen as a complement to that idea, not a contrast.

Prohibition of Images

This points to a different conception of the prohibition of images as well. As we have seen, Weinfeld maintains that the prohibition of images is necessary because Yahweh was *not* actually present at Horeb.[70] Accordingly, there is nothing to represent, and attempts to do so would ascribe a form to a God who was not present or visible. But, if Deut 4 is in fact advancing the idea that Yahweh's presence is somehow manifest at least in part through his word and *Torah*, then a different basis for the prohibition of images must be sought.

The prohibition of images and idolatry is set forth in Deut 4:15–24 (consequences of forbidden worship are dealt with in the next section, vv. 25–31). The section begins with the call for the Israelites to guard themselves carefully, because they saw no form at Horeb but heard a voice. This is followed by the warning against corrupting themselves by making an idol or any kind of image (vv. 16–18) or by worshiping the heavenly host (v. 19). The language in vv. 16–18 is reminiscent of

---

68. See pp. 102–103 above.
69. Mettinger, *Dethronement*, 46; see above, pp. 118–119.
70. Weinfeld, *Deuteronomy 1–11*, 204.

the creation account in Gen 1:14–27.[71] This serves two purposes in Deut 4. First, it serves to appropriate the theology of Gen 1:26, where human beings alone are created in the image and likeness of God.[72] This highlights the opposition to images because there is, for Israel, already an "image" of God in human beings. Additionally, the careful allusion to Gen 1 serves to highlight "heaven and earth," which points again to theological reflection on the nature of Yahweh's presence on earth and in heaven in Deut 4. As MacDonald notes, all the animals in Deut 4:16–18 are of the earthly sphere, whereas the concern in v. 19 is with the heavenly sphere.[73] This parallels the emphasis in Deut 4:36–39 on the fact that Yahweh is God in heaven above and on earth below.[74]

The logic, then, is that Yahweh alone is God and, therefore, it is illegitimate to worship any God but him. Worshiping anything but Yahweh on earth or in heaven is to worship what is created by Yahweh (as the Gen 1 allusion affirms); it is to worship the creation as opposed to the creator.[75] This, I believe, is the point being made in Deut 4:19, where it is said that the heavenly host consists of things that Yahweh has "allotted (חָלַק) to all the peoples under the whole heaven." Many interpreters understand this verse as saying that Yahweh has permitted or even ordained the worship of sun, moon, and stars on the part of other nations.[76] But this interpretation is based on the assumption that the heavenly host is allotted to all *other* people *for them to worship.* This is not stated in the text. The term חָלַק may mean "to assign," without the sense of dividing (cf. Job 20:29, 39:17; Jer 10:16; Hab 1:16).[77] Moreover, the text says that the sun, moon, and stars are assigned to all peoples under heaven, presumably including Israel, since no exception is noted. In this case, Deut 4:19 would be saying that

71. It is not, however, a precise reversal as, for example, Wright (*Deuteronomy*, 51) maintains. MacDonald (*Monotheism*, 196–97) notes that some elements in Deut 4:16–18 do not appear in Gen 1.

72. McConville, *Deuteronomy*, 108. This is seen as "aggadic exegetical adaptation" by M. Fishbane, *Biblical Interpretation in Ancient Israel* (Oxford: Clarendon, 1985), 321–22.

73. MacDonald, *Monotheism*, 197.

74. Ibid.

75. In Gen 1, there is an extended polemic against the beliefs of ANE cultures with regard to creation. Genesis in effect argues that everything that is worshiped as gods in other cultures was created by the one true God, Yahweh. (See G. J. Wenham, *Genesis 1–15* [WBC 1; Waco, TX: Word, 1987], 36–40.) If this is correct, and Fishbane's assessment of the relationship between Gen 1 and Deut 4:16–17 is accurate, then Deut 4 may be understood as adhering to the underlying ideology of Gen 1.

76. Weinfeld, *Deuteronomy 1–11*, 206; W. Brueggemann, *Deuteronomy* (AbOTC; Nashville: Abingdon, 2001), 55; Craigie, *Deuteronomy*, 137; Driver, *Deuteronomy*, 70.

77. M. Tsevat, "חָלַק *chālaq* II," *TDOT* 4: 451.

Israel is not to worship what is given to all people as a blessing from Yahweh. God created and assigned the sun, moon, and stars as light for all people, not as something to be worshiped. Israel is being reminded that they have a unique calling to be the people of Yahweh, and the people are to live out this calling first through the proper worship of Yahweh, not through the worship of what has been given to all people.[78]

More specifically with respect to images, the text points to the fact that Israel is to worship Yahweh as he has decreed. According to Deut 4:15, Israel is not to make idols, because they saw no form on the day that Yahweh spoke to them at Horeb. This ties image-prohibition to the previous emphasis (esp. in Deut 4:12) on the fact that the people saw no form but only heard the voice of Yahweh. As Wright aptly notes,

> the contrast is not between visible and invisible, or between spiritual and material, but *between the visible and the audible*. Idols have "form" but do not speak. Yahweh has no "form," but he decisively speaks. Idols are visible but dumb. Yahweh is invisible but eloquent.[79]

As we have seen, the words of Yahweh are the means by which his presence is manifest in Israel. So, making an image would be an attempt to actualize Yahweh's presence in a manner that is, first of all, contrary to the means he desires. It would be an attempt to substitute the speaking Yahweh, whose presence is manifest at least in part through his words, with a mute idol or image. Through his words, Yahweh confronts, rebukes, demands, and challenges. Attempting to represent Yahweh with a lifeless image would serve to "gag" him. "Idolatry therefore is fundamentally an escape from the living voice and commands of the living God."[80]

Second, constructing an image of Yahweh would serve to localize his presence in the place where the image is. But the very next section (Deut 4:25–31) indicates that even (from the perspective of the narrative of Deuteronomy) in the distant future, after the people have rebelled against Yahweh and worshiped him inappropriately or followed other gods, they can still realize Yahweh's presence by seeking

---

78. See Wright, *Deuteronomy*, 51–52; Merrill, *Deuteronomy*, 123 n. 174. The *Geneva Bible* (1560) advocated this understanding in a marginal note to this text, maintaining that God appointed the sun, moon, and stars to serve man (so they are therefore not to be worshiped). G. von Rad (*Wisdom in Israel* [Nashville: Abingdon, 1972], 185) argues that the polemic in wisdom literature against images is essentially that the creator cannot be represented in an image but is seen, rather, in what was created.

79. Wright, *Deuteronomy*, 50–51.

80. Ibid., 71.

him. Yahweh's nearness is thus stressed, because the people will "find him" (Deut 4:29). The role of *Torah* as the mode of actualizing Yahweh's presence is seen in v. 30, where it is said that the people will "obey his voice." It appears, then, that the presence of Yahweh is associated, not just with the words themselves, but also with the obedience of the people to the *Torah*. As MacDonald rightly observes, "To have the commandments, or even to obey the commandments is not 'to have Yʜwʜ,' but neither can Yʜwʜ be found by the people, that is, be present to them, unless they have the commandments and obey them. . . . [T]he presence of Yʜwʜ has both heavenly and earthly aspects."[81]

In this light, the prohibition of images is seen rather differently. Images are not proscribed because no form could have been seen but because images are an inappropriate way of actualizing Yahweh's presence.[82] Making images is inappropriate because it is contrary to Yahweh's will regarding the way his presence is to be manifested and also because it is too restrictive. Yahweh is God of *all* of heaven above and earth beneath. Therefore, his presence cannot be localized in an idol. To do so would be an attempt to place Yahweh under the "reach and control of the worshipers," which, having fixed his location, would make God available at the spot chosen by the people and on their terms.[83] This, however, is incompatible with the freedom and sovereignty claimed for Yahweh. So, rather than being a "digression"[84] from the primary interests of the chapter, the prohibition of images is central to the concerns of the chapter, and it is inextricably related to the issue of Yahweh's presence and how it is to be actualized.

This represents a rather sophisticated understanding of the presence of Yahweh that balances his transcendence and immanence. His immanence is apparent in his nearness to Israel, a specific people living in a particular time and place. At the same time, the transcendence of Yahweh is apparent in his ubiquity and freedom to choose how he will be worshiped and in the fact that his presence is manifest in *Torah* and its adherence, something that transcends the particularities of

---

81. MacDonald, *Monotheism*, 201.

82. Cf. Nelson, *Deuteronomy*, 65. R. P. Carroll ("The Aniconic God and the Cult of Images," *ST* 31 [1977]: 56) proposes another tantalizing possible reason underlying the prohibition of images. He suggests that Yahweh manifests himself to Israel in a relationship. He further notes that "a relationship characterizes a contiguity between two parties but is in itself highly abstract. As such it hardly permits of representation of a concrete nature. The god is experienced as a presence but not a presence that can be tangibly reproduced. So no images symbolize this relationship in the cult of Yahweh."

83. Cairns, *Word and Presence*, 59.

84. Nelson, *Deuteronomy*, 62.

time, space, and even, perhaps, the particularities of Israel itself (cf. Deut 4:6).[85]

The previous discussion suggests that the differences between the account of the revelation at Horeb in Exodus and the account in Deuteronomy are not of the sort that Weinfeld and others maintain. In contrast to the concerns of Exodus, one of the primary concerns of Deut 4 is to explicate the means by which Yahweh continues to be present with Israel after the people have departed from Horeb. The phenomenal manifestations (described as "meteorological and seismological" by Hurowitz[86]) of Yahweh's presence ceased after the departure from Sinai. In the narrative world of Deuteronomy, the people are about to enter the promised land, where their lives will change dramatically. At this important moment of transition, the people are assured that Yahweh will continue to be near them through *Torah* and their adherence to it. Idolatry, the elevation of image over word, would be an improper actualization of Yahweh's presence and would jeopardize their experience of that presence and also the possession of the land. So the accounts in Exodus and Deut 4 are not diametrically opposed to one another.

This emphasis on the moment of transition helps explain the somewhat puzzling mention of Moses' denial of entry into the land in Deut 4:21–22. In the middle of the discussion of the prohibition of images, the people are reminded that Moses will not go with them into the land. This has little to do with the issue of idolatry. But if the basis of the prohibition of images is the fact that the use of images would be an inappropriate attempt to actualize Yahweh's presence, the refusal becomes more clear. Ever since the departure from Horeb, Moses has been the mediator of Yahweh's words. This is one means by which Yahweh manifests his presence to the people. Moses' death means that he will not accompany the people into the land, and, more importantly, he will no longer mediate Yahweh's presence. The inclusion of this in the prohibition of images suggests that the Israelites were to recognize the supremacy of Yahweh in determining how his presence is to be experienced; they are not to resort to inappropriate means or cling to previous means that have been superseded.[87]

---

85. McConville and Millar, *Time and Place,* 135–37.

86. Hurowitz, "Storm God," 45.

87. MacDonald, *Monotheism,* 198. D. T. Olson (*Deuteronomy and the Death of Moses: A Theological Reading* [OBT; Minneapolis: Fortress, 1994], 35) suggests that the reminder of Moses' death outside the land appears here either because the land had become an idol for Moses (and his death outside the land serves as a warning) or because Moses may have become the object of idolatrous worship (and so his death serves as a warning to the people). But there is no solid textual evidence to support these possibilities. Entry into the land

Conclusions regarding Deuteronomy 4

Through its emphasis on *Torah*, Deut 4 shows that Yahweh's immanence is maintained, while his transcendent sovereignty is retained in
his ubiquity and in the fact that his presence, manifested somehow in
Torah and its adherence, is available at all times and places, and perhaps even to all people as well. From the narrative perspective of the
book, addressed to the people gathered on the verge of entering the
land, Deut 4 explains how the people may continue to experience the
presence of Yahweh in the land.

This understanding of the presence of Yahweh helps clarify the
purpose of the prohibition of images. I have argued that the emphasis
on aniconic worship serves to prevent illegitimate actualizations of
Yahweh's presence. He, as the God of heaven and earth, has determined that his presence will be manifest in *Torah* and its adherence.
Attempts to actualize his presence through the use of images would
be to manipulate him and to localize his presence inappropriately. It
would also serve to elevate images (which are lifeless) over the word
of Yahweh (which is living and powerful).

Deuteronomy 4, then, does deal with the presence of Yahweh but
not in a way that could be called demythologization. Deuteronomy 4
portrays Yahweh as actually present with his people at Horeb and explains the means by which he will continue to be present with them
in the near and distant future, while at the same time protecting his
transcendence.

This nuanced sense of Yahweh's presence has important implications for worship. Proper worship (i.e., aniconic worship in accordance with *Torah*) is vital in order for the nation to continue to experience Yahweh's presence. Aniconic worship is not incidental to
proper Yahweh worship but is, rather, central to it, because iconic
worship would be an inappropriate actualization of Yahweh's presence. Yahweh is to be worshiped as he truly is, the God of heaven and
earth who speaks. Proper worship, then, is necessary as the first step
toward demonstrating total loyalty to Yahweh.

---

may have become an idol for Moses, but it is equally possible that this remained a legitimate, heartfelt desire and never became idolatrous. The text does not state that Moses' desire was idolatrous. Similarly, there is no evidence in Deuteronomy that Moses was
worshiped by the people. Given the emphasis on the realization of Yahweh's presence in
Deut 4, it is better, in my estimation, to conclude that the reminder of Moses' death is related to the means by which Yahweh's presence is to be manifest, as I have argued.

Deuteronomy 5:1–6:9

We have examined Deut 4 and found that it has a sophisticated understanding of the presence of Yahweh and an emphasis on the role of *Torah* in the life of the nation. We will now turn our attention to the next section of the book that has been understood as representing demythologization and secularization. Once again, I will present several scholars' understanding of this section and evaluate it in an effort to determine if it represents the best interpretation of the data. I will then present an alternative interpretation of the section.

In Deut 5:1, a new section of the book begins. While it is common to argue that Moses' second speech begins at Deut 4:44,[88] there is nevertheless a break at Deut 5:1. The links between Deut 4:44–49 and Deut 1:1–5 suggest that these two texts form an inclusio, and the former section should be seen as marking the end of this section of the book. Lundbom notes that Deut 4:44–49 "prepares the audience for the giving of the law no more or less than all of chs. i–iii. It therefore has no preeminent claim to being the introduction" to Deut 5–28.[89] Moreover, the final verses of Deut 4 serve to bring to a close the historical remembrance that marks so much of Deut 1–4. Though the past is not forgotten or ignored, the concern from this point on in the book is more the future. Thus, chaps. 1–4 as a whole serve well as an introduction to the rest of the book, and they also serve to prepare the reader for the giving of the law in chap. 5.

My examination of this section will extend to Deut 6:9, because chaps. 5 and 6 represent a single, unified argument. This is supported by the fact that 5:27–6:3 demonstrates a chiastic structure.[90] In addition, the concern of chap. 6 is with the extension of the Decalogue, presented in Deut 5, into the lives of the people. The specific concern of Deut 6:4–9 is the explication of the relationship between loyalty to Yahweh and *Torah*, and this relationship highlights the priorities of Deut 5–6. Though the argument continues, all the key issues raised in chap. 6 are present by v. 9. Though a detailed examination of the

---

88. See, e.g., A. D. H. Mayes, *Deuteronomy* (NCB; Grand Rapids: Eerdmans / London: Marshall, Morgan & Scott, 1979), 159–60; Cairns, *Word and Presence*, 66; Brueggemann, *Deuteronomy*, 62–63. Some conclude that Deut 4:44–45 comprises two separate introductions to what were originally two separate speeches in Deut 5–11 (see C. A. Steuernagel, *Deuteronomium, Josua, Einleitung zum Hexateuch* [HKAT; Göttingen: Vandenhoeck & Ruprecht, 1900], 20–21, cited in McConville, *Deuteronomy*, 101). This, however, is unnecessary if, as I argue below, Deut 4:44–49 taken with Deut 1:1–5 is an inclusio, and the whole of chaps. 1–4 serves as an introduction to the giving of the law.

89. J. R. Lundbom, "The Inclusio and Other Framing Devices in Deuteronomy I–XXVIII," *VT* 46 (1996): 296–315.

90. Lohfink, *Hauptgebot*, 67–68.

entire book would demonstrate the need for and plausibility of an alternative understanding of the theology of Deuteronomy, the point may be made by looking at the initial verses of the chapter. Accordingly, my analysis will end at Deut 6:9.

Prevailing View: Demythologization and Secularization

Deuteronomy 5:1–6:9 continues the description of the encounter with Yahweh at Horeb that began in Deut 4. As a result, there are continued parallels with the Sinai narrative in Exodus. There are, however, important differences between the texts. The major differences have to do with the understanding of the presence of Yahweh and the presentation of the Sabbath law. We will examine these issues in turn and see how the presentation in Deuteronomy has been understood in terms of demythologization and secularization.

Presence of Yahweh

As was the case with Deut 4, the presence of Yahweh in Deut 5:1–6:9 has been seen as a contrast with the presentation in earlier sources. The earlier sources are held to be more anthropomorphic, stressing the immanence of Yahweh, whereas Deuteronomy seeks to deny the presence of Yahweh in favor of seeing him as remaining in heaven, thus stressing his transcendence.

In Deut 5, this may be seen in the description of the encounter with Yahweh at Horeb. Deuteronomy 5:4 says that Yahweh spoke "face to face" (פָּנִים בְּפָנִים) with the people at Horeb. Weinfeld maintains that the idea of a "face to face" experience with Yahweh is foreign to the thinking of Deuteronomy and cites as evidence the fact that Deut 4:12 and 15 maintain that no form was seen by the Israelites at Horeb.[91] In addition, he notes that the expression used (פָּנִים בְּפָנִים) is not the usual expression for "face to face," which would be פָּנִים אֶל־פָּנִים. The use of this less-common expression may, he argues, suggest an attempt on the part of the author to "obscure the more common phrase" because it did not comport with his understanding of divine presence.[92]

As in Deut 4, the present text appears to stress the aural over the visual, in Weinfeld's view. So, Deut 5:26 stresses the wonder of having heard the voice of the living God and survived. As we saw above (pp. 117–118), the danger of the revelation at Sinai in the Exodus presentation was seeing Yahweh. The aural is stressed in Deut 5 because

---

91. Weinfeld, *Deuteronomy 1–11*, 239.
92. Ibid.

the author(s) of the book could not conceive of being able to see Yahweh. This is another example of demythologization, because the conception of God is transformed from anthropomorphic into a more abstract idea.

Presentation of the Sabbath Law

Another area of difference between the accounts in Deuteronomy and Exodus has to do with the presentation of the Sabbath law. It will be helpful to examine the two accounts side by side in order to see the differences between them (differences in the Deuteronomic presentation are indicated in bold in the translation):

Exodus 20:8–11

Deuteronomy 5:12–15

8 זָכוֹר אֶת־יוֹם הַשַּׁבָּת לְקַדְּשׁוֹ׃

12 שָׁמוֹר אֶת־יוֹם הַשַּׁבָּת לְקַדְּשׁוֹ כַּאֲשֶׁר צִוְּךָ יְהוָה אֱלֹהֶיךָ׃

9 שֵׁשֶׁת יָמִים תַּעֲבֹד וְעָשִׂיתָ כָּל־מְלַאכְתֶּךָ׃

13 שֵׁשֶׁת יָמִים תַּעֲבֹד וְעָשִׂיתָ כָּל־מְלַאכְתֶּךָ׃

10 וְיוֹם הַשְּׁבִיעִי שַׁבָּת לַיהוָה אֱלֹהֶיךָ לֹא־תַעֲשֶׂה כָל־מְלָאכָה אַתָּה וּבִנְךָ־וּבִתֶּךָ עַבְדְּךָ וַאֲמָתְךָ וּבְהֶמְתֶּךָ וְגֵרְךָ אֲשֶׁר בִּשְׁעָרֶיךָ׃

14 וְיוֹם הַשְּׁבִיעִי שַׁבָּת לַיהוָה אֱלֹהֶיךָ לֹא תַעֲשֶׂה כָל־מְלָאכָה אַתָּה וּבִנְךָ־וּבִתֶּךָ וְעַבְדְּךָ־וַאֲמָתֶךָ וְשׁוֹרְךָ וַחֲמֹרְךָ וְכָל־בְּהֶמְתֶּךָ וְגֵרְךָ אֲשֶׁר בִּשְׁעָרֶיךָ לְמַעַן יָנוּחַ עַבְדְּךָ וַאֲמָתְךָ כָּמוֹךָ׃

11 כִּי שֵׁשֶׁת־יָמִים עָשָׂה יְהוָה אֶת־הַשָּׁמַיִם וְאֶת־הָאָרֶץ אֶת־הַיָּם וְאֶת־כָּל־אֲשֶׁר־בָּם וַיָּנַח בַּיּוֹם הַשְּׁבִיעִי עַל־כֵּן בֵּרַךְ יְהוָה אֶת־יוֹם הַשַּׁבָּת וַיְקַדְּשֵׁהוּ׃

15 וְזָכַרְתָּ כִּי־עֶבֶד הָיִיתָ בְּאֶרֶץ מִצְרַיִם וַיֹּצִאֲךָ יְהוָה אֱלֹהֶיךָ מִשָּׁם בְּיָד חֲזָקָה וּבִזְרֹעַ נְטוּיָה עַל־כֵּן צִוְּךָ יְהוָה אֱלֹהֶיךָ לַעֲשׂוֹת אֶת־יוֹם הַשַּׁבָּת׃

8 Remember the Sabbath day, to keep it holy. 9 Six days you shall labor, and do all your work, 10 but the seventh day is a Sabbath to Yahweh your God. On it you shall not do any work, you, your son or your daughter, your male servant or your female servant, or your cattle, or the alien who is within your gates. 11 For in six days Yahweh made the heavens and the earth, the sea and all that is in them, and he rested on the seventh day. Therefore, Yahweh blessed the Sabbath day and made it holy.

12 **Observe** the Sabbath day to keep it holy, *as Yahweh your God commanded you.* 13 Six days you shall labor and do all your work, 14 but the seventh day is a Sabbath to Yahweh your God. On it you shall not do any work, you, your son or your daughter, *or* your male servant or your female servant, or *your ox or your donkey, or any of* your cattle, or the alien who is within your gates, *so that your male servant and your female servant may rest as you do.* 15 *Remember that you were slaves in the land of Egypt, and Yahweh your God brought you out of there with a strong hand*

> *and outstretched arm.*
> *Therefore, Yahweh your God*
> *commanded you to keep the*
> *Sabbath day.*

The differences between the two presentations are readily apparent. In Exod 20:8–11, the rationale for the Sabbath is the fact that Yahweh worked for six days in creating and rested on the seventh day. In Weinfeld's view, the significance of the command in Exodus is that in remembering the Sabbath the people are reenacting Yahweh's rest on the seventh day.[93] This, he maintains, is an appropriate reflection of the Priestly view, in which the rituals of the sanctuary are seen as reenacting what takes place in the divine realm.[94] (Though the Decalogue in Exodus is usually considered largely to be part of E, or JE,[95] it is understood as representing the same world view as the P material related to the Sabbath in Gen 2:1–3 and Exod 31:17.[96]) It also represents a rather anthropomorphic view of God, in which he labors and has need of rest.

Deuteronomy alters this presentation to fit its conception of God. Weinfeld maintains that the idea of Yahweh's laboring or needing to rest did not fit the theological conception of the author(s) of Deuteronomy, so the rationale for the Sabbath was altered from "mythological" to social.[97] Thus, in Deut 5:14–15 the purpose of the Sabbath is so that humans may rest, but the basis for this is no longer the fact that Yahweh rested after creating the world but the historical fact of the deliverance from Egypt. Weinfeld concludes that "in Deuteronomy the Sabbath recalls an historical occurrence whereas in P it commemorates a sacral one."[98]

The desire on the part of the author of Deuteronomy to avoid a sacral connotation is also evident in the use of terminology in the two presentations. Weinfeld notes that the Sabbath commandment in Exod 20:8 begins with זָכַר ("remember"), which is associated with commemoration.[99] Thus, in Exodus, the motivation for the Sabbath is to commemorate Yahweh's rest on the seventh day in creation. The Sabbath command in Deuteronomy, however, begins in Deut 5:12

---

93. Weinfeld, *Deuteronomic School*, 222.
94. Ibid.
95. A. F. Campbell and M. A. O'Brien, *Sources of the Pentateuch: Texts, Introductions, Annotations* (Minneapolis: Fortress, 1993), 188.
96. Weinfeld, *Deuteronomic School*, 222.
97. Ibid.
98. Ibid.
99. Weinfeld, *Deuteronomy 1–11*, 303.

with the command to "observe" (שָׁמַר), which has no commemorative connotation. The use of זָכַר in Deut 5:15 points to the fact that the author wanted to avoid a sacral commemoration of Yahweh's rest in favor of the commemoration of a historical event.[100] This is further evidence that the author of Deuteronomy wanted to distance himself from earlier conceptions that do not comport with his thinking.

Weinfeld notes, however, that the situation is not entirely straightforward. He notes that the two motivations (social and sacral) could have existed together. Moreover, he recognizes that a social motivation for the Sabbath is provided in Exod 23:12. However, he sees significance "in the fact that the author of P selected specifically the sacral reason and developed it in his own way while the book of Deuteronomy chose the social motivation and formulated it in its own unique way, that is, humanistically."[101] The differences between the two presentations of the Sabbath law are interpreted as evidence of demythologization (earlier concepts of God are repudiated) and secularization (the Sabbath law is placed on a historical rather than sacral foundation).

It is appropriate at this point to evaluate the case presented for demythologization and secularization to determine if this interpretation is best supported by the data of the text.

Evaluation

There are some important considerations to be raised regarding Weinfeld and others' view that demythologization and secularization are at the core of Deut 5:1–6:9. We will examine these issues with respect to each of the major issues posited by Weinfeld.

Presence of Yahweh
As we noted above, Weinfeld and others have seen in Deut 5:1–6:9 a repudiation of earlier conceptions of the presence of Yahweh. However, as was the case with Deut 4 above, the evidence is capable of being interpreted differently.

Weinfeld's view of Deut 5:4 is based in large measure on his understanding of Yahweh's presence in Deut 4. Indeed, he argues that פָּנִים בְּפָנִים ("face to face") cannot be understood as referring to an actual experience of Yahweh's presence on the grounds that Deut 4:12 and 15 argue against this understanding. As we noted above, however, the evidence of Deut 4:12 and 15, as well as the chapter as a whole, points to an understanding of Yahweh's actual presence.

100. Ibid. See also idem, *Deuteronomic School*, 222.
101. Ibid.

In both Deut 4:12 and 15, the phrase "out of the midst of the fire" (מִתּוֹךְ הָאֵשׁ) appears. This is best understood as referring to Yahweh's presence, in that he speaks from within the fire, as we have seen. Moreover, the evidence from Deut 4 points toward an understanding of Yahweh's actual presence (though, as we noted above, this understanding does not mean Yahweh's presence is localized on earth; rather, Deut 4 conceives of Yahweh as present on earth and in heaven). Thus, it is not compelling to argue on the basis of Deut 4:12 and 15 that Deut 5:4 is inconsistent with actual presence, particularly since the very expression (מִתּוֹךְ הָאֵשׁ) used in Deut 4:12 and 15 to convey actual presence also appears in Deut 5:4.

Moreover, the phrase פָּנִים בְּפָנִים ("face to face") in Deut 5:4 is best taken as referring to an actual encounter with Yahweh. While Weinfeld is correct in noting that the form in which it appears in Deut 5:4 is unique in the Old Testament,[102] it is not clear that the author of Deut 5 used this form of the expression deliberately to distance himself from the usual form of the expression. First, it should be noted that the expression is considered by many interpreters to be a synonym for the expression פָּנִים אֶל־פָּנִים.[103] In three of the five instances in which פָּנִים אֶל־פָּנִים appears with reference to Yahweh, there is a clear sense that divine presence is in view.[104]

Second, there is a parallel to the expression פָּנִים בְּפָנִים in Num 14:14 and Isa 52:8, where the expression עַיִן בְּעַיִן ("eye to eye") appears. Weinfeld maintains that this expression means simply "directly" and is therefore adduced as evidence that פָּנִים בְּפָנִים should also be interpreted simply to mean "directly."[105] But both these instances involve the actual presence of God. In Num 14:14, Yahweh is said to be in the midst of the people, and manifestations of his presence are seen in the cloud that "stands over them." So, while there is, to be sure, a sense in which Yahweh is described as being experienced "directly" by using the phrase עַיִן בְּעַיִן in Num 14:14, it was actually an experience of Yahweh's presence.[106] Similarly, Isa 52:8 speaks of the people seeing "eye

---

102. Weinfeld, *Deuteronomy 1–11*, 239.

103. BDB 815; A. S. van der Woude, "פָּנִים *pānîm* face," *TLOT* 2: 1005.

104. The five occurrences of the phrase in which God is in view are Gen 32:31[30]; Exod 33:11; Deut 34:10; Judg 6:22; Ezek 20:35. The two instances in which divine presence is not explicit are Deut 34:10 and Ezek 20:35, but, as Wilson (*Midst of the Fire*, 78) notes, these latter two instances do not rule out the possibility of actual divine presence, and the sense of these texts may indeed include the idea of actual presence.

105. Weinfeld, *Deuteronomy 1–11*, 239–40.

106. See P. J. Budd, *Numbers* (WBC 5; Waco, TX: Word, 1984), 158, who notes that the expression עַיִן בְּעַיִן expresses the "closest of contact." See also T. R. Ashley, *The Book of Numbers* (NICOT; Grand Rapids: Eerdmans, 1993), 257; R. D. Cole, *Numbers* (NAC 3B; Nashville: Broadman, 2000), 230.

to eye" (עַיִן בְּעַיִן) the return of Yahweh to Zion. This, too, is describing
the actual presence of Yahweh in Zion that could be experienced "directly."[107] Thus, rather than undermining the understanding of פָּנִים
בְּפָנִים as referring to actual presence, the use of עַיִן בְּעַיִן appears to support the understanding that פָּנִים בְּפָנִים refers to actual presence. It is
likely, consequently, that the actual presence of an invisible God is in
view in Deut 5:4.

In addition, it is telling that in the narration of the giving of the
Decalogue in Exodus, the expression פָּנִים אֶל־פָּנִים (or, for that matter,
פָּנִים בְּפָנִים) is not used. Exodus 20:1, which, as an introduction to the
Decalogue, is parallel to Deut 5:1–5, says simply, "And God spoke all
these words, saying, . . ." There is no mention whatsoever of God's
speaking "face to face" with either Moses or the people. Compared
with the Exodus account, the author of Deuteronomy has added the
expression פָּנִים בְּפָנִים. This may be due to the author's desire to convey
the fact that the people heard the Decalogue directly,[108] but it is
noteworthy that in attempting to convey that fact, the author of Deuteronomy uses a term that could easily lead to the conclusion that
Yahweh was actually present. Given the similarities between the expressions פָּנִים אֶל־פָּנִים and פָּנִים בְּפָנִים, it is highly unlikely that Deuteronomy's use of the latter term was designed to signal an intention to
conceive of Yahweh's presence in a much different manner from that
conveyed by the former expression. In Weinfeld's view, the author of
Deut 5 *added* (in comparison with the Exodus account) a potentially
confusing expression that is remarkably similar to an expression con-
veying divine presence in an attempt (in part, at least) to deny Yahweh's actual presence. In short, it is a rather clumsy effort to obscure
the meaning of פָּנִים אֶל־פָּנִים by using the expression פָּנִים בְּפָנִים, which is
so similar that it invites misinterpretation. It seems more likely, instead, that the two terms are to be understood the same way, and both
convey the sense of being in the presence of another.

This is all the more likely when we remember that the expression
מִתּוֹךְ הָאֵשׁ ("out of the midst of the fire") appears in Deut 5:4 as well,
and is likely to convey the sense of actual presence, as we have seen.
It appears, then, that Deut 4:12 and 15 (particularly in light of the use

107. J. N. Oswalt, *The Book of Isaiah: Chapters 40–66* (NICOT; Grand Rapids: Eerdmans, 1998), 365, notes that עַיִן בְּעַיִן is used to speak of the "incontrovertible evidence of
God's presence." See also J. A. Motyer, *The Prophecy of Isaiah: An Introduction and Commentary* (Downers Grove, IL: InterVarsity, 1993), 420.

108. It is not exactly clear from the account of the theophany at Sinai in Exodus just
what the people heard directly. Deuteronomy, on the other hand, is clear that the whole
assembly heard the Decalogue. See below for more on this issue and its significance for the
interpretation of this section.

there of הָאֵשׁ מִתּוֹך) tends to *support* the view that פָּנִים בְּפָנִים indicates actual presence, rather than undermining this view, as Weinfeld main-
tains. While he rightly notes that Deut 4:12 and 15 make clear that
פָּנִים בְּפָנִים is to be understood idiomatically, since no form was seen,
the use of הָאֵשׁ מִתּוֹך points to an understanding of actual presence.
Since the expression הָאֵשׁ מִתּוֹך appears four times in Deut 5,[109] it
seems rather unlikely that there is a deliberate attempt in Deuteronomy to deny the presence of Yahweh and to repudiate the conception of his presence found in the Exodus account.

Moreover, the very next verse, Deut 5:5, says that Moses "stood between" (בֵּין עָמַד) Yahweh and the Israelites. This has usually been understood as referring to the fact that Moses served in a mediatorial role
in receiving the *Torah* from Yahweh and then presenting it to Israel.[110]
But there may be spatial dimensions to the use of the term as well.
Wilson notes that the use of the term elsewhere in the Old Testament
has a locative sense, and none of the other uses implies a mediatorial
role on the part of one who "stands between."[111] Deuteronomy 5:5,
then, is best taken as indicating Moses' physical location. He performs
a mediatorial role, of course, but not "by virtue of being between
them, but rather because of what he does when he stands there."[112]
Indeed, Nelson notes that there may be other explanations for Moses'
presence "between" Israel and Yahweh, such as keeping the people
from approaching the mountain for reasons of "ritual propriety."[113] If
this were the case, then this is also a spatial interpretation of the
phrase בֵּין עָמַד.

In addition, we should note that the entire chapter seeks to convey an encounter with Yahweh at Horeb. Thus, as we have seen in the
Deut 4 section above, noncorporeality and invisibility are not the
same as absence. As was the case in Deut 4, Deut 5:24–26 expresses
the idea of danger in hearing Yahweh's voice, which is consistent
with the idea that he is actually present. Israel's desire for a mediator
suggests that Yahweh's actual presence is understood, for it is only if
Yahweh is present and near that there would be danger of the sort that
a mediator could resolve. Indeed, in Deut 5:27, the representatives of

---

109. Deuteronomy 5:4, 22, 24, 26. Deuteronomy 5:23 says that Yahweh spoke out of
the "midst of the darkness," while the mountain was burning with fire, which also expresses his nearness.

110. Cf., e.g., Cairns, *Word and Presence*, 68; Craigie, *Deuteronomy*, 148; and Brueggemann, *Deuteronomy*, 65.

111. Wilson, *Midst of the Fire*, 79–81. The other uses of the phrase are Exod 14:19–20;
Num 17:13[16:48]; and 1 Chr 21:16.

112. Ibid., 81.

113. Nelson, *Deuteronomy*, 79–80.

the people come to Moses and ask him to "go near" (קָרַב) Yahweh. This makes sense only if Yahweh is thought to be actually present (though, as we have noted, invisible).

A final point to be mentioned in this regard is the discussion of Yahweh's writing of the Decalogue on tablets of stone. As Sonnet has observed, it is rather odd that the author of Deut 5, seeking (in Weinfeld's view) to repudiate corporeal notions of Yahweh's presence, would refer to Yahweh's engraving the words of the Decalogue on stone tablets.[114] This is all the more surprising since Deut 9:10 goes further and specifies that the tablets were written by the finger of God. While the two texts may, of course, have been written by different authors, it is rather curious that the final editor did not feel compelled to remove such anthropomorphic references, if indeed part of the purpose of the book was to repudiate more "primitive" conceptions of God.

It seems unlikely that this section is repudiating the actual presence of Yahweh. Rather, in this chapter, as in Deut 4, there is a conception that Yahweh is actually present (though the understanding is that Yahweh is present both in heaven and at Horeb) and that the people experienced a genuine encounter with him at Horeb. This is consistent with, rather than contrary to, the presentation of the revelation at Sinai in Exodus. The differences between the two accounts are not of the sort that Weinfeld posits.

Presentation of the Sabbath Law

We will now direct our attention to the differences between the presentations of the Sabbath law in Deut 5:12–15 and Exod 20:8–11. As we noted above, these differences are sometimes seen as evidence of a tendency toward secularization and demythologization in Deuteronomy, because the mythological idea of a God who needed rest was being rejected and a more humanitarian, social concern was replacing the original basis for the Sabbath law.

The major difference between the presentation of the Sabbath law in the two versions of the Decalogue is the motivation given in each instance. As we have seen, the Sabbath law in Exodus is explained on

---

114. J. P. Sonnet, *The Book within the Book: Writing in Deuteronomy* (Biblical Interpretation Series 14; Leiden: Brill, 1997), 49. Sonnet notes that this may in fact represent "demythologization" but of a different sort from what Weinfeld envisions. Sonnet notes (p. 50) that almost nowhere in ANE literature is there a portrayal of a deity writing without an intermediary, and none of the direct writing is of the sort that is portrayed in Deuteronomy. This may point to a polemic in Deuteronomy against the ideology of the neighbouring cultures: a case is being made that the authority immediately behind the Decalogue in Israel is Yahweh.

the basis of Yahweh's rest after creation, whereas in Deuteronomy the basis is the fact that the Israelites were slaves in Egypt. This is seen as an example of demythologization and secularization.

There are a number of problems with this understanding. First, it is not clear that the motivations in each law should be understood as mutually exclusive. Weinfeld himself notes that the Sabbath is depicted as having a social motivation in Exod 23:12.[115] Even if this passage derived from a hand different from the hand that produced Decalogue, the fact that a humanitarian motivation appears in connection with the Sabbath in the final form of Exodus argues against seeing social and creational motivations as mutually exclusive.[116] Moreover, Sonsino notes that the motivations given for various laws in the Pentateuch should not be considered the only possible motivations. Rather, multiple motivations are possible. He argues that the inclusion of motive clauses was "not to provide a motivation that would justify the law from all perspectives but to select from among all the possible rationales the one that would denote best the law's appropriateness in the eyes of the people to whom it was addressed.[117] We have seen that the final form of Exodus includes *both* a humanitarian/social motivation *and* a motivation based on creation. This suggests that multiple motivations are possible and that social and theological motivations are compatible with each other.

Second, the contention that the Sabbath law in Deut 5 rejects the motivations of the Exodus version of the Decalogue (while accepting the basic command) is undermined by the fact that Deut 5:12 seems to presuppose the Exodus account. Deuteronomy 5:12 commands the Israelites to observe the Sabbath כַּאֲשֶׁר צִוְּךָ יְהוָה אֱלֹהֶיךָ ("just as Yahweh your God commanded you"). The expression כַּאֲשֶׁר צִוָּה has been shown to function as a citation marker for sources that Deuteronomy has used.[118] The similarities between the presentation of the Decalogue in

---

115. Weinfeld, *Deuteronomic School*, 222.

116. Exodus 23:12 is considered by Campbell and O'Brien (*Sources*, 199) to be a "non-source" text. These are texts that are thought to be additions to a source or combined sources. Sometimes, texts are interpreted as a combination of sources and therefore cannot be said to belong to one or the other. The entire Book of the Covenant (Exod 20:22–23:33) is seen as a nonsource text.

117. R. Sonsino, *Motive Clauses in Hebrew Law: Biblical Forms and Near Eastern Parallels* (SBLDS 45; Chico, CA: Scholars Press, 1980), 116.

118. J. Milgrom, "Profane Slaughter and a Formulaic Key to the Composition of Deuteronomy," *HUCA* 47 (1976): 1–17, here 3–5. B. Lang ("The Decalogue in the Light of a Newly Published Palaeo-Hebrew Inscription [Hebrew Ostracon Moussaïeff No. 1]," *JSOT* 77 [1998]: 21–25) argues that כַּאֲשֶׁר צִוָּה should be thought of as anticipating something that follows rather than something that has gone before. Accordingly, he maintains that the

Exodus and Deuteronomy suggest that Deut 5 is based on Exod 20. But the presence of the citation marker כַּאֲשֶׁר צִוְּךָ shows that Deut 5 presupposes the Exodus account. That is, the author of Deut 5 was familiar with the presentation of the Sabbath law in Exod 20, and that account—including its theological motivation—is accepted in Deut 5, as indicated by the use of the citation marker.

This suggests that the theological motivation of Exod 20:11 is not rejected by the author(s) of Deuteronomy but is assumed and accepted. This is all the more likely when we consider that the citation formula is used "to indicate the sources which it assumes are so obvious to the reader that there is no need to quote them."[119] It is likely, then, that Deut 5 is aware of the theological motivation presented in Exod 20 and, moreover, presumes that the reader is also familiar with the presentation there. Rather than repudiating the theological motivation of the earlier law, Deut 5 presupposes it and seeks to emphasize elements appropriate to its audience.[120] In so doing, Deut 5 picks up on themes that are also known in the earlier material (e.g., Exod 23:12).

Third, we should note that the complementarity of the two versions of the Decalogue may extend beyond the citation in Deut 5:12 of the Sabbath law in Exod 20:8–11. Miller argues that the background to the Sabbath law in Deut 5:12–15 is not just the Decalogue in Exod 20:8–11 but also the account in Exod 5:1–9 of Pharaoh's refusal to allow the Israelites to go to worship Yahweh.[121] There, at the behest of Yahweh, Moses requests that the people be allowed to go three days' journey into the wilderness in order to worship Yahweh with sacrifices. This request is refused by Pharaoh, who rebukes Moses, noting that there is much work to be done and that the granting of Moses' request would give the people a rest (שָׁבַת) from their work. Yahweh then demonstrates his power over Pharaoh and all the gods

---

phrase should be translated "Thus Yahweh your God commands you." This is unlikely, however, because his interpretation fails to consider the evidence adduced by Milgrom that כַּאֲשֶׁר צִוְּךָ is a citation marker in Deuteronomy. In other words, the expression may well be used in Lang's ostracon to refer to something that follows, but this fact does not mean that the expression in Deuteronomy should be so translated, given the frequency with which the phrase appears to make reference to a source, as Milgrom documents. Furthermore, this translation would be awkward in Deut 5:16, where the phrase is followed by לְמַעַן. It is preferable, then, to see the expression as the marker of a citation that has preceded the text in question. See also McConville, *Deuteronomy*, 118.

119. Milgrom, "Profane Slaughter," 4.

120. Cf. Nelson, *Deuteronomy*, 82–83; G. F. Hasel, "The Sabbath in the Pentateuch," in *The Sabbath in Scripture and History* (ed. K. A. Strand; Washington, DC: Review and Herald, 1982), 21–43.

121. Miller, *Deuteronomy*, 81.

of Egypt (Exod 12:12) through the deliverance of the people from Egypt and bondage.

This incident points to the theological significance of the exodus in the Sabbath law in Deut 5. The Sabbath law calls upon the people to remember that they were once slaves, denied the privilege of worshiping Yahweh. Consequently, the people are to observe the Sabbath and allow *all*, including slaves—especially slaves—to have the opportunity to honor Yahweh by keeping the Sabbath holy. Miller maintains that, "if Exodus was God's redemptive activity to give sabbath to slaves, then Sabbath [in Deuteronomy 5] is human non-activity to remember the Exodus redemption."[122] Thus, there is a religious and theological purpose behind the law in Deut 5. It is not simply a humanitarian proscription but rather a call to the people to remember their own oppression, when they were denied the opportunity to worship Yahweh. Both presentations of the Sabbath law have at their center a concern to honor Yahweh as the sovereign creator-God. In doing so, however, they emphasize different things. Deuteronomy 5 seeks to ensure that *all* people are given the opportunity to honor Yahweh, regardless of their social status.

Moreover, parallels have often beeen drawn between the act of redemption from Egypt and creation.[123] Craigie notes that the motivation for the Sabbath law in Exodus is grounded in the creation narrative of Genesis. Resting on the Sabbath day functions, in part, to acknowledge humanity's dependence on the creator-God. Thus Craigie notes that "man's divinely appointed task to have dominion over the created order (Gen. 1:26) carried with it also the privilege of sharing in God's rest."[124] In the exodus-Horeb event, the people are, in effect, created as a nation.[125] The people's memory of their plight reminds them that they owe their existence as a nation to the redemptive actions of Yahweh in bringing them out of slavery. More recently, it has been argued that there are parallels to the creation account in the exodus in that a restoration of the created order from the disruption caused by Pharaoh's sinful oppression occurs through Yahweh's deliverance of Israel from Egypt. Yahweh's triumph over Pharaoh as

---

122. P. D. Miller Jr., "The Human Sabbath: A Study in Deuteronomic Theology," *Princeton Seminary Bulletin* n.s. 6/2 (1985): 88.

123. Craigie, *Deuteronomy*, 157.

124. Ibid.

125. N. Lohfink ("Reading Deuteronomy 5 as Narrative," in *A God So Near: Essays on Old Testament Theology in Honor of Patrick D. Miller* [ed. B. A. Strawn and N. R. Bowen; Winona Lake, IN: Eisenbrauns, 2003], 264) notes that Deuteronomy never refers directly to historical events that occurred prior to Horeb. Horeb is therefore best seen as a "primeval or primordial event."

evidenced by the plagues demonstrates that all of creation is under the sovereignty of Yahweh. The "outcome of this drama is that all should 'know Yahweh,' sovereign as creator and liberator."[126] In this way, the complementarity of the two presentations of the Sabbath law is evident. That is, though presented differently and with different emphases, the Sabbath law in Deut 5:12–15 nevertheless demonstrates important parallels with the theological emphasis on creation in Exod 20:8–11.

A fourth, related objection to Weinfeld's interpretation of the differences between the presentations of the Sabbath law has to do with the nature of the command in Deut 5. The Sabbath law in Deut 5:12 commands the people to "observe the Sabbath day to keep it holy (לְקַדְּשׁוֹ)." The next verse states that the seventh day is a Sabbath "to Yahweh." In this respect, it is identical to the fourth commandment as presented in Exodus. What is not fully appreciated in Weinfeld's treatment, however, is the religious significance of this command. The terminology draws on the language of holiness: the people are to observe the Sabbath to keep it holy. Hasel notes that this purpose is reiterated in Deut 5:12.[127] The usual motivation for Sabbath observance is Yahweh's command. Many commentators see the motivation expressed in Deut 5:14 ("so that your male servant . . . may rest," introduced by לְמַעַן) as the basis for the entire Sabbath law, but it has been argued that this is best seen as the motivation for the cessation of work, since "rest" is the main verb with which לְמַעַן is associated.[128] In

126. B. C. Birch et al., *A Theological Introduction to the Old Testament* (Nashville: Abingdon, 1999), 116. See also T. E. Fretheim, "Law in the Service of Life: A Dynamic Understanding of Law in Deuteronomy," in *A God So Near: Essays on Old Testament Theology in Honor of Patrick D. Miller* (ed. B. A. Strawn and N. R. Bowen; Winona Lake, IN: Eisenbrauns, 2003), 185–89.

127. It is not clear whether לְקַדְּשׁוֹ should be interpreted as referring to the purpose of שָׁמוֹר (with the sense of "observe the Sabbath day *in order* to keep it holy") or the means by which this is done ("observe the Sabbath day *by* keeping it holy"). Syntactically, both meanings are possible. See C. H. J. van der Merwe, J. A. Naudé, and J. H. Kroeze, *A Biblical Hebrew Reference Grammar* (BLH 3; Sheffield: Sheffield Academic Press, 1999), 155; and B. K. Waltke and M. O'Connor, *An Introduction to Biblical Hebrew Syntax* (Winona Lake, IN: Eisenbrauns, 1990), 608–9. The context of the Sabbath law in Deut 5, however, points toward purpose rather than means, because a means (namely, cessation from work) is made explicit in the following verses.

128. See Hasel, "Sabbath," 32–33; N. E. Andreasen, "Festival and Freedom: A Study of an Old Testament Theme," *Int* 28 (1974): 284–86; A. R. Hulst, "Bemerkungen zum Sabbatgebot," in *Studia Biblica et Semitica: Theodoro Christiano Vriezen qui munere Professoris Theologiae per XXV Annos Functus est, ab Amicis, Collegis, Discipulis Dedicata* (ed. W. C. van Unnik and A. S. van der Woude; Wageningen: H. Veenman, 1966), 155–56. On the use of לְמַעַן in Deuteronomy, see P. Doron, "Motive Clauses in the Laws of Deuteronomy: Their Forms, Functions and Contents," *HAR* 2 (1978): 61–77. For more general discussion of

this case, the motivation for the cessation from work is indeed so that rest is extended to all. But the motivation for observing the Sabbath in general, on the basis of Deut 5:12, is because Yahweh commanded it in order to keep the day holy.

The theological motivation for Sabbath observance is further seen when considering the structure of the law as a whole. The following structure may be posited:[129]

A	Introduction	Observe the Sabbath day to keep it holy, as Yahweh your God commanded you (v. 12)
B	Command (with motivation)	Six days you shall labor . . . but the seventh day is a Sabbath to Yahweh your God (vv. 13–14a)
B′	Command (with motivation)	On it you shall not do any work . . . so that (לְמַעַן) your male servant . . . may rest. Remember that you were slaves in the land of Egypt, and Yahweh your God brought you out (vv. 14b–15a)
A′	Conclusion	Therefore, Yahweh your God commanded you to keep the Sabbath day (v. 15b)

This structure highlights an important aspect of the Sabbath law and its motivations. It points to the fact that the command of Yahweh is the primary basis for the Sabbath law. Thus, there is a profound theological basis for the law in Deut 5, even though it does of course extend the observance of the Sabbath to all. Hasel maintains that

> the recognition of the theological motivation of the grounding of the Sabbath in a commandment of God cannot be emphasized enough, because it introduces an element that seems implicitly affirmed in Exodus 20:10a . . . and repeated in Deuteronomy 5:14a. . . . But in Deuteronomy 5 something is made explicit in the commandment itself for the

---

לְמַעַן, see Sonsino, *Motive Clauses,* 71; van der Merwe, Naudé, and Kroeze, *Reference Grammar,* 304–5.

129. This is somewhat similar, although not identical, to the structures proposed by Hasel, "Sabbath," 31; and Andreasen, "Festival and Freedom," 283. N. Lohfink ("The Decalogue in Deuteronomy 5," in *Theology of the Pentateuch: Themes of the Priestly Narrative and Deuteronomy* [trans. L. M. Maloney; Minneapolis: Fortress, 1994], 253) proposes a more detailed chiastic structure that highlights the role of rest for all in the household. However, he sees a turning point for the text as a whole in v. 15 on the basis of the presence of לְמַעַן. He thus takes לְמַעַן as being the motivation for the Sabbath law as a whole, which I believe is incorrect. He does, however, note the parallels between vv. 12 and 15 and, indeed, elaborates on the parallels.

first time: the Sabbath is to be kept because God has ordained it—nay,
commanded it—to be so.[130]

So, while Deuteronomy emphasizes certain aspects to accomplish its
own theological and rhetorical purposes, it includes in its presentation
of the Sabbath law a profound theological basis.

There is, of course, a humanitarian concern in the law in Deuteronomy, because it seeks to extend the observance of the Sabbath to all
in society. But it is important to recognize the theological foundation
on which this extension is based. This theological foundation in the
commandment of Yahweh dovetails with the emphasis on the exodus
from Egypt, which serves to "create" Israel as a nation. Both of these
theological themes highlight the centrality of Yahweh, for it is Yahweh
alone who is creator and redeemer in the world view of Deuteronomy.

This leads to a fifth and final objection to Weinfeld's understanding of the Sabbath law in Deut 5 and its relationship to the law in Exodus. I have argued that one of the theological bases for the law as
presented in Deut 5 is the fact that Yahweh commands obedience to
the law. As we saw in connection with our discussion of Deut 4
(pp. 127–134 above), one of the aspects of Deuteronomy's presentation of the revelation at Horeb is an emphasis on Yahweh's word, and
particularly *Torah*, as a means of actualizing his presence with the
people. We noted there that this is a special concern of Deuteronomy,
which portrays the people as being on the verge of entering the promised land and, therefore, about to experience dramatic changes in the
way in which Yahweh's presence is experienced. In contrast to Exodus, Deuteronomy is especially concerned with instructing the people
about how Yahweh will continue to be present with his people after
they enter and settle the land.

These considerations render it rather difficult to conceive of the
Sabbath law in Deut 5 as having been "secularized," since the observance of the Sabbath, in the thinking of Deuteronomy, is a means by
which Yahweh's presence may be actualized. Keeping the Sabbath is
not merely a matter of humanitarian concern (though this is, of
course, an important factor). Rather, there are religious implications
to Sabbath observance, just as *Torah*-keeping generally is conceived of
as a vital means of experiencing the presence of Yahweh. Thus, there
are profound religious implications to the Sabbath law, and it is difficult to conclude that secularization is at the heart of the Deuteronomic presentation of the Sabbath.

130. Hasel, "Sabbath," 31–32.

The unique emphases and perspective of Deuteronomy do, of course, call for investigation and explanation. It is to this endeavor that we now turn.

Alternative View: Yahweh's Torah *for All Generations*

I have argued above that Deut 5:1–6:9 is not best understood in terms of demythologization and secularization. At the same time, there are unique aspects to this material that do, indeed, point to the particular emphases and intentions of the book.

Generations and Journey

As we have noted elsewhere in this study, one important motif in Deuteronomy as a whole is the concept of *journey*.[131] The book presents itself as the speeches of Moses given to the people on the verge of entering the promised land, which was an important moment of transition. In the narrative perspective of Deuteronomy, the people have dramatically experienced Yahweh's presence through the pillar of cloud and fire, the tent of meeting, and the presence of Moses, the mediator of Yahweh's words. Now, on the verge of entry into the land, where so much will change, including the experience of Yahweh's presence, the people are reminded of their experiences. But this recitation of the past (including the presentation of *Torah*) is not mere repetition. Rather, the needs of the audience gathered on the plains of Moab are taken into account, and the presentation is tailored accordingly.

The presentation in Deut 5:1–6:9 picks up on certain aspects of the presentation in Deut 4, as I have argued above. In emphasizing obedience to *Torah*, this passage further highlights that obedience to *Torah* is a means of actualizing the presence of Yahweh. In the moment of transition, the people are told how they can continue to experience Yahweh's presence in a meaningful way.

The emphasis on the continuing journey of the people is found early in the chapter. Deuteronomy 5:2–3 says, "Yahweh our God made a covenant with us at Horeb. Not with our fathers did Yahweh make this covenant, but with us, all of us here alive today." Strictly speaking, this is not true, because Deut 1:34–39 and 2:16 make clear that the exodus generation (who experienced the covenant at Horeb) died out and was not allowed to enter the land. However, by emphasizing

---

131. See especially McConville and Millar, *Time and Place*, 15–88; and J. G. Millar, *Now Choose Life: Theology and Ethics in Deuteronomy* (NSBT 6; Leicester: Apollos, 1998). Miller ("Sabbath," 81) maintains that "one should never lose sight of the fact that Deuteronomy is the book of Scripture most self-conscious and explicit in its character as address to different generations in different times and circumstances."

that *this* generation entered into the covenant at Horeb, the author is stressing that Israel is always, in a sense, "at Horeb," hearing the commands of Yahweh and having to choose whether or not they will demonstrate total allegiance to Yahweh. This blurring of generational lines is an intentional rhetorical device used to highlight the responsibility of subsequent generations. That is, it is not enough that the ancestors[132] of the Moab generation entered into a covenant with Yahweh. The people of each generation must recognize their responsibility to demonstrate total loyalty to Yahweh through adherence to *Torah*.

The dynamic conception of generations may help explain the emphasis in Deut 5 on the actual presence of Yahweh. As we noted above (pp. 141–142), it is possible to read Deut 5 as promoting *greater* emphasis on the actual presence of Yahweh, since in the introduction to the Decalogue in the Sinai narrative in Exodus there is no use of the term פָּנִים בְּפָנִים ("face to face") as there is in Deut 5:4. By stressing the actual presence of Yahweh perhaps even more than does the Exodus account, Deut 5 highlights the responsibility of each generation. *This* generation, figuratively speaking, experienced Yahweh "face to face." Therefore, *this* generation must determine to live out loyalty to Yahweh through keeping *Torah*. It is telling, as well, that Deut 5:4 says that "Yahweh spoke with *you* face to face" at Horeb, shifting from the inclusive "us" of vv. 2–3. Elsewhere it is said that it was only Moses with whom Yahweh spoke "face to face" (cf. Exod 33:11; Deut 34:10). The emphasis on the experience of Yahweh's presence by Israel as a whole points to the concern of the author to emphasize the responsibility of this generation to obey Yahweh.

It is important to note, however, that this experience of Yahweh's presence is not absolute, as the next verses make clear. Deuteronomy 5:5 maintains that the people experienced Yahweh "face to face," but with Moses standing between. As we saw (pp. 143–144), this further points to Yahweh's actual presence at Horeb, but it also serves to demonstrate Moses' role as mediator of Yahweh's words. With respect to

---

132. The term אָבוֹת ("fathers") is sometimes used in Deuteronomy to refer to the patriarchs (e.g., Deut 1:8; 6:3). At other points, it refers more generally to ancestors, and the rhetorical purpose of these references is to highlight the responsibility of the present generation. This is the case here, where the context suggests that the contrast is not with the patriarchs (who indeed were not at Horeb) but with the previous generation, who, though present at Horeb, failed to demonstrate total allegiance to Yahweh. This highlights the responsibility of the present generation deliberately to live out loyalty to Yahweh, especially in the form of adherence to *Torah*. For further discussion of this, see C. J. H. Wright, "אָב," *NIDOTTE* 1: 219–23; T. Römer, "Deuteronomy in Search of Origins," in *Reconsidering Israel and Judah: Recent Studies on the Deuteronomistic History* (SBTS 8; ed. G. N. Knoppers and J. G. McConville; Winona Lake, IN: Eisenbrauns, 2000), 121–35.

the presentation of the Sinai narrative in Exodus, commentators are divided about what the people heard from Yahweh himself and what they heard through Moses. On the one hand, the text seems to imply that Moses alone heard Yahweh's voice, because Moses alone went up the mountain and heard Yahweh speaking in thunder (Exod 20:19–20). In addition, Exod 20:18, which comes after the Decalogue, says that, after seeing the thunder and lightning, the sounds of the trumpets, and the smoke, the people were afraid and begged Moses to serve as mediator. This could be taken to mean that they neither heard nor wished to hear the Decalogue.[133]

On the other hand, Exod 19:24–25 indicates that Moses descended the mountain to warn the people against approaching it, which implies that Moses was not on the mountain at the time when the Decalogue was spoken. In addition, Exod 21:1 refers to the people in the third person, indicating that Moses was now acting as intermediary on their behalf, in accordance with their request in Exod 20:18–21. This suggests that they heard the Ten Commandments, but the rest of the *Torah* was presented to them by Moses, who had received it from Yahweh. The result is that it is not entirely clear from Exodus what the people heard directly and what was mediated by Moses.

In Deuteronomy, however, the situation is much more explicit. With the exception of the possible ambiguity between Deut 5:4 and 5:5, the account in Deuteronomy is largely straightforward in affirming that the whole assembly (קָהָל) heard Yahweh's proclamation of the Decalogue and nothing more (cf. Deut 5:22). Why is Deuteronomy apparently so concerned to stress the fact that all of the people heard the Decalogue, particularly when the account in Exodus is, by comparison, ambiguous on this matter?[134]

The answer, I believe, lies in the fact that one of the priorities of Deuteronomy is to convey that all Israel is responsible before Yahweh for demonstrating covenant loyalty through adherence to *Torah*. The

---

133. See M. Noth, *Exodus: A Commentary* (OTL; London: SCM, 1962), 168, who maintains that the Decalogue is a later addition. Therefore, Exod 20:18–21 is not dealing with the fear of having heard the Decalogue but with the fear of the theophany more generally. See also M. Greenberg, "Decalogue (The Ten Commandments)," *EncJud* 5: 1435–36, and the much more detailed discussion in B. S. Childs, *Exodus: A Commentary* (OTL; London: SCM, 1974), 351–60.

134. There have been many attempts to explain the differences between the two presentations. Some have seen in the somewhat ambiguous account in Exodus and the perceived contradiction in Deut 5:4–5 evidence of different Sinai/Horeb traditions lying behind the various texts. (See, esp., E. Nielsen, *The Ten Commandments in New Perspective* [SBT 2nd series; London: SCM, 1968].) Rabbinic exegetes have said that the people heard the first two commandments but nothing more (see Weinfeld, *Deuteronomy 1–11*, 240–41).

blurring of generations, discussed above, helps convey the point that every Israelite is, in a sense, part of the Horeb generation and is consequently responsible to demonstrate loyalty to Yahweh. A similar motivation may lie behind the emphasis on the fact that all of the people heard the Decalogue. The Decalogue is, of course, identified as Yahweh's covenant in Deut 4:13. The fact that all the people heard the terms of the covenant shows that the "whole people is directly involved in the reception of the Decalogue as the basic conditions of the covenant."[135]

The Words of Yahweh for All Generations

In this way the responsibility of the entire Horeb/Moab generation is stressed, as also is the responsibility of subsequent generations. This is seen, first, through the blurring of generations that we have already noticed. Though the Moab generation was not actually present at Horeb, the account of the giving of the Decalogue brings the Moab generation into the picture. The appropriately reverent and fearful response of the people in Deut 5:23–27 (as well as Yahweh's approval of the sentiments expressed by the people in Deut 5:28–29) is credited to the Moab generation, though the response is still, strictly speaking, the actions of the Horeb generation. At no point following the melding of generations in Deut 5:2–3 does the rhetoric shift from "you" (whether singular or plural) to "they." It is not that "they" responded favorably, but rather "you" did.

The responsibility of future generations is also seen in the recording of the covenant and the requirement that the terms of the commandment be diligently taught to future generations. Deuteronomy 5:22 notes that Yahweh wrote the words on two stone tablets.[136] The recording of the terms of a covenant (בְּרִית), their deposition, and demand for public recitation are sometimes found in political treaties in the ANE. These actions were designed to ensure the loyalty of subsequent generations of vassal kings to the suzerain.[137] In Deuteronomy, the existence of a permanent record of the terms of the covenant

---

135. McConville, *Deuteronomy*, 131–32.

136. Deuteronomy 10:4 makes it clear that the words on the tablets were the words of the Decalogue. The context of Deut 5:22 suggests as much, but this fact is explicit in connection with the second set of tablets.

137. D. J. McCarthy, *Treaty and Covenant* (AnBib 21a; Rome: Pontifical Biblical Institute, 1981), 63–66; M. G. Kline, *Treaty of the Great King: The Covenant Structure of Deuteronomy—Studies and Commentary* (Grand Rapids: Eerdmans, 1963), 75–76; J. H. Walton, *Ancient Israelite Literature in Its Cultural Context: A Survey of Parallels between Biblical and Ancient Near Eastern Texts* (LBI; Grand Rapids: Zondervan, 1989), 103–4.

serves as a reminder to subsequent generations of their obligations in order to demonstrate loyalty to their suzerain, Yahweh.

There is, however, even greater significance to the fact that Yahweh himself wrote the words. Sonnet notes that there is in Deut 5:22 a "tight sequence" in terms of the relationship between Yahweh's speaking and his writing.[138] That is, Deuteronomy makes clear that Yahweh spoke and then wrote the words he had spoken. The account in Exodus is less clear regarding the time when the tablets containing the Decalogue were written, but Deuteronomy seems to be emphasizing that the words were unambiguously written by Yahweh himself immediately after the words were spoken. In addition, the words written by Yahweh were later given to Moses. But it is clear from Deut 9:9–11 that the giving of the tablets occurred only later. Why, then, did the author include a reference to the giving of the tablets to Moses in Deut 5:22, when it is clear from later texts that this occurred only after a rather substantial interval? Sonnet argues that the reference to the giving of the tablets in Deut 5:22 introduces another element to the sequence: speaking leads to writing, which is followed by giving.[139] The sequence may be graphically represented thus:

speaking → writing → giving

In presenting the giving of the law in this way, Deuteronomy establishes a paradigm by which the words of Yahweh are given to the people in written form through the mediation of Moses.

But the sequence does not stop here. Following the record of divine writing in Deut 5:22, there is a command that the people write words on their heart in Deut 6:6–9.[140] Included in this exhortation is the command to teach future generations of Israelites the words of Yahweh. So, the sequence is extended, and the giving of the words of Yahweh to the people (either directly or through the mediation of Moses) leads to the teaching of the words to subsequent generations. The graphic portrayal is thus extended:

speaking → writing → giving → teaching

The paradigmatic nature of this sequence may be seen in the fact that it is repeated later in the book.[141] Deuteronomy 10:4 is another depiction of the writing of the tablets, and this is followed, as in Deut 6:6–9,

---

138. Sonnet, *Book within the Book*, 42.
139. Ibid., 45.
140. Ibid., 51–54.
141. Ibid., 69–70.

with a command for the people to write the words on their heart and to teach them to subsequent generations in Deut 11:18–20.

It seems, then, that there is an important relationship between receiving the words of Yahweh and passing them on. The Israelites are expected to ensure the dissemination to future generations by diligently teaching to the children the words that were spoken by Yahweh. This, according to Deut 6:5–9, is the means by which love for Yahweh will be demonstrated.

Before considering the significance of receiving and passing on the words of Yahweh for the theology of this section, we now briefly will attend to two issues related to the interpretation of Deut 6:5–9. The first has to do with the nature of "loving" Yahweh in the context, and the second is the nature of the reference to "these words" (הַדְּבָרִים הָאֵלֶּה) in Deut 6:6.

The first issue is pertinent to this examination because it has to do with the obligations of each generation to live in obedience to *Torah* as a means of showing allegiance to Yahweh. In ANE political treaties, words for "love" are often used to describe the relationship between vassal and suzerain. So, for example, EA 158.36–38 speaks of the Pharaoh's love for the vassal.[142] In addition, the devotion of the vassal to the suzerain is described in terms of love. EA 53.40–44 says, "My lord, just as I love the king, m[y] lord, so too the king of Nuḫašše, the king of Nii, the king of Zinzar, and the king of Tunanab; all these kings are my lord's servants."[143] In this context, love is the terminology used to express total loyalty and devotion. Moran notes that "to love the Pharaoh is to serve him and to remain faithful to the status of vassal."[144]

This sheds light on the meaning of the command that "you shall love Yahweh your God" (וְאָהַבְתָּ אֵת יְהוָה אֱלֹהֶיךָ) in Deut 6:5. Given the general parallels between Deuteronomy and the ANE political treaties, it is likely that the sense of "love" as demonstrating loyalty is in view here.[145] This love is not primarily affective (though this is not to say that the affective sense is excluded[146]) but is instead "a personal, intimate, trusting relation."[147] Moreover, this love assumes that the

---

142. W. L. Moran, *The Amarna Letters* (Baltimore: Johns Hopkins University Press, 1992), 244–45. Other examples of the love of the suzerain for the vassal are found in EA 121.61; 123.23. See also idem, "The Ancient Near Eastern Background of the Love of God in Deuteronomy," *CBQ* 25 (1963): 77–87.

143. Moran, *Amarna Letters*, 125; idem, "Love of God," 79.

144. Ibid.

145. Nelson, *Deuteronomy*, 91; Brueggemann, *Deuteronomy*, 84. See also the introduction to the present book.

146. Cf. Wright, *Deuteronomy*, 98.

147. Miller, *Deuteronomy*, 102.

vassal's status as vassal is recognized and accepted. To "love" the "Great King" is to demonstrate obedience and allegiance to him.

This fits well with the theological understanding of the section of Deuteronomy that we are investigating. Yahweh is the sovereign who redeemed Israel from Egyptian bondage. As a result, he alone is deserving of the loyalty of the people. In hearing and accepting the basic terms of the covenant—the Decalogue—the people are committing themselves to complete and total allegiance to him alone.

A second issue that needs to be addressed is the nature of the דְּבָרִים ("words") that in Deut 6:6 are to be taught to succeeding generations. There are several options. This term could refer to: (1) only Deut 6:4, (2) the Decalogue, or (3) the whole of the *Torah* taught at Moab. The phrase "which I am commanding you today" (אֲשֶׁר אָנֹכִי מְצַוְּךָ הַיּוֹם) points toward seeing the דְּבָרִים as the whole of the teaching given at Moab, because there is much in Deuteronomy that fits into the category of commands. Moreover, Deut 5:31 and 6:1 refer to הַמִּצְוָה ("the commandment"), which points to the whole of what Yahweh commanded Moses to teach at Moab. It is likely, then, that the use of "words" in Deut 6:6 refers to the whole of Deuteronomy, because the entire book is presented as a record of Moses' teaching at Moab.[148]

The significance of the last point actually brings us back to the significance of the apparent emphasis on the sequence of speaking → writing → giving → teaching. As we have seen, the people are exhorted to keep Yahweh's דְּבָרִים ("words") in their hearts and, indeed, to impress them on their children. The words that are to saturate their lives are Moses' words of instruction given at Moab, as noted above. But it is significant that Moses' words at Moab represent a divergence from the presentation of the law at Sinai. I argued above (pp. 122–134) that the differences between the presentation of the theophany at Horeb in Exodus and in Deuteronomy are not of the sort that Weinfeld and others posit. But the two presentations are different in some respects.

Deuteronomy presents the Horeb event as foundational to the existence of Israel as a nation and as the covenant people of Yahweh. Further evidence for this is found in Deuteronomy's use of the term קָהָל ("assembly"). Deuteronomy 5:22 is explicit, noting that the whole assembly heard the words of the Decalogue. Subsequent references to the Horeb event in Deuteronomy refer to it as the "day of the assembly" (Deut 9:10; 10:4; 18:16). It is here that the whole people, as קָהָל, enter into the covenant with Yahweh. Thus the exodus-Horeb event is central to the foundation of Israel as the people of Yahweh.[149] This

148. Sonnet, *Book within the Book*, 52–55; Nelson, *Deuteronomy*, 91.
149. McConville, *Deuteronomy*, 131.

explains in part why the motivation for the Sabbath law is different in Deut 5:12–15, when compared with Exodus: the emphasis on the exodus points to the establishment of the people as the people of Yahweh. But, though the events at Horeb were foundational, the words of Yahweh are applicable in other times and in different situations. I argued above that the different motivations for the Sabbath law are not incompatible, nor are they of the sort that is sometimes claimed. But they do address the people of Yahweh at different times, facing different challenges and opportunities. The people addressed at Moab are, in the narrative perspective of Deuteronomy, on the verge of entering. the land. It is, as we have seen, a significant moment of transition.[150] In this moment, the events at Horeb are "re-realized" for the Moab generation in a way appropriate for them.[151] As Merrill notes, Deuteronomy presents "changing theological emphases for an unchanging God."[152]

This may also help to explain why Deuteronomy seems to be at pains to clarify exactly what the people heard directly and what they heard through the mediation of Moses. The terms of the covenant—the Decalogue—were heard directly by the people, because this event was foundational for the people and nation. The rest of Yahweh's words are explicitly said in Deuteronomy to have been spoken through Moses. To be sure, this does not undermine their authority, because Moses is established in Deut 5:31 as the official mediator of Yahweh's words.[153] But the very fact that the statutes and ordinances (הַחֻקִּים וְהַמִּשְׁפָּטִים) are clearly shown to have been presented through the mediation of Moses points to their different quality.[154] The fact that Moses, the official mediator of Yahweh's words, is able to interpret the law for the Moab generation points to the continuing relevance of the *Torah* in changing circumstances.

Conclusions regarding Deuteronomy 5:1–6:9

In the face of transition on the verge of entering the land of promise, the people of the Moab generation are instructed in the ways they can

---

150. See chap. 2 above.

151. McConville, *Deuteronomy*, 136.

152. Merrill, *Deuteronomy*, 152.

153. Moses is shown in Deuteronomy to have acted in this capacity prior to this time, of course (cf. Deut 1:6), but in the fabula of Deuteronomy, the official sanction of Moses as mediator occurs *prior* to the departure from Horeb, recorded in Deut 1:6.

154. This is further seen when Deut 10:1–5 is compared with Deut 31:24–26. The tablets written by Yahweh are stored in the ark, whereas the record of Moses' words are stored *next* to it. This suggests an important distinction between the direct and mediated words of Yahweh.

live out loyalty to Yahweh and continue to receive the blessings of the covenant relationship. They do so by keeping *Torah* and passing on the instruction to subsequent generations. The giving of *Torah* to the people is enshrined within Deuteronomy; it remains the foundational event for the people. But *Torah* is also shown in Deuteronomy to be capable of application to varying circumstances and situations. *Torah* itself does not change, but it is capable of being appropriated and applied by every generation in vastly different circumstances. The blurring of generations shows that each generation stands, figuratively speaking, "at Moab." The people of God in subsequent generations also must look to the foundational event at which *Torah* was given and the people constituted. At the same time, each generation is responsible before God to demonstrate total loyalty to him through adherence to *Torah*. And subsequent generations also have a responsibility to instruct future generations how to live a life marked by total allegiance to Yahweh.

Deliberate theological points are being made in this section, but they are not what Weinfeld and others propose. In Deut 5:1–6:9 the supremacy of Yahweh as creator of the people of God is stressed and demands for total loyalty are made. In addition, the relevance of *Torah*, the word of Yahweh, is emphasized for all generations. The foundation of the people of Yahweh is particularly stressed in this section, as it was through the covenant at Horeb: the people accepted the responsibility of living as the people of Yahweh. Thus, in the context of changing circumstances on the plains of Moab, a subsequent generation is approached as if they, too, were at Horeb and had assumed the same obligations. Through the blending of generations and the emphasis on teaching the words of Yahweh, this section seeks to demonstrate that *Torah* remains the foundation for every generation of the people of Yahweh.

Chapter 4

The Supremacy of the Giver of *Torah*: Deuteronomy 12

It is in Deut 12 that the three central tenets of the Deuteronomic revolution envisioned by Weinfeld are considered to be most readily apparent. In chap. 1 above, I presented and analyzed the broad contours of the arguments in favor of centralization, secularization, and demythologization. In this chapter, however, the focus will be on Deut 12 and the ways in which it supposedly contributed to the Deuteronomic revolution. It is here that centralization is explicitly commanded, necessitating alteration of previous practices and resulting in legislation permitting so-called "profane slaughter." In addition, there is in this chapter, in the view of many, a deliberate attempt to demythologize by means of the Name theology.

Deuteronomy 12 is the opening chapter of the legal corpus of Deuteronomy, following the historical remembrance and parenesis of chaps. 1–11. Like the beginning of the Covenant Code, the legal section of Deuteronomy begins with an altar law. Unlike the Covenant Code, however, the altar law in Deuteronomy demands a single place of worship, in direct contrast to the altar laws found elsewhere in the Pentateuch and in contrast to the practice of worship at the time that the book was ostensibly written.[1] This radical demand for centralization, when carried out by Josiah, resulted in the transformation of theology and practice in Israel.[2]

The unity of Deut 12 has long been questioned. While many argue that this chapter is the result of the compilation of various sources dating to various times, there is no consensus about the identification or dating of various strata.[3] Indeed, the various proposals regarding

---

1. M. Weinfeld, *Deuteronomy 1–11* (AB 5; New York: Doubleday, 1991), 37–44; idem, *Deuteronomy and the Deuteronomic School* (Oxford: Oxford University Press, 1972; repr. Winona Lake, IN: Eisenbrauns, 1992), 191–209.

2. Weinfeld, *Deuteronomy 1–11*, 78–81.

3. Some of the more recent studies include B. M. Levinson, *Deuteronomy and the Hermeneutics of Legal Innovation* (Oxford: Oxford University Press, 1997), 24–50; N. Lohfink, "Zur deuteronomischen Zentralisationformel," in *Studien zum Deuteronomium und zur*

the prehistory of the chapter have been challenged, and none is persuasive in its entirety.[4] As Levinson (who maintains that the chapter is best seen as composite) notes, "The problem with many such approaches is that . . . they overlook both the evidence for the secondary imposition of an editorial structure and the difficulties that such deliberate redactional reworking pose for reconstructing literary history in the first place."[5] Moreover, if it is granted that the redactor(s) of the final form of the book intended to communicate a coherent message to his/their audience, then certain diachronic questions become less compelling as the message of the final form is analyzed.

In addition, a positive case can be made for seeing the chapter as a unity. Most recently, McConville has argued that the requirements of the supposedly earliest form of the law (12:13–19) are incoherent on their own. In addition, he notes that the different forms of the centralization formula need not be considered to be different types, because the "short form" used elsewhere can be understood as presupposing a longer form (Deut 31:11; Josh 9:27). Finally, he argues that a coherent theological argument can be discerned in the chapter, and there are stylistic features that may point to unity.[6]

---

deuteronomistischen Literatur II (Stuttgart: Katholisches Bibelwerk, 1991), 147–77; A. D. H. Mayes, *Deuteronomy* (NCB; Grand Rapids: Eerdmans / London: Marshall, Morgan & Scott, 1979), 220–21; R. D. Nelson, *Deuteronomy* (OTL; Louisville: Westminster John Knox, 2002), 150–59; E. Reuter, *Kultzentralisation: Entstehung und Theologie von Dtn 12* (BBB 87; Frankfurt a.M.: Anton Hain, 1993); A. Rofé, "The Strata of the Law about the Centralization of Worship in Deuteronomy and the History of the Deuteronomic Movement," in *Deuteronomy: Issues and Interpretation* (OTS; Edinburgh: T. & T. Clark, 2002), 97–101; Y. Suzuki, "'The Place Which Yahweh Your God Will Choose' in Deuteronomy," in *Problems in Biblical Theology: Essays in Honor of Rolf Knierim* (ed. H. Sun and K. Eades; Grand Rapids: Eerdmans, 1997), 338–52. For a comprehensive bibliography on this issue, including some of the more important older studies, see D. L. Christensen, *Deuteronomy 1:1–21:9* (WBC 6a; Nashville: Thomas Nelson, 2001), 231–32.

4. See J. G. McConville, *Law and Theology in Deuteronomy* ([JSOTSup 33; Sheffield: JSOT Press, 1984], 40–42, 56–57), where the approaches of Steuernagel, Horst, and von Rad are critiqued; and idem, *Deuteronomy* (AOTC 5; Leicester: Apollos / Downers Grove, IL: InterVarsity, 2002), 214–16.

5. Levinson, *Legal Innovation*, 26.

6. McConville, *Deuteronomy*, 215–16. Levinson cautions that coherent literary structures do not necessarily point to literary unity but may, rather, be the result of an attempt on the part of an editor to obscure any seams that may have existed (Levinson, *Legal Innovation*, 27). While he is correct in urging caution regarding conclusions that may be drawn from the appearance of literary unity, he underestimates the possibility that rhetorical emphasis may explain certain features of the text, such as repetition and the *Numeruswechsel*. While rhetorical and stylistic unity do not *prove* literary unity, they certainly do not *disprove* it, and they certainly do not prove a literary composite.

Prevailing View: Radical Reform

Centralization

The first feature of Deut 12 to be examined is the demand for centralization.[7] After identifying the section to follow as the "statutes and ordinances" (וְהַמִּשְׁפָּטִים הַחֻקִּים) that were anticipated since chap. 4, Deut
12 orders the destruction of alien cults and commands (vv. 5–7) that
worship be centered on the "place that Yahweh your God shall choose
out of all your tribes to establish his name there as its dwelling place"[8]
(אֶל־הַמָּקוֹם אֲשֶׁר־יִבְחַר יְהוָה אֱלֹהֵיכֶם מִכָּל־שִׁבְטֵיכֶם לָשׂוּם אֶת־שְׁמוֹ שָׁם לְשִׁכְנוֹ). The exhortation continues, with repetitions of the demand for worship only
at "the place" in vv. 11 and 14, with some variation in wording.

Permission is then granted for the slaughter of animals for food
away from "the place," with the proviso that the blood of the slaughtered animal not be eaten (vv. 8–16). This is followed by another command to take all offerings to the place (vv. 17–19). The provision for
local slaughter is repeated, as is the requirement that all offerings and
sacrifices be carried out at the place (vv. 26–27). The section concludes
with an exhortation to worship Yahweh as he demands, repeats the
command to eradicate all vestiges of Canaanite worship, and demands that no alterations be made to the commandments given.[9]

The radical nature of the Deuteronomic program may be seen, it is
argued, by the way in which the demand for centralization in Deut 12
stands in stark contrast to the demands of other regulations in the Pentateuch. The requirements of Deut 12 are contrasted with Exod 20:24–
25 and Lev 17. Exodus 20:24–25 seems to permit multiple altars, while
Lev 17 restricts all sacrifice to the tabernacle during the wilderness period. This has been interpreted as showing that Deuteronomy was

---

7. For simplicity of analysis, I will examine the three aspects of the Deuteronomic revolution separately, though I realize that this is somewhat artificial; all three elements are
thought to run throughout the chapter and are indeed interrelated.

8. The translation of Deut 12:5 is problematic. The MT presupposes an otherwise un-
attested nominal form, שֶׁכֶן. This is often emended to לְשִׁכְנוֹ and interpreted as a *Piel* of שָׁכַן.
This is then seen as a doublet of לָשׂוּם (see, e.g., E. Tov, *Textual Criticism of the Hebrew Bible*
[Minneapolis: Fortress, 1992], 42, and n. 19). McConville (*Deuteronomy*, 211) notes that
there is "ambiguity concerning whether the suffix of לְשִׁכְנוֹ refers to 'it', that is, the 'name',
or to 'him', that is, Yahweh." But he rightly argues (ibid.) that the verb תִּדְרְשׁוּ is required to
complete the command begun at the beginning of the verse. This suggests that the verse
should be read as referring to its dwelling and refers to the name itself. This is in line with
v. 11, and I will use this translation in my analysis.

9. The chapter ends at v. 31 in the Hebrew versification, though it is generally
agreed that the thought of the chapter continues to 13:1[12:32]. See Christensen, *Deuteronomy 1:1–21:9*, 233–35.

seeking to transform the earlier law found in the Covenant Code, while the later Priestly material assumed the fact of centralization and sought to rescind the permission for profane slaughter granted by Deut 12.[10]

When compared with the altar law in Exod 20:24–25, the radical nature of Deuteronomy's requirements are held to be most readily apparent. Exodus 20:24 states:

מִזְבַּח אֲדָמָה תַּעֲשֶׂה־לִּי וְזָבַחְתָּ עָלָיו אֶת־עֹלֹתֶיךָ וְאֶת־שְׁלָמֶיךָ אֶת־צֹאנְךָ
וְאֶת־בְּקָרֶךָ בְּכָל־הַמָּקוֹם אֲשֶׁר אַזְכִּיר אֶת־שְׁמִי אָבוֹא אֵלֶיךָ וּבֵרַכְתִּיךָ:

An altar of earth you shall make for me, and you shall sacrifice on it your burnt offerings and your peace offerings, your sheep and your oxen. In every place where I cause my name to be remembered I will come to you and I will bless you.

In contrast, Deut 12:5, the most restrictive form of the centralization formula in the chapter,[11] says:

כִּי אִם־אֶל־הַמָּקוֹם אֲשֶׁר־יִבְחַר יְהוָה אֱלֹהֵיכֶם מִכָּל־שִׁבְטֵיכֶם לָשׂוּם אֶת־שְׁמוֹ
שָׁם לְשִׁכְנוֹ תִדְרְשׁוּ וּבָאתָ שָׁמָּה:

But you shall seek the place that Yahweh your God shall choose out of all your tribes to establish his name there as its dwelling place, and there you shall come.

---

10. J. Wellhausen, *Prolegomena to the History of Israel* (New York: Meridian, 1957), 35, 50. This view is advanced more recently in M. Noth, *Leviticus* (rev. ed.; OTL; Philadelphia: Westminster, 1965), 129–30. Many commentators now reject Wellhausen's reconstruction of the relative order of the pentateuchal source documents and argue that P precedes rather than follows D. Thus, Milgrom concludes that D overturns the more stringent regulations of Lev 17 (H), not vice versa. See J. Milgrom, *Leviticus 1–16* (AB 3; New York: Doubleday, 1991), 29; and idem, *Leviticus 17–22* (AB 3A; New York: Doubleday, 2000), 1454. Weinfeld, too, argues that P is prior to or at least concurrent with D; see Weinfeld, *Deuteronomic School*, 180–81. More recently, Wenham has argued that P is not just prior to D but the earliest of the pentateuchal sources; see G. J. Wenham, "The Priority of P," *VT* 49 (1999): 240–58.

11. Even Welch, who argues against seeing this chapter as centralizing, concedes that Deut 12:5 cannot be read as distributive ("in *any* of your tribes"), as is possible with Deut 12:14. He concludes that Deut 12:5 is a later insertion. See A. C. Welch, *The Code of Deuteronomy: A New Theory of Its Origin* (London: James Clarke, 1924), 58–62. Thus Manley, who follows Welch in seeing Deuteronomy as not requiring centralized worship in a single place, does not even deal with Deut 12:5 in his comparison of Deut 12 and Exod 20:24–25 but instead focuses exclusively on Deut 12:14. See G. T. Manley, *The Book of the Law: Studies in the Date of Deuteronomy* (London: Tyndale, 1957), 131–34. On the various forms of the centralization formula in Deuteronomy, see B. Halpern, "The Centralization Formula in Deuteronomy," *VT* 31 (1981): 20–38; and, more recently, R. D. Nelson, *Deuteronomy* (OTL; Louisville: Westminster John Knox, 2002), 152–53.

The altar law in Exodus appears to allow for a multiplicity of altars, while the law in Deut 12 restricts sacrifice to the single place that Yahweh would choose.

Levinson argues that Deut 12 represents a careful reworking of the altar law in Exod 20 and that the very syntax and lexemes of the earlier law are used in Deut 12 to promote its agenda.[12] His conception may be seen in table 1.[13]

Table 1

Exod 20:24	A	You shall sacrifice	וזבחת
		upon it	עליו
		your *burnt offerings.* . . .	את עלתיך
	B	*In every place* where . . .	בכל המקום אשר
Deut 12:14	B¹	In the place	במקום
		which Yahweh shall choose . . .	אשר יבחר יהוה
	A¹	there you shall offer	שמ תעלה
		your burnt offerings	עלתיך

Levinson argues that by using the very words of the earlier altar law, the authors of Deuteronomy have "tendentiously reworked [the earlier law] by means of studied, transformative exegesis, appropriating its very wording to express their own innovative agenda. Their implicit argument is that their innovation represents the actual force of that altar law, which they nevertheless replace by turning its own syntax and lexemes against it."[14]

Secularization

One of the most important examples of secularization in Deuteronomy, according to Weinfeld and others, is the law of profane slaughter presented in Deut 12. As we have seen, following the demand for centralization of worship to "the place" is a concession that animals may be slaughtered freely in the towns in which people live. This is, first of all, seen as a practical concession, since prior to the Deuteronomic reform all slaughter of non-game animals was to be carried out at an altar. The elimination of local sanctuaries meant that no altars were available to people living at a distance from the central sanctuary, so Deuteronomy allows for the nonsacrificial slaughter of domesticated

12. Levinson, *Legal Innovation*, 32–33.
13. Ibid., 35.
14. Ibid., 34.

animals. This contributed to secularization, in Weinfeld's view, because "a significant aspect of Israelite daily life [was freed] from its ties to the cultus."[15]

More important, however, is the notion that nonsacrificial slaughter is perceived as a rejection of the earlier conception that the blood of an animal possessed an inherently sacred quality. Weinfeld notes that Lev 17:6 demands that the blood of *all* slain non-game animals is to be brought to the Tent of Meeting and the blood sprinkled on the altar. The blood of game animals is to be poured out and covered with earth (Lev 17:13). The reason for this, he argues, is that all spilled blood demands "vengeance and satisfaction" and, since the blood of game animals cannot be atoned for by pouring it on the altar, it must be covered up.[16] But Deuteronomy presents a vastly different picture. Weinfeld argues that Deut 12 repudiates the notion of the sanctity of the blood, doing so by legislating that the blood of all animals slaughtered away from the sanctuary is to be poured out "like water" (Deut 12:16, 24). Demanding that the blood of animals slaughtered for nonsacrificial purposes be poured out like water asserts that the blood "has no more a sacral value than water has."[17]

Levinson supports this interpretation by once again noting the apparently deliberate way in which the very words of the earlier law are reworked in Deut 12 in support of the radical innovation of secular slaughter. He notes that certain key words are repeated in the Deuteronomic legislation and argues that this has been done in a way that has subtly shifted their meaning. Thus, where Exod 20:24 says, וְזָבַחְתָּ עָלָיו אֶת־עֹלֹתֶיךָ וְאֶת־שְׁלָמֶיךָ אֶת־צֹאנְךָ וְאֶת־בְּקָרֶךָ ("and you shall sacrifice on it [i.e., an earthen altar] your burnt offerings and your peace offerings, your sheep and your oxen"), Deut 12:21 says, וְזָבַחְתָּ מִבְּקָרְךָ וּמִצֹּאנְךָ ("And you may slaughter [זָבַח] from your cattle and from your sheep"). The changes in Deuteronomy are due to the fact that the law is here dealing with nonsacrificial slaughter. Levinson notes that

> local secular slaughter by definition cannot take place עליו 'upon it'—upon an altar—because Deuteronomy sanctions only the single altar at the cultic center. For the same reason, the lemma's reference to the cultic sacrifices את עלתיך ואת שלמיך 'your burnt offerings and your well-being offerings' is deleted from this noncultic context.[18]

He goes on to note that the elements omitted from the Exodus law are found in Deut 12:26–27, which deals with sacrifice and ritual at the

---

15. Weinfeld, *Deuteronomic School,* 214.
16. Ibid.
17. Ibid.
18. Levinson, *Legal Innovation,* 37.

central sanctuary and would be appropriate there.[19] He maintains that the authors of Deuteronomy have very carefully reworked the earlier law, even to the point of using the same words, even where problematic (such as the use of זָבַח to refer to nonsacrificial killing). This leads Levinson to conclude that the "author struggles to justify the innovation of secular slaughter in terms of prior textual authority, almost as if the older Exodus altar law itself lexically sanctioned the very innovation that overturns it."[20]

The legal justification for profane slaughter is debated. Deuteronomy 12:21 says that, if the place "is too far away from you, then you may slaughter your cattle and your sheep . . . *just as I commanded you* (כַּאֲשֶׁר צִוִּיתִךָ)." It is unclear just what commandment is referred to here. Many commentators see this as referring back to v. 15, where profane slaughter is first dealt with.[21] But this raises certain questions, because v. 15 is not a command but a granting of permission.[22] Moreover, there are no commands in the Pentateuch that specify the exact manner in which animals are to be slaughtered, and profane slaughter is not "commanded" anywhere else. This has led some to conclude that the citation in Deut 12:21 is a pseudoascription designed to harmonize Deut 12:13–19 with Lev 17,[23] a pseudocitation in which the authors of Deuteronomy attempt to give their innovations "the necessary textual pedigree,"[24] or a specific means of carrying out the slaughter.[25]

Demythologization

The final facet of the Deuteronomic revolution that is seen in this chapter is demythologization. Deuteronomy 12 is often thought to provide evidence for the view that Deuteronomy seeks to repudiate earlier conceptions of the presence of Yahweh through the "Name" theology. Weinfeld notes that Deuteronomy consistently defines the sanctuary not as the place in which Yahweh dwells but the place where his name is established. The purpose of this deliberate reference to the establishment of the "Name" of Yahweh is to "combat the

---

19. Ibid.

20. Ibid., 38.

21. See, e.g., Nelson, *Deuteronomy*, 161; S. R. Driver, *A Critical and Exegetical Commentary on Deuteronomy* (3rd ed.; ICC; Edinburgh: T. & T. Clark, 1901), 148.

22. As noted by J. Milgrom, "Profane Slaughter and a Formulaic Key to the Composition of Deuteronomy," *HUCA* 47 (1976): 1–17; and Levinson, *Legal Innovation*, 41–42.

23. M. Fishbane, *Biblical Interpretation in Ancient Israel* (Oxford: Clarendon, 1985), 534.

24. Levinson, *Legal Innovation*, 42–43.

25. Milgrom, "Profane Slaughter," 13–15.

ancient popular belief that the Deity actually dwelled within the sanctuary."[26]

Weinfeld maintains that this attempt at transforming earlier conceptions of the presence of Yahweh may be seen in the use of the phrase לְשַׁכֵּן שְׁמוֹ in Deuteronomy. This phrase originally had nothing to do with an abstract notion of the presence of God but was used by the authors of Deuteronomy in such a way as to imbue the term with an abstract sense of God's presence.[27] The fact that Deuteronomy and the Deuteronomi(sti)c literature never use שָׁכֵן שָׁם to refer to Yahweh's dwelling in the temple demonstrates, it is claimed, the intention of the authors to demythologize earlier concepts of Yahweh, specifically the idea that he was actually present.[28]

Evaluation

Deuteronomy 12 is a crucial chapter to scholars who hold the prevailing theory that Deuteronomy represents a radical reform program of centralization, secularization, and demythologization. It is necessary at this point to analyze the interpretations of Deut 12 as presented above in an effort to determine if the prevailing view is the best interpretation of the data of the text.

Centralization

One of the tenets of the prevailing view is that Deut 12, at least in some important respects, modifies earlier law and practice, most notably the altar law of Exod 20:24–25, as we have seen. But recent investigation has raised the possibility that the differences between the two sources are not as dramatic as Weinfeld and others maintain.

The Nature of the Altar Law in Exodus

Questions have been raised about whether or not the altar law in Exod 20:24–25 should be read as standing in stark contrast to the law in Deut 12. Crüsemann, for example, notes that the similarities between the altar laws in the Covenant Code and Deut 12 are more striking than most scholars assert. Like Deut 12, the altar law in Exod 20:24 says that a legitimate site is one that is associated with Yahweh's Name. More importantly, Exod 20:24 specifies that it is the place (or

---

26. Weinfeld, *Deuteronomic School,* 193. This view was advocated earlier by G. von Rad, *Studies in Deuteronomy* (trans. D. M. G. Stalker; Chicago: Henry Regnery / London: SCM, 1953), 37–44.

27. Weinfeld, *Deuteronomic School,* 193–94.

28. Ibid.

places) where Yahweh causes his Name to be remembered that are legitimate. Crüsemann notes that Yahweh

> does not promise his presence at even all sites with associated (ancient) traditions, but only on those where his name is still proclaimed. This is not a critique of the deuteronomic understanding, but rather an— incomplete—parallel to it. If we draw a correlation using the fact that the divine *name* is what constitutes a true shrine, then we are justified in speaking of a pre- or early form of the deuteronomic demand for centralization together with its underlying theology.[29]

In both altar laws, the legitimacy of a worship site depends, first, on its association with Yahweh's Name. Second, a legitimate worship site must be based on Yahweh's choice of it, either in causing his name to be "remembered" there (Exod 20:24) or in establishing it as a habitation for his name (Deut 12:5). So, although the two laws are different, they nevertheless share some important characteristics.

Others have questioned whether the altar law in Exod 20:24–25 should be read as dealing with a multiplicity of altars. Cassuto argues that the context of the passage suggests that multiple altars are *not* in view. From the narrative perspective of Exodus, the Israelites are leaving Sinai, where the people had experienced Yahweh's presence in profound ways. They may have felt that Yahweh was uniquely present at Sinai and that their departure was also a departure from Yahweh. The altar law of Exod 20:24, in this view, stresses that Yahweh will continue to be with his people wherever he causes his name to be remembered, not just at Sinai. Moreover, the specific provisions of the altar law refer to a single altar ("*an* altar of earth," not "altars of earth"), and so may be compatible with a single altar, as suggested by Deut 12:5.[30] Similarly, Bakon reasons that the emphasis in the Exodus altar law is on Yahweh's choice of the place and maintains that the pentateuchal literature is consistent in demanding a single place of sacrifice.[31] Finally, Van Seters argues that "it is entirely possible, if

---

29. F. Crüsemann, *The Torah: Theology and Social History of Old Testament Law* (Minneapolis: Fortress, 1996), 173.

30. U. Cassuto, *A Commentary on the Book of Exodus* (trans. I. Abrahams; Jerusalem: Magnes, 1967), 256–57. A similar view is presented in B. Jacob, *The Second Book of the Bible: Exodus* (trans. W. Jacob; Hoboken, NJ: KTAV, 1992), 752–53. This is, of course, not the mainstream view. See B. S. Childs, *Exodus* (OTL; London: SCM, 1974), 447 for an analysis of this view and a defense of the prevailing view of Exod 20:24 as dealing with a multiplicity of altars. See also the analysis of J. M. Sprinkle, '*The Book of the Covenant': A Literary Approach* (JSOTSup 174; Sheffield: JSOT Press, 1994), 47. The Samaritan Pentateuch on Exod 20:24b reads "in the place," which suggests that the requirements of the law were understood in terms of a single (Shechem) sanctuary.

31. S. Bakon, "Centralization of Worship," *JBQ* 26 (1988): 26–27.

not preferable, to interpret this whole law as having reference to a single altar."[32]

Of greater importance, however, is the fact that in the narrative context of the book of Exodus, the focus of Exod 20:24–25 is *not* on the number of altars. Rather, the emphasis is on how Yahweh is to be worshiped properly. Exodus 20:22–23, immediately preceding the altar law, draws a contrast between Yahweh's revelation of himself at Sinai and worship of icons. The exact nature of the relationship between the fact of Yahweh's speaking and the prohibition of idols is not provided here. But a contrast is drawn between worshiping Yahweh alongside gods of silver and gold and the rather simple, unadorned altar called for in vv. 24–25. The focus, then, is on proper Yahweh worship in contrast to idols, not on the number of altars. It is simply not the purpose of this text to establish the number of altars that could be considered legitimate. It is not the case, therefore, that the text unambiguously permits multiple contemporary altars.

The Nature of the Altar Law in Deuteronomy 12
Recently, scholars have also argued that Deut 12 itself is not necessarily limiting all worship to one sanctuary. Wenham has argued that Deuteronomy envisions a central, but not sole, sanctuary for Israel. That is, the legislation in Deuteronomy provides for a central sanctuary, but this does not preclude the possibility of other legitimate Yahweh sanctuaries elsewhere.[33] Evidence for this view is found in the fact that Deut 27 explicitly commands that an altar be constructed on Mount Ebal and that burnt offerings and peace offerings be offered there. Furthermore, Wenham notes, Deut 27 calls for the inscription of the law at the site on Mount Ebal, which is appropriate for a sanctuary.[34]

---

32. J. Van Seters, "Cultic Laws in the Covenant Code and Their Relationship to Deuteronomy and the Holiness Code," in *Studies in the Book of Exodus: Redaction-Reception-Interpretation* (ed. M. Vervenne; Leuven: Leuven University Press, 1996), 325. See also idem, *The Life of Moses: The Yahwist as Historian in Exodus–Numbers* (Louisville: Westminster John Knox, 1994), 280–82. In maintaining that the altar law in Exod 20:24–25 refers to a single sanctuary, Van Seters concludes that v. 24b is best conceived of as referring to a multiplicity of places where Yahweh's name will be invoked, though not where sacrifice will be carried out. The point here is simply that it is not *necessary* to conclude that the Exodus altar law envisions multiple altars.

33. G. J. Wenham, "Deuteronomy and the Central Sanctuary," *TynBul* 22 (1971): 103–18, especially 109–16; E. H. Merrill (*Deuteronomy* [NAC 4; Nashville: Broadman & Holman, 1994], 223–24) follows Wenham in this distinction. A similar view is advocated in McConville, *Law and Theology*, 28–29. Later, however, McConville (J. G. McConville and J. G. Millar, *Time and Place in Deuteronomy* [JSOTSup 179; Sheffield: Sheffield Academic Press, 1994], 117–23) altered his views, arguing that the legislation in Deuteronomy demands a sole sanctuary but one that could be located in a succession of places (see below).

34. Wenham, "Central Sanctuary," 114.

It has been noted that the wording of the command in Deut 27:5 regarding the construction of the altar is similar to the wording of the altar law in Exod 20:24. This has led some to argue that the command in Deut 27:5 is earlier than the altar law in Deut 12 and is, therefore, not Deuteronomic.[35] Others have claimed that this is a late addition.[36] But these proposed solutions do not explain how a final compiler could have included Deut 12 and Deut 27 in the same composition, particularly if, as is usually argued, Deuteronomy was written to advance the interests of Jerusalem and the royal administration. Moreover, the fact that Josh 8 records the construction of an altar at Mount Ebal suggests that this is not an afterthought but deliberate.[37] In any event, the presence of both chaps. 12 and 27 in the final form of Deuteronomy makes it difficult to argue that the book in its present form demands a single sanctuary without exception.

This question has been addressed in other ways as well. McConville and Niehaus[38] have argued that Deut 12 demands a single sanctuary but insist that the legislation provides that the location of that sanctuary could change. Shechem (and the ceremony described in Deut 27), then, is understood as one of the sites that serves as "the place" that Yahweh chose and was, therefore, a legitimate place of Yahweh worship. So, Deut 12 demands that there be a single sanctuary, but this requirement could be met in a succession of places, each of which is chosen by Yahweh. If this is the case, then the altar law of Deut 12 is not radically different from the altar law in Exod 20:24–25.

Another view has been advocated as well. Looking at the final form of Deut 12, Pitkänen argues that the chapter advocates centralization as an ideal to be lived out only when the nation has fully conquered the land and entered into the rest and safety that are promised (for the future, according to the narrative perspective of the book) in Deut 12:10.[39] He further notes that the "promise in v. 10 about the

---

35. See, e.g., G. von Rad, *Deuteronomy: A Commentary* (OTL; London: SCM, 1966), 165; and M. Anbar, "The Story about the Building of an Altar on Mount Ebal: The History of Its Composition and the Question of the Centralization of the Cult," in *Das Deuteronomium: Entstehung, Gestalt und Botschaft* (ed. N. Lohfink; BETL 68; Leuven: Leuven University Press, 1985), 309.

36. Mayes, *Deuteronomy*, 342.

37. Sprinkle, *Book of the Covenant*, 43.

38. McConville and Millar, *Time and Place*, 117–23. See also McConville, *Deuteronomy*, 230–32; J. J. Niehaus, "The Central Sanctuary: Where and When?" *TynBul* 43 (1992): 3–30.

39. P. M. A. Pitkänen, *Central Sanctuary and the Centralization of Worship in Ancient Israel: From the Settlement to the Building of Solomon's Temple* (Gorgias Dissertations: Near Eastern Studies 5; Piscataway, NJ: Gorgias, 2003), 97–98. Christensen (*Deuteronomy 1:1–21:9*, 249) notes that, according to "some [unnamed] scholars through the years, the text suggests some kind of intermediate step on the way to complete centralization of worship in

settlement, rest and safety is followed by the commandment in v. 11 that the people go and bring their offerings to the place Yahweh will choose."[40] Support for this view is found in Deut 26:1–2, where the requirement to bring firstfruits to the chosen place is subsequent to conquest of the land and settling in it. Prior to the point at which the people have conquered the land and obtained rest, and for those living at a great distance from the central sanctuary after that, additional Yahweh altars are permitted.[41]

We now take up Levinson's argument in favor of centralization. As noted, he maintains that Deut 12 radically changes the altar law of Exod 20:24 by using the very words of the earlier law but in such a way that the meaning is almost exactly the opposite of what the original law intended. We have already seen that the two fundamental premises of his approach (viz., that the Exodus altar law permits multiple altars and that Deut 12 envisions only one) are not as clear as he suggests. There is, however, an additional objection to be raised.

Levinson's argument is based on the use of the vocabulary and syntax of the earlier law. He sees in the use of the words of the earlier law a radical hermeneutical "transformation," so that the "lemma is viewed atomistically: legal or textual authority operates at the level of individual words that, even when recontextualized, retain their operative force."[42] But serious concerns may be raised about whether language functions in this way and, more importantly, whether the authors of Deuteronomy theorized about, or used, language in this way. Levinson sees a transformation of the word זָבַח in Deut 12: he notes that the word *always* has sacral connotations, except in Deut 12:5, 21 (elsewhere in Deuteronomy as well as in the Book of the Covenant). But if he is correct when he suggests that, in the hermeneutic of the authors of Deuteronomy, words function with their original "operative force" even when recontextualized, then זָבַח must be understood as a sacral term, the rewording of the earlier law notwithstanding.

It is simply not clear that the authors of Deuteronomy thought language functioned this way. The parallels between the altar law in Exod 20:24 and Deut 12 do not necessarily demonstrate what Levinson thinks they do. The topic of both texts is an altar law, and both texts are dealing with issues related to sacrifice. Therefore, it is not

---

ancient Israel." He claims (without elaboration) that "it is better to take the text at face value and to see here instructions from Moses for a people about to enter a new world."

40. Pitkänen, *Central Sanctuary*, 99.
41. Ibid., 104–9.
42. Levinson, *Legal Innovation*, 46.

surprising that the same terminology is used in both instances. Levinson sees evidence for his theory in the fact that terms such as מִזְבֵּחַ, מִבְקָרֶךָ וּמִצֹּאנֶךָ, and עֹלֹתֶיךָ וְאֶת־שְׁלָמֶיךָ appear in both texts but in different ways.[43] From this he concludes that the earlier text is being tendentiously reworked to alter its effect radically. But these terms are expected in this kind of context; it would be astonishing (to say the least) if they did not appear. The repetition of the terminology from the earlier law does not necessarily indicate that the later author(s) was/were recognizing an inherent "operative force." Rather, he/they may have been using words to convey their intentions in keeping with the overall context of their argument.

The fact that the terms appear in Deut 12 reversed in order from their appearance in Exod 20:24 is cited as evidence of the application of Seidel's law.[44] But some instances in which inverted quotations appear to be present may simply mark common terminology and context. For example, Gen 27:29 and Num 24:9 are cited by Beentjes as an example of inverted quotation due to the fact that the elements are reversed.[45] But the contexts of each are similar (blessing of Jacob/ Israel), so it is not surprising that the terms "blessed" and "cursed" appear.[46] It may not even be true that one text is actually quoting the other. Levinson concedes that repetitive resumption (another potential indicator of textual reuse) may "function as a compositional device and need not point to editorial activity or textual reworking."[47] It is likewise possible that some instances of apparent "inverted quotation" may be explained on contextual or rhetorical grounds.

43. Ibid., 36–37.

44. Ibid., 35. The theory is named for its first proponent, M. Seidel, "Parallels between Isaiah and Psalms," *Sinai* 38 (1955–56), 149–72, 229–40, 272–80, 335–55, as cited by Levinson, *Legal Innovation*, 18 n. 51. Other works that incorporate this theory into their analysis are P. C. Beentjes, "Inverted Quotations in the Bible: A Neglected Stylistic Pattern," *Bib* 63 (1963): 506–23; and M. Z. Brettler, "Jud 1,1–2,10: From Appendix to Prologue," *ZAW* 101 (1989): 433–35.

45. Beentjes, "Inverted Quotations," 509–10. Curiously, the examples cited by Levinson in his explanation of Seidel's law (*Legal Innovation*, 19–20) deal with a chiastic framing of an interpolation rather than a quotation in which the elements of one source are reversed in a subsequent source, as he claims in Deut 12. So, he cites as examples Exod 6:12–30, where the genealogy of 14–25 is framed chiastically by the repetition (in vv. 27–30, following the interpolation) of elements in the verses preceding it (vv. 12–13). The other example he cites is Lev 23:1–4, where the interpolation of the Sabbath law in v. 3 is framed chiastically through the repetition of elements from v. 2, which precedes the interpolation. Neither example is a particularly strong parallel to what he claims occurs in Deut 12: the source material itself appearing in reverse order in the new text.

46. Some of the other examples cited by Beentjes may be similarly explained.

47. Levinson, *Legal Innovation*, 19; he maintains that it is "more generally" the case that repetitive resumption indicates redactional activity or interpolation.

My primary concern with Levinson's contention that legal authority rests in individual words and phrases that retain their "operative force" even when recontextualized is that it does not seem to do justice to the significance of recontextualization. In terms of speech-act theory, when words from one context are used in a new situation, this constitutes a new speech-act.[48] How the speaker/author of the later speech-act intends the "operative force" of the words to be understood is a matter of interpretation based on the circumstances of the new speech-act. As Lohfink notes, "The individual speech-act [is] not determined only through words and syntax but instead is dependent on social, situational, and textual circumstances."[49] It cannot be assumed that the operative force of words from a former speech-act applies in the new context. Rather, it must be shown that the operative force does apply, and reuse of certain words (even if marked by inverted quotation) is insufficient proof, since the reuse of terminology may be explained on other grounds (contextual, rhetorical, etc.).

An additional objection may be raised. As we have seen above (see also chap. 1), Levinson envisions a program that is based on careful reworking of existing legal texts, using even the lemmas of the earlier works. This presupposes great familiarity with the existing texts. In addition, he notes that these texts "may not yet have had the status of actual public law; they may have been only prestigious texts, part of the curriculum of scribal schools."[50] Thus the texts being modified were, in some instances, familiar only to the scribes, so scribes are the audience (initially, at least) to which Deuteronomy addresses its hermeneutical and legal innovation. But as we noted in chap. 1, he never adequately explains why the scribes would need these texts so tendentiously reworked, if the texts being modified were not yet public law. The scribal audience, presumably themselves intimately familiar with the earlier law, would be readily aware that the new law was a radical departure from the requirements of the earlier law. Reuse of a lemma cannot disguise the fact that in this reconstruction the two laws are fundamentally at odds with one another. No one familiar with the earlier laws in question is likely to have been taken in by the fact that there was, due to reuse of a lemma, the appearance of continuity.

---

48. See, e.g., J. R. Searle, *Speech Acts: An Essay on the Philosophy of Language* (Cambridge: Cambridge University Press, 1969), esp. 22–53.

49. Author's translation from N. Lohfink, "Bund als Vertrag im Deuteronomium," *ZAW* 107 (1995): 221. Original German: "Der jeweilige Sprechakt [ist] nicht allein durch Wörter und Syntax bestimmt, sondern hängt genau so an gesellschaftlich, situativ und textlich vorgegebenen Umständen."

50. Levinson, *Legal Innovation*, 5.

Moreover, if the revised laws were well known, the change in practical terms would be unmistakable, regardless of the extent to which there appears to be continuity between the laws.

The preceding discussion demonstrates that the data of the text may be read in a variety of ways, and it is not clear that the differences between Deut 12 and the altar law in Exodus are as great as or necessarily of the kind that Weinfeld and others suggest. The fact that Deut 12 is not as clear on this issue as is sometimes claimed may suggest that the issue of the number of altars is not the primary emphasis of the chapter. If it is not, we must begin to determine what is primarily in view here.

In its present form, Deut 12 has important ties with the preceding material from chaps. 1–11. In the section immediately preceding chap. 12 is the call not to "go after other gods" (11:28), a topic that is at the fore of chap. 12. Moreover, in this conclusion to the framework of the legal material is a connection between loyalty to Yahweh and blessing on the one hand, and between disloyalty through disobedience and curse on the other. The emphasis in the preceding chapters has been on the need for loyalty to Yahweh in response to his acts on behalf of Israel, especially the act of electing them. Wright notes that

> all the sections of laws in chapters 12–26 are presented in the light of, or more precisely, in response to, the great truths and principles that have been so eloquently expounded in chapters 1–11. . . . There is a mirror-like effect in the way the earlier chapters present what God had done for Israel, while the later chapters present what Israel must do in response, often employing the same vocabulary to show this reciprocal relationship.[51]

The rhetorical effect is to raise the expectation that the means by which this can be done will be expounded.

The emphasis of the chapter may perhaps be discerned if we consider its structure. As we have seen, there is considerable debate over whether this chapter should be seen as a literary unity or as a compilation from various sources. For the present study, however, this question is less relevant. Rather, the focus here is on the theological and ideological implications of the text as it presently exists, regardless of the means by which it came to be in its present form. The chapter clearly possesses a thematic unity, and the fact that certain themes are repeated in 12:1–4 and 12:29–13:1[12:32] in the form of an inclusio

---

51. C. J. H. Wright, *Deuteronomy* (NIBC 4; Peabody, MA: Hendrickson / Carlisle: Paternoster, 1996), 158.

suggests that the chapter is a result of careful literary integration, as reflected in the following structure:[52]

A	Introductory Statement: "These are the laws you shall observe"	12:1
B	No God but Yahweh: destroy worship centers of false gods	vv. 2–4
X	Demonstrate loyalty to Yahweh alone in all aspectsof worship	vv. 5–28
B'	No God but Yahweh: do not imitate worship of false gods	vv. 29–31
A'	Closing Statement: "Observe all that is commanded"	13:1[12:32]

It appears, then, that one of the major issues is a contrast with practices depicted as Canaanite.

Following the introductory statement in v. 1, the Israelites are commanded to destroy all the places (מְקֹמוֹת) where the nations serve their gods. A polemical thrust seems to be directed at the multiplicity of pagan worship sites in v. 2, because worship is said to be "on the high mountains, and on the hills, and under *every* green tree." That is, the multiplicity of worship sites among the Canaanites is testimony to the lack of discrimination and discernment in selecting sites;[53] they simply are found everywhere. The implication, according to v. 3, is that the Canaanite sites must be destroyed and all vestiges of their worship eliminated. The intention is to destroy their name (שֵׁם) from that place (מָקוֹם).[54] All of this, according to v. 4, is in contrast to the kind of worship demanded by Yahweh.[55]

---

52. Cf. Christensen, *Deuteronomy 1:1–21:9*, 234–35; J. G. Millar, *Now Choose Life: Theology and Ethics in Deuteronomy* (NSBT 4; Leicester: Apollos, 1998), 109. Many interpreters see a more elaborate (though still chiastic) structure for the chapter, with profane slaughter as a separate category. As I will argue below, however, the so-called profane slaughter may actually be an act of worship, though not sacrifice. Accordingly, vv. 5–28 are a single section, dealing with the need for demonstrating loyalty to Yahweh in worship of every kind. For an alternative conception of the structure of this chapter, with profane slaughter as a separate element, see Nelson, *Deuteronomy*, 150.

53. Merrill, *Deuteronomy*, 220; McConville, *Deuteronomy*, 218. M. Greenberg ("Religion: Stability and Ferment," in *The World History of the Jewish People*, vol. 4/2: *The Age of the Monarchies: Culture and Society* [ed. A. Malamat; Jerusalem: Massada, 1979], 119) argues that in Deut 12 worship at multiple sites is portrayed as an inherently pagan practice and is, therefore, to be avoided.

54. The use of the singular in v. 3, though the plural was used in v. 2, shows that the singular can be used distributively and refer to a number of places. See below.

55. Nelson (*Deuteronomy*, 159) argues that כֵּן in v. 4 refers back to v. 2. It seems more likely, however, that both vv. 2 and 3 describe ways in which Yahweh is not to be worshiped,

There is a clear rhetorical emphasis in these verses on the contrast between the worship of the gods of the nations and the worship of Yahweh. Thus, there is a contrast between the "places" (מְקוֹמוֹת) in which the nations serve their gods (v. 2) and the "place" (מָקוֹם) that Yahweh chooses (v. 5). There is, moreover, a juxtaposition between the presence of the "names" of the gods at their holy sites, and the "Name" of Yahweh at his chosen site. The Israelites are commanded to eliminate every last vestige of the worship of the gods of the nations (vv. 2–3) and are commanded to obliterate the names of the gods from the places of worship. The Israelites are then told (v. 5) that they will "seek the place Yahweh your God will choose . . . to set his name." The emphasis of this passage is on the way Yahweh is to be worshiped by his people. The text is unequivocal that the Israelites are not to worship Yahweh in the same manner in which the nations worshiped their gods. Instead, they are to worship Yahweh in the manner and at the place he chooses. So the destruction of the "names" of the gods of the nations implies eradication of all their claims to legitimacy over the people of the land (including the Israelites). Similarly, the establishment of Yahweh's "Name" at the place of his choosing demonstrates that he has the right to establish his place, by virtue of his sovereignty and his ownership of the land.[56] As Wright notes, "To remove the names of Canaan's gods was to remove *their* presence and *their* power, just as the putting of Yahweh's name in a place was to fill it with *his* availability and *his* nearness."[57]

All of this suggests that the much-debated question of the number of worship sites is not primarily in view in this chapter. Rather, the emphasis is on the contrast between the false worship of Canaanite religion and the proper worship of Yahweh. Worship of Yahweh may be considered proper, according to Deut 12, only when it is carried out in accordance with his instructions and at the place of his choosing. Miller correctly notes that the emphasis in Deut 12

> is not upon *one* place so much as it is upon the place *the Lord chooses.*
> . . . The central activity of Israel's life, the worship of the Lord, is fully
> shaped and determined by the Lord. . . . The point is that there is an

---

because the presence of pillars, Asherim, and images are all contrary to proper Yahweh worship, which, according to the preceding chapters, is to be marked by (1) total devotion to Yahweh alone and (2) the absence of images (e.g., Deut 6:4; 4:15–24). A similar view to mine is advocated by J. H. Tigay, *Deuteronomy* דברים: *The Traditional Hebrew Text with the New JPS Translation* (Philadelphia: Jewish Publication Society, 1996), 120.

56. The issue of the use of "name" is dealt with below, pp. 192–197.

57. Wright, *Deuteronomy*, 159. See below for more on the issue of the "Name" of Yahweh in contrast to the "names" of the Canaanite gods.

appropriate place where the Lord may be found and worshiped, but that place is not arbitrary and anywhere. In the Lord's order, the Lord will choose and reveal the locus of dwelling and encounter with human life and with God's people.[58]

Unity in Israel's worship is achieved through the exclusive veneration of him as sovereign Lord, as opposed to any other gods, rather than through worship being offered at one place.

Seen in this light, the differences between the altar laws of Exod 20:24–25 and Deut 12 are not of the sort that is usually claimed. Both texts acknowledge that the validity of a place of worship is determined not by the inherent sanctity of a place as a result of longstanding tradition, previous veneration, or any other reason but by the endorsement of the site by Yahweh. The crucial issue is Yahweh's sovereignty in both altar laws. "The place" had to be one that Yahweh chose. Sacrifice was legitimate there because Yahweh had determined it to be so.

Whether Deut 12 refers to a central (but not sole) sanctuary or a succession of single sanctuaries that, in their day, were the only legitimate shrines is in my estimation an open question, because it is not the focus of the text. The centralization formula in Deut 12:5 is usually considered to be the most restrictive of the demands for a central sanctuary.[59] Even Welch, who argued for a distributive understanding of בְּאַחַד שְׁבָטֶיךָ ("in one of your tribes") in Deut 12:14 and was opposed to the idea of centralization generally, felt that Deut 12:5 could not be taken distributively and therefore demanded a sole sanctuary.[60] Thus it is argued that, while Deut 12:14 *could* be taken distributively, the fact that, in the present form, Deut 12:5 precedes Deut 12:14 means that the more restrictive sense of v. 5 will rule out the distributive sense that is possible in v. 14.[61]

---

58. P. D. Miller Jr., *Deuteronomy* (Interp; Louisville: John Knox, 1990), 131–32.

59. See, e.g., Nelson, *Deuteronomy*, 158; Mayes, *Deuteronomy*, 223.

60. Welch, *Code*, 58–62.

61. Nelson, *Deuteronomy*, 158; McConville, *Deuteronomy*, 225; Mayes, *Deuteronomy*, 223. E. W. Nicholson (*Deuteronomy and Tradition* [Philadelphia: Fortress, 1967], 53–54) argues that a distributive sense is *not* possible for Deut 12:14. He notes that the basis for reading Deut 12:14 distributively is often based on a comparison with the fugitive slave law in Deut 23:17, which says that a fugitive slave is to be allowed to dwell בַּמָּקוֹם אֲשֶׁר־יִבְחַר בְּאַחַד שְׁעָרֶיךָ ("in the place that he shall choose in any one of your towns"). This, he says, is simply an incorrect translation of the verse, and the correct translation can only be "in one of your gates" (p. 54). But he provides no evidence whatsoever for this assertion. He concedes, moreover, that, since Deut 23:17 is clearly referring to a class of people, the sense, if not the literal words, can be taken distributively. That is, a fugitive slave may live in any town he chooses, even if, in Nicholson's view, the law itself *must* be translated "in one of your gates." But since the text in Deut 12:14 has a sanctuary in view and Yahweh for its

What is less well recognized, however, is the fact that in this very pericope מָקוֹם is used of multiple sanctuaries.[62] As we have noted, v. 2 calls for the destruction of the places (מְקוֹמֹת) of Canaanite worship. This is often seen as drawing a contrast between the multiple places of worship of pagan gods and the single place (מָקוֹם) of Yahweh worship.[63] But the final clause of v. 3 says, "and you shall destroy their name from that place (מָקוֹם)." As Wright notes, מָקוֹם here is "just as *singular* as v. 5, and yet it clearly refers generically" to the Canaanite places of worship that are to be destroyed.[64] Since there is in the immediate context a precedent for the singular מָקוֹם to be taken distributively to refer to multiple sanctuaries, it is possible to take the singular in v. 5 in the generic sense, referring to a class or category.

If this is correct, then could the phrase מִכָּל־שִׁבְטֵיכֶם "out of all your tribes" in Deut 12:5 suggest that there is to be a Yahweh-chosen sanctuary in each of the territorial locations of the tribes of Israel? This is unlikely in light of subsequent legislation. Deuteronomy 17:8–13 seems to imply that there is just one central tribunal, not one in each tribal territory (note the comparison with Deut 1:17, where Moses is seen as the single person to whom appeal can be made). In addition, Deut 18:6–8 suggests that the rights of Levites to minister at a central sanctuary is in view—again, not simply to minister at one of many regional centers.[65]

On balance, I believe the evidence overall favors the view that Deut 12 envisions a single sanctuary, chosen by Yahweh, at which the Israelites could legitimately offer sacrifices. This requirement could be met in a series of places in succession, which accounts for the presence of the command to erect an altar on Mount Ebal in the final

---

subject, the distributive sense is impossible, even if it is possible in Deut 23:17. But as I note below, in Deut 12 there is an example of מָקוֹם as being used in a generic sense to designate a class (of places). If this is correct, then the meaning of the phrase in Deut 12:14 would be "in every place which Yahweh will choose in any of your tribes," and the fact that the subject of the verb is not distributive (as Nicholson rightly notes) is less compelling.

62. Wright, *Deuteronomy*, 170.

63. E.g., Nelson, *Deuteronomy*, 159–60.

64. Wright, *Deuteronomy*, 170. Other examples of generic reference to a class of things cited by Wright include Deut 17:14–20, where the singular מֶלֶךְ apparently refers to a succession of kings or even a divided kingdom. Also, Deut 18:15–22 refers to *a* prophet like Moses but clearly is referring to a class of prophets that can be considered true rather than false. Most telling for comparison with Deut 12 is the fact that what makes a prophet true or legitimate is his faithfulness to his calling to speak in Yahweh's Name. Similarly, "the king" (meaning more than one king) who is legitimate is one that is chosen by Yahweh. McConville (*Deuteronomy*, 219) also notes that the singular at the end of v. 3 must be taken distributively.

65. See Wenham, "Central Sanctuary," 111–12.

form of the book, in Deut 27. (This also best accounts for the presentation of worship in the historical books, which seem to conceive of a succession of sole sanctuaries.) It should be stressed again, however, that the primary emphasis is *not* on the number of sanctuaries but on the fact that Yahweh is to choose the location of legitimate places of sacrifice and that this stands in strong contrast to the practices depicted as Canaanite.

It appears, then, that centralization in Deut 12 can plausibly be conceived differently from the way it is usually conceived. I will present a more comprehensive interpretation of the chapter below (pp. 197–202). For now, we turn to an evaluation of the idea of secularization in the prevailing interpretation.

Secularization

A corollary to the idea of centralization, as we have seen, is the idea of secularization. The abolition of local sanctuaries meant that local sacrifice was no longer possible, so nonsacrificial (profane) slaughter was instituted.

The Sacral Nature of Predeuteronomic Slaughter
The primary evidence for the prevailing view of secularization is the idea that, prior to Deut 12, all slaughter was carried out at an altar and was, therefore, sacrificial. This argument is primarily based on 1 Sam 14:32–35. In this text, the people are said to be eating meat with the blood, to which Saul responds by bringing in a large stone and ordering the people to slaughter their animals on the stone. Verse 35 concludes the section by describing how Saul built an altar to Yahweh. The stone is understood to be an altar of the sort described in the altar law in Exod 20:25. The sin, then, was that the people were eating animals that had not been properly sacrificed, marked by their failure to give Yahweh his portion and by their failure to sprinkle the blood on an altar. This was rectified when Saul constructed an altar and sacrificed the animals properly. Accordingly, this text is seen as demonstrating that all slaughter was to be carried out at an altar and was considered to be sacrificial.[66]

There are, however, good reasons to question this interpretation. First, the text is explicit in identifying the sin of the people as eating

---

66. R. W. Klein, *1 Samuel* (WBC 10; Waco, TX: Word, 1983), 139; H. W. Hertzberg, *I and II Samuel* (OTL; Philadelphia: Westminster, 1964), 115–16; M. J. Evans, *1 and 2 Samuel* (NIBC 6; Peabody, MA: Hendrickson / Carlisle: Paternoster, 2000), 69–70; B. C. Birch, "The First and Second Books of Samuel: Introduction, Commentary, and Reflections," *NIB* 2: 1080. See also Weinfeld, *Deuteronomic School*, 213–14.

the meat with the blood.[67] There is no mention of any failure to withhold a portion for Yahweh or to have sprinkled the altar with the blood. Weinfeld sees the use of the phrase עַל־הַדָּם as a circumlocution for eating without first sprinkling the blood and cites Lev 19:26 as evidence.[68] But the prohibition in Lev 19:26 is simply about not eating the flesh with the blood. The law is not presented in the context of sacrifice, so it is not necessary to conclude that sacrifice, as opposed to blood manipulation, is in view in that text. In addition, Gen 9:4 prohibits eating meat with blood, again in a general, not sacrificial, context, as does Lev 17:10–14. Thus it seems likely that a more general principle about not eating blood (apart from any sacrificial implications) is in view, and it is likely that this principle lies behind 1 Sam 14:32–35. That this is a serious offense on its own terms, apart from any violations of sacrificial regulations, is beyond question, based on the association of blood and life made in both Gen 9:4 and Lev 17:11 as well as on the fact that the disposal of blood is important even in the case of nonsacrificial, game animals. It is therefore not unreasonable to think that the sin of the people in 1 Sam 14:32–35 was a failure to dispose of the blood properly and is not related to sacrifice.

Second, it is not clear that the stone brought by Saul and used for slaughter by the people should be seen as an altar. The construction of the altar is mentioned in v. 35. But if the stone brought by Saul in v. 33 is seen as an altar, then it is unclear why a second altar would need to be built. Some have said that the original stone was incorporated into the altar described in v. 35,[69] but this conclusion is highly speculative. The text indicates that the people were sacrificing on the ground (v. 32). This would make it impossible for the blood to drain properly, with the result that people would be eating meat with the blood. Bringing in a large stone would allow the blood to drain, thus ensuring that the commandments prohibiting the eating of blood were obeyed.[70] It is therefore unnecessary to conclude that the stone

---

67. Hertzberg (*Samuel*, 115–16) and Weinfeld (*Deuteronomic School*, 187) argue that the use of the phrase עַל־הַדָּם should be understood as "on the blood" rather than "with the blood." In their view, the sin was that the people failed to sprinkle the blood on the altar as required. But Exod 12:8 employs a similar construction: the people are instructed to eat the flesh *with* bitter herbs (עַל־מְרֹרִים). It is rather unlikely that the command in Exod 12:8 is for the people to eat the meat *on* the herbs, so it is better to conclude, with P. K. McCarter Jr. (*1 Samuel* [AB 8; New York: Doubleday, 1980], 249), that the expression אָכַל עַל "means simply 'eat with,' the prepositional phrase referring to something eaten along with the main food."

68. Weinfeld, *Deuteronomic School*, 187.

69. Hertzberg, *Samuel*, 116.

70. Cf. J. M. Grintz, "'Do Not Eat on the Blood': Reconsiderations in Setting and Dating of the Priestly Code," *ASTI* 8 (1972): 78–105.

in v. 32 is to be seen as an altar.[71]

The significance of this for the interpretation of Deut 12 is due to the fact that 1 Sam 14:32–35 is normally understood as preceding the composition of Deut 12. The fact that 1 Sam 14:32–35 may plausibly be read as dealing with blood manipulation, not sacrifice, suggests that slaughter was not always considered sacrificial. If this is so, then the case for secularization in Deut 12—that what was previously sacral is radically altered and removed from the realm of the cult—is weakened significantly.

Profane or Sacral Slaughter?

Use of זבח *in Deuteronomy 12.*   In addition, an argument can be made for seeing Deut 12 as expanding the realm of the sacred, not narrowing it. In Deut 12:15 and 21, people in the towns (i.e., away from the central sanctuary) are permitted to slaughter and eat meat. What is unusual, however, is the fact that the term זָבַח is used in connection with this ostensibly profane slaughter. The word זָבַח is used consistently throughout the Old Testament in connection with sacrifice. Of the 134 times the word appears, all but 8[72] are indisputably related to sacrifice and, therefore, have sacral connotations. Apart from Deut 12:15 and 21, all the remaining exceptions have been seen as probably bearing sacrificial connotations or as emulating or imputing a sacrificial sense.[73] This leaves only Deut 12:15 and 21 as perhaps having a nonsacral sense.

The fact that all the other uses of זָבַח in the Old Testament (including elsewhere in Deuteronomy) have a sacral connotation raises the question of whether a sacral implication may be present in Deut 12 as well. Milgrom concludes that the use of the term זָבַח in Deut 12:15 and 21 was to specify that the manner in which the animal was to be killed for profane slaughter was the same as for sacrifices, namely, by slitting the throat.[74] In support of this view, Milgrom notes that there are three terms related to slaughter in the Old Testament: זָבַח, טָבַח,

---

71. Hertzberg (*Samuel,* 116) maintains that the use of a large stone for sacrifice in 1 Sam 6:14 suggests that the stone here also was used for sacrifice. In that case, however, the text explicitly states that a sacrifice—a burnt offering—was made to Yahweh on the stone. The sacrificial connection is therefore explicit in 1 Sam 6:14, whereas it is at best only implicit in the present text, if indeed it is there at all.

72. Numbers 22:40; Deut 12:15, 21; 1 Sam 28:24; 1 Kgs 19:16, 21; Ezek 34:3; 2 Chr 18:2.

73. See Milgrom, "Profane Slaughter," 2; Levinson, *Legal Innovation,* 38 n. 29; R. E. Averbeck, "זבח," *NIDOTTE* 1: 1069. Ezekiel 34:3 is the one case that is seen as being a true example of a nonsacral use of the term. However, as Milgrom ("Profane Slaughter," 2) notes, the exilic setting of this text, where true sacrifice was impossible, makes it difficult to say with certainty whether any sacral connotation is implied.

74. Ibid., 13–15.

and שָׁחַט. As noted, זָבַח always refers to slaughter in a sacred context. On the other hand, טָבַח always refers to profane slaughter. The third term, שָׁחַט, is used in much the same manner as זָבַח, to designate sacrificial slaughter. Thus, he concludes, Hebrew is unique among its cognate languages in having two terms that designate sacred slaughter, unless שָׁחַט actually had a more technical meaning of slaughtering by cutting the throat.[75] Interestingly, Arabic has a verb, *saḥaṭa*, meaning "to slit the throat," and a complementary noun meaning "throat."[76] Moreover, Deut 12:21 indicates that sacrifice is to be done as Yahweh commanded (כַּאֲשֶׁר צִוִּיתִךָ). Since there are no commands in the Pentateuch that specify the exact manner in which animals are to be slaughtered, Milgrom concludes that this allusion is not to a specific command but to the verb שָׁחַט and specifies that all slaughter is to be carried out by slitting the throat. In this view, then, Deut 12:15 and 21 specifies that in every case in which an animal is slaughtered, the same procedure (slitting the throat) is to be used, whether the slaughter is in a cultic context or not.

Levinson, following Hoffman, objects that this reconstruction is untenable because there are no specific rules for the slaughter of sacrificial animals in the Old Testament; the ritual procedures for sacrificial slaughter are found only in later rabbinic materials.[77] This is of course correct. But it is also the case that many of the problems related to the interpretation of sacrificial ritual have to do with the fact that many of the details that would lend clarity to a later audience are left unsaid because they were readily apparent and familiar to the original audience.[78] That specific procedures were spelled out in Jewish law much later certainly does not mean that the procedures were known in the time of Deuteronomy's composition. At the same time, however, the fact that specific procedures were made explicit only later does not mean there were originally no procedures.[79] It may

75. Ibid., 14.

76. Ibid. See also R. E. Averbeck, "שחט," *NIDOTTE* 4: 78.

77. B. M. Levinson, *The Hermeneutics of Innovation: The Impact of Centralization upon the Structure, Sequence, and Reformulation of Legal Materials in Deuteronomy* (Ph.D. diss., Brandeis University, 1991), 181; idem, *Legal Innovation*, 42 n. 46. He cites D. Z. Hoffmann, *Das Buch Deuteronomium* (vols. 1–2; Berlin: Poppelauer, 1913–22), 1.167–68.

78. G. J. Wenham, "The Theology of Old Testament Sacrifice," in *Sacrifice in the Bible* (ed. R. T. Beckwith and M. J. Selman; Grand Rapids: Baker / Carlisle: Paternoster, 1995), 76–77.

79. While Milgrom asserts that the procedure in view in Deut 12:15 and 21 is the slitting of the throat, he acknowledges that this does not mean that "the rabbinic technique of ritual slaughter, i.e. a clean, transverse cut of both the oesophagus and the trachea so that all the main blood vessels are severed . . . stems from biblical times" (Milgrom, "Profane Slaughter," 15 n. 48).

simply mean that they were familiar to the audience to whom the text was addressed.

Thus, caution should be exercised in concluding what is intended by the use of זָבַח. Milgrom's hypothesis that זָבַח refers to slitting the throat is a tantalizing and intriguing possibility but not a certainty. What seems much more likely, in my estimation, is that the use of זָבַח in Deut 12:15 and 21 points to a sacral, not secular, connotation for the procedure. The fact that זָבַח always (including elsewhere in Deuteronomy itself) has a sacral connotation, coupled with the fact that the verb שָׁחַט, which is always used of profane slaughter, is not used suggests that the author(s) were not describing a ritual that they considered secular.

To be sure, we cannot come to a conclusion on this matter solely on the basis of the vocabulary used (or not used). A conclusion must be supported by additional evidence that, in the present context of the chapter as a whole, a sacral connotation is likely. That is, the determination of the meaning of זָבַח depends mostly on one's view of Deut 12 as a whole, not just on one's examination of the word itself. I believe that the evidence of the chapter in its context supports an understanding of זָבַח as a sacral term.

Holiness of the Land in Deuteronomy.   As we saw in chap. 1, a case has been made for seeing in Deuteronomy an *expansion* of the concept of holiness, in contrast to the idea of secularization.[80] While the general outline of the argument is presented there and does not need to be repeated, it is necessary here to consider how certain aspects of that view are germane to the issue of secularization in Deut 12.   .

In Lohfink's important analysis, there are two instances of the expansion of holiness in Deuteronomy generally that may assist in the interpretation of Deut 12. First, he notes that in Deuteronomy there is a particular emphasis on the holiness of the entire people, not just the priests.[81] This is evident in the way in which statements of the holiness of Israel appear in contrast to the people of the world as a whole. Deuteronomy 7:6 says of Israel, עַם קָדוֹשׁ אַתָּה לַיהוָה אֱלֹהֶיךָ ("you are a people holy to Yahweh your God"). But this is followed by the phrase לְעָם סְגֻלָּה מִכֹּל הָעַמִּים אֲשֶׁר עַל־פְּנֵי הָאֲדָמָה ("a people for himself, a treasured possession out of all the peoples who are on the face of the earth"). No mention is made anywhere in Deuteronomy of the people

---

80. N. Lohfink, "Opfer und Säkularisierung im Deuteronomium," in *Studien zu Opfer und Kult im Alten Testament: Mit einer Bibliographie 1969–1991 zum Opfer in der Bibel* (ed. A. Schenker; Tübingen: Mohr [Siebeck], 1992), 15–43.

81. Ibid., 35.

being a "kingdom of priests," as they are designated in Exod 19:6. Priests are not set apart in Deuteronomy as models of holiness. Rather, holiness is a quality of Israel as a whole (not just king or priest) in contrast to the peoples of the earth.[82] Other texts draw similar distinctions between Israel and the nations (e.g., Deut 14:2; 26:18–19; 28:9–10).

Second, it can be argued that there is in Deuteronomy an expansion of holiness to encompass the land as a whole, not just the sanctuary. There is, first of all, the command in Deut 12:1–2 to destroy *all* pagan worship sites throughout the whole land. This implies that the entire land is the realm of Yahweh (because only his duly-designated site[s] is to be sought). Moreover, all of Deut 7 makes the case for the incompatibility of pagan worship with Yahweh worship and explicitly notes that vestiges of pagan worship throughout the land must be destroyed due to the fact that the Israelites are a holy people (Deut 7:6). Pagan worship practices are described as תּוֹעֵבָה ("abomination") in Deut 7:25–26; this is a negative sacral term in Deuteronomy.[83] The presence of pagan worship anywhere in the land is incompatible with the presence of the holy people of Yahweh.

Laws of warfare may point in a similar direction. Deuteronomy 20 differentiates between the treatment of cities far off and those nearby. Deuteronomy 20:13–15 says that when cities far away (i.e., outside the land) are conquered, the Israelites may allow the women to live and may take the conquered people's property as booty. But in the case of cities nearby, within the land, the חֵרֶם (ban) is to apply; accordingly, nothing is to be allowed to live. The rationale provided (Deut 20:18) is to prevent the corruption of Israelite worship with another people's abominable practices. It is likely, however, that the war envisioned beginning in Deut 20:10 is a war of conquest outside the land of Canaan. Therefore, the women and children taken as booty would

---

82. Cf. E. Regev, "Priestly Dynamic Holiness and Deuteronomic Static Holiness," *VT* 51 (2001): 246–47; W. Eichrodt, *Theology of the Old Testament* (London: SCM, 1961), 1: 412.

83. Lohfink, "Säkularisierung," 36–37. Regev ("Holiness," 249–50) argues that abomination in Deuteronomy is "something faulty or flawed, but since its implications are not given, it is possible that it does not really affect the sacred and endanger the holy." In contrast, he argues that תּוֹעֵבָה in P "pollutes the land of Israel and destroys the sinner himself." But this does not really do justice to the fact that things that are תּוֹעֵבָה in Deuteronomy are almost all actions that either demonstrate disloyalty to Yahweh through association with pagan worship or violate his commandments or both. This places the nation as a whole in danger of being expelled from the land, which in turn would be a disruption of the relationship between Yahweh and Israel. So, the implications of תּוֹעֵבָה in Deuteronomy are severe and have a tremendous impact on the access of the people to the land and, therefore, the holy presence of Yahweh.

be subject to the Israelites and also in a position to entice them to follow other gods. There is no apparent qualitative difference between
the people far away (who could, perhaps, entice the Israelites to follow after other gods but are not subject to the ban) and those nearby
(who are subject to the ban) except that the latter reside in the land
while the former do not. It could be countered that women and children would not be in a position to entice the Israelites to follow after
other gods, and therefore the captured women from far away were
not a threat to the purity of Yahweh worship. But the same could be
argued vis-à-vis the women and children captured within the land,
yet the command is that they are to be annihilated with the men.
This suggests that the land itself is somehow considered to be holy.

Additional explicit statements of the holiness of the land itself are
found in: Deut 21:23, where the body of an executed criminal is to be
taken down so as not to defile (טָמֵא) the land; Deut 24:4, where the re-
marriage of a divorced woman by her first husband is said to be an
abomination (תּוֹעֵבָה) before Yahweh, and the practice is forbidden lest
it bring sin upon the *land*, not the people involved.[84] Finally, Deut
21:1–9 mandates that the ceremony of the broken-necked heifer is to
be carried out in the case of an unsolved murder. Weinfeld rightly
notes that, in this text, expiation is for the people, not the land.[85] But
according to Deut 21:1 it is in the land that this law becomes important,[86] and Milgrom notes that the ceremony is "incomprehensible
without the assumption that blood does contaminate the land on
which it is spilt and that this ritual transfers the contamination to untillable land."[87] Since the three cases in which Deuteronomy speaks
of the defilement of the land are not found in P, it is difficult to conclude that Deuteronomy seeks to curtail the realm of the holy; in fact,
it could be said to expand it.[88]

---

84. Lohfink, "Säkularisierung," 37; J. Milgrom, "The Alleged 'Demythologization and
Secularization' in Deuteronomy (Review Article)," *IEJ* 23/3 (1973): 157.

85. Weinfeld, *Deuteronomic School*, 210–11.

86. Lohfink, "Säkularisierung," 37. Note, as well, that the expression "the land" frames
the chapter (vv. 1, 23).

87. Milgrom, "Alleged 'Demythologization and Secularization,'" 157.

88. Ibid. In his response to Milgrom's review article, M. Weinfeld ("On 'Demythologization and Secularization' in Deuteronomy," *IEJ* 23/4 [1973]: 232) maintains that the presence of laws dealing with the contamination of the land in Deut 21 is due to the fact that
these laws constitute "an ancient layer preserved in the Deuteronomic code." Weinfeld further maintains (ibid.) that the Deuteronomic interpretation of these laws betrays the authors' true ambivalence toward the idea, in that only one expression (טָמֵא) from P is used
to convey the idea of the contamination of the land, and then only once (21:23). But this
does not address the issue of why a Deuteronomic redactor, ostensibly attempting radically
to alter the conception of earlier texts in favor of a new understanding would permit such

The law of Passover and the Feast of Unleavened Bread in Deut 16:1–8 also contains elements that may point toward the holiness of the land as a whole. As is well known, the presentation of the combined feast in Deuteronomy emphasizes the participation of the people at "the place" (16:2, 6), in apparent contradiction to the earlier practice of celebrating Passover in the home (Exod 12).[89] But Deut 16:4 mandates that leaven is to be removed from the entire territory (גְּבוּל), that is, from the whole land. This suggests that, while the focal point of the festival is, of course, the central sanctuary, where sacrifices are carried out (Deut 16:2), the whole land is somehow understood as being within the realm of the feast and accordingly must be cleansed of leaven.

In addition, there is some ambiguity about what is intended by the use of the word אֹהֶל ("tent") in v. 7. It may be used in the sense of "to go home," implying that, following the sacrifice, the people were to return to their homes (cf. Josh 22:4, 6; 1 Kgs 8:66).[90] A problem with this understanding is that Deuteronomy consistently envisions the people as living in houses and uses the term אֹהֶל to refer to their temporary dwellings in the desert (Deut 1:27; 5:30; 11:6). Some have therefore concluded that this refers to temporary shelters erected in the vicinity of the central sanctuary in which the participants would live during the week of the festival.[91] Both interpretations are possible. Regardless of which is the case, the celebration of the festival is not limited to the boundaries of the central sanctuary but extends (as demonstrated by v. 4) into the whole of the land, including even the women and children, who need not make the pilgrimage to the central sanctuary according to Deut 16:16, as well as the men who may not have made the journey.[92] The ambiguity surrounding the sense of

---

ancient concepts to remain unaltered. Neither does it address Deut 24:4, in which the contamination of the land is also in view.

89. The issues surrounding the interpretation of Deut 16:1–8 are many and complex. Among the debated elements are the literary sources that may lie behind the text, the relationship of these texts to other pentateuchal legislation, and the religiohistorical question of the relationship between the Passover and the Feast of Unleavened Bread. For the purposes of this study, it is not necessary to attempt to treat these issues. For an extensive bibliography on them, see Christensen, *Deuteronomy 1:1–21:9*, 326–28. See also J. G. McConville, "Deuteronomy's Unification of Passover and *Maṣṣôt*: A Response to Bernard M. Levinson," *JBL* 119 (2000): 47–58; and the reply of B. M. Levinson, "The Hermeneutics of Tradition in Deuteronomy: A Reply to J. G. McConville," *JBL* 119 (2000): 269–86.

90. Adopting this view is Tigay, *Deuteronomy*, 155.

91. P. C. Craigie, *The Book of Deuteronomy* (NICOT; Grand Rapids: Eerdmans, 1976), 244; Merrill, *Deuteronomy*, 253.

92. Deuteronomy 16:16 makes clear that only males are required to attend the thrice-yearly festivals at the chosen place. Given the emphasis in Deuteronomy on the inclusion

אֹהֶל is seen by McConville as a deliberate effort to convey the "extension of the worship life of Israel into the land."[93]

Deuteronomy 16:8 may point in the same direction. On the seventh day there is to be an עֲצֶרֶת ("sacred assembly") to Yahweh. At issue is the location of this assembly. If the tents in v. 7 are understood as being the homes of the people throughout the land, then the law apparently would require the people to return to the מָקוֹם at the end of the week for the assembly.[94] This seems rather implausible in practical terms, because for some the journey could be quite long. This may point toward the view that the pilgrims lived in tents at the central sanctuary for the week, participated in the assembly, and then returned home. There is, however, another possibility.

I have argued above that it is possible to read this section as seeking to extend the worship of Israel into the land itself. Deuteronomy 16:8 may be another example of this, because the location of the עֲצֶרֶת is not entirely clear. If the tents in v. 7 are understood as being the people's homes, it is unlikely that they would be required to return to the מָקוֹם later in the week, as we have seen. It is possible, therefore, that what is envisioned is the holding of an assembly in the towns throughout the land.[95] If this is so, the festival would be celebrated throughout the land, though sacrifice would be peformed only at the central sanctuary. This is somewhat problematic, because the term עֲצֶרֶת is usually used in connection with the central sanctuary.[96] The final clause of v. 8, however, may help clarify the situation. This clause commands that no work is to be done on the day of the assembly. This can, of course, apply to pilgrims "dwelling" temporarily at the sanctuary but has greater relevance for people who either did not go the sanctuary in the first place or who have returned home prior to the seventh day. Those who have made the journey to the sanctuary are,

---

of women in the religious life of the nation (cf. Deut 12:12, 15; 15:12, 17; 16:11, 14) it seems best to conclude that women were not required to participate in the pilgrimage festivals but may have done so.

93. McConville, "Unification," 56. Levinson ("Reply," 276–77) argues that this hypothesis is untenable due to the fact that sacrificial worship is restricted to the temple, according to Deut 16:5–6. But this misses the point entirely, since what McConville (rightly, in my estimation) argues is not that *sacrifice* is intended here to be practiced throughout the land but rather that *worship* is not limited to the central sanctuary and therefore may be seen as extending into the land as a whole. A similar point is made by Tigay, *Deuteronomy*, 156; and W. S. Morrow, *Scribing the Center: Organization and Redaction in Deuteronomy 14:1–17:13* (SBLMS 49; Atlanta: Scholars Press, 1995), 145 n. 44.

94. Levinson, *Legal Innovation*, 79–80.

95. Tigay, *Deuteronomy*, 156.

96. Leviticus 23:26; Num 29:35; 2 Chr 7:9; Neh 8:18; Joel 1:14; 2:15–17.

more or less by definition, unable to carry out their normal work.[97]
Those in the towns, however, could conduct normal work throughout
the week (while abstaining from leaven, as required by v. 4), but they
would observe the conclusion of the festival by abstaining from work
on the seventh day.

So, regardless of whether or not the tents are envisioned as homes
or as actual tents at the sanctuary or whether the assembly is local or
centralized, the celebration of the feast is not limited to the confines
of the מָקוֹם but is, rather, extended into the land, at least by means of
cessation from work on the seventh day and through abstention from
leaven in the entire land.[98] If the tents should be thought of as homes
and the assembly is carried out locally, the extension of holiness to
the entire land is even more pronounced. In any event, the religious
celebration at the מָקוֹם extends into and is paralleled by actions taken
throughout the land. This suggests that sanctity in Deuteronomy is
not limited to the מָקוֹם but is a quality of the entire land.[99]

A final text in Deuteronomy that may indicate an extension of holiness to the land is Deut 14:28–29.[100] There it is commanded that, at
the end of three years, the tithe is to be maintained in the towns. In

---

97. Morrow, *Scribing the Center*, 145.

98. It is quite likely that many people did not journey to the sanctuary. Women and
children, as we noted, were not required to attend but may have done so (Deut 16:16). In
addition, it is likely that in practice an assembly consisted of representatives from the entire nation, given the problems associated with having all the men journey to a potentially
distant sanctuary and remaining for seven days. See Tigay, *Deuteronomy*, 372 n. 24; and
B. Halpern, *The Constitution of the Monarchy in Israel* (HSM 25; Chico, CA: Scholars Press,
1981), 190. Thus, the requirement for cessation from labor on that day would allow non-
pilgrims to participate in the end of the festival.

99. The relationship between the "center" and the "periphery" has been evaluated
from a sociological perspective by S. Grosby, "Sociological Implications of the Distinction
between 'Locality' and Extended 'Territory' with Particular Reference to the Old Testament," *Biblical Ideas of Nationality: Ancient and Modern* (Winona Lake, IN: Eisenbrauns,
2002), 69–91. Grosby notes that concepts of *territoriality* include the existence of a center
and a periphery and the recognition of the sovereignty of the territorial deity throughout
the area of the land. This may support the idea that the worship and presence of Yahweh
is to be localized in a "place" but nevertheless extends throughout the entire territory that
is thought to belong to him.

100. There are other texts outside of Deuteronomy that seem to point in a similar direction. Joshua 22:19, for example, draws a contrast between the "uncleanness" of the
Transjordanian regions and the cleanness of the entire Cisjordanian land, based explicitly
on the presence of the tabernacle. Thus, Yahweh's presence (associated with the tabernacle) has the effect of rendering the entire land clean. So, sanctity is not limited to the pre-
cincts of the tabernacle. Similarly, Isa 11:9 refers to the holy mountain of Yahweh but also
refers to the fact that the land/earth (הָאָרֶץ) is filled with the knowledge of Yahweh, pointing to the parallels between the center and the periphery. See, again, Grosby, "Implications," 76–78.

this way, the celebration of the blessings of Yahweh is carried out throughout the land—not just at the sanctuary—as is the case for the other years. It could be argued that this law is an example of the humanitarian concerns of Deuteronomy, in that it specifically calls for the sharing of this tithe with the Levite, alien, orphan, and widow (v. 29).[101] But this overlooks the fact that the tithe law in Deut 14:22–27 also contains in it a humanitarian concern for the Levite (v. 27). More important, however, is the fact that Deut 26:12–15 highlights the sanctity of this portion (v. 13) and the inherently religious nature of the requirements of this law. Thus, something that is seen as inherently sacred and normally associated with the central sanctuary is shared throughout the land as a religious observance. The profound religious significance of this action and the complex interrelationship between sanctuary and land are evident in the fact that faithfulness to the law in Deut 14:28–29 must be declared before Yahweh at the central sanctuary (26:2, 13).[102] This, as ever in Deuteronomy, results in blessing of both people and land (Deut 26:15).

The foregoing discussion of texts in Deut 14 and 16 demonstrates that an expansion of holiness in Deuteronomy is plausible. It is all the more telling that this expansion is found in two of the chapters that are considered to be most heavily influenced by centralization.[103] Since other texts in Deuteronomy show an expansion of holiness, it is reasonable to evaluate the data of Deut 12 in this light.

As I argued above, it would be an anomaly if זָבַח referred to a profane practice in Deut 12. Since at least some other texts in Deuteronomy, including the texts that most obviously deal with centralization, appear to reveal an expanded concept of holiness, it is possible that זָבַח in Deut 12 refers to a sacred, not profane, practice. The exact nature of this practice is not entirely clear. I further argued that caution should be exercised in concluding that זָבַח in Deut 12 refers to the slitting of the throat. At the same time, it is apparent that the

---

101. Weinfeld, *Deuteronomic School*, 290.

102. McConville, *Deuteronomy*, 252. W. Brueggemann (*Deuteronomy* [AbOTC; Nashville: Abingdon, 2001], 162) maintains that this legislation represents "a profound secularization of the practice in which the owner, YHWH, does not even insist on the visible gesture of presentation at the sanctuary, but wants the 10 percent set aside in the community for its use. Thus the religious rite is transposed into an act that concerns the local economy, a 10 percent infusion of extra goods into the community." This overlooks the religious implications of Deut 14:28–29 and the integral relationship between it and Deut 26:12–15.

103. As I noted in chap. 1, von Rad (*Commentary*) argues that the effects of centralization may be seen most clearly in chaps. 12, 14, 15, 16, 17, 18, and 19 in the Deuteronomic law code.

practice is not to be equated with sacrifice, since Deut 12:15 and 22 are explicit that both the unclean and clean may eat of it.

What seems most likely, then, is that the sacral term זָבַח is deliberately used to highlight the religious significance of the act of slaughter by the Israelites in the land, and therefore that Deut 12 is teaching that all of life lived in the land before Yahweh has religious significance. Deuteronomy 14 and 16 expand the scope of holiness in Deuteronomy so that the entire people and the land are within the realm of the holy; holiness in Deuteronomy, as has long been recognized, is not limited to the central sanctuary and its environs. Deuteronomy 12, in my estimation, contributes to this understanding by stressing the inherent holiness of all actions lived out before Yahweh, and the nonsacrificial slaughter of animals is to be understood in this way. Lohfink maintains that "in keeping with Deuteronomy, nothing is released into the realm of the profane. . . . Somehow, nothing remains any longer in Israel that is not holy."[104]

Support for this view may be seen in the fact that elsewhere in Deuteronomy the term זָבַח refers to sacral actions. But it is also telling that Deut 28:31 uses the term טָבַח to refer to actions taken by enemies of Israel. As we have noted, טָבַח always refers to profane slaughter. Its use in Deut 28:31 is expected, because the actions of Israel's enemies would not be of religious significance to Yahweh, unlike the actions of Israelites. Thus, even in the land, the slaughter of animals by the enemies of Israel is profane. For Israel, as the סְגֻלָּה of Yahweh and subject to the terms of the covenant, all of life has religious implications. This is not true for others, so the normal term for profane slaughter is used.

That זָבַח and nonsacrificial slaughter generally have sacral implications is further seen when the prohibition of eating the blood is considered. As we have seen, Weinfeld and others have maintained that in Deuteronomy there is no sacral significance to the blood, and it can be poured out like water in the context of nonsacrificial slaughter (Deut 12:16, 24). But this overlooks the fundamental religious basis for the blood prohibition and the fact that even in the context of nonsacrificial slaughter an absolute prohibition on eating blood is maintained.

It has been noted that the absolute prohibition of eating blood is unique to Israel among the cultures of the ANE, and only Israel main-

---

104. Lohfink, "Säkularisierung," 36; author's translation; original German: "im Sinne des Deuteronomiums wird nichts ins Profane entlassen. . . . Irgendwie gibt es in Israel nichts mehr, was nicht heilig wäre."

tained that the "life" of a creature was in its blood.[105] Thus, Milgrom concludes that the blood prohibition "cannot be passed off as an outlandish vestige of some primitive taboo; it must be viewed as the product of a rational, deliberate opposition to the prevailing practice of its environment."[106] If this is the case, then the rejection of the practice of eating blood had theological and religious significance as the Israelites sought to distance themselves from the thinking and practice of surrounding cultures. The fact that the blood prohibition is emphatically stated in Deut 12 suggests that this practice has religious significance. The pouring of the blood on the ground "like water" (which is stated in terms reminiscent of the pouring of the blood on the altar) may be designed to highlight the contrast between sacrificial blood manipulation and nonsacrificial blood manipulation rather than to imply anything about the sanctity of the blood itself. What is emphasized is not the nonsacral character of blood but the importance of properly disposing of it in every instance. The fact that the blood prohibition appears three times in Deut 12 as well as elsewhere in the book (Deut 15:23 and perhaps implied in 14:21 as the basis for the prohibition on the consumption of the נְבֵלָה, because an animal that died on its own would not have had the blood drained properly) suggests that this is not incidental or devoid of religious significance. It is hard to conceive of secularization in the context of the blood prohibition that is grounded on the uniquely Israelite religious association of blood and life, particularly since the author(s) of Deuteronomy could easily have purged any elements of earlier theology that did not conform to their thinking, as has been argued is the case elsewhere in Deuteronomy.

All of this suggests that Deut 12 emphasizes the profoundly religious nature of life lived before Yahweh in the land. Levinson argues that Deut 12 creates a "new, noncultic procedure" for nonsacrificial slaughter that is in some ways reminiscent of the ritual carried out at the altar; it is religious, though noncultic.[107] This, I believe, is entirely correct. But instead of a transformation of the lemma of the earlier altar law, I believe it is more likely that Deut 12 is highlighting the religious nature of this noncultic action through the blood manipulation

---

105. D. J. McCarthy, "The Symbolism of Blood and Sacrifice," *JBL* 88 (1969): 166–76; idem, "Further Notes on the Symbolism of Blood and Sacrifice," *JBL* 92 (1973): 205–10; J. Milgrom, "Ethics and Ritual: The Foundations of the Biblical Dietary Laws," in *Religion and Law: Biblical-Judaic and Islamic Perspectives* (ed. E. B. Firmage, B. G. Weiss, and J. W. Welch; Winona Lake, IN: Eisenbrauns, 1990), 159–91.

106. Ibid., 161–62.

107. Levinson, *Legal Innovation*, 49.

and the use of the sacral term זָבַח. In this way, Deut 12 supports the theology of other parts of the book, which highlight the fact that all of life lived in the land is in the realm of the holy and is, therefore, religiously significant.

We will return to the topic of nonsacrificial slaughter when a more comprehensive interpretation of Deut 12 is provided (below, pp. 197–202). We will now examine the arguments in favor of demythologization in Deut 12.

Demythologization

The final element to be evaluated in the Deuteronomic revolution envisioned by Weinfeld is demythologization. The general thesis of demythologization was evaluated in chap. 1, so here I will focus more intently on the particulars of Deut 12.

As noted above, a crucial aspect of the theory of demythologization is the idea of the use of שֵׁם in Deut 12. This is thought to be part of a deliberate effort to repudiate the idea that Yahweh was actually present with his people. Instead, his "Name" is present at the central sanctuary, as a sort of hypostasis.

I noted in chap. 1 (see pp. 84–86) that the use of שֵׁם has been connected with ordinary worship, in contrast to the term כָּבוֹד, which is used for special manifestations of God's presence. This undermines Weinfeld's general premise that the earlier sources were inherently anthropomorphic and that Deuteronomy seeks to repudiate the earlier conceptions of Yahweh's presence in the midst of his people. Moreover, the use of שֵׁם in the centralization formula in Deuteronomy often appears in the phrase לְשַׁכֵּן שְׁמוֹ. But because this phrase *always* appears in the same form in Deuteronomy (a *Piel* infinitive construct of שָׁכַן with שֵׁם as the direct object), it should be regarded as an idiom.[108] So, the meaning of the phrase may be greater than the sum of its constituent parts. Thus, "to pull one component of an idiomatic phrase (in this case *name*), reassign to that component a broader meaning because of its occurrence in other contexts . . . and to reinsert that redefined component into what should be a closed syntactical unit . . . is simply grammatically untenable."[109]

The Name theology has been challenged on other grounds as well. Mayes, for example, argues that the use of שֵׁם is best understood as affirming Yahweh's actual presence in the midst of his people and notes

---

108. S. Richter, *The Deuteronomistic History and the Place of the Name* (Ph.D. diss., Harvard University, 2001), 46.

109. Ibid.

that "when Yahweh is said to have caused his name to dwell at a sanctuary the intention is to indicate the real and effective presence of Yahweh himself at that sanctuary."[110] This may be seen at least in part in the fact that the phrase לִפְנֵי יְהוָה appears frequently in connection with the establishment of Yahweh's name (Deut 12:7).[111] Earlier, examination of Akkadian parallels led several exegetes to reject the notion of a "name theology," at least in Deuteronomy itself. Wenham has demonstrated parallels between the Hebrew phrase לְשַׁכֵּן שְׁמוֹ and the Akkadian phrase *šakan šumšu*.[112] He notes that the Akkadian phrase, as used in other documents from the ANE, stresses ownership and often includes overtones of conquest. The Akkadian phrase appears in the Amarna letters with a king or an overlord as the agent of the action. In EA 287, for example, the prince of Jerusalem, Abdu-Heba, says that the king, Akh-en-Aton, "has set his name in the land of Jerusalem forever."[113] Similarly, the same prince writes that the king "has set his name at the rising of the sun and at the setting of the sun."[114] Wenham notes, further, that the term appears in ANE literature in connection with the inscribing of a name on a foundation stone of a sanctuary, a practice that was "essential to the validity of the temple."[115]

Building on this argument, van der Woude claims that the name formulas in Deuteronomy stress the proclamation of Yahweh's Name at the chosen place, on the basis of Akkadian parallels that use cognate words to describe the proclamation/pronunciation of a name.[116] He also criticizes the Name-theology thesis on the grounds that it presupposes a universal ANE conception of "name"—one that always

---

110. Mayes, *Deuteronomy*, 59–60.

111. Cf. I. Wilson, *Out of the Midst of the Fire: Divine Presence in Deuteronomy* (SBLDS 151; Atlanta: Scholars Press, 1995), esp. 164–65, 191–97.

112. Wenham, "Central Sanctuary," 112–13. See also idem, *The Structure and Date of Deuteronomy: A Consideration of Aspects of the History of Deuteronomy Criticism and a Reexamination of the Question of Structure and Date in the Light of That History and of the Near Eastern Treaties* (Ph.D. diss., University of London, 1970), 248–50. Wenham is here following R. de Vaux, "Le lieu que Yahvé a choisi pour y établir son nom," in *Das ferne und nahe Wort: FS L. Rost* (ed. F. Maass; Berlin: de Gruyter, 1967), 219–28; idem, "Review of *God and Temple*, by R. E. Clements," *RB* 73 (1966): 447–49. This understanding of שָׁכַן is also defended by F. M. Cross, *Canaanite Myth and Hebrew Epic: Essays in the History of the Religion of Israel* (Cambridge: Harvard University Press, 1973), 245–46.

113. EA 287: 60–63, in *ANET*, 488.

114. EA 288: 5–7, in *ANET*, 488.

115. Wenham, "Central Sanctuary," 114. This observation is based on the work of S. D. McBride, *The Deuteronomic Name Theology* (Ph.D. diss., Harvard University, 1969).

116. A. S. van der Woude, "שֵׁם," *TLOT* 3: 1361–62.

defines the entity named[117]—and because the theory presupposes rather than proves a dichotomy between Yahweh's immanence and transcendence.[118]

Further evidence for this view comes from Richter. She argues that the idiom לְשַׁכֵּן שְׁמוֹ was used in the ANE to state that one had inscribed his name on a victory stele or a foundation stone for a temple. The purpose of such an inscription was to claim ownership, "victory," or even "to become famous by heroic deeds."[119] In the context of temples, the use of the phrase *šuma šakānu* indicated that the construction of the place of worship was not the result of human initiative but came from obedience to a divine command. This ensured that the place of worship was regarded as a legitimate cult site. Thus, Richter argues, the "establishment of the name" in Mesopotamian temple foundation deposits had nothing to do with the nature of divine presence at the cult site but was concerned with the legitimacy of the site as determined by the deity's choosing it.[120]

It is important to note, however, that the ANE parallels, while shedding light on how the idiom לְשַׁכֵּן שְׁמוֹ could be understood, cannot be determinative in themselves. Barr writes that "lexicographic research should be directed towards the semantics of words in their particular occurrences and not towards the assembly of a stock of pervasive and distinctive terms which could be regarded as a linguistic reflection of the theological realities."[121] Failure to consider the specific context of the centralization formula and the idiom לְשַׁכֵּן שְׁמוֹ has been a problem with many earlier efforts at interpreting Deut 12. Similarly, caution must be exercised to avoid reading parallel Akkadian usage into the text of Deuteronomy unless there is sufficient textual warrant for doing so.[122]

In terms of Deut 12:1–7, there are important exegetical reasons for questioning whether a "Name theology" (and therefore demythologization) is the best understanding of the text. The term שֵׁם first appears in v. 3 in connection with the gods of the Canaanites. Verse 3 commands the Israelites to "tear down their altars and smash their pillars and burn their Asherim with fire. You shall chop down the carved images of their gods and obliterate their name (שֵׁם) from that place." Fol-

---

117. Ibid., 1350–51.
118. Ibid., 1360–62.
119. Richter, *Place of the Name*, 243.
120. Ibid., 165–70.
121. J. Barr, *The Semantics of Biblical Language* (Oxford: Oxford University Press, 1961), 274.
122. Cf. J. H. Walton, "Principles for Effective Word Study," *NIDOTTE* 1: 163.

lowing the command that the Israelites should not worship Yahweh
in that way (v. 4) is the command that the Israelites should "seek the
place that Yahweh your God shall choose out of all your tribes to establish his name (שָׁם) there as its dwelling place" (v. 5). The juxtaposition of the term שָׁם in vv. 3 and 5 points to a deliberate attempt to
contrast the presence of Canaanite gods and the presence of Yahweh
following the destruction of the Canaanite worship sites. It is an integral part of the rhetoric of contrast that was noted in conjunction
with the use of מָקוֹם in our examination of centralization above.

The contrast is further evident when the structure of Deut 12:2–7
is noted. This section has the following structure:

A	Eliminate the places and name of Canaanite gods	vv. 2–3
X	"You shall not worship Yahweh your God in that way"	v. 4
A'	Seek the place and Name of Yahweh for worship	vv. 5–7

In this section, a sharp contrast is drawn between the worship of Canaanite gods and the proper worship of Yahweh. The Israelites are not
to seek the places and names of the indigenous gods; to do so is contrary to proper Yahweh worship (v. 4, the central element). Rather,
they are to seek Yahweh at the place he chooses, which will be marked
by his establishment of his name there.[123]

The contrast is even more evident when one considers the purpose
of the elimination of Canaanite cultic sites. The destruction of the Canaanite sites serves to eliminate their claims of legitimacy over the
people of the land (and the land itself). The names of the gods of Canaan are to be replaced by the Name of Yahweh in the place he
chooses. For Israel, Yahweh, the giver of the land, is to be worshiped
according to his own desires and at the place of his choosing. Miller
rightly notes that

> replacing one divine name with another serves two functions. First, it
> indicates that here we deal with the functioning reality of the other
> gods. Their names are gone; one may no longer call upon the name of
> any of those gods. They may not be acknowledged or worshiped and are
> thus rendered ineffectual as far as Israel is concerned. . . . Further, ne-
> gating one group of names and establishing another name in effect calls
> for a new order, a transformation: a shift from an order where there are
> multiple claims for human allegiance and where the worship of god or
> gods is done in arbitrary and accidental fashion. . . . This order is to give
> way to another, wherein divine control is placed over human worship
> and one name replaces all other names.[124]

123. Cf. Craigie, *Deuteronomy*, 217.
124. Miller, *Deuteronomy*, 131.

In this respect, then, the use of שֵׁם in Deut 12 should be seen as part of the rhetorical emphasis of the chapter, highlighting the supremacy of Yahweh in contrast to the gods of Canaan.

This same argument is taken up in Deut 12:29–13:1. We noted above (pp. 174–175) that the structure of the chapter as a whole is chiastic. Thus there are parallels between vv. 2–4 and 29–31. In the latter section, the need for eliminating all vestiges of Canaanite worship is again at the fore; the justification for this action is to prevent the religious practices of the Canaanites from luring the Israelites away from exclusive loyalty to Yahweh. So, although the term שֵׁם is not used in this section, the rhetorical emphasis is the same. The point in each section is that Canaanite worship is to be eliminated because it is incompatible with exclusive loyalty to and veneration of Yahweh. The competing claims of the foreign gods (represented in vv. 2–4 by the use of שֵׁם and in the latter section by a description of the ways in which their influence could be felt) must be eliminated.

A deliberate theological point is being made, but it is not about the nature of the presence of Yahweh, as Weinfeld and others argue. The point is that Yahweh alone is to be worshiped in the place and manner he chooses, and anything that could compete for the loyalty of the people is to be eliminated.

The use of the term "Name" also may signal a profound emphasis on who Yahweh is. McConville has argued that the name of Yahweh is associated with "who he truly is."[125] Who Yahweh is may be known only in the context of his acts in relationship and in response to his creation and, more specifically, Israel.[126] McConville concludes that "the relationship between the name of God and his saving actions means that there is something ongoing about it. His name can be fully known only in the context of the unfolding biblical story."[127] So, the emphasis in Deut 12 on the Name of Yahweh may stress his continuing relationship with his people as he reveals more of who he is in the context of the ongoing history (especially in the conquest), as well as in the covenantal terms described in this very chapter.

---

125. McConville, *Deuteronomy*, 230.

126. C. R. Seitz ("The Call of Moses and the 'Revelation' of the Divine Name: Source-Critical Logic and Its Legacy," in *Word without End: The Old Testament as Abiding Theological Witness* [Grand Rapids: Eerdmans, 1998], 229–47) argues that Yahweh's enigmatic revelation of his Name to Moses in Exod 3:14 and 6:3 is best understood in the context of the subsequent acts of deliverance and power, culminating in the exodus. That is, Yahweh is known more fully as "Yahweh" only in his deliverance of his people from Egypt and in the destruction of those who oppose him (pp. 243–44).

127. McConville, *Deuteronomy*, 230.

The preceding discussion suggests that Weinfeld and others who have posited a demythologization in Deut 12 in which the actual presence of Yahweh is repudiated fail to account adequately for the data of the text. Nelson notes that "any concept of Yahweh's 'real absence' seems to be excluded by Deuteronomy's repeated references to the performance of sacral acts 'before Yahweh,' that is, in Yahweh's presence."[128] In addition, the contrast between the names of the gods of Canaan and the name of Yahweh, coupled with the strong statement that Yahweh is not to be worshiped in the manner of the Canaanite gods, suggests that the emphasis in this chapter is not on the presence of Yahweh per se but on the necessity of demonstrating loyalty to Yahweh alone by worshiping him at the place and in the manner of his choosing.

Alternative View: The Supremacy of Yahweh

Deuteronomy 12 marks an important transition in the rhetoric of the book as a whole. Deuteronomy 1–3 deals with the historical experience of the nation and highlights the faithfulness of Yahweh toward Israel as well as Israel's failure to trust him properly and receive the fulfillment of his promises. Deuteronomy 4 emphasizes the need for complete loyalty to Yahweh and builds on the historical reflections of the earlier chapters. The Decalogue is then presented as the terms of the covenant (Deut 5:2). In that moment, as we have seen in chap. 3, Yahweh is establishing the terms of the covenant relationship between Israel and himself. Yahweh, the "Great King," is dictating the terms of the relationship, the terms by which Israel must live and the only means by which they can experience Yahweh's continued blessing and favor. The exhortation following, in Deut 6–11, focuses primarily on the need for living out this relationship properly, which in these chapters means showing exclusive loyalty to Yahweh. Accordingly, these chapters have been interpreted as an extended exposition of the first commandment.[129]

Within the chapters prior to Deut 12, there is an anticipation of the law that is to be revealed. Deuteronomy 4:1, for example, commands the Israelites to listen to the הַחֻקִּים וְהַמִּשְׁפָּטִים ("statutes and ordinances") that Moses teaches. But as Millar rightly notes, there is nothing in

---

128. Nelson, *Deuteronomy*, 153.

129. J. H. Walton, "Deuteronomy: An Exposition of the Spirit of the Law," *Grace Theological Journal* 8 (1987): 214–15.

Deut 4 that seems to qualify as הַחֻקִּים וְהַמִּשְׁפָּטִים.[130] Despite this, the phrase appears five times in Deut 4,[131] which suggests that its use is deliberate and contributes to the rhetorical or communicative intention of the author. It occurs again in Deut 5:1 and 31, which is understandable, given the presentation of the Decalogue in Deut 5. But the reappearance of the phrase in Deut 6:1, 20; 7:11; and 11:31, all with the sense of something yet to come, creates a sense of anticipation in the reader/listener. That is, the first three chapters have confronted the Israelites with their failures and highlighted the need for the present Moab generation to make better choices than their forebears. The introduction of הַחֻקִּים וְהַמִּשְׁפָּטִים in Deut 4:1, coupled with its frequent use in that chapter, register the fact that the nature of Israel's response will be in keeping the statutes and ordinances to come. The repetition of the phrase after the Decalogue has been presented, in the context of an exhortation to demonstrate complete loyalty to Yahweh, points further to the connection between living a life of loyalty to Yahweh and keeping הַחֻקִּים וְהַמִּשְׁפָּטִים.

These chapters emphasize the need for demonstrating total allegiance to Yahweh and anticipate the חֻקִּים וְהַמִּשְׁפָּטִים that will be the means by which this will be accomplished.[132] Through the rhetoric of Deut 1–11, the reader anticipates the means by which loyalty to Yahweh may be lived out, in order to live and receive the blessings promised to the Israelites.

In Deut 12, the presentation of the specific terms of the *Torah* begins. In light of the context just discussed, it is telling that the very first command given (following the identifying statement in Deut 12:1 that "these are the חֻקִּים וְהַמִּשְׁפָּטִים" that have been anticipated) is to destroy all vestiges of Canaanite worship. Canaanite worship is incompatible with exclusive allegiance to Yahweh, as v. 4 indicates. Moreover, a deliberate contrast is drawn between the worship of the gods of Canaan on the one hand and Yahweh on the other, as we have seen. This suggests that the primary means of demonstrating loyalty to Yahweh is through proper worship of Yahweh.

The importance of demonstrating loyalty to Yahweh in worship is marked by the command in v. 5 to seek the place that Yahweh will

---

130. McConville and Millar, *Time and Place*, 37.

131. Deuteronomy 4:1, 5, 8, 14, 45.

132. The phrase הַחֻקִּים וְהַמִּשְׁפָּטִים should not be taken to refer *only* to the legal material in chaps. 12–26. Rather, as G. Braulik ("Die Ausdrücke für 'Gesetz' im Buch Deuteronomium," *Bib* 51 [1970]: 40–66) has shown, the phrase refers to the whole of Mosaic preaching in chaps. 5–26. But the legal material of chaps. 12–26 is, of course, a vital part of the preaching of Moses, so the use of the phrase still contributes to the sense of anticipation of the means by which Israel is to demonstrate total covenant loyalty to Yahweh.

choose for worship. But the use of דָּרַשׁ with the preposition אֶל has the sense of "turning to" or "choosing" and often entails the choosing of either God or "false religious intermediaries."[133] Thus, what is commanded here is not simply to identify the place (or even the number of places) but to choose to worship only at the place where Yahweh determines he will be worshiped, and in so doing, to reject the places and names of the gods of Canaan.

A major focus, then, is on Yahweh's right to determine where and how he will be worshiped. The location of the place is not specified here, primarily because it is unimportant compared with the fact that Yahweh alone has the right to say where he is to be worshiped. In the view of Deut 12, there is nothing especially sacred about the site of the מָקוֹם ("place"). Its sanctity and legitimacy derive from the fact that Yahweh has chosen it. Indeed, by commanding the destruction of Canaanite worship sites, Deuteronomy is maintaining that those sites have no inherent sacred quality, and they can be destroyed without fear of repercussion from those gods (who, in the view of Deuteronomy, are nonexistent anyway). They are not to be maintained as cultic sites for Yahweh, because sanctity of a Yahweh worship site is based only on his election of it and because maintaining those sites could become a snare for the Israelites (Deut 12:30).

The interpretation of the text itself points to the fact that Yahweh's sovereignty in choosing the place of worship is being emphasized in this chapter. This, in turn, suggests that there may be warrant for understanding the use of לְשַׁכֵּן שְׁמוֹ ("to establish his name") in light of the ANE parallels. That is, the author may have had in mind the implications of the parallel Akkadian idiom when he used the phrase לְשַׁכֵּן שְׁמוֹ in Deut 12. Richter notes that the use of this idiom is quite appropriate in this context, despite the difficulties involved in applying a parallel foreign phrase. She claims that it is appropriate to this context

> because it emphasizes YHWH's role as conquering king by communicating hegemony in the context of kingship, allegiance in the context of sovereignty, and fame due to battles won. Moreover, in many ways this idiom serves as a shorthand reference to the historical prologue of Israel's covenant with her God which served as the theological catalyst for the proper cultic behavior detailed in the old law code.[134]

---

133. McConville, *Deuteronomy*, 219. Examples of this use include Deut 18:11; Job 5:8; Isa 8:19; 19:3.

134. Richter, *Place of the Name*, 256.

It is conceivable that the author chose this idiom and used it consistently because it helped convey the nature of Yahweh's sovereignty so effectively.

We saw above that Deut 12 draws a contrast between rightful Yahweh worship and the false worship of Canaanite gods. This highlights the main concern of the chapter, which is the requirement of total loyalty to Yahweh. This becomes evident when one reviews the structure of the chapter (see also pp. 174–175 above):

A   Introductory Statement: "These are the laws you
          shall observe"   12:1
  B   No God but Yahweh: destroy worship centers of
            false gods   vv. 2–4
      X   Demonstrate loyalty to Yahweh alone in all aspects
            of worship   vv. 5–28
  B′   No God but Yahweh: do not imitate worship of
            false gods   vv. 29–31
A′   Closing Statement: "Observe all that is
          commanded"   13:1[12:32]

Allegiance is expressed, first, through seeking Yahweh at the place he chooses. Sacrifices and offerings are to be carried out only at the place that Yahweh designates. The sacrifices and offerings are to be the focus of corporate worship, as the people gather there. The worship at the central sanctuary is also to be marked by inclusiveness, because all Israel is envisioned as gathering there (male and female, slaves [both male and female], and the Levites) according to Deut 12:12. In addition, worship at the place is to be marked by joy.

But while sacrifice is restricted to the central sanctuary, worship is not. Instead, the entirety of life in the land is to be lived before Yahweh and, therefore, is religiously significant and is considered as falling to some degree in the realm of worship. This is, I believe, the significance of the regulations concerning nonsacrificial slaughter. In the narrative of Deuteronomy, Moses addresses the people on the plains of Moab, on the verge of entering the promised land. Most of the generation gathered there have never known any life other than a nomadic life in which worship was centered on the tent of meeting and in which the people experienced Yahweh's presence in remarkable and dramatic ways (Deut 2:14–16; 31:14–15). Now, however, the people are about to enter into the land itself, and corporate worship is to be at the central sanctuary. This will mean that, for those living some distance from the sanctuary, opportunities to participate in corporate worship will be limited, perhaps just to the thrice-yearly festivals. For all the people, moreover, entry into the land means a shift in their experience of the presence of Yahweh. The symbols of Yahweh's presence will no longer be visible to the vast majority of them on a daily basis. This has the effect, as Weinfeld notes, of separating a significant portion of life from ties to the cult.[135]

Weinfeld, as we have seen, argues that this means that Deuteronomy is seeking to secularize life that has been freed from its ties to the cult. I believe, rather, that in the practice of nonsacrificial slaughter, Deuteronomy is seeking to remind the people that, though they are perhaps far from the visible symbols of Yahweh's presence, their presence in the land of promise is a tangible reminder of Yahweh's faithfulness. As people in covenant with Yahweh, the people are to live every aspect of their lives in demonstration of loyalty to him. Even when slaughtering meat for consumption in the towns throughout the land, the people are to demonstrate their loyalty to Yahweh. This is achieved first by conceiving of it as a religiously significant act, marked in Deuteronomy by the use of the sacral term זָבַח. Second, it is accomplished through the disposal of the blood, which may never be eaten (Deut 12:16, 23–25).

In this way, Deuteronomy creates a nonsacrificial ritual that highlights the religious significance of life lived in the land in allegiance to Yahweh. It is, to be sure, not a sacrifice, because both clean and unclean may eat of it (Deut 12:15, 22). In addition, the author is at pains to make clear the distinction between sacrifice and nonsacrificial slaughter in vv. 25–26. But in my estimation, the author is also trying to highlight the religious significance of nonsacrificial slaughter. It becomes a means by which even people who live far away from the central sanctuary and from the visible reminders of Yahweh's presence are able to demonstrate loyalty to Yahweh on a daily basis and to be mindful of his sovereignty and presence.

This explanation is also in keeping with the Deuteronomic conception of the holiness of the land, as discussed above. Just as the entire land becomes a site for the Passover celebration through the elimination of leaven throughout the land, nonsacrificial slaughter reflects the holiness of the entire land and is a parallel to the sacrifices carried out at the sanctuary. Support for this may also be found in the parallel expressions that describe the blood manipulation in the sacrificial and nonsacrificial contexts. Deuteronomy 12:16 and 24, for example, command that the blood be "poured out" on the earth (עַל־הָאָרֶץ תִּשְׁפְּכֶנּוּ) in the practice of nonsacrificial slaughter. Later, in v. 27

---

135. Weinfeld, *Deuteronomic School,* 214.

in the context of sacrificial slaughter, the people are told that the blood of their sacrifices are to be "poured out" on the altar (יִשָּׁפֵךְ עַל־ מִזְבַּח). The parallel actions (though not an exactly parallel grammatical construction) suggest that the author intended to see the two spheres similarly. Levinson argues that Deut 12:27 represents a tendentious re-use of lemmas from Exod 20:24, based on the fact that certain terms appear in both laws. But in Deuteronomy's present form it is possible to see a parallel between the pouring of the blood on the ground in nonsacrificial slaughter and on the altar in sacrificial slaughter. The blood prohibition marks the religious significance of the former.

This nonsacrificial ritual, moreover, is intimately connected with Yahweh's blessing. Deuteronomy 12:15 states that the people are allowed to eat meat in the towns "according to the blessing of Yahweh your God which he is giving you" (כְּבִרְכַּת יְהוָה אֱלֹהֶיךָ אֲשֶׁר נָתַן־לְךָ). Thus the provision of the meat itself, as well as the permission to eat it in a nonsacrificial setting, is seen as part of Yahweh's blessing of the people and the land. The conception of this slaughter as religiously significant and the prohibition of eating blood may be designed in part to remind the consumer of the fact of Yahweh's blessing and that every aspect of life is under his sovereignty. Reverent slaughter and abstinence from eating blood are, then, part of the response of the people to the blessings Yahweh has given, just as is the consumption of the tithe, sacrifices, and offerings at the central sanctuary.

Once again, there is an emphasis on changing circumstances at a moment of transition. As we saw in chap. 2 above, the inclusion of Deut 1:9–18 in the historical narrative serves in part to highlight the constancy of *Torah* in the midst of changing circumstances. Here, at the beginning of the legal section of Deuteronomy, there is further emphasis on the need for constancy in the midst of changing situations. The narrative of Deuteronomy portrays the people as entering the land and settling in it. This change has important implications for experiencing Yahweh's presence and living out loyalty to him, as required of people in covenant relationship with him. Once again, Deuteronomy emphasizes that no matter how the circumstances change, Yahweh's faithfulness in blessing will be constant (vv. 7, 15). More important, however, is the need to demonstrate loyalty to Yahweh in every aspect of life. Deuteronomy's conception of nonsacrificial slaughter provides a means by which the people throughout the land may do so, even in the radically altered circumstances of settlement presupposed by the narrative.

Conclusions regarding
Deuteronomy 12

In this chapter, we have examined the evidence that Deut 12 supports a radical program of centralization, secularization, and demythologization. This evidence, I have argued, may be interpreted differently and in fact leads to different conclusions.

I have argued that, rather than pointing toward centralization of all worship at a single sanctuary, the evidence demonstrates that Deut 12 emphasizes the supremacy of Yahweh by his choice of where and how he is to be worshiped. A careful reading of the text in its context shows that the number of altars is not the main point of Deut 12, so there is no conflict with Exod 20:24–25. The primary emphasis is on Yahweh's sovereignty and the contrast between proper Yahweh worship and the false worship of Canaanite gods. Choosing Yahweh means a fundamental rejection of the Canaanite gods and Canaanite worship practices.

Rejecting the Canaanite gods must be followed by an embrace of Yahweh and by living lives totally devoted to him. In the narrative world of the text, the people are about to undergo a change in the way they experience Yahweh's presence and the way they demonstrate allegiance to him. For Deuteronomy, all of life in the land is of religious significance, as evidenced by the extension of holiness to the land itself, not merely the environs of the central sanctuary. Consequently, the law of nonsacrificial slaughter establishes a means by which the people can conceive of life as religiously significant and demonstrate loyalty to Yahweh. But it is not to be considered "profane," since in the view of Deuteronomy there is no activity of the people in the land that is to be considered profane. All of the actions of the people of Israel in the land have covenantal and religious significance.

Worship emerges as a fundamental theme in this chapter. Heading the laws of the legal section is concern for proper Yahweh worship. If the entire legal section is seen as the means by which the people respond to Yahweh's blessings and gracious acts on their behalf, Deut 12 makes explicit that proper worship is at the heart of this response. The first way in which allegiance to Yahweh may be shown is through a rejection of all false worship and a dedication to worshiping Yahweh as he has commanded.

The emphasis is not on the nature of Yahweh's presence or absence from the central sanctuary. Rather, the emphasis is on the need for the people to demonstrate loyalty to Yahweh by rejecting false worship and living lives of obedience to him and to *Torah*.

Chapter 5

Political Administration and *Torah*: Deuteronomy 16:18–18:22

The final section of Deuteronomy we will be considering in this study is Deut 16:18–18:22. Like the previous texts we have examined, Deut 16:18–18:22 is often seen as a text that supports a radical program of centralization, secularization, and demythologization. This text deals with the offices of judge, king, priest, and prophet, and it is often considered to be one of the key texts advancing the Deuteronomic program; some of the unique emphases of Deuteronomic theology are most clearly discerned in this passage.

This passage served as the basis for our broad consideration of centralization in chap. 1 above. There, five views of centralization were presented and analyzed on the basis of the laws regarding offices. It is not necessary, therefore, to repeat that discussion here. Rather, I will summarize here the contours of the arguments that elements of centralization, secularization, and demythologization are present in Deut 16:18–18:22 and some concerns raised with regard to that understanding. The bulk of this chapter will consist of my presentation of an alternative understanding of this section.

Prevailing View: Centralization and Secularization

As we saw in chap. 1, Deut 16:18–18:22 has been read as evidence for Deuteronomy's program of centralization. Though they conceive of it differently, all five of the representative scholars considered above believe that centralization is an important aspect of this part of the book.

This section of Deuteronomy is widely recognized as a separate unit.[1] It deals with the political and religious organization of life in

---

1. See, e.g., R. D. Nelson, *Deuteronomy* (OTL; Louisville: Westminster John Knox, 2002), 213; J. G. McConville, *Deuteronomy* (AOTC 5; Leicester: Apollos / Downers Grove, IL: InterVarsity, 2002), 280–81; W. Brueggemann, *Deuteronomy* (AbOTC; Nashville: Abingdon, 2001), 178–79; R. E. Clements, "The Book of Deuteronomy: Introduction, Commentary, and Reflections," *NIB* 2: 416–18.

Israel, which has led many to describe this text as a "constitution" for Israel.[2] While this is an apt description, because this section clearly provides instruction regarding the major offices and institutions that will govern the nation, it is nevertheless a part of the book as a whole and must be interpreted in light of its broader context. There is no evidence that Deut 16:18–18:22 was ever an independent text.[3] Regardless of the origin of these laws, they are now presented in Deuteronomy in the context of Moses' address to the people gathered on the plains of Moab, on the verge of entering the land. The topics covered in this address are:

Judges and Legal Administration	16:18–17:13
Law of the King	17:14–20
Levitical Priests	18:1–8
Prophets	18:9–22

The appointment of judges in Deut 16:18–20 is often thought to be a direct result of centralization. Prior to Deuteronomy, it is usually argued, priests in local sanctuaries adjudicated certain cases. With the elimination of local sanctuaries as a result of the Deuteronomic reform under Josiah, local priests were no longer available to serve in this capacity.[4] As a result, two transformations take place in the legislation in Deuteronomy. First, professional judges are to be appointed to adjudicate local cases, according to Deut 16:18–20. Second, appeals are to be brought to a central tribunal, where priests and judges render verdicts (Deut 17:8–13). The law related to judges also indicates secularization, because the priests who rendered judgment at local sanctuaries are replaced by a professional judiciary, removing legal decision-making from the realm of the cult. Thus it is considered significant that, despite the inclusion of a priest at the central tribunal, sacral media are not mentioned in the resolution of difficult cases.[5]

2. S. D. McBride, "Polity of the Covenant People: The Book of Deuteronomy," *Int* 41 (1987): 229–44; B. Halpern, *The Constitution of the Monarchy in Israel* (HSM 25; Chico, CA: Scholars Press, 1981), esp. 226–33.

3. McConville, *Deuteronomy*, 281. McConville rightly notes that the "separate existence of the laws, and even their pre-deuteronomic grouping as a body of laws governing aspects of the constitution of Israel, cannot be ruled out." The fact remains, however, that the precise origins are unknown, and the section has been thoroughly integrated into the rhetoric and argument of the book as a whole.

4. See M. Weinfeld, *Deuteronomy and the Deuteronomic School* (Oxford: Oxford University Press, 1972; repr. Winona Lake, IN: Eisenbrauns, 1992), 233–36; B. M. Levinson, *Deuteronomy and the Hermeneutics of Legal Innovation* (Oxford: Oxford University Press, 1997), 98–143.

5. Weinfeld, *Deuteronomic School*, 233–34.

The law of the king (Deut 17:14–20) is also understood as support-ing the unique nature of the Deuteronomic program. The limitations on the role of the king are considered radical, although there is no consensus among scholars regarding the significance of these limita-tions. Some consider the law of the king to be an elevation of the cen-tral tribunal,[6] while others think that it is a rejection of certain abuses of kingship (by specific kings) as well as an emphasis on the impor-tance of the institution of the monarchy itself.[7] Still others see the law as a reflection on the institution of the monarchy and a reduction in the significance of the king.[8]

The law related to priests in Deut 18:1–8 also reflects Deuteron-omy's program of centralization. Centralization is especially evident in the regulation about priests serving at "the place" in Deut 18:6–8: the elimination of local sanctuaries resulted in displacement of the lo-cal priests and this law ensured their participation in the ministry of the central sanctuary.[9] This law, then, like the law requiring the ap-pointment of judges, is directly related to the centralization of wor-ship in Jerusalem and the concomitant elimination of all altars in other locations. It is evidence that centralization was a far-reaching aspect of the Deuteronomic program.

I raised some objections to this view in chap. 1. I argued that Wein-feld's interpretation of the law about judges (Deut 16:18–20) is based on assumptions about the role of elders that are not supported by the data of the text. That is, Weinfeld argues that the judicial reform ad-

6. Levinson, *Legal Innovation*, 142.

7. Weinfeld, *Deuteronomic School*, 169–71.

8. N. Lohfink, "Distribution of the Functions of Power: The Laws concerning Public Offices in Deuteronomy 16:18–18:22," in *A Song of Power and the Power of Song: Essays on the Book of Deuteronomy* (ed. D. L. Christensen; SBTS 3; Winona Lake, IN: Eisenbrauns, 1993), 346–48.

9. I. Cairns, *Word and Presence: A Commentary on the Book of Deuteronomy* (ITC; Grand Rapids: Eerdmans / Edinburgh: Handsel, 1992), 170. Since J. Wellhausen, *Prolegomena to the History of Ancient Israel* (New York: Meridian, 1957), 121–51, esp. 139–40, some have seen in Deut 18:6–8 a reflection of 2 Kg 23:8–9 and identify the Levite in Deut 18:6 as be-ing a priest of one of the high places who was denied a role at the temple in Jerusalem according to 2 Kg 23:8–9. However, the relationship between Deut 18:1–8 and 2 Kg 23:8–9 is far from clear. Deuteronomy 18:6–8 reads more like a description of an occasional pil-grimage to the central sanctuary, not a major migration. In addition, it is unlikely that the author of the DtH, who holds Josiah up as a model Israelite and king, would portray him as disobeying a law from Deuteronomy, which is considered to be the book of the law that served as the basis for his reforms. On this, see R. D. Nelson, "The Role of the Priesthood in the Deuteronomistic History," in *Congress Volume: Leuven, 1989* (ed. J. A. Emerton; VTSup 43; Leiden: Brill, 1991), 132–47; J. G. McConville, *Law and Theology in Deuteronomy* (JSOTSup 33; Sheffield: JSOT Press, 1984), 132–35; R. Abba, "Priests and Le-vites in Deuteronomy," *VT* 27 (1977): 257–67.

vocated by Deuteronomy leaves only "patriarchal and family litigation" within the sphere of influence of the elders and mandates that
all cases requiring the establishment of guilt or innocence be brought
to the newly-appointed professional jurists.[10] But Deut 19:11–12 gives
the elders responsibility for determining the guilt or innocence of the
manslayer, and other cases assigned to elders (Deut 21:19–20; 22:15–
21; 25:8–9) also deal with the establishment of guilt or innocence.

This leads to a further concern about Weinfeld's reconstruction.
Weinfeld believes that centralization created a judicial vacuum because local altars were eliminated.[11] But Weinfeld himself recognizes
that prior to Josiah's reform there was a local civil judiciary at which
elders and judges officiated.[12] His interpretation does not consider
the possibility that local officials (elders and judges) could have continued to adjudicate matters that arose despite the elimination of the
local altars. His contention that the Deuteronomic reforms combined
the two institutions of the judiciary (sacral and civil) at the central tribunal is possible; but why are judges to be appointed in the city
gates? In Weinfeld's own view, judges previously had officiated there;
why could they not have continued to do so?

The law of the king in Deut 17:14–20 raises additional questions
about whether centralization and secularization are the primary concerns of this section. As we noted in chap. 1, there is at present no
consensus regarding whether this text, and Deuteronomy as a whole,
supports or opposes the institution of the monarchy. At the same
time, most interpreters think that the book of Deuteronomy originated in or near the time of Josiah and associate the book with his
reforms. But the law in Deut 17:14–20 may plausibly be read as presenting kingship as a governmental option, not as a necessity. Kingship, after all, is not commanded by the law of the king but is, rather,
permitted. If kingship is in fact vital to the centralizing program envisioned by Deuteronomy,[13] it is surprising that kingship is not more
directly supported or even required. In addition, the powers of the
king are dramatically circumscribed when compared with the powers
of ANE kings in general or the powers actually exercised by Judahite
and Israelite kings (see below). This raises the question whether the

10. Weinfeld, *Deuteronomic School*, 234; idem, "Elder," *EncJud* 6: 578–80.
11. Weinfeld, *Deuteronomic* School, 234. See also B. M. Levinson, "The Reconceptual-
ization of Kingship in Deuteronomy and the Deuteronomistic History's Transformation of
Torah," *VT* 51 (2001): 520.
12. Ibid., 235–36.
13. M. Weinfeld, *Deuteronomy 1–11* (AB 5; New York: Doubleday, 1991), 55; idem,
Deuteronomic School, 298–306.

law of the king is best associated with the kinds of reforms carried out by Josiah who, if he followed the letter of the law of the king, would have found himself in a remarkably less-powerful position. In its present form, at least, the Deuteronomic law code, with its inclusion of the law of the king, does not seem to fit squarely with the centralizing reforms of Josiah.[14] This does not, of course, prove that the law should not be associated with the Josianic reforms, but it does raise the possibility that at the heart of this section in its present form is something other than the centralizing and secularizing reform posited by Weinfeld and others.

This apparent problem has led some to conclude that the law of the king is not a part of the law book that served as the basis of Josiah's reforms but that it is, rather, a deuteronomistic addition to the earlier work.[15] This solution, however, is hard to reconcile with the fact that DtH portrays kings in Israel and Judah as exercising the powers denied them in the law of the king.[16] It is difficult to conceive of a Deuteronomistic editor who would include in the final form of Deuteronomy stipulations that could serve at least in part to undermine his efforts to highlight the positive aspects of the monarchy.

The law of priests in Deut 18:1–8 does not indicate that it anticipates a major influx of priests. Rather, it seems at best to envision an occasional, "voluntary movement of Levites to serve at the central sanctuary,"[17] perhaps along the lines of a "temporary tour of duty at the sanctuary by a Levite who comes from one of the cities set aside for him in any part of the land."[18] Accordingly, caution should be exercised in attributing this law to the effects of centralization.

---

14. A. D. H. Mayes ("Deuteronomistic Ideology and the Theology of the Old Testament," *JSOT* 82 [1999]: 68–69) notes that the reforms of Josiah also tended to bypass the social law of the Deuteronomic code. This raises further questions about whether the book in its present form is best seen as supporting the type of reforms carried out by Josiah, and consequently whether the kind of radical program posited by Weinfeld and others is really the best interpretation of the text as it presently stands.

15. See, e.g., idem, *Deuteronomy* (NCB; Grand Rapids: Eerdmans / London: Marshall, Morgan & Scott, 1979), 273; U. Rüterswörden, *Von der politischen Gemeinschaft zur Gemeinde: Studien zu Dt 16,18–18,22* (Frankfurt am Main: Athenäum, 1987), 94–111; and E. Otto, "Von der Programmschrift einer Rechtsreform zum Verfassungsentwurf des Neuen Israel: Die Stellung des Deuteronomiums in der Rechtsgeschichte Israels," in *Bundesdokument und Gesetz: Studien zum Deuteronomium* (ed. G. Braulik; HBS 4; Freiburg: Herder, 1995), 93–104.

16. G. N. Knoppers, "The Deuteronomist and the Deuteronomic Law of the King: A Reexamination of the Relationship," *ZAW* 108 (1996): 336–44; idem, "Rethinking the Relationship between Deuteronomy and the Deuteronomistic History: The Case of Kings," *CBQ* 63 (2001): 393–415.

17. Nelson, *Deuteronomy*, 232.

18. McConville, *Deuteronomy*, 299.

Moreover, whether Deut 18:1–8 knows of the distinction between priests and Levites or, indeed, whether this text is referring to priests of the high places is the wrong question. The emphasis in this section is not on the nature of the priesthood per se but on the means by which the Levitical tribe, having no allotment of land, will be supported. Thus, McConville rightly notes that the emphasis is on offering the Levites more than "mere crumbs" and actually allowing them to accumulate wealth.[19] Deuteronomy 18:6–8, then, emphasizes the rights of all members of the tribe of Levi to enjoy the wealth that Yahweh will provide when they serve at the central sanctuary. In this way, the Levites, along with the aliens, orphans, and widows, serve as a measure of the extent to which Israel is truly living as the people of Yahweh, which also results in sharing with all the people the abundant blessings promised by Yahweh.[20]

Alternative View: Supremacy of Yahweh and Torah

In my estimation, interpreters of Deut 16:18–18:22 such as Weinfeld and others are correct in their assertion that this section of Deuteronomy sets forth a radical, even revolutionary, program. The nature of the program, however, is rather different from what is usually claimed. In this section, I will present an alternative interpretation of the text in an effort to identify what may be at the heart of the radical Deuteronomic program. To accomplish this I will examine separately the various subsections of the passage.

Judges and Legal Administration (Deuteronomy 16:18–17:13)

The section dealing with offices opens with the command that judges and officers (שֹׁפְטִים וְשֹׁטְרִים) are to be appointed in all the towns in the land.[21] Following the instruction to appoint judges, there is an

---

19. Ibid., 297.

20. See McConville, *Law and Theology*, 151; N. Lohfink, "The Laws of Deuteronomy: A Utopian Project for a World without Any Poor?" Lattey Lecture 1995 (Cambridge: St. Edmund's College, 1995); and idem, "Das deuteronomische Gesetz in der Endgestalt: Entwurf einer Gesellschaft ohne marginale Gruppen," *BN* 51 (1990): 25–40. Cf. also C. J. H. Wright, *Deuteronomy* (NIBC 4; Peabody, MA: Hendrickson / Carlisle: Paternoster, 1996), 213–15.

21. The expression שֹׁפְטִים וְשֹׁטְרִים may simply be a hendiadys referring to judges ("judging officials"), since the only activity in question here is judicial in nature. See E. H. Merrill, *Deuteronomy* (NAC 4; Nashville: Broadman & Holman, 1994), 257–58. On the other hand, it may refer to two different offices, where שֹׁטֵר is a reference to some type of scribal activity. See Nelson, *Deuteronomy*, 217; and McConville, *Deuteronomy*, 286; and the more

exhortation to pursue justice and to avoid partiality and bribes (Deut 16:19–20).

In interpreting this text, it is important to note specifically who is addressed here. Generally, it is recognized that the community as a whole is instructed to appoint judges.[22] But the significance of this, as well as how consistent this principle is throughout the section on offices in Deut 16:18–18:22, has not been as readily appreciated.

Deuteronomy 16:18 commands the people to appoint judges and officers, using a second-person singular verb, which is usually understood in Deuteronomy as addressing the whole people.[23] In the next verses, Deut 16:19–20, most commentators argue that the individual judges, not the community as a whole, are being addressed.[24] But there is no change in the form of address: the second-person singular is used in these verses as well. I think it more likely, therefore, that the entire community is still being addressed.[25] As members of the wider community, those who would serve as judges are included, but the primary addressee in these verses is Israel as a whole.[26]

This view is supported by the fact that v. 18 ends with a reference to the judges in the third-person plural: וְשָׁפְטוּ אֶת־הָעָם מִשְׁפַּט־צֶדֶק ("and

---

elaborate treatment of the offices in M. Weinfeld, "Judge and Officer in Ancient Israel and in the Ancient Near East," *IOS* 7 (1977): 65–88.

22. See, e.g., Clements, "The Book of Deuteronomy," 419; J. H. Tigay, *Deuteronomy* דברים: *The Traditional Hebrew Text with the New JPS Translation* (Philadelphia: Jewish Publication Society, 1996), 160; P. D. Miller, *Deuteronomy* (Interp; Louisville: John Knox, 1990), 143; R. Brown, *The Message of Deuteronomy: Not By Bread Alone* (BST; Leicester: Inter-Varsity, 1993), 176. Other scholars, however, claim that some other entity is being addressed. G. von Rad (*Deuteronomy: A Commentary* [London: SCM, 1966], 118) argues that the king is to appoint the judges. Mayes (*Deuteronomy*, 264) posits that an unspecified "centralized authority" has responsibility for appointment. Similarly, Y. Suzuki ("Deuteronomic Reformation in View of the Centralization of the Administration of Justice," *AJBI* 13 [1987]: 34) maintains that the addressee here is "an organization of the administration."

23. On the use of second-person singular and plural in Deuteronomy, see T. A. Lenchak, *"Choose Life!": A Rhetorical-Critical Investigation of Deuteronomy 28,69–30,20* (AnBib 129; Rome: Pontifical Biblical Institute, 1993), 12–16, and the references there.

24. E.g., Miller, *Deuteronomy*, 143; P. C. Craigie, *The Book of Deuteronomy* (NICOT; Grand Rapids: Eerdmans, 1976), 247; Merrill, *Deuteronomy*, 258; Wright, *Deuteronomy*, 204; I. Cairns, *Word and Presence: A Commentary on the Book of Deuteronomy* (ITC; Grand Rapids: Eerdmans / Edinburgh: Handsel, 1992), 159–60; von Rad, *Commentary*, 114–15; S. R. Driver, *Deuteronomy* (ICC; Edinburgh: T. & T. Clark, 1895), 200–201.

25. This view is supported by Tigay, *Deuteronomy*, 160; Nelson, *Deuteronomy*, 218; F. Crüsemann, *The Torah: Theology and Social History of Old Testament Law* (Minneapolis: Fortress, 1996), 238–40 (ET of *Die Tora: Theologie und Sozialgeschichte des alttestamentlichen Gesetzes* [Munich: Chr. Kaiser, 1992]).

26. Contra Craigie, *Deuteronomy*, 247, who argues the opposite: these verses, "although applying in principle to all men, are addressed particularly to the officers of the law."

they shall judge the people with righteous judgment"). This clearly shows that the entire community, not the judges, is being addressed in v. 18. That there is no alteration in the form of address in vv. 19–20 suggests that the same audience, the community as a whole, is in view there as well. This is all the more likely in view of the well-established fact that Deuteronomy frequently alternates between the singular and plural forms of the second person. That is, if the judges were being addressed, one might expect a shift to the plural form of the second person, which is often used to address a collection of individuals.[27]

The LXX reading supports the view that the community continues to be addressed in vv. 19 and 20 (though it does, admittedly, suggest that the primary referent here is the judges themselves rather than the people as a whole). The LXX shifts into the third-person plural, stating that *"They* [i.e., the judges] shall not distort justice. . . . *They* shall not take bribes."* This is, perhaps an attempt to harmonize v. 19 with the last phrase of v. 18, which is also in the third-person singular.

Identifying who is being exhorted in vv. 19–20 is important for understanding what is at the heart of the theology of this section. Those who think the judges are being addressed rightly recognize an emphasis on justice, which is clearly important to life lived in relationship with Yahweh. Frequently, however, the admonition to the judges is seen as evidence of a secularization program in Deuteronomy. In this view, it is significant that *judges* are being addressed. Prior to the centralization of worship in Jerusalem and the abolition of local sanctuaries, it is argued, local disputes would often have been resolved through the mediation of priests in the local sanctuaries. The abolition of sanctuaries required that secular judges be appointed. Accordingly, the fact that judges are being addressed rather than priests highlights the revolutionary nature of Deuteronomy's program of centralization and secularization.

If, however, the people as a whole are being addressed, a different picture begins to emerge. In this reading, the entire community is responsible to ensure that justice is done in Israel. This is a truly revolutionary aspect of the Deuteronomic program. Throughout the ancient Near East, the king was responsible for the administration of justice, but Deuteronomy places this responsibility squarely in the hands of the community as a whole. Moreover, the pursuit of justice (or perhaps, better, "righteousness"; see below) is of supreme importance, for it permits the people to "live and possess the land" that Yahweh is giving them (v. 20). Those who will be judges are included in this

---

27. Lenchak, *"Choose Life,"* 13.

exhortation, to be sure, but the entire community is responsible before Yahweh for the maintenance of justice.[28]

What does it mean to "pursue righteousness" (v. 20)? Most translations gloss the Hebrew word צֶדֶק as "justice" in this verse. "Justice" is certainly part of the semantic range of the word, but careful examination of the term as it is used in this context suggests that the judicial sense is not primarily in view.

As we saw in chap. 2 above, the nominal forms צֶדֶק and צְדָקָה in Deuteronomy do not usually appear in judicial contexts. Rather, the broader sense of "righteousness" appears to be connected with these nominal forms.[29] It has also been noted that צֶדֶק entails adherence to some fixed standard known to the community.[30] Thus, for example, Deut 25:15 calls for weights and measures that are שְׁלֵמָה וָצֶדֶק, that is, in conformity with a known standard and not compromised in any way. Similarly, Deut 33:19 speaks of זִבְחֵי־צֶדֶק, meaning sacrifices that conform to some known standard. The use of the adjectival form צַדִּיק in Deut 16:18 refers to people whose lives and behavior conform to certain standards. Deuteronomy 16:18 further says that the newly appointed judges are to judge the people with מִשְׁפַּט־צֶדֶק, which refers to judgment that is in conformity to a standard. Reimer concludes that צֶדֶק "terminology indicates right behavior or status in relation to some standard of behavior expected in the community. It also entails the adjudication of such behavior or status as well as the more abstract sense of some claim to it."[31]

The fact that the people as a whole are addressed in Deut 16:19–20 suggests that "righteousness" (in a broader sense) rather than "justice" (in the forensic/legal sense) is in view here.[32] Few of the people being addressed are likely to engage in the adjudication of cases as judges. But all of the people have opportunity to pursue צֶדֶק in the

---

28. Nelson, *Deuteronomy*, 218.

29. See above, pp. 101–102.

30. D. Patrick, *Old Testament Law* (Atlanta: John Knox, 1985), 117; D. J. Reimer, "צדק," *NIDOTTE* 3: 750; H. G. Stigers, "צדק," *TWOT* 2: 753; N. Snaith, *The Distinctive Ideas of the Old Testament* (London: Epworth, 1944), 73.

31. Reimer, "צדק," 750.

32. Weinfeld rightly notes that the broader understanding of righteousness "does not exclude the juridical sense of the expression. . . . '[J]ustice and righteousness' is not a concept that belongs to the jurisdiction alone, but is much more relevant for the social-political leaders who create the laws and are responsible for their execution" (M. Weinfeld, *Social Justice in Ancient Israel and in the Ancient Near East* [Jerusalem: Magnes, 1995], 44). In Weinfeld's view, however, the responsibility for the maintenance of a "righteous" society lies with the king.

course of their lives.[33] They do so by living out every aspect of their lives in conformity to a known standard.

The standard to which Israel is expected to conform is expounded, beginning in the next verse. Scholars have often regarded these verses as an abrupt interpolation that has little to do with the context. Levinson, for example, argues that Deut 16:21–17:1 "bear[s] no relationship whatsoever to justice. They deal with cultic issues—the topic of the previous section of the legal corpus."[34] But the charge of irrelevance can be sustained only if judges are addressed in Deut 16:19–20 and if the narrower, judicial sense of צֶדֶק is assumed in v. 20. If, however, we see the entire community as being involved in the pursuit of righteousness (in the broader sense), then these verses are not an interruption. Rather, they provide a vivid description of unrighteousness: syncretism in the form of the construction of an אֲשֵׁרָה and the withholding of sacrifices that rightfully belong to Yahweh. In short, unrighteousness is portrayed as a violation of Yahweh's commandments (both in the Decalogue and the commandments already given in Deut 15:19–23). This, according to Deuteronomy, is the nadir of unrighteousness.

The nonjudicial sense of צֶדֶק is also evident in other places in the Deuteronomic law. Deuteronomy 15:9 warns against failing to lend to a needy brother because the year of release is near. As a result, the needy person will cry out to Yahweh against the would-be lender. It is striking that it is not from judges or the judicial system that the needy person will seek justice but from Yahweh. Since generosity of this sort cannot be legistlated or its absence adjudicated, the focus seems to be wider than the confines of forensic justice—on righteousness in the broadest sense.[35]

Some of the laws of Deut 24 point in a similar direction. Included in this section are laws about recovering the forgotten sheaf or olives while harvesting (Deut 24:19–22), paying wages on time (vv. 14–15), not keeping a pledge when making a loan, or even entering someone's home to collect a pledge (vv. 10–13). None of these laws is likely to be enforced effectively through appeal to judges, as is evident from the

---

33. A similar perspective may be seen in Lev 19:11–18, where commands relating to the pursuit of righteousness/justice are contained within commands having nothing to do with the judicial sphere. As in Deut 16, the people as a whole are called upon to see that every aspect of life, including the maintenance of the legal system, is carried out in conformity to Yahweh's standards of righteousness.

34. Levinson, *Legal Innovation*, 100. Similarly, Driver (*Deuteronomy*, 201) argued that this section has no connection to the preceding material and suggests that Deut 16:21–17:7 may originally have been located before Deut 13:2.

35. Cf. Nelson, *Deuteronomy*, 196.

fact that it is to Yahweh that the needy person who is deprived of his pledge overnight appeals (v. 15). Perhaps the community could have informally brought pressure to bear on the violator and thus ensured that צֶדֶק was maintained. It is particularly noteworthy that Deut 24:13 specifically identifies proper treatment of a needy person as צְדָקָה ("righteousness"). It seems, then, that צֶדֶק is more than simply forensic justice and includes a broader sense of righteousness.[36]

This understanding of righteousness is consistent with a general perspective in Deuteronomy of collective responsibility.[37] Deuteronomy 21:1–9 is a case in point: the actions of the elders and priests are described in third person ("*they* shall go"), while the addressee remains Israel as a whole, in the second-person singular ("*your* elders [זְקֵנֶיךָ]"). The prayer of the elders in the nearest city is that the guilt will be removed from *Israel*, not only their locale (v. 8). There is a distinct sense in which the actions of individuals (or small groups within the whole) affect the well-being of the whole. Accordingly, the community as a whole has a responsibility to maintain justice. The rhetoric of Deuteronomy, including its unique emphasis on the role of the people as a whole, serves to "[construct] the consciousness of the people and [situate] them in their 'world.'"[38] Similarly, Deut 12 addresses the need for total allegiance to Yahweh to the people as a whole, not to a subgroup. By including the entire community in the exhortation, the author shows that the people as a whole are responsible for the maintenance of purity in worship.

In light of this, we may describe Deut 16:21–17:1 not as an interruption but as part of the rhetorical thrust of Moses' speech. By following a plea for the pursuit of צֶדֶק with a description of actions contrary to the desired goal, the author throws into sharp relief the contrast between loyalty and obedience to Yahweh and the dark alternative (behavior described in vivid terms as things that Yahweh hates [שָׂנֵא] and as abominations [תּוֹעֵבָה]). The purpose is to persuade the audience to pursue righteousness zealously, and the use of negative ex-

---

36. For a different perspective, as well as discussion of the implications for modern language translation of the Hebrew text, see S. M. Voth, "Justice and/or Righteousness: A Contextual Analysis of *ṣedeq* in the KJV (English) and RVR (Spanish)," in *The Challenge of Bible Translation: Communicating God's Word to the World* (ed. G. G. Scorgie, M. L. Strauss, and S. M. Voth; Grand Rapids: Zondervan, 2003), 321–45.

37. D. Patrick, "The Rhetoric of Collective Responsibility in the Deuteronomic Law," in *Pomegranates and Golden Bells: Studies in Biblical, Jewish, and Near Eastern Ritual, Law, and Literature in Honor of Jacob Milgrom* (ed. D. P. Wright, D. N. Freedman, and A. Hurvitz; Winona Lake, IN: Eisenbrauns, 1995), 421–36.

38. Ibid., 435.

amples serves both to illustrate the nature of צֶדֶק by showing what it is not and to motivate the hearers to avoid its opposite.

In the same way, Deut 17:2–13 illustrates what it means for the people to pursue righteousness. Here, as in Deut 16:18–20, it is the people as a whole who are addressed in second-person singular. Deuteronomy 17:2–7 has been understood as an example of the type of case that the newly appointed judges might face.[39] Instead, I believe it describes a situation in which the community is to uphold standards of justice and righteousness. Here, as in Deut 16:21–17:1, the offense involves violation of the first commandment by worshiping other gods.[40] The entire community is to be diligent in ensuring that loyalty to Yahweh is demonstrated in every facet of life. In addition, the procedures outlined in 17:2–7 demonstrate that, while the community is expected to uphold standards of righteousness and to prosecute those who fail to demonstrate loyalty to Yahweh, they are expected to do so in a way that demonstrates fundamental fairness (vv. 4–6). This interpretation renders unnecessary both the "standard solution" (in which Deut 17:2–7 is moved to the context of Deut 13) as well as Levinson's hypothesis that 17:2–7 is a readaptation of lemmas from Deut 13:7–12.[41]

The standard of righteousness that the community is to uphold is further revealed in Deut 17:11, where the authority of the judges is affirmed in the strongest of terms, because the death penalty is prescribed for a person who fails to abide by the decisions of the court. It is interesting to note, however, the language that is used. Verse 11 says that parties to a court case are to "do according to the terms of the law (תּוֹרָה) taught you and according to the decisions (מִשְׁפָּט) announced to you." The juxtaposition of these terms highlights the fact that both תּוֹרָה and מִשְׁפָּט are understood as part of the revealed will of Yahweh and therefore must be strictly adhered to.[42] As Millar has argued, the Ten Commandments, given directly by Yahweh to the people; the specific stipulations of chaps. 12–26, given through the mediation of Moses; and even the parenesis in Deuteronomy are conceived of as

---

39. See Miller, *Deuteronomy*, 143–44; Wright, *Deuteronomy*, 205–6.
40. This is suggested by the fact that the verbs "serve" (עָבַד) and "worship" (חוה) are used in reverse order from their appearance in Deut 5:9. See Merrill, *Deuteronomy*, 260.
41. See Levinson, *Legal Innovation*, 104–7, 119–20. Levinson's arguments are presented and criticized more fully in chap. 1 above.
42. Cf. Snaith, *Distinctive Ideas*, 75; B. Lindars, "Torah in Deuteronomy," in *Words and Meanings: Essays Presented to David Winton Thomas* (ed. P. R. Ackroyd and B. Lindars; Cambridge: Cambridge University Press, 1968), 128–31.

"law" for Israel and represent the standards to which the entire community is expected to conform.[43]

In light of this, it is reasonable to conclude that a central concern of the law regarding judges is to illustrate how the entire community should uphold righteousness and the things that may threaten it—not to promote a secular institution due to changes wrought by centralization. Indeed, the fact that false worship is cited as the parade example of unrighteousness and the fact that righteousness is conceived of more broadly than ordinary forensic justice point to the religious significance of this legislation. If my interpretation is correct, the revolutionary nature of Deuteronomy's program lies not in the secularization of the judiciary as a result of centralization but in the rejection of ancient Near Eastern models of government (especially kingship) in favor of the elevation of *Torah*.

The Law of the King (Deuteronomy 17:14–20)

The truly revolutionary nature of the Deuteronomic program is seen most clearly in the law of the king, in Deut 17:14–20. Deuteronomy presents a king with significantly circumscribed powers. Indeed, the very office of the king is not required but is permitted, if the people desire it. In contrast, the offices of judges (Deut 16:18–20, 17:9), priests (Deut 17:9, 18:1–8), and prophets (Deut 18:9–22) are required by Deuteronomy.[44] Moreover, these offices are presented as more significant in the life of the nation than the king, according to Deuteronomy.[45]

The role assigned to the king in Deuteronomy is rather remarkable. He is prohibited from accumulating large numbers of horses (Deut 17:16), which is best understood as limiting his power to establish a large standing army equipped with a powerful chariot force.[46] Thus, the common ANE role as military leader is denied the king. In addition, he is prohibited from amassing great wealth or a harem (Deut 17:17), which, McConville argues, is understood as "opposing a centralized royal administration, which concentrates a nation's wealth by means of a tax system, and which uses royal marriage as a

---

43. See McConville and Millar, *Time and Place*, 36–57. What constitutes "law" in Deuteronomy is also taken up in N. Lohfink, "Die *'ḥuqqîm umišpāṭîm'* im Buch Deuteronomium und ihre Neubegrenzung durch Dtn. 12:1," *Bib* 70 (1989): 1–27; and G. Braulik, "Die Ausdrücke für 'Gesetz' im Buch Deuteronomium," *Bib* 51 (1970): 40–66. This is similar to the use of דְּבָרִים ("words") that was posited in chap. 3 above.

44. Cf. Miller, *Deuteronomy*, 147.

45. McBride, "Polity," 241.

46. See Craigie, *Deuteronomy*, 255; Lohfink, "Functions of Power," 345.

tool of international diplomacy."[47] In addition, he is denied a judicial function.[48]

Equally telling is what this law, and Deuteronomy generally, do *not* say about the king. Nowhere is the king referred to as the son of God, as is sometimes true of ANE kings and as Israelite kings were referred to in the context of the so-called "Jerusalem Cult Tradition" or Zion theology.[49] In Deuteronomy, Israel as a whole is described as sons of God (Deut 1:31). The king is specifically presented as a "brother Israelite" (17:15, 20), who easily might elevate his heart above his brothers. Adherence to *Torah* is presented as the means by which the king is kept humble and in his place as part of the community of brothers.

This stands in stark contrast to the role of kings in the ANE or, indeed, the role actually played by Israelite monarchs. The centrality of the king in ANE political systems is highlighted by Whitelam, who notes that

> the king's role in the protection of society as warrior, the guarantor of justice as judge and the right ordering of worship as priest are the fundamental roles which cover all aspects of the well-being of society. It is well known that this triple function of kingship, with particular emphasis on the roles of the king as judge and warrior, is common throughout the ancient Near East and is expressed in a great deal of royal literature from Mesopotamia through the Levant to Egypt.[50]

While there undoubtedly were practical limitations on the king's power, and political realities surely necessitated the sharing of the

47. J. G. McConville, "King and Messiah in Deuteronomy and the Deuteronomistic History," in *King and Messiah in Israel and the Ancient Near East: Proceedings of the Oxford Old Testament Seminar* (ed. J. Day; JSOTSup 270; Sheffield: Sheffield Academic Press, 1998), 276.

48. Lohfink, "Functions of Power," 340; see also Rüterswörden, *Gemeinschaft zur Gemeinde*, 90–91.

49. On the Zion tradition, see G. von Rad, *Old Testament Theology*, vol. 1: *The Theology of Israel's Historical Traditions* (trans. D. M. G. Stalker; New York: Harper & Row, 1962), 46–48; R. E. Clements, "Deuteronomy and the Jerusalem Cult Tradition," *VT* 15 (1965): 300–312. For a critique of this understanding, see J. G. McConville, "Jerusalem in the Old Testament," in *Jerusalem Past and Present in the Purposes of God* (ed. P. W. L. Walker; Carlisle: Paternoster / Grand Rapids: Baker, 1994), 21–51.

50. K. W. Whitelam, "Israelite Kingship: The Royal Ideology and Its Opponents," in *The World of Ancient Israel: Sociological, Anthropological and Political Perspectives: Essays by Members of the Society for Old Testament Study* (ed. R. E. Clements; Cambridge: Cambridge University Press, 1989), 130. Cf. also W. von Soden, *The Ancient Orient: An Introduction to the Study of the Ancient Near East* (Grand Rapids: Eerdmans, 1994), 63–71; W. W. Hallo and W. K. Simpson, *The Ancient Near East: A History* (San Diego: Harcourt, Brace, Jovanovich, 1971), 172–78; and W. G. Lambert, "Kingship in Ancient Mesopotamia," in *King and Messiah in Israel and the Ancient Near East: Proceedings of the Oxford Old Testament Seminar* (ed. J. Day; JSOTSup 270; Sheffield: Sheffield Academic Press, 1998), 54–70.

responsibilities of power, the fact remains that nowhere in the ANE is the power of the king limited by a written document, as the power of the Israelite king is limited by the regulations in Deuteronomy. The Code of Hammurabi, for example, is clearly directed from the king to his people and seeks to regulate their conduct, not his.

The only positive function assigned to the king in Deuteronomy is reading a copy of "this law" (הַתּוֹרָה הַזֹּאת) and being guided by its precepts. This allows the king to learn to fear Yahweh and live a life of obedience (Deut 17:19–20). The result will be a secure future for him and his sons (Deut 17:20). In this way, according to Deuteronomy, the king serves not as a representative of the people before their god, as is the case in some ANE contexts,[51] but as the model Israelite.[52]

The significance of the king's exemplary role warrants further consideration. As noted, the law of the king presents a very limited role for the king. The only positive function for the king is writing a copy of the law, reading it, and living in adherence to it. The purpose of this is לְבִלְתִּי רוּם־לְבָבוֹ מֵאֶחָיו ("so that he might not be lifted up above his brothers"). This warning against pride follows a caution against the multiplication of possessions: Deut 17:16–17 prohibits the king from acquiring (רָבָה) for himself horses, money, or wives. This echoes the warnings in Deut 8:11–14 in a remarkable fashion:[53] the people are exhorted to keep the *Torah* lest their hearts be lifted up (רוּם) as a result of their having acquired (רָבָה) for themselves livestock, silver and gold, and other material possessions. The triple repetition of רָבָה and the presence of the "silver and gold" motif in both locations suggests that the echo is deliberate.[54]

The parallel between the king and the people is further evident in the command in Deut 17:20 that the king not "depart from the commandment either to the right or to the left" (סוּר מִן־הַמִּצְוָה יָמִין וּשְׂמֹאול). This echoes the command delivered to the entire people at the beginning of the giving of the law that they are to do all that Yahweh commanded them, not departing from it either to the right or to the left (Deut 5:32).

These deliberate verbal echoes highlight the exemplary role of the king. Just as the people received the oral *Torah* that is the means by which they demonstrate loyalty to Yahweh and receive the blessings of the land, the king receives the written *Torah* that emphasizes his

---

51. Hallo and Simpson, *Ancient Near East,* 175.

52. Miller, *Deuteronomy,* 147.

53. J. P. Sonnet, *The Book within the Book: Writing in Deuteronomy* (Biblical Interpretation Series 14; Leiden: Brill, 1997), 81–82.

54. Ibid.

loyalty to Yahweh (since the law of the king requires a rejection of the normal role played by an ANE king, thus marking Yahweh's kingship over Israel[55]) and secures blessing for his house and nation. The king thus serves as a model Israelite by his adherence to *Torah*, thus acknowledging Yahweh's supremacy and receiving the blessings of being Yahweh's elect.

The importance of *Torah* is further demonstrated by the law of the king. As we noted, there is no parallel in ANE legal texts to the law of the king: a king's power limited by a written text. Thus, Deuteronomic law is unprecedented in what it intends to accomplish. Whereas in ANE societies the king was supreme, Yahweh is the "fountainhead" of law, and *Torah* is an expression of his will.[56]

Finally, the role of the people as a whole must be mentioned once again. As in the case of judges, the people, still addressed in second-person singular, have an important role to play. Although Yahweh is the one who will choose the king (Deut 17:15), there will be no king until the people decide that they want one. When they do, they are also given a role in "setting the king" (תָּשִׂים עָלֶיךָ מֶלֶךְ; Deut 17:15) over themselves. That is, in accordance with the decision they have made, they set Yahweh's choice over them and in so doing relinquish certain aspects of their communal power to the king. Whereas in the ANE "kingship descended from heaven," in Deuteronomy it derives from the desire of the people and the permissive will of Yahweh.[57]

Thus, the radical nature of Deuteronomy's program is highlighted in this passage. There is a radical difference between the role of the king in ANE royal ideology and the role prescribed in Deuteronomy. Indeed, Deuteronomy consistently and carefully highlights the role of the people as a whole. The result is that Deuteronomy emerges as a powerfully countercultural text;[58] by opposing the prevailing models of political leadership, especially through its emphasis on the role of

---

55. G. V. Smith, "The Concept of God/the Gods as King in the Ancient Near East and the Bible," *Trinity Journal* n.s. 3 (1982): 36–38. See also Miller, *Deuteronomy*, 148.

56. M. Greenberg, "Some Postulates of Biblical Criminal Law," in *Studies in the Bible and Jewish Thought* (JPS Scholars of Distinction Series; Philadelphia: Jewish Publication Society, 1995), 28.

57. H. Frankfort, *Kingship and the Gods: A Study of Ancient Near Eastern Religion as the Integration of Society and Nature* (Chicago: University of Chicago Press, 1948), 237. See also W. E. Evans, "An Historical Reconstruction of the Emergence of Israelite Kingship and the Reign of Saul," in *Scripture in Context II: More Essays on the Comparative Method* (ed. W. W. Hallo, J. C. Moyer, and L. C. Perdue; Winona Lake, IN: Eisenbrauns, 1983), 72.

58. Wright, *Deuteronomy*, 210. Cf. also M. Greenberg, "Biblical Attitudes toward Power: Ideal and Reality in Law and Prophets," in *Studies in the Bible and Jewish Thought* (JPS Scholars of Distinction Series; Philadelphia: Jewish Publication Society, 1995), 56–58.

the people in assembly,[59] Deuteronomy demonstrates itself to be a truly revolutionary text.

But the revolutionary program cannot be separated from the emphasis on *Torah*. First of all, the revolutionary program is described and developed in the midst of a text that claims authoritative status for itself. More important, however, is the emphasis on sustaining the relationship with Yahweh. The people are chosen by Yahweh to be his people but with this great privilege comes the responsibility to demonstrate Yahweh's supremacy in every aspect of their lives. This lies at the very heart of the message of Deuteronomy.

Levitical Priests and Prophets (Deuteronomy 18:1–22)

The final portion of this section of the book takes up the offices of priest and prophet. Like the offices of judge and king, the offices of priest and prophet contribute to a society marked by the unique vision of Deuteronomy.

Priests (Deuteronomy 18:1–8)

Deuteronomy 18:1–8 specifies that the Levitical priests, who have no tribal inheritance of land, are to be supported from the offerings and sacrifices of the people as a whole. Verses 6–8 also provide that the Levite is to be provided for at "the place" when he chooses to go to minister. As we noted above, this provision is often understood to be a direct result of the centralization of worship, when local altars were abolished and the priests who served them were displaced. At the beginning of the present chapter, I argued that there were good reasons to question the interpretation that an influx of priests at the central sanctuary due to centralization lies behind this section.

This section contributes to the articulation of the radical vision of Deuteronomy in which the normal structures of ANE polity (which emphasizes the role of the king) are rejected. The office of priest is here identified as important for the life of the nation. Priests have already been mentioned in connection with the central tribunal (Deut 17:9), and here their role comes up again. The radical nature of Deuteronomy's vision becomes apparent when we note that the priest is explicitly given a role in the administration of justice (though the king is not). This is not, however, their only function.

The role of the priests in society is clearly religious, because they minister in the name of Yahweh at the place he chooses (Deut 18:6–7). But it is important to note that priests are rather pointedly said to

---

59. See chap. 3 above.

have no inheritance in Israel. The term נַחֲלָה ("inheritance") in Deuteronomy usually refers to the land itself, describing allocations to individual tribes: Deut 29:7 states that Transjordanian land was given to
Reubenites, Gadites, and the half-tribe of Manasseh as an inheritance.
The word is also used to refer to allocations to individual families
within the tribal divisions.[60] Moreover, other texts in Deuteronomy
speak of the Levites' having no inheritance, specifically, no allotment
of land (e.g., 10:9; 14:27, 29).

In contrast to the other tribes, Deut 18:2 says of the Levites that
"Yahweh is their inheritance" (יְהוָה הוּא נַחֲלָתוֹ). Wright notes that this
expression

> was not a pious spiritualization of a life of ascetic poverty but a state-
> ment of the principle that they would receive the full material bless-
> ing of their inheritance to the extent that the people of Yahweh were
> faithful in their worship of him and in covenant commitment to one
> another.[61]

Thus in addition to their religious service, the Levites have a role to
play as a measure of the people's obedience. McConville notes that the
Levites are intended in Deuteronomy to be prosperous, not poor. He
notes that "a poor Levite could not be an ideal figure, for his poverty,
far from portraying devotion to Yahweh, would actually be a consequence of disobedience and godless independence on the part of the
whole people, and a harbinger of their deprivation of the benefits of
the land."[62]

In addition, Deuteronomy envisions the priests as teachers of *Torah*. It is they who are keepers of copies of the *Torah* (Deut 17:18;
31:9), and it is they who are to read the law to the people every seven
years (Deut 31:10–13). The religious priorities of Deuteronomy are
emphasized by the fact that the priest is portrayed as an integral part
of the administration of the nation. As teachers of *Torah*, the priests
foster all of the people's awareness of their obligation to live lives that
demonstrate total allegiance to Yahweh. As a tribe without inheritance and dependent on the willingness of others to share their
bounty as commanded in the *Torah*, the Levitical priests serve as a
measure of the extent to which that loyalty is exhibited in the every-
day lives of the people. Brueggemann notes that "the anticipated
covenant community requires priests at its center in order to resist

---

60. C. J. H. Wright, "נחל," *NIDOTTE* 3: 77.
61. Wright, *Deuteronomy*, 213.
62. McConville, *Law and Theology*, 151.

the profanation of life."[63] All of this marks the fundamentally religious concerns of the Deuteronomic program.

Prophets (Deuteronomy 18:9–22)

The final administrative office is that of the prophet. Deuteronomy 18:9–22 begins with a rather lengthy description of the practices of the inhabitants of the land that are forbidden for Israel on the grounds that they are "abominations" (תּוֹעֵבֹת). This is followed by the promise that Yahweh will raise up a prophet for the people and a discussion of the role of Yahweh's word in the ministry of the prophet (18:15–22).

The list of prohibited practices covers a host of practices known from the ancient world. The practices that are forbidden for the Israelites share in common the attempt to gain "knowledge or guidance, or to exercise power over the deity or other people by magic and secret procedures."[64] Thus, child sacrifice should be seen not merely as the sacrifice of the child but also as an attempt to direct events or obtain guidance. An example of this function of child sacrifice is seen in 2 Kg 3:26–27.[65]

These "abominations" are said to be the reason the Canaanites were to be driven out of the land (Deut 18:12). In light of this, it is significant that the references to Yahweh's gift of the land in vv. 9 and 14 frame the discussion of forbidden practices, thus emphasizing the importance of proper worship. Attempts to manipulate Yahweh or to obtain guidance in unauthorized ways are an abomination, the very thing that resulted in the expulsion of the Canaanites from the land. The implication is that improper worship will lead to the expulsion of the Israelites as well.

In contrast to the Canaanites, the Israelites are to be blameless (תָּמִים) before Yahweh (18:13). This term usually appears in sacrificial contexts to note the condition of animals that are acceptable for sacrifice. But it also may be used to denote truth more generally or to refer to ethical qualities.[66] The use of terms such as תָּמִים and תּוֹעֵבָה reveals the religious foundation of the issue.[67] Yahweh alone has the right to dictate how he is to be worshiped, and proper worship must acknowledge his sovereignty. For the people to engage in the worship practices of the Canaanites would be to demonstrate disloyalty to Yahweh.

---

63. Brueggemann, *Deuteronomy*, 190.
64. McConville, *Deuteronomy*, 300.
65. Craigie, *Deuteronomy*, 260.
66. McConville, *Deuteronomy*, 301–2.
67. Cf. Merrill, *Deuteronomy*, 270.

The office of prophet is presented as the Yahweh-ordained means by which his voice will continue to be heard. The emphasis on Yahweh's voice is recognizable in the contrast between the Canaanites' "listening" (שָׁמַע) to fortune-tellers (Deut 18:14) and the command to "listen" (שָׁמַע) to the Yahweh-chosen prophet (v. 15).[68] This contrast is also seen in the parallels between the prophet to come and Moses, because vv. 16–18 state that the coming prophet will be "like Moses" in terms of being the authorized mediator of Yahweh's words.[69]

Again, we note the significance of the addressees of Moses' speech. The audience of Moses' speech in Deuteronomy's narrative is on the verge of entering the promised land. This is, as we have seen in our examination of other texts, a moment of transition. As in other cases, provision is made for a dramatically different life in the land. Moses will not enter the land with the people, but Yahweh will raise up a prophet to serve as mediator of his words. Given the already-observed tendency in Deuteronomy to look to the distant future while addressing the Moab generation, it is likely that what is envisioned here is a succession of prophets who will serve to mediate Yahweh's word to the people, rather than a single individual. This conclusion becomes more evident when we compare the reference to a prophet in Deut 18:15ff. with the references to a king in Deut 17:14, where more than one is clearly intended.[70] Thus, Moses' speech addressing the audience at Moab provides for the continued, Yahweh-sanctioned mediation of Yahweh's own words. Unlike the offices of judge and king, however, the office of prophet will exist completely at the initiative of Yahweh. The people have no role in choosing the prophet himself or choosing whether or not there will be a prophet. In the moment of transition, Yahweh provides a means by which his words will continue to be heard.

The importance of Yahweh's words is seen in the discussion of true and false prophets. The true prophet is one who speaks what Yahweh commands him to speak, and he has the authority of Yahweh (18:18–19). In contrast, the false prophet is one who presumes to speak in

---

68. McConville, *Deuteronomy*, 302.

69. There is no real contrast between the statement in Deut 18:15 that the coming prophets would be "like Moses" and the statement in Deut 34:10 that no prophet has yet arisen who is "like Moses." The latter text is emphasizing the unique nature of Moses' relationship with Yahweh ("whom Yahweh knew face to face," Deut 34:10). The emphasis in Deut 18 is on Moses' mediatory role, and it is in this respect that the future prophets may be described as "like Moses." At the same time, it is clear that Moses' role was unique (not least because of the statement to that effect in 34:10) in that he was mediator of the initial giving of *Torah* and the establishment of the people as the people of Yahweh.

70. Nelson, *Deuteronomy*, 234.

Yahweh's name but says things that Yahweh has not commanded. Alternatively, a false prophet may be one who speaks in the name of a god other than Yahweh. In either case, the offense is punishable by death, presumably because such actions serve to make it more difficult for the people to hear the words of Yahweh and demonstrate covenant loyalty to him by obeying his commands.

The office of prophet, then, is important in Israelite society, because within Deuteronomy is the recognition that, while Yahweh and *Torah* do not change, situations and circumstances do. The prophets serve as interpreters of *Torah* in changing circumstances. The fact that their office is instituted within the *Torah* suggests that an expansion of *Torah* should not be expected. Rather, the prophets serve as a "means of concretizing and actualizing the will of God, as set out in general terms in the Torah."[71] In addition, the fact that the *Torah* itself (including the basic terms of the covenant, the Decalogue) is given at Horeb, the foundational event for Israel as the people of Yahweh, indicates the subordination of future prophets to *Torah*. The true prophet speaks only at Yahweh's initiative and only his words.[72]

Conclusions regarding
Deuteronomy 16:18–18:22

In this chapter, we have seen that there are good reasons to question interpretations of Deut 16:18–18:22 as a program based in large measure on centralization and the changes wrought by the abolition of local sanctuaries. I have argued that an alternative interpretation of the data of the text is more likely. Rather than being radical in its centralization and associated secularization, Deut 16:18–18:22 is radical in its opposition to ANE models of administration that emphasize the role of the king.

In Deut 16:18–22 a radically different political administration is presented. The assembled people have remarkable powers. It is the people who appoint judges, and it is only when they desire a king that Yahweh will appoint one. Moreover, in this model, the community as a whole is responsible before Yahweh for ensuring righteousness, which is more than "justice" (although it includes justice). It is only by giving Yahweh his due, beginning with worship, that the people are able to demonstrate righteousness and total loyalty to Yahweh, as required.

71. Lohfink, "Functions of Power," 351.
72. Nelson, *Deuteronomy*, 236.

The revolutionary nature of the administration is seen perhaps most dramatically in the law of the king. The king is described as having remarkably limited powers in comparison with the power wielded both by ANE monarchs and the actual kings of Israel and Judah. The king, according to Deut 17:14–20, is to be a model Israelite and is to study *Torah*. He is not even first among equal Israelites but is, like all the people, subject to *Torah*. None of the usual roles of an ANE king are given to the king in Deut 17:14–20. By circumscribing the powers of the king, Deuteronomy highlights the supremacy of the true king, Yahweh, and demonstrates that the nation's success will not be achieved through any of the means used by surrounding nations (such as, for example, military might) but only through the demonstration of total allegiance to Yahweh.

The offices of priest and prophet round out the presentation of the administration of the nation lived in dedication to Yahweh. The Levitical priests, having no land inheritance, are dependent on the obedience of their countrymen for their survival. Yahweh has promised to bless the people abundantly. If the people obey him and give the Levites (as well as the alien, orphan, and widow) their due, there will be no poor Levites. (Indeed, if the people take seriously their obligations to their neighbours, there should be no poor at all, according to Deut 15:4.)

Priests, however, are more than religious servants and the measure of the obedience of the people. They also are the keepers of copies of the *Torah*, which implies that they also have a responsibility to teach the people the terms of *Torah*. To a remarkable degree, their success (or even survival) depends on the extent to which the people as a whole know and obey *Torah*.

The office of prophet is also an important one in this revolutionary vision of life under Yahweh. If the priests have the responsibility to keep and teach *Torah*, the prophet is called to interpret *Torah* and the word of Yahweh in the face of changing situations. In the midst of change and the human desire for control and knowledge, Israel is called to eschew divination and magic in favor of heeding *Torah* and the words of the true (i.e., Yahweh-sanctioned) prophet. At Horeb, the people entered into relationship with Yahweh and committed themselves to demonstrating loyalty to Yahweh. At Moab, this commitment is reaffirmed, and the *Torah* is emphasized as a means of living out this commitment. The prophet reminds the people of their obligations and calls them to account, in Yahweh's name, when they fail.

This section of Deuteronomy, then, highlights what I believe is at the heart of the Deuteronomic program. The supremacy of Yahweh is firmly established, because it is he who gives *Torah*, commands its obedience, enforces its terms, and chooses king and prophet. This section highlights the ways in which the people of Yahweh are to live and govern themselves in order to show complete loyalty to Yahweh.

At the same time, *Torah* is emphasized. It is *Torah* that contains the standards of righteousness to which the people are expected to aspire. The *Torah* provides for the offices that will assist the community in attaining those standards. Even the king, who is the highest authority under the gods in ANE cultures, is subordinate to *Torah*, as seen by the fact that he must read from it daily and by the fact that he is not a recipient or promulgator of it. No one in Israel is greater than *Torah*, for all are held to its standards.

It is significant that *Torah* is emphasized especially to the Moab generation, which is on the verge of transition. For in this moment of transition, *Torah* is emphasized as the means by which the people will experience Yahweh's presence and be able to honor him appropriately. Moses, the mediator of Yahweh's words thus far, will not go into the land with the people. Significantly, there is no single replacement for Moses, because the role of prophet (even one said to be "like Moses") is not defined as having all of the functions that Moses performed. Instead, the successor to Moses is *Torah* itself: the *Torah* provides for the various roles that Moses filled.

This vision for life in relationship to Yahweh is truly radical. It contains such a fusion of the political and religious that it is hard to see in it an attempt at "secularization," as Weinfeld claims. Indeed, the life of every Israelite is infused with religious import as part of a community responsible for the maintenance of righteousness. Rather than being a program of centralization and secularization as usually conceived, Deut 16:18–18:22 represents a truly radical rejection of ANE models of administration in favor of a political administration that emphasizes the supremacy of Yahweh, with his *Torah* being obligatory for all his people.

Implications and Conclusions

Centralization in Deuteronomy is best envisioned as the centralization of sacrifice, while the conception of holiness is expanded so that all of life is lived before Yahweh and is, therefore, religiously significant. Thus, while sacrifice is centralized, worship is not. Moreover, I have set forth here the idea that Deuteronomy is radical in its rejection of ANE conceptions of administration, which have at their center an all-powerful king. Instead, Deuteronomy presents a vision of a community in which the people in assembly are given tremendous responsibility. This perspective is an alternative to the five views of centralization surveyed in chap. 1. Like Driver, I argue that Deuteronomy has a realistic program for the administration of the nation. I see elements in the Deuteronomic vision that are utopian, but unlike Lohfink, I do not see it as thoroughgoingly utopian.

Texts reflect ideology (which is largely synonymous with world view), and Deuteronomy is no different. What remains to be considered in this final chapter are the theological and ideological implications of the alternative conception of Deuteronomy presented in the preceding chapters. My perspective on Deuteronomy suggests the presence of a world view rather different from the one posited by Weinfeld and others.

At the heart of the Deuteronomic world view is the supremacy of Yahweh. One of the primary goals of the book is to inculcate a sense of total loyalty to him. The emphasis on Yahweh's uniqueness leads to the conclusion that he alone is able to bless the people and guarantee their security and prosperity. The rhetoric of Deuteronomy consistently presents Yahweh as unique among the gods (the very existence of other gods is denied in Deut 4:39). This rhetorical emphasis highlights the requirement for demonstrating total allegiance to Yahweh. He alone is God; therefore he must be obeyed and honored.

The supremacy of Yahweh is also evident in the fact that it is Yahweh who commands. He dictates the terms of the covenant relationship between himself and Israel. Indeed, parallels with ANE political treaties highlight the supremacy of Yahweh. In the ANE suzerain-vassal treaties, the "Great King" did not negotiate terms with the vassal. In the same way, Yahweh does not negotiate terms with Israel. Rather, he sets forth the stipulations by which loyalty to him is to be demonstrated. That Deuteronomy, like some ANE political treaties, includes a historical prologue in which Yahweh's generous actions on behalf of Israel are recounted further highlights the supremacy of Yahweh. He has shown himself willing and able to act on Israel's behalf in the past. The blessings of covenant relationship with Yahweh will be achieved only through obedience to the terms of the covenant.

Yahweh's supremacy extends beyond the establishment of the covenant relationship and its implications, significant as they are. Deuteronomy also portrays Yahweh as a God who is present with his people. We have seen that Deuteronomy guards Yahweh's transcendence while at the same time highlighting his presence with his people Israel. The people experienced Yahweh in profound ways at Horeb, but another of Deuteronomy's concerns is to note that his presence will not end when the people enter the land of promise. Rather, they will continue to live out their relationship with Yahweh in the land. Through obedience to *Torah*, they will be able to experience and actualize Yahweh's presence. Deuteronomy is at pains to stress the aniconic nature of Yahweh worship, because worship incorporating images would deny his singularity and also realize his presence in ways that are contrary to his desires. Yahweh is a God who is present with his people but only in the ways that he chooses. Living as the people of God means realizing Yahweh's presence as he determines.

Yahweh's determination of the means by which is presence is realized is shown by the significance attached to the "place that Yahweh your God will choose." Yahweh has a right to choose where he will be worshiped and how. Deuteronomy consistently requires the people to repudiate practices depicted as Canaanite, in part because worshiping Yahweh in that way would be to deny his supremacy and sovereignty in determining how he is to be worshiped. The supremacy of Yahweh must be acknowledged in every facet of life.

The idea of the supreme and present God leads to an expansion of the realm of holiness in Deuteronomy. All of life in the land is lived "before Yahweh" and therefore has religious significance. Nonforensic "righteousness" is made the responsibility of the community as a whole. The extension of the celebration of the Passover into the land also points to the religious significance of every aspect of life. The extent of religious significance is seen most clearly in Deuteronomy's treatment of nonsacrificial slaughter: the slaughter of all animals is religiously significant and another means by which allegiance to Yahweh may be demonstrated. In the Deuteronomic world view, every activity of the people in the land has covenantal and religious significance; every activity demonstrates either allegiance to Yahweh or lack of commitment to him.

The supremacy of Yahweh thus is at the very heart of the theology and ideology of Deuteronomy. Equally important, however, is the role of *Torah*, because it teaches the means by which Yahweh's supremacy is lived out by his people.

It is significant, therefore, that both the Decalogue in Deut 5 and the explanation of *Torah* in Deut 12–26 begin with the proper way to worship Yahweh. Only when Yahweh is properly honored through worship in accordance with his commands can the rest of the *Torah* be carried out, for proper worship means, first, acknowledging the absolute supremacy and sovereignty of Yahweh. The danger of improper worship is that it directs attention and loyalty to a deity other than the one true God or to a false conception of the true God. Because the means by which Yahweh's supremacy is lived out generally is through adherence to *Torah*, worship is at the heart of *Torah*.

More generally, *Torah* describes a mode of living. As such, it presents a vision for the people of Yahweh living in harmony with one another and in dedication to their God. This vision is remarkably egalitarian: Deuteronomy provides for just and righteous treatment for all people, including even slaves. Deuteronomy, and the *Torah* at its heart, envisions a society in which the whole of the people of God are considered "brothers" to one another. Slaves, the marginalized, women, and even the king are considered brothers, and all members of the society strive to live out loyalty to Yahweh. The extent to which they are able to do this determines their success—and even their survival—in the land.

The mode of living described in Deuteronomy is flexibile and adaptable in the face of changing circumstances. Indeed, the rhetoric of Deuteronomy is, in many respects, timeless, because it addresses the Moab generation as though they were at Horeb. In this way, subsequent generations of the people of Yahweh are included in Deuteronomy's appeal to demonstrate total allegiance to Yahweh through adherence to *Torah*; though they face different challenges and threats, they are called to demonstrate total loyalty to Yahweh.

Equally significant is the fact that the whole of Deuteronomy is presented as an address to the Israelites gathered on the verge of entering the promised land. At this moment of transition, the assembled people are told how they will experience Yahweh's continued presence and how they can obtain prosperity and security in the new situation.

Deuteronomy provides for the continuing applicability of its vision to future generations. The great mediator of Yahweh's words will not accompany the people into the land. But Yahweh's words will go with them, in the form of the tablets of the Decalogue and the written

Torah. At the same time, Deuteronomy provides for the office of the prophet who is to interpret the *Torah* in the changing circumstances. Thus the mediated voice of Yahweh will be heard among the people of God, despite Moses' death outside the land. Through the prophet who is called by and speaks at Yahweh's initiative, the words of Yahweh will continue to be interpreted and applied in the community. At the same time, the Levitical priests are called to be keepers of *Torah* and to teach the law to the people, thus ensuring that every generation is aware of the requirements of covenant loyalty.

The significance of *Torah* is further seen in the fact that there is no single successor to Moses. Rather, *Torah* itself emerges as the successor to Moses, because it provides for the offices that will partly fill Moses' various roles. No single person, office, or institutional arrangement is absolutely essential to living in relationship to Yahweh. Rather, the people of Yahweh must seek to live their lives in accordance with *Torah* as it is revealed and interpreted by Yahweh-sanctioned interpreters. Deuteronomy's world view includes a God who is greater than all others and who is not limited by the circumstances of the present. Accordingly, Yahweh and his *Torah* alone are the constants for the people of God.

The emphasis on the supremacy of Yahweh expressed through adherence to *Torah* leads to a remarkably countercultural ideology in Deuteronomy. Against the backdrop of ANE cultures, the Deuteronomic program stands in stark relief. In contrast to the centralized power structures of ANE monarchies, Deuteronomy provides for a system in which powers are distributed and in which the people in assembly have a genuine, responsible role to play.[1] The king, so central to political administration in ANE societies, is not even required in the political administration envisioned by Deuteronomy, and, if the people choose to have a king, he is greatly limited in his powers. He is subject to (and is to be a student of) *Torah*, and he is not to exalt himself above his brother Israelites. The function of this dramatically limited kingship is to highlight the fact that Yahweh is the true king in Israel; it is intended to ensure that the success of the nation is credited to Yahweh and not to the abilities of the king to carry out the usual ANE functions of power. Thus, the supremacy of Yahweh and *Torah* are again emphasized.

---

1. B. M. Levinson ("The Conceptualization of Kingship in Deuteronomy and the Deuteronomistic History's Transformation of *Torah*," *VT* 51 [2001]: 532–33) notes that the literature of the Bible and the ANE is usually overlooked when one examines the influences that led to Western judicial thought and concepts of limited government.

At the same time, Deuteronomy is not so utopian as to be unaware of the reality of human nature. Chapters 27 and 28 set forth blessings and curses, but it is clear in subsequent chapters that the curses are likely, if not certain, to be experienced by the nation. Even prior to chaps. 27–28, there is an awareness of the likelihood that the people will fail to live out their responsibilities to Yahweh. The expulsion of the people from the land of promise is spoken of as a near-certainty in Deut 4, and the portrait of the people in Deut 9 as "stiff-necked" and "stubborn" is not flattering and hardly inspires confidence that the people are willing and able to obey Moses' commands.[2] Thus, Deuteronomy is, in a sense, "eschatological"[3] in its outlook. That is, it envisages a society as it ought to be. At the same time, it is fully cognizant of the realities of human life and of all the difficulties that arise in human society. Tension between the ideal and the present reality is maintained. Thus, Deuteronomy is *both* realistic and utopian.

The understanding of the ideology of the book outlined here is consistent with the data of the text. Deuteronomy can hardly be read as supportive of the kind of royal reforms that Weinfeld and others propose. In its elevation of the people in assembly and their responsibility before Yahweh, the limitation of the role of the king, and the distribution of the functions of power, Deuteronomy cannot be seen as seeking to advance the power and role of the monarchy. Indeed, Deuteronomy is radical precisely in its *rejection* of models of administration that have at their center an all-powerful king, as well as its emphasis on the holiness of all of life lived in adherence to *Torah* and its elevation of the supremacy of Yahweh and his *Torah*.

2. For further development of this idea, see J. G. McConville, "Deuteronomy: Torah for the Church of Christ," *European Journal of Theology* 9 (2000): 39–42.

3. Cf. C. J. H. Wright, *Deuteronomy* (NIBC 4; Peabody, MA: Hendrickson, 1996), 189; J. G. McConville, *Deuteronomy* (AOTC 5; Leicester: Apollos / Downers Grove, IL: Inter-Varsity, 2002), 35–36.

Indexes

Index of Authors

233

Index of Scripture

237